STORIES
OF OKA

STORIES
OF OKA

LAND, FILM, AND LITERATURE

ISABELLE ST-AMAND
TRANSLATED BY S.E. STEWART

UNIVERSITY OF MANITOBA PRESS

Stories of Oka: Land, Film, and Literature
© Isabelle St-Amand 2018
Foreword © Katsitsén:hawe Linda David Cree 2018

Originally published as *La crise d'Oka en récits: territoire, cinéma et littérature*, by Presses de l'Université Laval in 2015

22 21 20 19 18   1 2 3 4 5

University of Manitoba Press
Winnipeg, Manitoba, Canada
Treaty 1 Territory
uofmpress.ca

Cataloguing data available from Library and Archives Canada
ISBN 978-0-88755-819-1 (PAPER)
ISBN 978-0-88755-552-7 (PDF)
ISBN 978-0-88755-551-0 (EPUB)

Cover design by Sébastien Aubin
Cover image: Martin Akwiranoron Loft, *Haudenosaunee Tattoo #1*, Serigraph, hand pulled, 11x16 inches, 2015 Edition of 25.
Interior design by Jess Koroscil

Printed in Canada

The University of Manitoba Press acknowledges the financial support for its publication program provided by the Government of Canada through the Canada Book Fund, the Canada Council for the Arts, the Manitoba Department of Sport, Culture, and Heritage, the Manitoba Arts Council, and the Manitoba Book Publishing Tax Credit.

We acknowledge the financial support of the Government of Canada through the National Translation Program for Book Publishing, an initiative of the *Roadmap for Canada's Official Languages 2013–2018: Education, Immigration, Communities*, for our translation activities.

Funded by the Government of Canada | Canadä

TO LÉON, MY CHILD

CONTENTS

FOREWORD

I met Isabelle many times, either at the Kanehsatà:ke Cultural Center or a Youth Art Show in the community. She struck me as being genuine in her interest to understand the underlying causes of the "Oka Crisis, 1990." I wasn't surprised when I learned that she had taken on the daunting task of writing about the ongoing Kanehsatà:ke resistance in 1990. Remember that this unresolved historical conflict and Mohawk resistance are twice as old as Canada, which claims that in 2017 is its 150th year of nationhood. Isabelle has created a powerful, clearly written narrative of what was happening behind the barricades, in front of the barricades, and in the offices of Canada's politicians.

Isabelle took a different path from previous individuals who chose to take a focused snapshot of the summer of 1990. The inclusion of poetry, films, plays, and other literary works by Indigenous and non-Indigenous writers added a multi-dimensional perspective that was missing in prior narratives. The reader benefits from the author's perception as it is evident that she has spent an enormous amount of time searching, finding, analyzing, internalizing, and seeking out key informants who have contributed previously unknown stories.

I will admit that I had a difficult time. I would read a chapter or a few pages and suddenly my mind would be flooded with images, memories, and feelings of anger, sadness, fear, and, yes, at times, laughter. Many of the community residents were confined to the Food Bank at our elementary school when the Canadian Army moved into the territory. They blocked roads on their way to surround the treatment centre. Meanwhile, the Sûreté du Québec police rode slowly up and down Route 344, attempting to intimidate us. I am one of the women who decided to taunt the Sûreté du Québec with signs that said how many more laps to get free doughnuts. I also helped to start a milkweed seed-pod throwing game, just like throwing snowballs—both spontaneous activities meant to relieve the stress of restricted mobility and the threats of the unknown.

I love reading about history, Indigenous peoples, human rights, social equity, culturally responsive education, and any research materials that tackle racism and derogatory stereotypes. As I read Isabelle's book, I came to the conclusion that she was writing about all these issues. My personal beliefs and understanding come through when she quotes Patrick Wolfe's term "the settler-colonial logic of elimination [of the Native]," driving home the depraved indifference of the ongoing Indigenous genocide by white privileged adherence to papal bulls, the Discovery Doctrine, and *terra nullius*.

The author later quotes Lee Maracle's novel, *Sundogs*, in reference to our honourable warrior men and women of our Nations: "They take up arms, not to deprive anyone of their life but to show the world they are dead serious about living."

These words sum up the unmistakable truth that Indigenous peoples throughout the world have always been given but two choices: elimination or survival!

And, while many in Canada believe that we are on the path to reconciliation, I believe that we have missed a few critical steps to achieving justice, respect, and dignity for all Indigenous peoples. Collectively, we as peoples sharing this place called Turtle Island must first resolve and identify our conflicts; we then seek to restore or create positive and reciprocal relationships; we must provide restitution for any wrongs and it must be agreed upon by all. Finally, and with great hope in our collective future, we can then achieve reconciliation.

Isabelle's book, *Stories of Oka*, is a gathering of stories, from a myriad of sources, full of emotion and reconnection to family and ancestral histories that have been silenced for too long. As I read this book, I shared my feelings with others, and with family who were present in the Pines on July 11. I saw the potential of this book as a learning tool and as a chance to share the burden of our trauma.

I have been a staunch advocate for Indigenous culturally responsive education to be included at every level of education from early childhood to post-secondary. This book should be required reading at all post-secondary institutions, especially for those who plan to become teachers. Invite those voices who are included in this book to speak directly to your students in your classrooms.

Isabelle St-Amand presents an opportunity for readers to become part of "Karihwatà:tie," or the continuing stories or events.

Niawenhkó:wa, Isabelle.

Katsitsén:hawe Linda David Cree
Kanien'kehá:ke ne Kanehsatà:ke

NOTE ON THE TEXT

This book is the updated English-language version of the book *La crise d'Oka en récits: territoire, cinéma et littérature*. Differences between the two language versions are therefore not due to translation, but to a revision of the original material.

This study draws on both French- and English-language sources, some of them interviews, unpublished archival materials, and film dialogue or transcripts. It also makes reference to literary works that have not previously been translated into English, as well as some that were originally written in English.

The original translation for this publication of an extensive citation of French material is identified in the text. Translations of one sentence or less are not identified, for ease of reading, but the fact that the material has been translated is clear from the reference information. In a limited number of cases, where the citation is brief and gaining access to the original document is difficult, there has been a retranslation of material that was originally written or spoken in English.

In this book, the spellings of *Kanehsatà:ke/Kanehsatake* and *Kahnawà:ke/Kahnawake* were deliberately not standardized. Over the course of my research, I heard people from these two communities discussing the reasons for using one or the other, and I also observed in my readings a diverse use of terms, Kanien'keha or English, in written and published works by Mohawk authors. In this book I tried to reflect as much as possible the spellings that tend to be used in different contexts, while inflecting the tone of my writing through these different uses.

INTRODUCTION

how many times do I have to tell you
how many times do I have to shout it!
how many times scrawl for you I will survive!

I will survive because I have to fight
to hear at last the beating of our hearts
filled with hope
the beating of our drums
from another time
we must no longer look back but look forward
while I nonetheless must cast away the hide scrapers
that are wearing away my brothers' resistance.

north of my famine, my barricades will become demands.

I am not a skin for sale
a nation to hang on the living room wall
I'll tell you right off:
I will not just be an Oka Crisis
locked up in a history book no matter what.

and when they look at me
they'll be looking at a people united and standing straight with the
power of thunder!
my songs of peace will be the sap of my proud survival!

when they look at me
they'll be looking at a people united and standing straight
before the dawn's sacred fire!

I will not just be
an Oka Crisis
locked up in a history book
no matter what.

and if you sleep
it's because my songs of peace
will have been your lullabies

and the sap of my proud survival.

—*Natasha Kanapé Fontaine, "L'âme en tannage [Soul tanning]" (translation)*

Innu slam poet Natasha Kanapé Fontaine performs this piece at Indigenous political, literary, and cultural events in Quebec and elsewhere in the country. With a strong presence and urgency, she uses these words to reiterate speech that is hard to hear, interpellating the colonial subject and declaring a firm intention to make herself visible and active in the contemporary world. Her words evoke the ongoing struggles of Indigenous peoples, among them the Mohawks of Kanehsatake who, nearly thirty years after the so-called Oka Crisis, still have to defend their rights and actively protect their land from encroachment. The young Innu poet's performance of this territorial slam has served as the soundtrack and visual intertext for the video piece *Je ne resterai pas une crise d'Oka* [I will not just be an Oka Crisis]. The video deals with a demonstration held at Oka as a protest against fracking, the tar sands, and moving bitumen through pipelines, as well as bills C-38 and C-45, which reduce protection of land and watercourses while infringing on Indigenous rights.[1] Through her engaged poetry and politics, Fontaine draws attention to the role of artists in the Indigenous struggles for land and nation, pride and survival, unity and peace. The video, constructed around the poet's words, sketches the obvious links between the 1990 territorial conflict, the continuity with the struggles manifest in the Idle No More movement since 2012, and the flowering of Indigenous artistic expression in Quebec. It evokes the central themes of this book—territory, film, and literature.

I came to the Oka Crisis somewhat by accident and after many detours. By placing me explicitly in the colonizer's position, the event challenged the basic tenets of the society I belonged to, forcing me to engage in a more fundamental re-examination than I had at first anticipated. Why look at Oka and how it was represented? It was a violent, dramatic, traumatic conflict, significant and yet rarely symbolized. I was drawn to it spontaneously and intuitively, and it was only when my research was well advanced that I found among my childhood souvenirs a box full of newspaper clippings about two particular events: the explosion of the *Challenger* space shuttle in 1986 and the Oka Crisis in 1990.[2] The political crisis that had been central to my research for over two years had therefore affected me more at the time than I realized. There was something imperative and defining in the crisis and its armed conflict that I had experienced as a kind of mystery, something overwhelming that I couldn't understand and that gave rise to searching questions. I remember schoolyard discussions, with dubious stories about taxes and snowmobiles and noisy accusations brandished like incontrovertible truths. I also remember suspecting that something else lay hidden behind the sweeping declarations, but I was left feeling perplexed and fascinated, unable at that stage to know more. I was then living in Shawinigan, with its Indigenous name, where I grew up in near-total ignorance of the Atikamekw communities in Opitciwan, Manawan, Wemotaci, and surrounding towns, whose traditional territories I, and my own people, occupied on the shores of the Saint-Maurice River, Atikamekw Sipi.

It was only many years later that I came to renew my relationship to the crisis. My research was intended to cast the political event in a new light by relating it to documentary films and literary narratives that had never yet been examined in this way. At the outset, to orient my thinking, I asked myself three main questions: What happened during the Oka Crisis? What does it mean to film an event as it is taking place, and then tell the story in a documentary film? How has the event been symbolized in settler and Indigenous literary works? By answering these questions, I intended to gain a better understanding of the conflict-ridden relationships that unite and separate Indigenous peoples and settler societies within Canada. As I explain in the first chapter, I quickly realized that a study of Oka and its various representations could not be separated from the deeply conflictual colonial dynamic driving the political event. It was therefore necessary to develop a theoretical approach that could not only include the perspectives of settler and Indigenous peoples in their specific contexts, but also relate the two and identify points of contact and intermingling.

Therefore, for the purposes of this book, I resolved to take a multi-perspective approach that would enable me to grasp the many dimensions of meaning attached to this deep-rooted conflict. The idea of "the event" provided the guiding principle in untangling the concentrated knot of intersecting aspects that made up the Oka Crisis, whether during the siege in action, in documentary films, or in literary narratives. Conflict was another important element in my reflection. I drew on the thinking of German sociologist Georg Simmel in *Le conflit* [The Sociology of Conflict] to understand more specifically how the crisis affected not only reciprocal relations among the peoples and each one's internal structure, but also the overriding relationship that unites them in a single entity. My thinking gradually led me to the Indigenous research paradigm proposed by Cree scholar Shawn Wilson in *Research Is Ceremony: Indigenous Research Methods.* According to Wilson, viewing research as a ceremony consists in strengthening the connections and bridging the distance between disparate elements so that they share the same space and illuminate one another. In the same way, the approach I have chosen for this book looks at the event from different angles, angles that contrast and conflict but gradually start to make sense by themselves and in relation to one another. Following the particular concept of the ceremony, research reaches its point of culmination when all the ideas have been brought together and acquire meaning from the connections established among them.

Like the event around which it is constructed and thus helps to reactivate, this book presents various dimensions of the political crisis as seen from contrasting points of view. It seeks a better understanding of what drove and shaped the conflict; what gave it its strategic and symbolic power; and how the siege exposed the parties' relations to each other and their own community, to third parties, and to the conflict itself. In so doing, it enables us to define the event in all its intense antagonism, with awareness of its negative and positive poles and its potential for violence and healing, affirmation and explosion. It also offers a better understanding of the painful, alarming intertwining of relationships between the Indigenous peoples and the settler societies, made even more tangled by Oka.

THE PROCESS OF REFLECTION

The particular approach I have taken was driven, on the one hand, by the nature of this significant political event and, on the other, by recent research in Indigenous film and literature. When I began to write the book, I already had a long-standing interest in society's sites of debate, far-reaching political events, and varied expressions and representations of power and protest. In 2011, after working on the massive demonstrations against the Summit of the Americas held in Quebec City in 2001, I had co-edited an interdisciplinary collective work that interrogated the figures of siege in a minority context, more specifically that of Quebec, in relation to their various expressions of consultation and conflict.[3] I pursued this avenue of study by focusing on the Oka Crisis and how it has been represented. I therefore approached the event from a very specific place of utterance, looking at it first from the Quebec and Canadian settler perspective that is part of my personal heritage.

At the same time, failing to consider the perspectives, experiences, and accounts of the Mohawk communities directly affected by the conflict was inconceivable. Even more than leaving a central part of the conflict obscure, relegating the Mohawk voices to the sidelines of the debate, downplaying or ignoring them, would have the effect of replaying an old colonial dynamic of marginalizing and denying Indigenous realities, expression, and knowledge. At the same time, I found myself in a literary studies department, without any specialization in Indigenous studies or particular connection to those communities, and so the project's relevance seemed far from obvious. How to approach this kind of event when I was at such a remove from one of the parties involved? And, above all, how to negotiate, without reinforcing it, the blatantly colonialist relation inevitably set up by the research process?

My first step was to visit the language and cultural centres of Kanehsatake and Kahnawake. I did this in the hope of gaining a better understanding of how the conflict of summer 1990 had been experienced, thought about, and imagined from the point of view of the Mohawk communities. As a literary scholar, I was obliged to adopt a new way of learning, different from that I had been trained in, and as a result to develop new methodological tools. My process includes a conceptual exploration that has evolved over the course of meetings and research. I gradually introduced concepts that would allow me to comprehend the various elements of the political crisis during the siege in action, in documentary films, and in literary narratives. Examples of these concepts are performativity and counter-performativity; sovereignty, whether political, rhetorical, visual, or literary; exile and reterritorialization; the fragility of the settler state; and eyewitness accounts and the role of personal stories. I went back and forth through my manuscript in order to revise, alter, remove, or add concepts as the research moved forward.

The visits to Kanehsatake and Kahnawake produced concrete results. In a fundamental way, they immediately made me aware of my position as a settler researcher and of the heavy colonial baggage I was carrying, willingly or not. Over time, my various encounters also made me more sensitive to the Mohawk context and better informed about it, not to mention helped me to grasp aspects that might otherwise have gone unnoticed: for example, the unexpressed trauma of the armed conflict, the fundamental importance of sovereignty, and such critical moments as resisting the Canadian military who landed on Tekakwitha Island. Other aspects are the extreme seriousness of the political issues at the core of the crisis, the violent nature of the enduring colonial relationship, and the crucial significance of the territory or land when viewed in its close connection to culture, language, and storytelling. In dealing directly and immediately with the research's ethical and political dimensions, I thought in very concrete terms about my research background and its implications. For instance, as a non-Indigenous researcher, I could not ignore the fact that I was working in a context, and still do, in which Western theories of knowledge and its validity have for a long time served to delegitimize and marginalize Indigenous peoples. Neither could I dismiss the fact that these theories have too often been developed in the absence of the principal stakeholders, as Maori researcher Linda Tuhiwai Smith explained very clearly in *Decolonizing Methodologies: Research and Indigenous Peoples.* In particular, this relationship to the production of knowledge has motivated Indigenous peoples to arm themselves with ethical protocols requiring, notably, that the research be designed in the community in question, be developed in a close relationship to that community, and respond to the community's needs.[4]

When it came to preparing my ethical clearance request, I quickly realized that my research project did not meet the requirements. Further, my project did not deal with the Mohawk communities per se, but rather with a conflict that affected the Mohawks, First Nations, Québécois, and Canadians. As well, the study of filmed and written narratives by Indigenous and non-Indigenous people from all across the country extended the analysis to multiple perspectives that had to be interpreted without lumping them together or reducing them within an excessively rigid analytical framework. From there, I asked myself how my research, which brought an interdisciplinary, intercultural lens to bear on the conflict, could grasp the event's full complexity. How could it be useful—rather than harmful—to the Mohawk communities that lived through this difficult event? In what way could I carry out this research ethically and responsibly, without either re-engaging in a colonial dynamic or specializing in Iroquois studies?

In *Travelling Knowledges: Positioning the Im/Migrant Reader of Aboriginal Literatures in Canada*, the literary scholar Renate Eigenbrod emphasizes that the reader (or researcher) who finds herself in a position of exteriority in relation to the Indigenous cultures involved as the subject of her study must come to "the realization of being excluded from knowing fully."[5] My initial discussions with members of the Mohawk communities quickly gave me to understand that I would never completely grasp what the 1990 crisis represents from a Mohawk point of view. For that matter, the event was never within my reach. It occurred here and there, in bits and pieces, such that I spent most of my time perceiving it at a distance and immersing myself in the context essentially through film and literature, in order eventually to achieve some degree of understanding. In a fundamental way, my various encounters and my participation in the organization of different Indigenous events, conferences, and activities allowed me to grasp the living aspect of Indigenous cultures, cinema, and literature. In the Anishinaabe scholar, writer, and filmmaker Armand Garnet Ruffo's view, it is not so much a matter of whether non-Indigenous researchers accumulate background information and anthropological readings, but rather "a question of cultural initiation, of involvement and commitment."[6] In my case, it was obvious that I could not proceed as if I were an Indigenous researcher, or a non-Indigenous ethnohistorian or anthropologist working in an Indigenous community. I therefore adopted the stance of engaging in an interaction with various individuals and cultural sites from the acknowledged, overt position of an outsider. It was from this external stance that I came to elaborate my theoretical reflection. It is located at the outer limits of the conflict, which set in opposition identities that were antagonized by territoriality, in what the literary and cultural studies scholar Mary Louise Pratt calls "contact zones" or, to be more accurate, in what the urban studies and critical race theory scholar Kevin Mumford terms "interzones"[7] to bring out the inequality of power relations that define the terms of engagement.

The detailed examination of the siege's scenography in Chapters 2 and 3 sheds light on how interactions between the peoples were negotiated and made visible throughout the armed conflict. The conflict's setting and staging informed how the siege in action was analyzed, shaped in documentary films, and recounted in literary works. It therefore became less a question of having to know everything than managing to arrive at a fair, relevant reflection based on what could be accessed.

TELLING THE STORY OF A HARSH POLITICAL CONFLICT

This study of the Oka Crisis, or Kanehsatake resistance, was a challenge, owing to the political conflict's magnitude and complexity, the intensity of antagonism and the impossibility of neutrality, and political legitimacies that are still in tension. This is all the more emphatic because, nearly three decades later, the conflict is still alive. In the Mohawks' view, the Oka Crisis is not the stuff of movies or fiction, but a tough political conflict around issues that remain as real as they are urgent. The summer of 1990 was further marked by the intensification of overt racism across the country and the brutal attacks with volleys of stones against the Mohawk families being evacuated from Kahnawake. This violence directly interpellates the settler societies of Quebec and Canada, as do the historical and contemporary injustices brought to light by the event.

In *L'événement et le temps* [The event and time], the philosopher Claude Romano maintained that the event is revealing because it encourages us to judge the situation from a perspective that it has itself created. It is precisely this question of judgement and responsibility that emerges from the analysis of the documentary film *Okanada: Behind the Lines at Oka.*[8] The documentary records the words of the last people left behind the barricades as interviewed by Albert Nerenberg, the Canadian journalist who managed to get past the military lines towards the end of the armed conflict. The film reminds viewers of the partiality of viewpoints and thus leads them to ask new questions. For example, what can explain the glaring difference between how the warriors were represented in the media and the accounts delivered to the camera by the Mohawk protesters behind the barricades? Which version of the truth about the event comes closest to the experience of the people involved? When speech has been discredited, what can an individual viewpoint, that of the historical eyewitness, contribute to a comprehensive understanding of the conflict? These questions are central to the content of Chapter 4.

Throughout this book, I have been careful to ground the theoretical analysis in the concrete reality of the event that occurred during the siege in action, and in the filmed and written narratives by settlers and Indigenous peoples. In putting forward my own narrative of the event, I have drawn some directions from the reflection of Sto:lo writer and critic Lee Maracle. In the chapter "Oratory: Coming to Theory" of her book *Memory Serves*, Maracle considers that a story engaged with "the process of thought/feeling and being,"[9] is preferable to a dry theory disconnected from context and human experience. While wishing to take account of Quebec and Canadian perspectives, including those of the authorities, I chose to use the methodological device of shifting Quebec and Canadian literary studies onto the terrain of Indigenous studies.

THE IDEA OF SOVEREIGNTY

Where the resistance at Oka and its representations are concerned, it has proved to be instructive to relate certain concepts of sovereignty to one another—that evoked by the Kanien'kehà:ka communities during the siege in action; the concept of visual sovereignty discussed in turns by Tuscarora art curator and scholar Jolene Rickard in journal articles[10] and Seneca scholar Michelle Raheja in *Reservation Reelism: Redfacing, Visual Sovereignty, and Representations of Native Americans in Film* in order to theorize Indigenous control over representations; as well as related concepts of rhetorical, cultural, and literary sovereignty advanced by Indigenous researchers like Scott Richard Lyons, Beverley R. Singer, Craig S. Womack, and Daniel Heath Justice. The siege and the multiple accounts of the event, like the various ideas of sovereignty associated with them, imply different forms of reterritorialization: that is, as argued Cree researcher Neal McLeod, to occupy a space and impose in that space a discourse that matches the physical reality surrounding it. The Indigenous narratives of the siege counteract the process of exile described by McLeod, by which Indigenous peoples are dispossessed of their land and become relegated to a situation of spatial exile, just as they are cut off from their families, stories, languages, and collective memory and placed in a situation of ideological exile.[11]

Similarly, it is not surprising that the concept of visual sovereignty should lend itself so easily, and in such an instructive way, to an analysis of the documentary film *Kanehsatake: 270 Years of Resistance* by the Abenaki filmmaker Alanis Obomsawin, which is treated in Chapter 5. The documentary renders the event by making Mohawk cultural and political power its centre, while highlighting words and images that alter the representations conveyed in the mass media. In the film, issues of land and survival, historical resistance and contemporary Indigenous struggles, humour and spirituality become linked around the event. These issues reappear in other forms in the Indigenous literary narratives.

LITERARY REPRESENTATIONS

I chose to focus my analysis of literary narratives on the issue of representation in order to continue making connections with other elements that showed up frequently in my study of the event. Furthermore, as demonstrated by media representations of the Oka Crisis or Kanehsatake resistance, the effective action of representations is an issue that must be taken seriously in a colonial context. Research in Indigenous studies has inventoried the debilitating projections and belittling representations communicated in everyday life and in politics, as well as in films and books. In her 2010 book *When the Other Is Me: Native Resistance Discourse 1850–1990*, Métis researcher Emma LaRocque demonstrated that the stereotypical images of Indigenous identity line up along what she described as the dehumanizing "civ-sav dichotomy." In addition to engendering and justifying racist aggressions, these stereotyped representations tend to eradicate any potential for genuine recognition and exchange. It is in this regard that many Indigenous researchers and writers have envisioned words as weapons. Literature's role in changing representations as well as realities was put forward already in 1978 by Anishinaabe literary theorist Gerald Vizenor's *Wordarrows: Native States of Literary Sovereignty*. Similarly, a strong belief in the visionary power of art has driven the work of Huron-Wendat playwright Yves Sioui Durand,[12] who co-founded in 1985, with Catherine Joncas, the francophone theatre company Ondinnok. Like Vizenor and Sioui Durand, many Indigenous literary artists have creatively engaged with the Indigenous cultural and political struggles against settler colonialism and neoliberalism. As Métis scholar, writer, and filmmaker Warren Cariou pointed out in *The Oxford Handbook of Indigenous American Literature*, "The appropriation of voice controversy can now be seen as a kind of discursive build-up to the Oka Crisis, a sign that Indigenous people had reached a point at which they would no longer be passive recipients of colonial representation or objectification."[13] This can be clearly discerned in the ways in which Indigenous writers have taken on the event in their creative works following the resistance of 1990.

Literary narratives of Oka more specifically can promote the circulation of other images and accounts of the event and, to an extent, have the power to redefine what it has represented. As demonstrated by cultural studies scholar Claudine Cyr regarding the celebrations and protests of the 500th anniversary of the Americas in 1992,[14] an event can be reanimated and reinterpreted in different ways, such that it remains open to transformation and negotiation as long as it keeps being expressed and replayed. This is what happens in, for example, *Voleurs de cause* [Cause robbers], the poetry collection inspired by the Oka Crisis by Québécois poet Yves Boisvert that is treated in Chapter 6, along with the narratives of other Québécois and Canadian writers. Rather than offering a clear, simple rendition, Boisvert clouds the issues and thus keeps the event's lack of definition in play throughout the book's eighty-odd pages. On the Indigenous side, as we will see in the final chapter, written narratives that mention the 1990 resistance share a strong conceptual link to politics and history in literary expression. While narratives of the event rely on fiction, they also constitute a form of resistance that operates by refashioning representations from an Indigenous place of utterance. Many of the Indigenous writers' narratives, such as those by Dan David, Lee Maracle, Douglas Raymond Nepinak, and Richard Wagamese, rely on a reactivation of family connections and stories shared during the event, making direct reference to a relational paradigm.

In *Taking Back Our Spirits: Indigenous Literature, Public Policy, and Healing*, Métis scholar Jo-Ann Episkenew discussed how "Indigenous literature is able to construct a common truth about our [Indigenous peoples' and settlers'] shared past."[15] After sociolinguist Charlotte Linde, she viewed speaking out, whether in a public forum or a literary narrative, as a "relational act" that makes it possible to move from isolation to shared stories, thus convening a community.[16] Then again, French philosopher François Flahault reminded us, in his essay *La méchanceté* [Malice], that the reader shares in the responsibility for how the narrative is produced, insofar as it is in the act of reading that it is actualized. The narrative's essential quality, he explained, is to constitute a shared life experience.[17] In the same spirit, this book is intended to make a contribution towards constructing a shared story, without, however, obliterating the reality and harshness of power relations determined by the settler colonial context that is still our own.

CHAPTER 1

The Event and the Impossibility of Neutrality

Public sentiment was deeply perturbed by the events that took place in the Oka region during the summer and fall of 1990: a 78-day stand-off with armed Natives posted behind the barricades, closure of the Mercier Bridge for some 55 days, intervention of the Canadian Armed Forces at the request of the Quebec government, an extremely traumatizing situation for the local populace, and above all, the death in the line of duty of a Sûreté du Québec officer.

—*Coroner's Office*, Rapport d'enquête du coroner Guy Gilbert sur les causes et circonstances du décès de monsieur Lemay [*Report on the Inquest by Coroner Guy Gilbert into the causes and circumstances of Mr. Lemay's death*]

Overt conflicts over territory and its resources are complex and emotionally charged, going to the very foundation of the settler states. They are at the root of serious confrontations among the police, Indigenous protestors, and non-Indigenous populations in recent history across Turtle Island. In the United States, this was made tangible in 2017 by the state repression directed at the Sioux water protectors and their supporters who had gathered at the Oceti Sakowin Camp, North Dakota, to halt the construction of the Dakota Access Pipeline, a crude oil pipeline endangering sacred sites and crucial water sources. In Canada, Idle No More, "one of the largest Indigenous mass movements in Canadian history," has been praised since 2012 for its ability to conduct a grass-roots, relatively non-confrontational social and political resistance through multiple teaching-ins, rallies, and protests for Indigenous sovereignty and environmental protection.[1] It is nonetheless a fact that Indigenous resistance has repeatedly been faced with state repression across the country. Some examples of the violent clashes sparked by forceful police intervention in Indigenous communities that reclaimed, defended, and asserted their land or fishing rights were seen in Listuguj (Restigouche), Quebec, in 1981; Gustafsen Lake, British Columbia, in 1995; Ipperwash, Ontario, also in 1995; Caledonia, Ontario, in 2006; and Elsipogtog, New Brunswick, in 2013.

The Oka Crisis, which exploded in 1990, without a doubt remains the territorial conflict in recent history that most deeply affected Indigenous and settler relations in this country. Following immediately on the failure of the Meech Lake Accord negotiations, the seventy-eight-day armed standoff drew much media attention and rendered visible an Indigenous presence that the Quebec and Canadian society believed had faded away. The event challenged the status quo and exposed a colonialist violence that underlies relations among the peoples making up Canada. It raised glaring political and legal questions, and was part of an expanded cultural context that encourages us to consider the many different ways in which history and stories are performed, utilized, staged, and recited. While it caused feelings of belonging to become fiercely polarized, Oka offered a common field of action on which this conflict could be played out.

Through its form and structure, this book attempts to reveal progressively what, in this political crisis, moved the Quebec and Canadian settler societies to realize that the status quo is not self-evident, but is based on a colonial power relation that normalizes the settler state order as it eliminates for specific purposes the political legitimacies of the peoples indigenous to the land. The book replicates the process of reflection I undertook when I ran up against fundamentally divergent interpretations in the many documentary sources and reference materials that deal with this territorial conflict.

STATE OF THE ISSUE

The Oka Crisis stimulated a substantial amount of discursive and audiovisual production, which has become an integral part of the event and its aftermath. Throughout the summer of 1990, the disturbing, dramatic armed conflict generated intense media coverage in a steady stream of television reports, information updates, and articles in daily and weekly newspapers, news magazines, radio broadcasts, and public forums, along with press releases and media conferences, letters, petitions, and posters that circulated in different places and networks. Day after day, the entire country avidly followed the reporting of an event that had captured the attention of the broader public as well as local residents. During the siege and in the months following its denouement, backgrounders on the land dispute, testimonies, and numerous other accounts were published. They represented many different voices attempting to report on the event, to communicate and symbolize what was happening in the moment and what had come before.

I argue that the Oka Crisis can be understood as an event. In that perspective, I agree with Onondaga scholar David Newhouse, who concluded from the various terms in use, "It is hard to know what to call the events at Oka. It has been variously described as crisis, incident, uprising, rebellion, and insurgency in the journalistic and academic literatures. I use the more neutral term 'events' to reflect this multiple perspective."[2] The notion of event can also point to specific impacts produced. According to historian Pierre Grégoire, the event is subjected to explanatory procedures that require us to locate it at least schematically in the context of its emergence, define how it proceeded, and specify a number of its effects.[3] Most of the media reports and publications dealing with the 1990 crisis make an attempt in this direction. The reports written by independent observers called to the site in summer 1990, such as representatives of Quebec's human rights commission, the Commission des droits de la personne du Québec, and the International Federation for Human Rights, followed such explanatory procedures—they located the conflict in its broader context and then assessed the situation and the actions of the various players according to the terms of the specific mandate their organization had been given regarding the crisis. The police intervention on 11 July, which is what triggered the overt armed conflict, clearly called for elucidation—the shots fired in the grove called the Pines and the death of Corporal Marcel Lemay have since generated an aura of violence and mystery around the political event.

Significantly, all parties directly affected by the police intervention (namely, the Sûreté du Québec's chief executive officer, the Quebec association of provincial police officers, the municipalities of the village and parish of Oka, as well as the Mohawk communities of Kanehsatake and Kahnawake) demanded a public inquiry into "the events" of 11 July 1990.[4] The following year, the Quebec government launched a public inquiry with a social and preventive mandate to shed light on the causes and circumstances of Corporal Lemay's death. As distinct from a police inquiry or a civil or criminal case, the procedure was "neither accusatory nor adversarial, but inquisitorial" (Quebec 1995, 3). It meant that the mandate received by the government-appointed coroner was not to identify a guilty party by name or to assign blame, but to understand what had happened, with the specific aim of preventing such a sequence of events from happening again.

Moreover, since the event in question was an armed conflict causing a death, the explanatory procedures to which it was subject tended to report, locate, and assess it from the perspective of adjudication and the law. There would be no accusation levelled or individual identified as responsible for taking the fatal shot, with the result that Corporal Lemay's death will never be resolved. At the same time as the coroner's inquest was proceeding, a criminal trial was being held at Montreal's courthouse. Various charges were brought against some thirty-five Indigenous activists who had been behind the barricades at Kanehsatake in September 1990.[5] The Crown cited counts of taking part in a riot, obstructing peace officers in the performance of their duty, and possessing firearms for a purpose dangerous to the public peace. The defence recast the trial in a political light. In addition to insisting that the accused had committed none of these crimes, defence lawyers maintained that their actions were justified by the need to protect land belonging to their people and to ensure their safety against violations of human rights committed by the authorities.[6] At the end of the lengthy trial, the jury rendered a verdict of not guilty on all counts. In a press release issued in response to their acquittal and addressed to the media, the Mohawk activists and their allies described the decision as "the jury's recognition that issues of territory and jurisdiction should not be decided in a criminal court, but by nation-to-nation negotiation between the Canadian government and the Six Nation Iroquois Confederacy" (translation).[7] The deliberations and judgement associated with this criminal trial raise critical political questions that lie at the root of the territorial conflict of summer 1990.

In addition to prompting a public inquiry and a trial, the event generated numerous political interrogations within the framework of the state itself. The Quebec government's request to the Canadian Armed Forces under Aid to the Civil Power—in other words, the government's calling out of armed forces as support for the provincial police—raised many questions. The responsibility of the Government of Canada for the degeneration of a land dispute into an armed confrontation also remained a principal subject for interrogation. Why, for example, did the federal government wait until the conflict degenerated to that point before intervening? Why didn't it redeem the disputed land from the town of Oka before the crisis erupted, as suggested in March 1990 by John Ciaccia, Quebec Native Affairs minister at the time?[8] It is in response to questions like these that in 1991, the federal government held hearings of the Standing Committee on Aboriginal Affairs to understand the crisis that had recently rocked the country. Like the coroner's inquest, these hearings were intended to clarify "the complex issues underlying this conflict and the confusion and bitterness felt in its aftermath"[9] in order to avoid further violence and promote healing.

The troubled period following the rejection of the Meech Lake Accord and the confrontations at Oka also saw the creation of the Royal Commission on Aboriginal Peoples. Its mandate was to "investigate the evolution of the relationship among aboriginal peoples (Indian, Inuit and Métis), the Canadian government, and Canadian society as a whole"[10] with the goal of suggesting concrete solutions to the challenging problems that had hindered these relationships. The commission engaged in consultations to explore "the basis of an equitable, honourable relationship between Aboriginals and non-Aboriginals in Canada," and underlined the importance of understanding the origins of the conflicts between the different peoples in order to work towards a resolution. "But the barricades will not fall until we understand how they were built," reads the report, in which the commission clearly noted a common interest in settling disputes: "Every Canadian will gain if we escape the impasse that breeds confrontation between Aboriginal and non-Aboriginal people across barricades, real or symbolic."[11] The event calls for understanding, introspection, and analysis, at all levels.

In the years following the crisis, various social and political actors continued to talk about and explore the event in a variety of publications: learned articles, essays, memoirs, and theses. These publications recount their author's unique relationship to the event. Many years after the crisis, provincial and federal government ministers, in particular John Ciaccia and Harry Swain, who had taken part in negotiations with various Mohawk political actors published accounts of the conflict based on their personal experience. What were the issues associated with this territorial conflict, from the governments' perspective? How did the political climate of the time influence their representatives' decisions? What actions might have been taken to avoid the conflict or hasten a resolution? Their accounts described the constraints implicitly placed on the political actors who, at the time of the crisis, proceeded in accordance with state machinery. Similarly, research in the field of military studies emphasized the strategic and logistical considerations governing the denouement of the armed conflict. In *Oka: A Convergence of Cultures and the Canadian Forces*, historian Timothy C. Winegard looked at the legal framework and political significance of deploying Canadian troops under Aid to the Civil Power during the crisis.[12] Like other works in this field, it explicitly situates the military's role in the structure of Canadian law and statehood, revealing the blueprint of the government framework that was exposed by the siege in the summer of 1990.

While they pursued a similar process aimed at understanding the event, the publications produced by Mohawk scholars, political activists, and community members who had experienced the siege close up addressed other concerns and frames of reference. In *At the Woods' Edge: An Anthology of the History of the People of Kanehsatà:ke*, Mohawk authors Brenda Katlatont Gabriel-Doxtater and Arlette Kawanatatie Van den Hende established the presence of the Kanehsata'kehró:non on the land since time immemorial. They cited the 1990 resistance as a sequel to the historical struggles against a pernicious, insistent colonization process, and presented eyewitness accounts of the siege by community members. From Kahnawake, Donna Goodleaf published the non-fiction account *Entering the War Zone: A Mohawk Perspective on Resisting Invasions*, in which she looked back at the summer of 1990 to locate the activities of Mohawk political actors—especially the women in charge of communications—in the framework of Mohawk and Haudenosaunee political and spiritual structures. Goodleaf honoured her community's resistance to colonial government policies as well as its courage when faced with police and military repression.

Many other forms of inquiry have appeared in Indigenous and non-Indigenous scholarly works that treat the crisis as a continuation of colonial history, discuss images and media representations of the conflict, examine the geography of the siege, study the historical struggles of the Indigenous peoples, and highlight how the Mohawk people's political and social structures were affirmed. Nonetheless, this handful of examples from a vast number of settler and Indigenous accounts reveals certain divergences, which point to fundamental issues that were central to the conflict that blew up in 1990.

AN INTERDISCIPLINARY APPROACH

Oka speaks to the colonial and therefore deeply conflicted nature of the settler-Indigenous coexistence on the levels of historiography, territoriality, politics, and culture. In a magnifying mirror, it reflects a continental context in which the First Peoples and settlers are, to borrow the phrasing of Chippewa media studies scholar Gail Guthrie Valaskakis, "shackled to one another in cultural conflict and political struggle." Regarding this difficult cohabitation, Valaskakis continued: "Today, Natives and newcomers are engaged in conflicts over land and treaties, stories and stereotypes, resources and policies, all interrelated issues that arise in collapsed time and continuing discord. The threads of this discord are formed from dissimilar memories, images and meanings, each string entangled in struggles over territory, history, and ideology."[13] The crisis that exploded in summer 1990 provides a single point of focus for the multiple threads of discord that inescapably bind and separate peoples positioned on either side of a long process of colonization that is still active.

The issue of territory is of primary importance in the resistance at Kanehsatake. It implies a political dimension concerning how the very narratives that give the land's occupation meaning and legitimacy can come into conflict. In his book *If This Is Your Land, Where Are Your Stories? Finding Common Ground*, literary scholar J. Edward Chamberlin stressed how essential it is to understand "how stories give meaning and value to the places we call home; how they bring us close to the world we live in by taking us into a world of words; how they hold us together and at the same time keep us apart."[14] The element of conflicting stories mentioned by Chamberlin has been an integral part of the history of the Americas since colonization began. From the first contact, the imperial European powers have relied on the Doctrine of Discovery and on the principle of *terra nullius* to carve up among themselves the territory they set foot on, dismissing the existence of the peoples who were indigenous to those lands. Institutionalization of this international jurisdictional construct reinforced and legalized the dehumanization of the Indigenous peoples and the concomitant persisting appropriation of their lands.[15] The structural effects of what anthropologist and ethnographer Patrick Wolfe has termed "the settler-colonial logic of elimination"[16] continue to be felt today. This is notably indicated by the loss of territory, gulfs between generations, and deep-seated injustices, along with the harsh socio-economic conditions and multifaceted violence that result from ongoing settler colonization. Contrary to the rational dimension generally associated with the law, this principle includes an undeniable element of fiction, as underscored by Chamberlin when he states that "the settlers quickly invented a myth of entitlement—a constitution, a creation story—to match their myth of discovery."[17] Canada, like other settler countries, is based on a constitution that was developed in the absence of Indigenous peoples. The constitution is shored up by a judicial and legal structure that reduces the First Peoples to inferior status and seeks their assimilation. *The Report of the Royal Commission on Aboriginal Peoples,* requested by the federal government following the Oka Crisis, clearly states as much.

The siege in action exposed a land dispute that had persisted at Oka-Kanehsatake for nearly three centuries.[18] Moreover, it partook of a dynamic of conflict that has dictated the nature of relationships between the Indigenous peoples and the settler colonial and government authorities in Canada generally. By actualizing, in physical space, "the confrontation of two theses: that of legality and that of legitimacy," as it was put by Coroner Guy Gilbert (Quebec 1995, 77), the siege demonstrates why the power to define is fundamental to relationships between Indigenous peoples and the Canadian government. The siege maintained by Mohawk people against police and the military reminds us that Canada as we know it is built on the marginalization, delegitimization, and, very often, interdiction of Indigenous forms of knowledge and expression.

In 1990, the event erupted on the disputed land at the root of the conflict that had been growing increasingly poisonous for months and even centuries in Oka-Kanehsatake. The issues involved go back to the very foundations of settler societies: the appropriation of the land and the basis for its legitimacy. The territorial dispute touches on and cuts across dimensions of politics and law as well as culture and identity, making an examination of the ways in which the historical, personal, and imagined accounts contradict one another very telling. The causes of conflict that became incendiary during the siege reappear in other forms on film and in literature, which is why this book connects film and literary narratives with the political event they report on or from which they draw inspiration. Ultimately, as we will see, the conflict that resulted in the siege shows up in a very concrete way in the research.

AN INEVITABLE PARTIALITY

The Oka Crisis, or the resistance at Kanehsatake, grew out of what is called a "deep-rooted conflict" by specialists in conflict studies, such as Vernon W. Neufeld Redekop. According to him, such conflicts, which are closely linked to identity, touch on "beliefs, values, culture, spirituality, meaning systems, relationships, history, imagination, and capacity to act that are at the core of an individual or group."[19] Intense and charged with emotion, they connect with a variety of fields and disciplines that cluster together and overlay one another. It is precisely this clustering that makes it difficult to understand these conflicts in all their complexity. In an immediate way, Coroner Guy Gilbert said, Oka involved "a confrontation between Indigenous peoples and a municipality, a complex legal situation, a case with a 250-year timeframe" (Quebec 1995, 398). The event, which the coroner described as being "of extraordinary complexity" (Quebec 1995, 30), brings into play some significant political and strategic considerations. The scope is that much greater because the conflict was intensified by several elements. Among these are the armed intervention of the Sûreté du Québec and the Canadian Forces; the involvement of municipal, provincial, and federal governments; the active, strategic engagement of Mohawk people from Kahnawake, Akwesasne, and other Haudenosaunee communities; the mobilization of First Peoples across the country and at the international level; as well as the repeated display and enactment of intense racial hatred towards the Mohawks and other Indigenous peoples.

An event is by definition hard to grasp as it is going on, and the deeply conflicted nature of the one concerning us here has produced numerous grey zones that have persisted after the fact. In his study of the military intervention in the crisis, historian Timothy C. Winegard stated, "The truth is obscured by the numerous factions present within the conflict, each vying to protect their cause. For those involved it was and still is a matter of perspective. The same can be said for those who have previously written on the Oka crisis."[20] In this respect, researchers ultimately run up against the same kind of difficulties that had to be overcome by coroners, prosecutors, and investigators, among others. All the same, it is to be noted that distance from the armed siege has a significant influence on the questions asked about it. The further we are from it, the more we tend to direct our attention to its structural and symbolic aspects; the closer we get to the conflict's epicentre, however, the more we become mired in the details of issues that grow in number, complexity, and intensity.

As demonstrated in the public inquiry intended to shed light on the causes and circumstances of Corporal Marcel Lemay's death during the shooting on 11 July 1990, accounts of the conflict drew in parties with diverging interests in relation to the evidence to be used in a criminal trial and, more broadly, to the assignment of ethical and political blame for poisoning the conflict. Given what was at risk, both personally and politically, all of the parties were motivated to report the event in such a way as to avoid compromising themselves. In his report, Coroner Guy Gilbert remarked on a lack of transparency that made his job much more complicated. He deplored the fact that the public inquiry should have "gradually become the arena for a common front of police officers" who put aside their differences and made a "display of complacent submission regarding the upper management of the Sûreté [du Québec]," which was called upon to account for the decision to intervene at Oka-Kanehsatake on 11 July 1990 (Quebec 1995, 10). To add to the difficulties, holding the criminal trial at the same time as the inquiry had the effect of inhibiting testimony. Reporting a "difficult, even impossible situation for the Mohawks," the coroner observed that they "gave testimony with restraint and reticence," knowing that the prosecutors, in their cross-examinations, were collecting material that could be useful to the police investigation (Quebec 1995, 18). In addition to having such considerations hamper clarification of the event, numerous factors would long remain obscure as a result of the secrecy that protected many official documents connected to the conflict. This added to the element of the unknown that persisted after the event itself had ended.

Such a strategic partiality in constructing our relation to reality is all the more apparent when we are clarifying a territorial conflict that owes its conflictual nature to an armed confrontation, and, as well, involves settlers and Indigenous peoples in Canada as a whole. Given this situation, the partiality is not limited to understanding a disaffected element within the same, single society. Rather, it applies to different political legitimacies in a continuing state of tension. From the perspective of the discipline of history, for example, it is especially significant that numerous historians work as consultants to governments and band councils involved in legal disputes over the basis and validity of land claims by First Nations, Métis, and Inuit; or, to take the opposite perspective, that of land claims by Quebec and Canada. At Oka-Kanehsatake, as far back as the first disputes between the Sulpicians and the Mohawks in the eighteenth century, the issue of land gave rise to unequal power relations that are impossible to ignore in the context of settlement. This is striking in the context of a siege that underscores the historical motives and political means of colonial governments, and the settler states of Quebec and Canada that succeeded them, for pronouncing in favour of colonial ownership of the land.

The armed conflict in the summer of 1990 disturbed public law and order. For that reason, it was put down by the police with the support of the Canadian Armed Forces under Aid to the Civil Power, as provided for in the National Defence Act. Deploying the resources of the Sûreté du Québec and the Canadian Army at the siege site demonstrates how the status quo can be maintained by resorting to force, which raises various questions on moral and political levels.

Having reviewed numerous books on the Oka Crisis, military historian Timothy C. Winegard concluded that many questions still remain unanswered for lack of information or agreement in versions of events. In his view, none of the publications he found "represents a historically complete and unbiased representation of the events that transpired before and during the summer of 1990."[21] In any case, the matter of perspectives and, by extension, of sources constitutes a crucial issue in the conflict, whether regarding the basis for the legitimacy of the occupation of the land, or how the conflict was experienced, understood, and assessed.

On examining the various sources, one quickly realizes that it would not be possible to do this conflict justice by designing a compromise that would provide seamless reconciliation of the various interpretations, divergent interests, and antagonistic stances. Just as an all-embracing synthesis would threaten to compromise the integrity of the different parties, it would be hazardous to choose between versions that not only diverge but often do not tally. The governments' accounts and those of the Mohawk Nation often conflict directly, all the more because the legitimacy of the former establishes itself in large part to the detriment of the latter. To add to the complexity, these accounts coincide on many of the same points, although discordant voices can be heard from both sides of the barricades.

During the 1990 conflict, the authorities and the media made much of the divisions within the Mohawk communities, but the communities were not the only ones to have experienced disagreements and dissension—deep divisions also showed up in the Quebec and Canadian populations. Convincing examples are provided by the differences that pitted the Municipality of Oka against the non-Indigenous environmental groups, or the diametrically opposed attitudes of the white residents who took part in the racist riots on the approaches to the Honoré-Mercier Bridge, on the one hand, and the white demonstrators who marched in the streets to support the Mohawks' land struggle, on the other. Dissension could also be seen within the governments. The coroner's report clearly recognized a divergence in perspective on the part of the Quebec authorities during the investigation: "Briefly, between the Sûreté, the public service, the political authorities and the office of Minister Elkas, views and opinions were disparate and incomplete" (Quebec 1995, 396). Although it may be hard to find agreement in versions of the facts, one thing is certain—the Oka Crisis was a source of uneasiness and confusion.

A close study of this territorial conflict makes it clear that neutrality was and still is impossible. This is all the more obvious in that, nearly thirty years later, the conflict still has not been resolved. Regarding Oka, media studies scholar Lorna Roth concluded that "accounts of the events and background about the issues could not adequately be analyzed and/or synthesized in an 'objective,' neutral fashion." However, she added that researchers who are "concerned with finding new ways of speaking and writing take into account the complexity and multiplicity of perceptions around this historical event."[22] The complexity and multiplicity of perceptions regarding this event are very real and must indeed be taken into account. Nonetheless, it is appropriate to recognize that, in addition to being heterogeneous, these perceptions are heavily polarized. In other words, it is not enough to say that there are multiple versions; the polarization at work and the conditions for effectiveness of different versions must also be considered. Furthermore, the unattainable neutrality mentioned earlier does not mean that we should exclude all reflection on the conflict as a whole. In fact, it is possible to think in, with, and through conflict; the recurring elements that we are able to discern in these multiple versions point to certain avenues of understanding.

In *Narrating Our Pasts: The Social Construction of Oral History*, anthropologist Elizabeth Tonkin pointed out that, in the oral tradition, several versions often exist of the same story, but despite that, we can still perceive core consistencies. In her view, collecting and considering multiple versions together makes it possible to identify these consistencies, as well as minor variations that might emerge. The specific variations to be found in a given story locate the narrator, the audience, and the entire society in a particular climate. In a similar way, rather than sorting through the details to resolve the extreme complexity of this political crisis, this book draws out the core consistencies to be found in the multiple versions of the crisis. At the same time, it offers a unique version of the event that locates the researcher, political actor, filmmaker, and writer, by turns, along with the reader and the entire society, in the particular climate of the Oka Crisis, or resistance at Kanehsatake. What stands out in the perspectives of governments, Canadian soldiers, Mohawk protestors, and Indigenous communities? What can be discerned in the perspectives developed by different documentary filmmakers, writers, poets, and playwrights? In what ways does research after the fact influence an event that continues to be so active? What should we do with what the event reveals to us?

This book does not reveal new information about Oka. Far from providing a political or historical analysis as such, the study of the siege in action is to be viewed in relation to the documentary films and literary narratives and serve as their context. This book does not study the Mohawks, Québécois, or Canadians per se, but rather a conflict-ridden political event in which they were all involved and through which they all took action and expressed themselves. The idea is not to suggest a relativity that has the effect of dissolving and absolving the colonial violence now that the injustices have been exposed and it is time to assign responsibility. This danger has frequently been pointed out by Indigenous studies scholars, in particular Craig W. Womack in his 1999 work *Red on Red: Native American Literary Separatism*, and Renate Eigenbrod in her 2005 book *Travelling Knowledges: Positioning the Im/Migrant Reader of Aboriginal Literatures in Canada*.

At the same time, this book does not pretend to provide a definitive response to the event. Instead, it strives to develop its reflection in light of the "truth-telling" proposed by Anishinaabe writer Basil H. Johnston. In his text "One Generation from Extinction," Johnston explained that the expression *w'daeb-awae* is used in his language to affirm that what someone says is true. It constitutes a philosophical proposition that very specifically challenges the existence of an absolute truth: "But the expression is not just a mere confirmation of a speaker's veracity. It is at the same time a philosophical proposition that, in saying, a speaker casts his words and his voice only as far as his vocabulary and his perception will enable him. In so doing the tribe was denying that there was absolute truth; that the best a speaker could achieve and a listener expect was the highest degree of accuracy. Somehow that one expression 'w'daeb-awae' set the limits of a single statement as well as setting limits on all speech."[23] In the spirit of this proposition, which requires of a speaker the greatest accuracy she can achieve within the limits of her vocabulary and perception, I tried to define the topic and the theory for this book so as to articulate the strongest possible argumentation according to my specific place of utterance, research process, and perspective.

Further, Oka's breadth and complexity—politically, culturally, and as an event—oblige us to "recognize that we will never see the whole thing completely," to borrow from theatre and performance studies scholar Josette Féral.[24] The idea is not to produce a final answer to the questions raised by the 1990 conflict, but rather, as suggested by literary scholar Jonathan Culler in reference to a completely other context, to "attempt to throw things into question and redirect our thinking into areas other than those where [the works in question] are presumed to belong."[25] In the context of settlement more specifically, the idea is also to make what is familiar foreign, and ask, following Culler, "readers to do another take on their own way of thinking and the institutions to which that thinking subscribes."[26] In this sense, I wanted to offer a dynamic interpretation of Oka by looking at the event from both general and particular viewpoints, based on what was said and done at the site of the siege and in the public space, and was then to be found in other forms in documentary films and literary narratives. This approach is all the more appropriate because first of all it is the event, with what it shakes up or breaks open, that throws a situation into question and makes us see it differently.

RESEARCH AS A SITE OF TENSION

In tackling the proliferation of meaning and significance surrounding a deep-rooted conflict, the notion of "the event" provides an effective critical tool in untangling the concentrated knot of intersecting aspects of the Oka Crisis. An event springs from an unprecedented coincidence of circumstances. As American anthropologist Raymond D. Fogelson pointed out in "The Ethnology of Events and Nonevents," "events involve processes, changes, happenings, acts, transformations and other features that are essentially different from physical objects or concrete things."[27] Unforeseen and unforeseeable, an event produces a break from what is normal, throws things into suspense, and takes the various actors by surprise, leaving them caught against their will in the breach it opens. With its elements of danger and risk, the event is enigmatic and induces passion. A defining phenomenon, it brings out something that without it would not have been revealed and that materializes suddenly, contrary to expectations. Claude Romano further observed that the event is characterized in part "by the non-sense of what appears, at first glance, to be incomprehensible," but also in part "by the excess of meaning [the event] itself generates."[28] The event that erupted on 11 July 1990 manifested itself in this paradoxical way.

The Oka Crisis, or resistance in Kanehsatake, is often described as a fissure or break in the established order, a crisis of legitimacy or hegemony, and sometimes as an opening up of possibilities.[29] At first elusive, the event excites a need to find meaning and grasp an occurrence that, while long dreaded, arrives without warning. Mohawk political scientist Gerald Taiaiake Alfred referred to that tension between incomprehension and an excess of meaning in explaining that the crisis and its consequences provided him with the context for researching and writing *Heeding the Voices of Our Ancestors*: *Kahnawake Mohawk Politics and the Rise of Native Nationalism.* He went on to say that Oka "forced me to search for deeper meaning to what seemed, from the inside, an incoherent or contradictory set of events."[30] While the conflict was confounding, it was also eloquent. In Claude Romano's terms, we can state that the Oka Crisis, like the event, is revelatory because it exhorted us to judge the situation according to a perspective it engendered. The siege, a veritable stage set for antagonistic identities, accentuated and made visible tensions that occur in a more or less attenuated way in daily life.

During the Oka Crisis, the Quebec and Canadian societies saw their troubled relationship with Indigenous peoples exposed; they appeared as the heirs to a less than brilliant colonial history and settler colonial present, and were therefore seen in an unflattering and even alarming light. By contrast, Indigenous peoples who had long had their identity denied, had been unjustly dispossessed and marginalized, suddenly saw their presence affirmed at the centre of these settler societies. They were still more fundamentally confirmed and validated among the First Nations, who immediately recognized themselves in the land struggles and political assertions made by the besieged Mohawks. As Romano wrote, the event resembles us; it is "the point of crystallization from which there emerges an understanding of who we are."[31] In this sense, the Oka Crisis, or resistance at Kanehsatake, can be viewed as a focal point that reveals the overall relationship among all peoples in the country.

Whenever an event occurs, argued Claude Romano, it makes manifest something about its own context that would remain hidden without it; what's more, it sets the limit on possible interpretations for determining and deciding its meaning.[32] For a proper interpretation of events with an intercultural dimension, ethnohistorian Raymond Fogelson insisted, it is not enough to put historical information in context. Since the context itself is problematic, it must be explained. What context are we talking about? According to what place of utterance has this context been defined? How does a given context influence the interpretation of an event? In the matter of the Oka Crisis or the resistance at Kanehsatake, are we talking about a context that is Mohawk, Québécois, Canadian, or global, taking in all parties?

Fogelson explained that when an ethnohistorical approach is used, "events may be recognized, defined, evaluated, and endowed with meaning differentially in different cultural traditions."[33] The fact of this differentiation means that a situation considered to be an event by some could go virtually unnoticed by others. The violent dissension that shook the Mohawk community of Akwesasne in the spring of 1990, for example, did not unduly disturb Canada's broader general public.[34] That conflict was nonetheless very serious and involved exchanges of fire that cost the lives of two Mohawk men, Harold J.R. Edwards and Matthew Pike. By contrast, Oka was an event for everyone. The Mohawks and other Indigenous peoples, as well as the Québécois and Canadians, were all aware of the dispute over land that, in the middle of a constitutional crisis, suddenly degenerated into a protracted armed conflict and major media event. As the attitudes of the various parties demonstrate, the ways of recognizing, defining, and assessing the event and assigning it meaning vary with the perspective. Although some may see it as a repetition and others as a new phenomenon, the event loses none of its power to reveal the overall relationship that unites and opposes them.

This book approaches the Oka Crisis, or the resistance at Kanehsatake, not from a relativist position that places all forms of knowledge on the same plane, but rather from one that works with comparisons, contrasts, colonial relations, and, necessarily, conflict. It purposively presents multiple, conflicting, Indigenous, and non-Indigenous theories and worldviews so that the tension, malaise, and violent affect played out during the siege will be replayed in the writing. It interrogates not only the historical facts, but also what informs the various bodies of knowledge that determine their interpretation. Thus, on the one hand, the book attends to the actions and utterances of the various political actors that accompanied the siege's progress; on the other, it refers to different theories and traditions of thought in order to examine these perspectives in a fair and relevant way.

If, in reporting on the actions of various players, we interpret them only in terms of the dominant theoretical and cultural framework, we inevitably empty some of these actions of their meaning and thus support a process of erasing certain realities and understandings. Who are the Mohawks, in the story of the Canadian or Québécois Nation? For that matter, who are they in the story of the Mohawk Nation or the Iroquois Confederacy? It takes little reflection on this question to realize what the effects of different interpretative positions might be.

In a very fundamental way, studying the Oka Crisis also encourages the realization that the status quo is not a neutral position, but a dominant colonial stance that is most often taken to be the natural order. This distinction is all the more important because one of the features of the political crisis of summer 1990 is its capacity to expose the constructed nature of this established order.

If it is crucial to recognize that the status quo reflects power relations derived from colonial history, then examining the Canadian and Quebec governments, Western social institutions, and all the traditions of thinking that lie behind them is equally critical in gaining a better understanding of the dynamics of conflict at work in the Oka Crisis. Of course, the aforementioned elements do not derive from a monolithic structure and are similarly integral in many ways to the lives of Indigenous individuals and peoples. They nonetheless represent the political and symbolic order to which settler societies subscribe and by which they benefit, whether implicitly or explicitly. As a result, understanding how they influenced the development of the 1990 conflict is relevant. If we proceed from the realization that the settler populations exist within a national state framework, recognize the authority of the courts, are governed by municipal, provincial, and federal laws that in part regulate their existence, and have received a certain history and an undeniable privilege as a legacy, then we are better able to understand how they have interpreted, experienced, recounted, and imagined the event. Further, we must take Métis scholar Emma LaRocque very seriously when she cautions us that by "contextualizing offensive literature—or policy or outcome," especially one that is colonialist and racist, we risk ending up "defending, normalizing, neutralizing, or even legitimizing it."[35] This is certainly one of the major challenges posed by this interdisciplinary and intercultural study of Oka.

By revisiting the event from perspectives that are both intertwined and antagonistic, the book opens up a space in which different interests and forms of knowledge regarding the conflict become related and opposed. It builds on the work of Maori scholar Linda Tuhiwai Smith who, following scholar of postcolonial studies Edward Said, defined research as "a significant site of struggle between the interests and ways of knowing of the West and the interests and ways of resisting of the Other."[36] In the book's publishing context, in Canada and Quebec, it is crucial to acknowledge and generate a space for Mohawk and Indigenous perspectives and traditions of thought. Without that, the position of the Mohawk protesters in summer 1990 would remain devoid of meaning or, which might be worse, be explicable only through its distance from the dominant society, often with reference to an imaginary figure associated with the criminal world. This was the case when the Québécois and Canadian populations saw armed Mohawk warriors appear at the top of the Saint-Michel Hill in Oka-Kanehsatake as well as in the middle of the Honoré-Mercier Bridge in Kahnawake.

Over the last decades, Mohawk scholars have generated transformative knowledge and understandings in the fields of Iroquois and Native studies. By orienting the thinking of scholars who do not belong to their nations, they have simultaneously acted as cultural and political ambassadors. The work of such contemporaries as Gerald Taiaiake Alfred, anthropologist Audra Simpson, and literary scholar Rick Monture, to name just a few, can make it easier for scholars from other Indigenous nations, and also for settler scholars, to perceive the besieged Mohawk people's stance in all the complexity of its broader context. By reading their work along with many other Mohawk narratives that corroborate and supplement one another, whether it is in the realms of arts, politics, film, or culture, one becomes able to gradually gain some insight into these communities' continued opposition to encroachment and their historical and political realities, as well as the meaning that can be assigned to the siege of 1990. In addition to laying bare the injustices at the basis of settler societies, their work brings out the consistent strategy of the Mohawk people, who refuse to bow down to Canadian authority but reaffirm the sovereignty of the Mohawk Nation and Iroquois Confederacy. Simpson's and Alfred's theoretical work especially exposes how the siege of summer 1990 generated tension between the state paradigm, which views the territorial conflict essentially in terms of Canadian law, and the Indigenous resistance and resurgence, or those of the Mohawk people more specifically, which inscribe it in an Indigenous narrative of legitimacy.[37] In so doing, they shed light on the inherent conflict in a situation of coexistence shaped by a long, sustained process of colonization. They can be understood as being part of what Taiaiake Alfred calls the "New Indigenous Intelligentsia," one that "is trying to get settlers to understand that colonialism must and will be confronted and destroyed."[38] And thus, in addition to making the Mohawk protestors' position stronger by placing it squarely on theoretical and historical levels, Mohawk scholars and artists also provide conceptual tools that make it possible to define the event within the perspectives of their communities and nation.

In this book, I take into account the differentiated stories that dovetail with power relations made manifest during the Oka Crisis or Kanehsatà:ke resistance. I simultaneously acknowledge that these stories have cut across and influenced one another in various ways since the first contact, although in accordance with unequal and unjust colonial relations. As well as generating a strong polarization, the event reveals a tangle of inextricable relationships; as in Georg Simmel's theory of conflict, it paradoxically unites the antagonists around a single object claimed by both. Just as conflict creates a relationship between the parties it unites and opposes, revisiting Oka means referring to theories that are both particular and shared and in a state of interaction as much as tension. By the same token, just as the siege sets the stage for establishing a space for agreement in which a confrontation can take place, this book sets out to construct a story that is shared and yet does not negate inherent elements of conflict and highly fraught colonial power relations.

While this book gives due consideration to the questions that arise when Indigenous knowledges and Western academic knowledges intersect, as discussed, for instance, by scholars George J. Sefa Dei, Rauna Kuokkanen, Devon Abbott Mihesuah, and Angela Cavender Wilson,[39] it also proposes interpretative tools that would enable us to identify unique features and bring different fields into dialogue, in order to create conditions for mutual understanding even in the absence of agreement. As the violent exacerbation of a deep-rooted settler colonial conflict, the Oka Crisis never ceases to remind us of the potential of such a process and the practical and theoretical difficulties inherent in it. On this point, Renate Eigenbrod remarked that the aim of reconciliation favoured in books produced in Indigenous studies constitutes "a goal that requires a paradigm shift in *all of* society."[40] On a very modest scale, this book makes an effort to outline a reflection that moves in the direction of such a paradigm shift, or, at the very least, attempts to make its relevance and necessity felt. At the same time, when examining the Oka Crisis or Kanehsatà:ke resistance, it strives to take into account not only a colonial past but also a colonial present, one that requires, as Dene political scientist Glen Sean Coulthard argued, that we acknowledge and throughly understand "the current entanglement of settler coloniality with the politics of reconciliation."[41]

CHAPTER 2

The Siege in Action: Settler Crisis and Indigenous Resistance

The Mohawk people have been waiting for over 300 years for a peace that never seems to come. A peace blocked by arrogant, racist governments and their forced assimilation policies concealing their coveting of our lands and resources through their legislation.

—*Ellen Gabriel, "Epilogue. Fraudulent Theft of Mohawk Land by the Municipality of Oka"*

In the spring of 1990, the First Nations made the weight of their opposition felt in the Meech Lake constitutional discussions, notably through the intervention of Cree Manitoba Member of the Legislative Assembly Elijah Harper, who refused to give his consent to the ratification of the accord. As soon as summer came, the Mohawks asserted their sovereignty in a political conflict that captured the headlines and, by the time it ended, had undermined the national myth of Quebec and Canada: the Oka Crisis.[1] The local occupation of a dirt road launched at Kanehsatake several months before the crisis blew up is one of the "flashpoint events" described by political scientist Peter H. Russell. According to Russell, "the flashpoint event occurs when members of the Aboriginal community see that government, without settling the long-standing dispute, is permitting activities to take place that ignore Aboriginal interest in the area, and, in effect, deny Aboriginal or treaty rights. Under these conditions, members of the Aboriginal community may decide to take direct action to stop the activity and produce a flashpoint event."[2] This was the scenario played out at Kanehsatake. In 1990, the federal government repeatedly refused to suspend a municipal development project slated to take place on land that the Kanehsata'kehró:non had been defending for nearly three centuries. Faced with the government's failure to take action, community members decided to occupy the site in order to prevent the felling of trees, the first phase of the planned project, and to put pressure on the Municipality of Oka. The occupation of the grove called the Pines that had been ongoing since 9 March 1990 corresponds in all respects to a flashpoint event. However, it is the police intervention of 11 July 1990 that makes it an "event" in the full sense of the term. The morning on which the firing broke out, a land dispute that had been bogged down and growing increasingly poisonous for months, if not years, suddenly veered out of the actors' control and became driven by a dynamic of its own.

The notion of "the event" was theorized by philosophers Gad Soussana, Alexis Nouss, and Jacques Derrida in *Dire l'événement, est-ce possible?* [Is it possible to say the event?].[3] After their work, among that of others, it can be said that the Oka Crisis constitutes an event in that it erupted unexpectedly, its final outcome was unknown, and it demanded a response. Indeed, the peaceful occupation of the Pines had lasted for four entire months when the Sûreté du Québec, Quebec's provincial police, in response to a third request by the Municipality of Oka's mayor, forcefully intervened to dismantle the Mohawk barricades. On the morning of 11 July 1990, 125 members of the tactical intervention team arrived on the site and, faced with the occupiers' determination to stay, began an assault on the Pines. The chaotic shootout that followed resulted in the tragic death of one of the officers, Corporal Marcel Lemay. In the midst of this violent altercation, the event was born, marking the beginning of a lengthy period of suspense. Against all expectations, the police then withdrew, and the Mohawk protestors reinforced the barricades with the abandoned police vehicles; this time they blocked an actual road, Route 344, that runs through Oka and Kanehsatake. That same morning, protesters from Kahnawake came to the aid of those in Kanehsatake by blocking access to the Honoré-Mercier Bridge, a principal traffic artery connecting Montreal to its suburbs on the St. Lawrence River's South Shore. The Sûreté du Québec immediately surrounded the two communities and returned to set up barricades of its own facing those of the Mohawks. The two camps were armed and tension was high, causing fears that further violence would break out.

The siege that was then established would result in an intervention by the Canadian Armed Forces at the end of the summer. It sent a shock wave across the country, particularly into Indigenous communities, which felt directly

Mohawk women blocking the Honoré-Mercier Bridge, which connects Montreal to Kahnawake, the day of the shootout, 11 July 1990. Courtesy of Kanien'kehá:ka Onkwawén:na Raotitióhkwa Language and Cultural Center.

affected by a land dispute that had degenerated to such an extent. The populations of Quebec and the rest of Canada, who were also interpellated by the crisis, were stunned and confused, and expressed an alarming degree of racial hatred. The siege did not end until 26 September 1990, after seventy-eight days of open conflict that saw the mobilization of more than 1,000 Sûreté du Québec officers, officers of the Royal Canadian Mounted Police, and, as backup, in the function of the Aid to the Civil Power, "the deployment of the Canadian Forces, 4,500 strong," or more specifically "2,500 regular and reserve troops from the Thirty-Fourth and Thirty-Fifth Canadian Brigade Groups and the Fifth Canadian Mechanized Brigade Group."[4] Beyond the physical and material confrontation, the Oka Crisis ultimately threw the symbolic territory constituting the national space into question.[5]

There was a loud outcry against the stance of the Mohawk protestors, who carried weapons to defend their territory. The ins and outs of the police operation in the Pines, however, were gradually lost to view in the subsequent media circus. Clearly, striking images of masked warriors perched on upended Sûreté du Québec vehicles lying across the road, and brandishing weapons as a sign of victory, presented a more powerful draw for the media than the political and ethical complexities of coexistence shaped by a lengthy colonization process. And yet, two days before the armed conflict exploded, Quebec's minister of Native Affairs John Ciaccia had written to Oka's mayor, asking him to suspend the golf course project indefinitely so that the barricades could be lifted and the necessary time given to negotiating a solution acceptable to all parties.

In his letter of 9 July 1990, two days before the fatal intervention, Ciaccia declared outright that the situation was growing more complex and "risk[ed] degenerating into a confrontation." Referring to the injunction obtained by the municipality to force the protestors to lift the barricades, he explained that the issues surrounding the territorial conflict "go beyond what is strictly legal in the situation as interpreted by the courts." They principally concerned "1) the historical claims of the Aboriginal peoples, 2) the cultural context and the Aboriginals' perception of this situation, 3) the relationships between the Aboriginal communities and our society, 4) the message sent out into the world that this is how we treat the Aboriginals."[6] The letter was published in its entirety in the next day's issue of the daily newspaper *Le Devoir*. It stated that the dispute over the respective interests of the Municipality of Oka and Kanehsatake's Mohawk community was part of the larger history of colonization and the settler state formation that still shapes relations among the different peoples in Canada as a whole. Further, Ciaccia anticipated that the international community could not help but take a negative view of such hasty, forceful recourse to police intervention, when the purpose was to make room for the expansion of a golf course and a housing development on land adjacent to the cemetery of a small Indigenous community, whose historical land claims would be cavalierly ignored. Relations among Canada, Quebec, and the First Nations had just been damaged by the failure of the Meech Lake Accord, and here were the Indigenous peoples again making their voice heard, this time in the middle of an armed conflict that would resound as far away as Europe, where Canada's reputation would be tarnished.

THE OKA CRISIS

The force with which the event exploded cannot be separated from the deep-seated causes of the territorial conflict, which in turn point to the history of oversight and negligence underpinning the event. As put by French historian

Mohawk warrior Richard Livingston Nicholas standing atop an overturned police vehicle blocking a main road in Kahnesetake at the beginning of the Oka Crisis, on 11 July 1990, after a police assault to remove Mohawk barriers failed. Canadian Press/Tom Hanson.

Pierre Nora, the event becomes the site of the brutal emergence of a constellation of social phenomena that rise up from the depths.[7] Narratives based on events reveal power relations, political objectives, and social values; they are intended to construct a coherent image of the past, whose heft depends largely on how visible or invisible it becomes.

In the summer of 1990, the siege gave visibility to a dispute whose origins date all the way back to the establishment of the Oka municipality, a dispute that to this day has not yet been resolved. Its immediate cause was a contested project to expand the golf course and build a housing development. More largely, the siege attests to a colonial history featuring repeated encroachment on the land, intensive Christianization, and assimilation policies with the aim and expectation of making the Indigenous peoples disappear in order to better naturalize settlement. In Canada and Quebec, this obliteration of the peoples indigenous to the land is an inherent, yet largely unacknowledged, part of the national stories of the settlers, who have long given themselves the credit for founding the country. In a completely different context, American literary critic Shoshana Felman talks about an "historical attack on the act of vision"[8] to denote the determination to render invisible not just the presence one seeks to obliterate, but also the genocidal acts themselves and the party responsible for them. The breach produced by the event in summer 1990 sheds light on the violence the settler nations have perpetrated on the Indigenous peoples behind the scenes, and thus helps to produce a brief alteration in the field of vision. According to American cultural studies scholar Amelia Kalant, a crisis like Oka opens up a "space for extended experimentation" in which relationships are redrawn. These transformations, Kalant added, are limited by the extent to which re-establishing the status quo is part of resuming the daily routine.[9] That is why it is still important to go back and revisit the event in such a way as to change how the discourse is constructed and to do so in order to counter invisibility.

The representations put forward to justify the process of appropriating Indigenous lands have at their core a figure of exclusion called the "Invented Indian" or the "Imaginary Indian." The articulations of this colonial figure in the United States, Canada, and Quebec were notably expounded by writers James A. Clifton in the collection *The Invented Indian: Cultural Fictions and Government Policies*, Daniel Francis in his work *The Imaginary Indian: The Image of the Indian in Canadian Culture*, and Jean-Jacques Simard in his book *La Réduction: l'Autochtone inventé et les Amérindiens d'aujourd'hui* [The Reduction: The

Invented Indian or Today's Aboriginals]. As Simard has explained, the entire historical edifice for what he calls the "reduction" of Indigenous peoples rests in a very concrete way on a business of appropriating the territory and expropriating resources. Its cohesiveness is ensured by a powerful set of symbols, images, and fictions describing the authentic Aboriginal in terms of the "Noble Savage" imagined by eighteenth-century European philosopher Jean-Jacques Rousseau. Based on an inverted image of Western society, continues Simard, this imaginary construct conceives of the Indian as a primitive being linked to an unspoiled natural world, untouched by civilization and heir to an ancient cultural heritage that must remain immutable, under pain of disappearing.[10]

And so, in 1990, the Indigenous peoples were still seen as destined either to disappear or to remain faithful reproductions of an imaginary figure relegated to ineffectuality on the margins of history, politics, and territory. As that figure, Indigenous people would be beings on the periphery required to stay in remote regions, if not in museums, where their petrified image would provide a substitute for authenticity to colonizing nations short on legitimacy. In this context, as Kalant further explained in her book *National Identity and the Conflict at Oka*, Indigenous peoples living close to metropolitan areas would become figures of false Indians, assimilated individuals who would be hard to recognize. This discursive construction involves an implicit refusal to recognize in Indigenous peoples the ability to change with contact.[11] These fixed concepts of identity were still present and active at the close of the twentieth century, associating Indigenous peoples with a form of knowledge that erases subjectivity—knowledge being, according to Kalant, "that which allows us to act upon and change our environment and produce ourselves."[12] During the Oka Crisis, the Mohawks broke into the public space in an unprecedented way, where they succeeded in imposing an image that combined what is Indigenous, contemporary, and urban in a coherent, effective whole. Counter to essentialist, rigid representations that relegate them to an ineffectual past, they were projecting, on the doorstep of the city of Montreal, the image of an Indigenous community that can make use of urban infrastructures crossing its land as well as the international political structures and communications technologies operating in the contemporary world. Breaking the imaginary link between Indigeneity and a bygone era, the protesters took the stage as Indigenous subjects who could appropriate forms of knowledge adapted to the circumstances.

In the summer of 1990, power relations that had seemed generally accepted were suddenly on the line and, due to the event's unique nature, could be seen from a different angle. The Mohawks managed to make their presence felt in the public space in unexpected ways, the Municipality of Oka ran up against resistance it had thought it could overcome, and the provincial and federal governments had to deal with a crisis that forced them to take a stance in a territorial dispute receiving massive media attention. Protests supporting the Kanehsatake Mohawks' land struggle replicated that conflict across the country, highlighting contemporary political solidarity among Indigenous peoples. In Quebec, the government feared that "the inception of a process that could become extremely complex and embarrassing,"[13] in the terms of Quebec politician Jacques Parizeau, could have repercussions for negotiations with other Indigenous nations, then ongoing or to come.

The country was shaken when relations that the Quebec and Canadian settler societies had until then believed to be harmonious, if not non-existent, were revealed to be colonial relationships fraught with intense conflict. Wendat scholar George E. Sioui observed that Oka occurred at a time when the Indigenous peoples were still largely viewed as a myth, "popularly thought of as false, illegitimate Nations, or merely, tribes."[14] By contrast, he added, "the Oka crisis, in 1990, has so much shocked the public feeling, by raising the terrifying possibility that we might, in fact, be existing for real, that it has triggered a very severe backlash from the Québécois and Canadian societies."[15] Redrawing real and symbolic boundaries was profoundly distressing to the settler society. Quebec's human rights commission commented that the land dispute in Oka-Kanehsatake "took on a completely unprecedented, virulent tone and a quality of extreme urgency."[16] In the title of its report on the crisis, it went so far as to evoke a genuine "collective shock."

THE RESISTANCE AT KANEHSATÀ:KE

Whereas in the eyes of the Québécois and Canadians, the Oka Crisis might seem like a revelation, from the perspective of the Mohawks and other Indigenous peoples, who have been battling various forms of encroachment for centuries, the event feels like a repetition. *At the Woods' Edge: An Anthology of the History of the People of Kanehsatà:ke* underlines a pronounced contrast in Indigenous and settler perceptions of the 1990 conflict: "To many Canadians, the events of the summer of 1990 seemed unprecedented in the history of Canada. In fact, everything that happened that summer has parallels in Kanehsatà:ke history and the history of Aboriginal peoples across Canada. The attitudes prevailing among the different levels of government, the police, and the armed forces towards the issues raised were merely a continuation of an historical pattern of avoidance."[17] The context in which the event erupted involved many elements of a scenario whose different versions have been replayed over and over in the history of Kanehsatà:ke and numerous Indigenous communities across the continent. These include the projected municipal appropriation of disputed land; a complete lack of consultation with the Kanehsata'kehró:non, who learned of the town's project through the media; court decisions endorsing the municipal development despite unsettled land claims; the call to police action to force the Indigenous occupiers to make way despite ongoing negotiations; the reluctance of provincial and federal governments to intervene; and the criminalization of Indigenous political activity.

At the heart of this scenario is the propensity of settler societies to want to get rid of the colonial question by ignoring, distantiating, or erasing the Indigenous peoples who refuse to be assimilated. This is despite the fact that, from the first contact, the Indigenous peoples had formed strategic political and military alliances with the newly arrived Europeans, who depended on their support to maintain trade and establish the French and British colonial regimes. The Indigenous loss of military influence, especially following the War of 1812, brought a change in attitude on the part of successive colonial authorities and governments, who stepped up the process of colonization and land appropriation while backing out of the terms of their agreements and treaties with the First Nations.

According to Neal McLeod, the process of alienation experienced by Indigenous peoples can be understood as a dual exile, both spatial and ideological (McLeod 2001, 18–19). These concurrent and interrelated processes have a direct impact on the daily life of individuals and communities. The siege that was lived through not only in Kanehsatà:ke but also at Kahnawà:ke represents this dual process in an emphatic way. As in the past, some members of the community were forced to leave because the situation had become untenable. The threat of encroachment, the extreme danger posed by the armed conflict, the checks by police, the frequent, intrusive searches, the disquieting military presence, the lack of food supplies inside the perimeter, the verbal and physical aggression on the part of neighbouring settler populations, and the intense political pressure— all these factors together created a high-tension situation for the Mohawk communities and individuals, who were forced to live their daily lives under a state of siege. As described in *At the Woods' Edge*: "As circumstances evolved in an often surreal and shocking manner, the Kanehsata'kehró:non had no choice but to react. Sometimes in anger or fear, with caution, often with humour. People were forced to make difficult choices for themselves and their families. For some that meant staying to the end whatever that end might be. Others faced with the threat of a full scale military intervention, had no choice but to leave" (Gabriel-Doxtater and Van den Hende 1995, 248). Whatever the reasons,[18] the decisions that must be made in such a situation are painful not only for the individuals but also for the community, which sees its unity compromised.

Over the centuries, many generations of Kanehsata'kehró:non had been forced to choose whether to leave under pressure or stay where they were and face adversity. The process of spatial exile caused by colonial settlement could be seen in operation at Hochelaga, or Montreal, or Tiohtià:ke (which means in Kanien'keha "where the group splits") (Gabriel-Doxtater and Van den Hende 1995, 381).[19] The church authorities made efforts to distance the Indigenous peoples from that important strategic centre within traditional Iroquois territory. Approximately two decades after having been encouraged to move from the Catholic mission they occupied at the foot of Mount Royal to the mission at Sault-du-Récollet along the Rivière des Prairies, the group of Mohawks who had gathered there were again pushed off the land they occupied. This time, the move was towards the west of the Island of Montreal, to the Lake of Two Mountains, where the Séminaire de Saint-Sulpice had obtained a deed from the King of France in 1717 and 1735 to establish an "Indian mission" for the use of the Mohawks (and Nipissings and Algonquins).

Although they were not enthused about having to relocate their families and move away from the main trade routes, the group of Mohawk people chose to leave in the hope of finally being able to establish a home in a place where they would no longer be disturbed. At a council held late in the eighteenth century, Chief Aghneetha addressed Sir John Johnson, General Superintendent of the Department of Indian Affairs at the time, and reminded him of what motivated his people:

> If we would consent to go and settle at the Lake of Two
> Mountains we should have a large tract of land for which we
> should have a Deed from the King of France as our property, to
> be vested in us and our Heirs for ever, and that we should not
> be molested again in our habitations.

Altho' it was very inconvenient for us to be quitting our houses
and small clearings, yet the desire of having a fixed property of
our own induced us to comply, and we accordingly set out and
took possession of the land assigned to us. (Gabriel-Doxtater
and Van den Hende 1995, 30)

In accordance with Iroquois diplomatic protocol, the finalized agreement was
recorded in a beaded belt called Two Dog or Two Wolf Wampum. Ethnohistorian Kathryn V. Muller explains that in the oral tradition, the wampum belts
constituted a contract and an archive that "situated peoples/nations on a particular territory and depicted their relationship to one another."[20] Huron-Wendat
historian Jonathan Lainey also explains that they were "offered at formal meetings to back up what has been said and make it legitimate and official."[21] At one
time, they were understood and used by colonial authorities in their political
relations with Indigenous nations.

In 1781, when the priests from the Séminaire de Saint-Sulpice were hound-
ing the Kanehsata'kehró:non over their occupation of the land, eleven Mohawk
chiefs made speeches to British army officer Colonel Campbell in which they
recalled the agreement that had been concluded and recorded in the wampum.
The chiefs, Enita, Anewariis, Wisekowa, Kekarontasha, Ottarakehte, Satiotenola, Kamon, Warakwanentahon, Niwaniaha, Tirdesha, and Chawin,[22] asked
that their title to the seigneury at the Lake of Two Mountains therefore be
honoured. They reminded the seminary of its obligations to them: "here is our
contract: the white line you see on this belt shows the length of our land: the
figures holding hands by the cross represent our faithfulness to our religion: the
two dogs, placed at the ends, guard the boundaries of our land. And if someone
wishes to disturb us in our possession, they must alert us by barking: and that is
what they have been doing for three years."[23] In keeping with colonial logic, the
British authorities refused to consider the wampum a legal document. Throughout the history of settlement, explained Kathryn V. Muller, the issue of land
ownership would create many difficulties, "since it depended upon vastly different understandings of ceremonies of possession, or the means by which people
articulated and legitimized their existence in a particular landscape."[24] Wampum and their diplomatic function were denied by successive colonial authorities and Canadian governments as they appropriated the land and established

their dominion over it. Some wampum belts were even seized by settler colonial police forces in the process. Nonetheless, wampum is still used by Indigenous peoples in international diplomatic relations, as well as in their oral history and cultural life. The work of Mohawk historian Warren Bonaparte, including in the form of his public talks and *Wampum Chronicles*, offers a telling illustration of this continuing use of wampum.

The origins of Kanehsatà:ke are ancient. As recounted in *At the Woods' Edge*, it was one of the first villages to embrace the message of the Peacemaker, the prophet who, after a long period of strife, established the Kaianene'ko:wa, the Great League of Peace, which is at the founding of the Iroquois or Haudenosaunee Confederacy. The confederacy dates back to between 1100 and 1300 CE (Gabriel-Doxtater and Van den Hende 1995, 9). It was at first made up of five nations: the Kanien'kehà:ka, the People of the Flint, the Mohawks; O'nientehá:ka, the People of the Standing Stone, the Oneidas; Ononta'keháka, the People of the Hill, the Onondagas; Kaionkeháka, the People of the Great Pipe, the Cayugas; and Shenekeháka, the People of the Great Mountain, the Senecas (6); and, beginning in the eighteenth century, Tehatiskaró:ros, the People of the Shirt, the Tuscarora. *At the Woods' Edge* explains that the village of Kanehsatà:ke is mentioned by name in ancient condolence ceremonies, indicating the community's historical, political, and spiritual relationship with the other clans and nations making up the long-standing confederacy (23–24). The book deconstructs the myth that the Séminaire de Saint-Sulpice founded an Indian mission in uninhabited territory. It explains that it was rather the Mohawks living in the region, which for a long time had been part of their hunting territory, who welcomed their brothers and sisters from the religious mission (20–23). The book adds that the St. Lawrence Iroquoians were not only related to the Kanien'kehà:ka, but that they belonged to their people (28–29). Ignoring this history, the colonial authorities saw the region called Lake of Two Mountains as an integral part of the colony. By the same reasoning, they also saw the Indian mission established there as coming entirely under the authority of French rule and, after the conquest, that of the British regime.

Faced with this situation, the Kanehsatà:ke Mohawks stood by their ancestral occupation of the land and the political agreements reached with colonial authorities. They recalled the agreement by which the lands ceded by the King of France were initially reserved for them, and they persisted over time to assert and exercise their rights. In 1781, 1788, 1794, 1802, 1818, 1828, 1839, 1848, 1869, and on up until the twentieth century, they petitioned the colonial authorities and then the Canadian politicians for recognition of their right to the seigneury lands.[25] They repeatedly pleaded their cause in the courts and to political and ecclesiastical authorities, but in vain.

In 1902, Chief Jos Kennatosse Gabriel travelled to England to present King Edward with a petition that he and eight other Mohawk leaders had signed. Although he did not obtain an audience with the king, his process made the community's grievances more widely known. The petition was published in the *Montreal Star* of 28 April 1902 and described the situation of spatial exile that was tormenting the Kanehsata'keró:non. It attested to the repression reserved for any act of resistance and restated the land rights of the Mohawks. These were the rights that Chief Kennatosse was asking the king to restore:

Owing to our rights being stolen by the Seminary of St. Sulpice we have not enough land left to support our families. We are poorer now than when you first took us under your protection. The reserve is full of French, and over thirty years they have taken us and put us in prison for cutting our firewood and timber for buildings. The 28th of February, 1902, a policeman came to my home to arrest me for cutting my firewood to keep my family warm. I went to Ottawa to get protection from the Government, but they refused to protect me, so yesterday, March 7, 1902, policemen came again to take me, but I refused to go with them. We know that the Seminary has no right on our reserve, as you will see from the following quotation from the words of J. Stuart, Attorney-General at Quebec City, December 10, 1826: "The pretended deed of gift of April 20, 1764, must be considered an absolute nullity" (Robert Christie, *History of Lower Canada*, vol. 6). With such knowledge of the matter I cannot conceive that the Seminary of St. Sulpice could hold our estate as held by them at present in Canada with no right of possession in these lands. I have not told you one-half of our troubles, but will now beg of you to have our rights restored. And I also beg of you to drive out the French that are in our reserve. I also beg to have the deeds of our lands given to us.

The petition carried across the ocean referred to a local situation caused by colonial settlement that had been festering for many years. In fact, throughout the nineteenth century, on a daily basis, the Kanehsata'keró:non had to deal with increasingly draconian restrictions imposed by the Séminaire de Saint-Sulpice. In addition to forbidding the Mohawks to cut or sell wood without permission, the seminary called on the police to enforce its own authority. It also illegally sold seigneury land to French-Canadian settlers who, in return, showed no hesitation in violently assailing the Mohawk residents.[26] In protest against this untenable situation, which undermined their dignity as it dispossessed them of their lands and means of survival, the men of Kanehsatà:ke defiantly continued to fell trees and sell the products without the seminary's permission. Like Chief Kennatosse, many were arrested, ordered to pay a fine, and often even imprisoned for having transgressed colonial authority, which increased their bitterness and frustration.

As well as watching their territory shrink beneath their feet, the Kanehsata'keró:non saw their connections to one another deteriorate as a result of growing economic pressures and the internal dissension sown by the church authorities. This alienation would soon become more acute owing to the residential schools set up by the British government in the 1840s and further institutionalized by Canada following its settler colonial foundation in 1867. These institutions, explicitly aimed at assimilating the Indigenous peoples, were attended by many children from Kanehsatà:ke. Using the image of a tightening noose, the narrator of *At the Woods' Edge*, Tiononte'kó:wa ("the mountain") expresses anxiety over the survival of the people, who saw their land and their existence threatened by the priests: "These Roti'kharahón:tsi want to keep breaking the land and the people into smaller and smaller parts till only bits and pieces remain to be easily scattered by the winds" (100). The breaking up referred to by Tiononte'kó:wa exemplifies the dual process of exile by which, in Neal McLeod's view, a people's ability to govern itself and tell its stories becomes compromised.

Tensions between the Sulpicians and the Kanehsata'keró:non intensified and in 1877 culminated in a serious clash to which the 1990 crisis would be disturbingly similar. Following the historical model of avoidance mentioned above, the church and government authorities attempted to resolve the colonial conflict, not by protecting the Indigenous lands from encroachment, but by once again encouraging the Mohawks to leave Kanehsatà:ke and take up residence in another region (128). Some families finally accepted land offered by the federal government at Gibson, in the Muskoka region of Ontario; however, the vote to leave was far from unanimous, which created further tension within the community: "By the summer of 1880, Kanehsata'kehró:non showed signs of breaking under the pressure. The proposed removal created dissension in the community, and there were hard feelings between those who would go and those who would stay. While the vast majority remained opposed to removal, there were those who believed that leaving would give them their only chance for a peaceful and prosperous life" (133). When they arrived in Gibson in late fall 1881, the displaced Mohawk families found neither the housing nor the provisions promised by the government. As a result, their situation during the first winter was precarious. To top it all, the land proved to be less suited to farming than hoped, and white squatters who had settled there attacked members of the Mohawk families, leaving them in a similar situation to the one they had just left (158–59). Upon returning to Kanehsatà:ke, some of them found that, during their absence, the Sulpicians had sold their houses and property to white colonists.[27] In the meantime, the Kanehsata'kehró:non who had remained behind continued to resist mounting pressure from the Sulpicians and the government to relocate the entire community.

The possibility of having to leave as a result of increased outside pressure also affected the Kahnawa'kehró:non throughout the nineteenth century. This was demonstrated by historian Daniel Rück (also spelled as Rueck in previous publications) in a recent article on "the external pressures that caused a breakdown in land governance in Kahnawake and led to a wood crisis in the 1870s."[28] The community and nation, he further explained in that article, faced major challenges from the increased intrusion of the federal government and the establishment of an assimilative and appropriative federal legislation at a time when they also had to deal with the effects of industrialization and a population explosion in Montreal. In another text titled "When Bridges Become Barriers: Montreal and Kahnawake Mohawk Territory," Rueck also wrote, "Once Kahnawakehró:non realized that governments would not consider their interests over the interests of the Montreal business elite, they took serious steps toward abandoning the territory."[29] Some of them considered selling the reserve and relocating the community to such areas as Cherokee territory. Rueck continued, "Between 1860 and 1875, Kahnawakehró:non made four documented efforts to sell the entire reserve." In the absence of a government reply, however, they recommitted themselves to their existing territory.[30] Despite repeated

efforts from the federal government to undermine the power of the chiefs and
impose that of the state, Rück states, "Mohawks understood that their nationhood was under serious threat and used various strategies to attempt to maintain their own laws and government."[31]

In *At the Woods' Edge*, the narrator Tiononte'kó:wa observes that in these
historical circumstances, the patience and good will of the Kanehsata'kehró:non
were exemplary. She also predicts that one day they will reach their limit, given
the unjust and oppressive character of the laws imposed by the government:
"The laws of the land have been applied to the Kanehsata'kehró:non in the
meanest manner, without even the pretense of justice or fair play, and the people
of Kanehsatà:ke have been expected to submit obediently to the 'Rule of Law.'
Despite setbacks and losses, the Kanehsata'kehró:non demonstrated incred-
ible patience and goodwill. A time would come, however, when their patience
would finally run out, and all of Canada would feel the effects of the hundreds
of years of persecution and oppression endured by the people of Kanehsatà:ke"
(164). In this regard, *At the Woods' Edge* reminds us that the Oka Crisis, or the
resistance at Kanehsatà:ke, represents only a small part of the community's collective history. It points out, "Each and every family living in Kanehsatà:ke has
its own personal history of human rights violations, illegal land seizures by so-
called authorities, and unwarranted imprisonment" (263). Thus, if the event
appeared from the dominant colonial perspective to be a case of the margin's
bursting into the centre, from the Mohawk point of view it was a continuation
of the community's experience and history of battling against the colonial project to eliminate it and appropriate its land.

THE MYSTERY AT THE HEART OF THE SHOOTOUT

The event's symbolic charge was abruptly intensified by the violent death at the
heart of the crisis. For that reason, it became hard to channel. In point of fact,
the person who fired the shot that took the life of Corporal Lemay will never
be identified; as a result, without a guilty party to blame, questions continue
to hover, and the mystery that hung over the siege all summer will likely never
completely fade away. The few images of the shootout that were recorded show
police officers in combat gear entering the Pines, followed by a bulldozer to
knock down the barricades. Then, during the twenty-second exchange of fire
that ensued, we see the ground, trees, and sky rushing past chaotically, shrouded
in a fog of tear gas. When the shooting stops, leaving one of the officers from the

tactical intervention team wounded by a bullet, the officers beat a retreat, abandoning their vehicles at the site and carrying away their colleague, who would later die from his wounds.

The eruption of the armed conflict and the death of an officer during the resulting shootout immediately sparked questions that could not be overlooked. What set off the shooting? Why were there armed Indigenous activists in the pine grove? Why did the Sûreté du Québec intervene with force? And, above all, of course, who killed Corporal Lemay? Elements of the mystery hanging over the event remained shut away on the siege site until the crisis ended in late September 1990, since investigators and medical examiners, among others, were unable to cross the line and collect their evidence until then. The inability to visit the scene of the shooting left a crucial part of the investigation pending, and the prolonged siege increased the possibility that evidence would be compromised or suppressed.

Another revealing aspect added to the element of the unknown that was central to the event: operational communications during the police intervention on 11 July 1990 were not recorded as required, despite an explicit Sûreté du Québec directive that had been in force since 1985 (Quebec 1995, 20 and 425). In his report, the coroner therefore considered the argument that team members lacked the necessary technology to record Operation Doré 90-4 to be "unacceptable" and "even comical," and he expressed grave doubts about the plausibility of "such a gross omission" (426). Noting that it was a major operation, planned and carried out not in a remote region but just outside the city of Montreal, the coroner clearly suggested that the recording existed but was deliberately suppressed: "Isn't it more likely that the operation was recorded but the reels could no longer be found?—It has been known to happen in the Americas" (426). The mystery surrounding the non-existence or disappearance of the recordings, the confused testimonials of the officers at the coroner's inquest, and their repeated memory lapses can be added to the other obscure or missing elements on either side that maintain the uncertainty and leave the case open to speculation.

THE EVENT THAT DEFIED ALL EXPECTATIONS

The mounting social tension had been anxiously monitored for months and, despite additional warnings issued by Indigenous leaders in the years before Oka,[32] no one could have predicted the scale of the conflict that was about to erupt.

As Glen Sean Coulthard specified in *Red Skins, White Masks: Rejecting the Colonial Politics of Recognition*, the 1990 crisis took place in the wake of "near a decade-long escalation of Native frustration with a colonial state that steadfastly refused to uphold the rights" recently enshrined in the Constitution Act of 1982, "resulting in a marked rise in First Nations' militancy and land-based direct action."[33] In Quebec, the resistance at Kanehsatake occurred in a context of extremely tense relations between the province's police forces and Indigenous communities. In May 1990, Quebec's human rights commission had asked the government to hold public hearings on the police forces' discriminatory, racist actions against Indigenous people. The commission was acting in response to the complaints lodged by Indigenous communities across the province, including the Algonquin in Lac Barrière, the Innu in Les Escoumins, the Labrador Inuit, and the Kanehsatake Mohawks.[34] In the spring, federal and provincial police and armed forces were deployed in Akwesasne after armed confrontations had broken out in the community, with fatal results. These state forces remained alert to what was happening at Oka-Kanehsatake, fearing that the conflict would spread from one community to the other.[35] Between May and July, a series of court injunctions ordering the dismantling of the barricades at Kanehsatake had progressively increased the probability of a police assault. Activists from Kahnawake, Akwesasne, and other Haudenosaunee communities converged on the Pines to support the original occupiers. Disagreements over the changing methods of resistance incited some of the occupiers to take the decision to leave. Gradually, barricades of logs were installed and fortified.

On 5 July 1990, Quebec's minister of Public Security Sam Elkas alluded to the injunction to dismantle the barricades and declared in a threatening tone, with reference to the occupiers in the Pines: "They have until the 9th [of July], and after that it all comes down" (quoted in Quebec 1995, 416). His inopportune declaration implied harsh intervention by the police and added to the tension. On his side, Quebec's minister of Native Affairs John Ciaccia attempted to defuse the situation by asking the mayor of Oka—in vain—to postpone his request to the Sûreté du Québec. At dawn on the fatal day, the Mohawk occupiers were informed that a police operation was imminent. According to an account by the Tsi Niionkwarihò:ten Cultural Center, the camp was plunged into "a climate of impending danger and foreboding" that had the protestors "once again shoring up the defences."[36] Responding to the media, Mohawk spokesperson Ellen Gabriel said that in the case of a police operation, the people in the Pines were determined to take up a defensive stance: "We are not seeking violence, but we will defend ourselves if attacked." She underscored the political legitimacy of this position: "International laws recognize our right to be armed. For us, these negotiations are conducted nation to nation."[37] It was in this climate of social and political tension that the police intervention took place on 11 July 1990.

Shooting did not break out as soon as the police arrived at the site. According to the coroner's report, three hours elapsed between the tactical squad's arrival at the pine grove at 5:30 a.m. and the tragic exchange of fire, which broke out at 8:53 a.m. (Quebec 1995, 345–54). The intense violence of the confrontation rattled the police and the people in the Pines. It also unnerved the members of the small Mohawk community, who saw the everyday lives of their families brutally disrupted. One Kanehsata'kehró:non reported: "Starting from the 11th, when whoever it was, called at home to say that the cops were attacking our people, I found it so unreal. I couldn't believe that in a place like Canada, they would attack native people that way. My disbelief turned to anger and disgust. I don't think anybody really expected it to happen that way. Maybe the ones dealing with the cops that morning expected it to some extent, but not the way it happened. They thought they would be arrested, not shot at, or beat up like people were later" (Gabriel-Doxtater and Van den Hende 1995, 254). With its unpredictable outcome, the evolving siege opened up a space for a tense interplay that raised fears of further violent confrontation. Anticipating another police offensive in the Oka region, the local hospitals engaged in joint emergency planning; it was reported in the media that they called on the Red Cross for more blood units and assigned an extra team to the emergency department to treat bullet wounds.[38] Suffering from shock and appalled by the police presence in their community, the Kanehsatake Mohawks worried about what was happening and what was to come. They often expected the worst, as illustrated by these accounts gathered after the event, in *At the Woods' Edge*:

> The morning it happened, I was on my way to work and there was
> a road block and all the firing was going on, for a moment you
> have that terrible feeling and you wonder what is going on. (255)

> The heavy presence of sq [Sûreté du Québec] and army—for me
> it was the worst thing. Even now, I go by that ferry, I can still see
> the sq lined up with their guns. There couldn't have been worse

than that. For me, they played a wicked and important role. I felt
so insecure. We didn't know what they were going to do, pull the
trigger or what? Would they invade our houses? Or what? (248)

The first impact was when Corporal Lemay was killed. My
immediate concern was: "They're going to massacre our people."
(249)

The neighbouring community of Kahnawake also found itself propelled
into the event. The Mohawk activists who suddenly blocked the Honoré-Mercier Bridge received immediate support. Kenneth Deer, spokesperson for the
Mohawk Warrior Society of Kahnawake, explained the situation as follows:
"There was no plan, no coordination. . . . We had to stand behind them, but
we didn't have any idea what it would mean."[39] In part, the barricades across
the bridge were intended to dissuade the Sûreté du Québec from launching a
second assault on the protestors at Kanehsatake, who had at that point closed
off the main road crossing Oka and Kanehsatake and reinforced their defences
in anticipation of another incursion.

The Sûreté du Québec officers were also surprised by the undeniably disastrous outcome of Operation Doré 90-4. They had no doubt been prepared to use
force to dismantle the barricades and arrest the occupiers, but they most probably did not expect to lose one of their colleagues or to have to beat a retreat, as
they did that morning. The next day, on 12 July 1990, a story on page 3 of *Le
Devoir* reported that the armed police intervention at Oka produced "the effect
of a bomb going off in this peaceful community in the country." The shock waves
immediately travelled across Canada, and many voices were raised in condemnation of the police operation. In a press release of 18 July 1990, the Human Rights
Institute of Canada expressed the widespread perplexity and incomprehension:
"Why were the Police called? Why did they come? Why did they bring guns and
tear gas and create a crisis?" In a similar vein, five days after the shooting, *Le Devoir* observed on page 9 that "the decision to authorize the police to conduct an
assault remains shrouded in obscurity, at least for the time being."

On the other hand, one thing is certain: the negotiations concerning the
land at Kanehsatake had suddenly taken a new turn. The fact that a man had
died radically changed the conflict's dynamics, and the further fact that the victim was a police officer on duty gave the tragedy a particular symbolic dimension.

On 16 July 1990, a civil funeral was held in the presence of representatives from police forces across the country and the grieving family of Corporal Lemay. A guard of honour made up of twenty Sûreté du Québec officers assembled on the church square and, to the beat of a drum, eight of Corporal Lemay's fellow officers shouldered the coffin draped in the Quebec flag. After six days of siege, the Sûreté du Québec's director, Robert Lavigne, addressed the 1,500 people who had gathered in the church. His speech, which was carried on the front page of *Le Devoir* on 17 July 1990, encouraged his men to resist giving in to anger and resentment: "We will not find any answers to our questions in revenge, reprisal, revolt." This appeal for calm invites speculation about the mood among members of the police force following the disastrous intervention.

By creating a breach in the established order, the armed conflict distinguishes itself from a court battle. As explained by Georg Simmel, the court battle "rests on a broad base of unity and consensus among the adversaries."[40] Legal argument, added Simmel, can take place without the intrusion of a personal moment, the intervention of a third party, or a more or less fatal incident.[41] This is not the case for an armed conflict that erupts from a fatal, unforeseeable reversal, calls for intense personal commitment, and involves the strategic intervention of third parties.

THE SIEGE AT KANEHSATAKE AND KAHNAWAKE

A strategic police cordon was set up on the highway and the river around Kanehsatake and Kahnawake, and roads leading to the village of Oka were closed off to keep out anyone but the residents.[42] At the foot of Saint-Michel Hill in Oka itself, sandbags were piled up to form a barricade and police vehicles were lined up in rows on the site. In Kanehsatake, at the summit of the hill, the Mohawk barricade had been installed. It overlooked the village of Oka on the shore of the Lake of Two Mountains. The two barricades were roughly 100 metres apart. Mohawk activists blocked the main street in Kanehsatake and certain access points. An almost impenetrable barrier was also created around Kahnawake to protect the community from incursions. In both communities, barricades made of banks of earth, overturned cars, and tree trunks placed across the roads kept the police from entering the territory. A genuine siege began, evoking all at once the "state of exception" theorized by Giorgio Agamben,[43] major disruptions caused by events, and wars of attrition. The "state of siege" evoked here alludes to a public authority's control enforced at the expense of individual liberty.[44] Similarly,

Audra Simpson wrote, in reference to the settler state's forceful intervention against the Mohawk defiance of both settler citizenship and land expropriation in 1990: "The state of exception was official, and colonial law was strangely, violently, and very precariously reinscribed."[45] This could be seen, added Simpson, in the presence of the Sûreté du Québec, the Royal Canadian Mounted Police, and, later on, the Canadian Armed Forces on the site of the standoff.

From the outset, the police cut off deliveries of food and medicine to the Mohawk communities, thus violating human rights. The police also prevented or seriously limited all movement in and out of people and vehicles, sometimes including ambulances, and stepped up the searches, along with arrests and interrogations that were often abusive.[46] To relieve a shortage of supplies that was rapidly being felt in Kanehsatake and Kahnawake, people from the Mohawk communities brought in food through the woods or in boats. Others organized food banks in community halls, which had become places for refuge and gatherings.[47] Exasperated by the constant searches, and even more by the assault on their dignity the searches represented, the people decided to counteract the humiliation by taking action on a daily basis to obstruct the police repression. As Chief Joe Norton of the Kahnawake Band Council explained to Abenaki documentary director Alanis Obomsawin, while he had been held up at one of the many annoying police barriers, "We decided if we had to suffer that kind of indignity, *we* in turn would retaliate with our own plan of action to create as much resistance as we could."[48] In front of Obomsawin's camera, Norton demonstrated what he meant by refusing a police officer's request to open his car trunk, causing an even longer delay, and by instead telling the officer to do it himself if he insisted on making a search. His subtle yet effective action evokes the resistance tactics described by political scientist and anthropologist James C. Scott in *Domination and the Arts of Resistance: Hidden Transcripts.* His subtle yet effective action evokes the resistance tactics described by political scientist and anthropologist James C. Scott, in *Domination and the Arts of Resistance: Hidden Transcripts*, as acts of resistance that can be expressed and perceived, but not clearly enough for them to be punished or sanctioned.

Through July and August 1990, the routines of local non-Indigenous populations were also disrupted by the conflict. Every day, some 200,000 South Shore residents used the Honoré-Mercier Bridge as their main point of access to the Island of Montreal; they now saw their daily commute made two to three hours longer by the barricades. From the outset, settler residents expressed great irritation at having to make long detours and negotiate the resulting bottlenecks on the Victoria, Champlain, and Jacques-Cartier bridges. Many said they felt they had literally been "taken hostage" by the Mohawk barricades and forced to pay the price, even if, in their view, they were not directly involved in the territorial conflict at Kanehsatake. Outraged by the situation and frustrated by government inaction, many non-Indigenous citizens were determined to take the law into their own hands by directly lashing out at Mohawk communities and individuals as a group, one they vehemently blamed for the situation. A number of white residents, filled with resentment, prevented members of the Kahnawake Mohawk community from leaving and entering the reserve, checking cars and ambulances at points of entry and exit. They harassed and verbally abused the Mohawks they met outside Kahnawake, at times brutally attacking them physically and most often without police intervention of any kind. The impunity granted to these heinous acts against Indigenous people is indicative of the violent settler backlash that occurred in the summer of 1990 in the society of Quebec and, in a more general way, that of Canada, as indicated by other blatant acts of racism across the country.

The mayors of Châteauguay, Saint-Constant, Delson, Sainte-Catherine, and Mercier were concerned about the significant loss of wages and revenue caused by the siege. They consequently agreed to try to hasten a return to normal conditions by putting pressure on the entire community of Kahnawake. In a move that also served to legitimize the racist acts of the settler residents who literally besieged the Mohawk community, they wrote to the government of Quebec to demand that it "maintain the complete impenetrability of the barricades on routes 132–138 until the block is removed."[49] Night after night, white protesters gathered on the approaches to the Honoré-Mercier Bridge, at first by the hundreds and then by the thousands, to demand that the police and the governments force "the warriors" to remove the barricades. At the top of their voices, they called for the intervention of the Canadian Army and violently cursed and insulted the people they called "the Indians." More than once, the effigy of a masked Mohawk warrior was hung from a lamppost and burned, to the cheers of the white crowd. An effigy of Premier Robert Bourassa suffered a similar fate at the hands of the same crowd, and white rioters repeatedly attacked Sûreté du Québec officers, who replied with a barrage of tear gas. These chaotic race riots went on day after day and were echoed across the country as oppression and racism against Indigenous people intensified.

The Sûreté du Québec was soon overwhelmed by events: the failed police operation of 11 July had strengthened the resolve of the Mohawk occupiers to maintain their positions; negotiations with the governments were not progressing; the Sûreté du Québec did not have the resources they needed to confront the armed activists in case of an exchange of gunfire; and the authorities had to conclude that the long-standing animosity between the provincial police and the Mohawk communities would only be detrimental to another police operation.[50] In addition, the aggressive, racist demonstrations, which now included several local members of the white supremacist organization the Ku Klux Klan, grew so intense on the South Shore that the 14 August edition of *Le Devoir*, a leading independent newspaper in Quebec, carried the following banner headline: "The SQ Apologizes and Pronounces Itself Overwhelmed." With endorsement of this conclusion by the Royal Canadian Mounted Police, the Sûreté du Québec alerted the Quebec government, which then officially asked the Canadian Armed Forces to lend their assistance to the police.[51] While military troops had been deployed from the beginning of the conflict, it was only now, when the social order had been so severely disrupted, that the Canadian Army officially intervened. Quebec Premier Robert Bourassa addressed a request to Chief of Defence Staff General John de Chastelain, who responded with the following statement: "The government has now gone to the court of last resort, which is us. We cannot fail, because we are all that is left."[52]

The feeling of having reached the limit is also mentioned by the Mohawk warriors, although from their point of view it was not so much the social order that was threatened as the very core of their collective existence. As explained after the event by Dale Dion, a member of the Mohawk Warrior Society of Kahnawake:

> There are times when you need to use violence, especially
> when the very core of your existence is being threatened. We
> cannot allow the future of the Mohawk nation to be decided by
> outsiders . . . the issue of Mohawk nationhood is not a debatable
> issue, just as our aboriginal right to land is not. Violence is
> respected . . . they listen . . . they fear violence. Violence has
> given us bargaining power. It seems that when we [the Warrior
> Movement] use violence then we are a threat . . . then we are
> taken seriously . . . then they say, well let's talk about the issues.[53]

In this case, direct action appeared to be a solution of last resort to be used against a temporary threat, certainly, but also to oppose a process of colonization that had been sustained and ongoing for centuries. Dion's framing of Mohawk armed resistance speaks to a political awareness of "the intolerable ideational challenge to sovereignty" that "Indigenous violence"[54] can come to pose in settler colonial contexts in which, to further use scholar Lisa Ford's reflection, "attempts to assert criminal law jurisdiction over Indigenous peoples, including the process of bringing them into criminal courts as both offenders and victims of crimes, were at the core of redefining 'sovereignty and its relationship to territory and jurisdiction.'"[55] The summer of 1990 brought to light in the Canadian context several elements of these nineteenth-century colonial dynamics.

In mid-August, following the Sûreté du Québec's declaration that it was overwhelmed, the Canadian Army announced its intervention and the military took up a position around the besieged communities. At that point, the slightest error at the site of the armed conflict, whether made by a Canadian soldier or an Indigenous protestor, could have provoked a confrontation with absolutely disastrous consequences. The state and military authorities feared triggering Indigenous resistance across the country. On the Indigenous side, there was dread of sparking a military offensive against the Mohawk communities. Although a determination in both camps to avoid triggering an offensive kept the situation under control, the armed conflict included a significant element of uncertainty and instability. The strategies employed by the parties to intimidate their adversary and play on power relations increased the conflict's intensity. For example, throughout, the Mohawk warriors deliberately left room for doubt and ambiguity about their intentions and the size of their force. "We played on their fears and let their imaginations play games with them," explained warrior Cookie McComber after the crisis.[56] Early on, a threat to blow up the Honoré-Mercier Bridge had been formulated to dissuade the police from attempting a second assault on the barricades at Kanehsatake. This threat would haunt everyone's consciousness all summer. It would also produce an effect on the military, who would need to take into account the possibility thus introduced.

On the other hand, the impressive, massive deployment of military was a display of strength intended to deliver a psychological blow to the Mohawk occupiers. As Winegard specified: "Again the move, complete, was designed to show overwhelming force to induce an element of shock on the Warrior [*sic*] who were monitoring CF movements and deployments."[57] It would simultaneously serve as visible, concrete evidence that the Canadian Army had all the resources it needed to reach its objectives. While admitting that a military assault was out of the question, the army's upper echelon, who were in communication with the Mohawk warriors on the Honoré-Mercier Bridge, exerted pressure to get the barricades dismantled. They let hover the possibility that the government would order the army to force an entry into the territory of Kahnawake.[58] The evolution of these strategic relations between the Canadian military and the Mohawk warriors sent ripples through the public discourse and the media's imagination, and the conflict's dynamic drew in different actors whose deeds, gestures, and words came to intersect and influence one another in various ways.

MILITARY ADVANCE AND STONE THROWING

At the end of August, when the siege had lasted almost two months, two movements coincided in an extremely disturbing way: the announcement of the Canadian Army's advance and the stoning of Mohawk families by the crowd of white settlers. On 27 August, Quebec's premier made an official request to the Canadian Armed Forces to begin operations that would force the dismantling of the barricades and restore law and order in the Mohawk communities and the surrounding region.[59] Beginning the next day, 28 August, the military and the government held media conferences to announce the imminence of a direct intervention. On that same day, one of the most terrifying episodes in the crisis took place. A crowd of white settlers from the region hurled stones and insults at a convoy of vehicles carrying Mohawk elderly people, women, and children who were being evacuated from Kahnawake in fear of the army's announced assault.

It was as if the settler population were mimicking and interpreting for itself the offensive that had been outlined in the authorities' speeches and then reformulated and relayed in various ways by television, radio, and print media. Conveying the tension that coloured the period, the front page of *Le Devoir* of 29 August reported anticipatory statements by the Canadian military saying that "if they are obliged to mount the fortifications one by one, the operation will be very costly in terms of human lives and ammunition." The dire possibility that the siege would end in a bloodbath was very present and frequently cited. *Le Devoir*'s front page for 28 August announced, "The army has received the order to advance." It went on to repeat the fatalistic, quietly threatening prediction by George Erasmus, then chief of the Assembly of First Nations, about the

Mohawk protesters: "They will defend their territory and there will be deaths, that's certain, and they will be heroes and martyrs for the entire world."

While the Canadian Army prepared to engage in the operation, the social and media discourses created a climate of gloom, antagonism, and violence that combined explosively with the impatience, frustration, and aggression prevalent among the settler populations. On the morning that the Canadian Armed Forces relieved the Sûreté du Québec at Kahnawake, many white residents of the region gathered on the approach to the Honoré-Mercier Bridge, some of them binoculars in hand, waiting for "something to happen"; in other words, waiting for the army to mount an assault on the Mohawk barricades. The crowd set up a noisy booing when they saw Lieutenant-Colonel Robin Gagnon, who was in charge of sector operations, shake hands with the Mohawk warriors he met in the buffer zone on the bridge, namely "Red Turtle, Skywalker, and Omega Man, as well as a political representative of the Band Council Irwin Goodleaf."[60] While the military authorities favoured dialogue as a means of resolving the conflict, as explained by Lieutenant-Colonel Gagnon, the horrifying scenarios inspired by the announced launch of military operations continued to be active in the space of conflict.

These scenarios tallied with the authorities' discourses, which depicted the warriors as criminals and terrorists, thus negating the political legitimacy of the demands made by Mohawk negotiators. In a media conference held on 28 August 1990, immediately following that held by the Canadian Armed Forces, Prime Minister Brian Mulroney called the Mohawk demands "unacceptable." He went on to announce that the army would carry out its mission, which was to dismantle the barricades. In speaking about the Mohawk protestors, he said: "They [the Mohawks] have put on the table a series of totally unacceptable claims, including immunity from criminal law. . . . In short, they have sought to give themselves the status of an independent nation within the boundaries of Canada. . . . Obviously there will be no pleasure in this task, but the Canadian Forces will do their duty and the barricades will come down."[61] In order to convince the population of the military intervention's legitimacy, the prime minister concluded his speech by detailing the threat the authorities supposed was presented by the Mohawk activists. He listed and described the kind and quantity of weapons estimated to be in their possession, condemned their "illegal smuggling" operations, and finally deplored the fact that many members of the Mohawk communities refused to reject what he called the rhetoric and violence of the Mohawk Warrior Society.[62]

The longer the siege went on, the more frequently the government discourses referred to the warriors as criminals and terrorists,[63] as if "there was no authorizing text for their action, besides vice and violence."[64] The effect of these discourses was to isolate the action of the warriors at the barricades and deprive it of its meaning, which of course had repercussions for the entire population of the Mohawk communities. It is a fact that the actions of the Mohawk Warrior Society members were far from receiving unanimous support in the Haudenosaunee communities. This was clearly and tragically shown by that spring's conflict at Akwesasne. A criticism of the actions of the Mohawk Warrior Society was also distinctly expressed by Cayuga Chief Jake Thomas, among others, in relation to his understanding and appreciation of the Great Law and Code of Handsome Lake in the context of the armed resistance at Kanehsatà:ke.[65] However, it is also true that the image created by the governments placed the warriors essentially in the settler colonial frame of reference, which completely obviated their political and historical position within the Haudenosaunee Confederacy as well as the connection to their communities. One must simply compare the government discourses with that of someone like Jake Thomas to see the colonialist, racist undertone that permeated official and common settler discourses in 1990. The dehumanization inherent in these negative government representations tended to make racism towards Mohawk communities and individuals, and by extension all Indigenous peoples, seem accepted, and even to endorse it.

Social discourses steeped in a deep-seated racial hatred were often heard in the summer of 1990. Reflecting the feelings of at least a portion of the non-Indigenous population, radio host Simon Bédard of CJPR's *Réaction* in Quebec City propagated hateful ideas and an attitude of hostility regarding the Mohawk warriors, with complete impunity. He set out to dissociate them from other Indigenous leaders, so as to make it easier to call for their annihilation at the hands of the military:

> As for me, the only thing I see now ... right now, is that there
> are 200 Indian chiefs in Winnipeg. Brian Mulroney should go
> meet them with Bourassa and tell them: Are you for what the
> Warriors are doing, or against it? Take a vote for us. If you're

against, we can clean it up right away. And have the support of
other Indian chiefs because they say that it's only a small group
over there, they say that all the Indian nations in the country are
against what the Warriors are doing. If that's the case, you go
in with the army and you clean it all up. Fifty dead, a hundred
dead, a hundred and twenty-five dead, it just dies out. We bury
the whole thing and get on with our lives.[66]

This genocidal statement, which the host considered to be justified by the fact
that the "warriors" may not have generated unanimity regarding their position,
had repercussions among certain segments of the population, whose reaction
was virulent. The colonial backlash was all the more worrisome because this
poisoning of the social climate coincided with the widely publicized increase in
military pressure.

When the Mohawks learned that the Canadian Army would be advancing
on Kahnawake, they had ample reason to fear that the soldiers would enter their
territory in force and that community members would be killed in the course
of the operation. The decision to evacuate was made with the intention of putting the people out of harm's way. The Peacekeepers, Kahnawake's police force,
obtained confirmation from the controlling forces that the safety of evacuated
members would be ensured, and they organized a convoy of fifty to seventy vehicles containing families from the community who had decided to seek refuge
outside the besieged area. The convoy headed for the other side of the Honoré-
Mercier Bridge, to Ville LaSalle on the Island of Montreal.

While the Sûreté du Québec officers took the time to search each vehicle,
the populace was informed of the evacuation and a local crowd of white settlers
rushed to the bridge's exit to await the "Indians." At the exit, when the vehicles
emerged onto a section of roadway bordered by concrete walls and embank-
ments, several dozen clusters of men attacked the convoy with large rocks they
had picked up from a nearby construction site. The cars including women, children, and elderly people from Kahnawake drove in a straight column through
a dense cloud of dust, showered with racist insults and furious shouts from the
crowd that were punctuated by the shattering of car windows. The provincial
and federal police officers who had lined up between the crowd and the convoy
did not intervene to stop the stone throwing.

In one of the cars was Allison Jacobs, then an administrative secretary and communications officer in Kahnawà:ke. She described this very difficult scene with restraint and emotion to Alanis Obomsawin, who covered the violent episode in her documentary *Rocks at Whiskey Trench*:

> I sat there, during that time, and thought about . . . if I was
> gonna tie my son in the seat next to me, in a seatbelt, or hold
> him. For some reason I said no, I'm gonna hold him. I felt more
> comfortable putting him on my lap and holding onto him than
> strapping him in, which I normally would have done. This time
> I didn't. All you could see was like an avalanche of rocks, and
> it wasn't small rocks, it was large rocks. Rocks like this. [Using
> her hands, she indicates the size of a large grapefruit.] You
> could see what was happening to the cars in front of you, so
> we were terrified. My sister-in-law was crying and shaking, and
> a rock hit the back of my sister-in-law's window. The window
> shattered. We were covered in glass. . . . It's something that I
> have suppressed, I think, until now.

Like other Mohawk women, Jacobs expresses her dismay and a certain disbelief at the sight of these serious acts of violence perpetrated against people from her community. She continues by describing a disturbing murderous intent behind these gestures: "I couldn't believe how many people gathered there, how many people hated us, so much, that. . . . They weren't there just to throw rocks to scare us. These were rocks to kill us!" Many people had to be taken to the hospital's emergency department for treatment of lacerations and wounds caused by shards of glass. A seventy-one-year-old man, Joseph Armstrong, was hit in the chest by one of the rocks and his untimely death has been described as directly related to this violent assault.

This experience was completely traumatic for the people in the cars and for the entire Mohawk community. So say the women, men, and children who remember with distress what they underwent that day. Alanis Obomsawin would herself remark that she could find a kind of peace only by making her documentary film, *Rocks at Whiskey Trench*, the last in a series of four, because until then "we had not heard what the people in the cars had to say."[67] Faced with the violence perpetrated against their community that day, the Mohawk women reaffirmed their determination to stand up and resist, even under attack. In Obomsawin's film, Caireen Cross Montour, a registered nurse in Kahnawake who was a teenager at the time, recounts her experience:

> I was just staring out of the window. Really, I could have been hit in the face. I was there with my brother in the back seat with me and I just, I decided that whoever was there, they weren't gonna see me hiding. They were gonna see my face staring out at them, you know . . . strong face. They weren't gonna see me back down. Fifteen is quite an age to be going through that. That was one of the things I knew I had to do. I felt almost like I was taking care of the family in my father's place because I knew my mother was very nervous.

People speak of feeling both betrayed by the Quebec and Canadian authorities and guilty for having carried out the evacuation without knowing of the danger that awaited the people in the convoy. Again, in *Rocks at Whiskey Trench*, several people speculate that the Sûreté du Québec and the Royal Canadian Mounted Police (RCMP) had been informed that the convoy might be the target of an attack, but they did nothing to prevent it. Others note that the police let the convoy go ahead into the hail of rocks instead of advising them to turn back when they saw that a furious crowd had gathered at the other side of the bridge. In short, everything points to Quebec's and Canada's controlling forces deliberately letting the convoy cross the bridge when they knew that an enraged crowd was waiting at the other end, making themselves accomplices in these serious attacks.

Others from Kahnawake express regret at having left the community; they make an explicit connection between their experience on the bridge and their daily battle to preserve their identity. In *Rocks at Whiskey Trench*, Allison Jacobs again explains: "I should never have left. I would never leave again. I feel safe in Kahnawake, and I feel safe nowhere else, but here. I'm proud to live in this community. Kahnawake to me shows how very strong and determined our people are to maintain our identity. I'm proud to be Mohawk. I think that no matter how the governments or the outside communities try, they could never beat that out of us, not even with a rock."

With this, Jacobs is reaffirming her pride in being Mohawk and the determination she shares with her people to display their strength and maintain their identity, no matter how much adversity they have to endure. That experience was for several people a defining moment of the summer of 1990 that generated renewed, yet in many ways disturbing, understandings. In a 2017 Canadian Broadcasting Corporation (CBC) interview, Tracey Deer, the director of the TV show *Mohawk Girls*, remembered being in a car with her mother, sister, and cousin, and trying, amidst the noises, angry crowd, cloud of dust, and rocks pelted, to grasp what was happening at that frightening moment:

> My mother started screaming and crying because she was
> so afraid. I remember also being afraid but also wanting to
> understand: What is this? What's happening? I remember
> getting up from the floor, to look, and I could see, off the back
> of the window, all of these men on a rise with the rocks. They
> were throwing them, they were cheering, and they were happy.
> And I could see the policemen, just standing there, not doing
> anything. Then our back window smashed open. My sister
> and my cousin got covered in glass, and they started screaming.
> Then just like that, we were out. That moment changed
> everything for me and has really shaped my entire life.[68]

Tracey Deer's account, which retraces her path as a Mohawk filmmaker, alludes to the way the violent scene she experienced and witnessed that summer brought to her mind a clarified vision of the material embodiment of settler colonialism in her life.

During the Oka Crisis, or the resistance at Kanehsatake, the positions adopted by the authorities aroused a latent racism feeding on the dehumanizing representations of Indigenous peoples that remain embedded in the public mentality and thus central to North America's settler structures. Further, it is as telling as it is troubling to ask what might have happened if the reverse scenario had been played out. What might have been the reaction of the security forces and non-Indigenous Quebec population if a worked-up crowd of Mohawks had gathered at the end of the bridge and hurled rocks, accompanied by insults, at white settler residents in cars being evacuated from a Montreal neighbourhood? The response, which we can too easily imagine, would say much about the colonial violence that structures the Quebec and Canadian societies. In this regard, Indigenous scholars such as Taiaiake Alfred, Emma LaRocque, and Jo-Ann Episkenew have targeted the feelings of cultural superiority, patriarchal arrogance, and white privilege that continue to feed into and legitimize this type of attack. The episode as told by Tracey Deer of Indigenous women fleeing their community in fear of a military intervention, only to be attacked by a crowd of white male settlers, is revealing. In fact it can be thought of as a localized, momentary materialization of a gendered dynamics of settlement according to which, as Audra Simpson contended, "Canada requires the death and so called 'disappearance' of Indigenous women in order to secure its sovereignty."[69] The rocks thrown on the Kanien'kehà:ka women and children in the summer of 1990 disturbingly appear to reinscribe a gendered settler violence that intensified in the face of the forceful, public, and politicized Mohawk resistance.

In 1990 the armed siege projects the clearly focused image of a profound dissonance inherent in the Quebec and Canadian societies. It makes a break with dominant representations of a social order that is considered to be a given, in which Indigenous people are hardly to be seen, except on the margins. In this regard, the siege evokes the heterotopia conceived by French philosopher Michel Foucault.[70] In fact, by changing the familiar reality into an Other Space, the siege exposes the space to which settlers belong in a new light; by making a violent hostility towards Indigenous peoples concrete within this space, it changes the self-constructed image of the Quebec and Canadian societies. As discussed above, it also confirms to Indigenous peoples many of their observations and worst suspicions regarding settlement. While the event creates a breach in the order of things, causing eruptions, violence, and confusion, the siege's scenography accentuates and polarizes the territorial conflict, redrawing it in broad strokes.

AT THE PINES' EDGE

The rivalries that were brought into focus in the siege space developed around representations and issues associated with occupation of the land. In defiance of an economic development plan arrived at in the absence of the Kanehsatake Mohawks, the initial occupation of the Pines and the siege that followed produced the specific result of inhabiting the land to be protected and making it seen to be inhabited. By restoring the human element to what was conceived of in the settler imagination as a landscape, the occupation forced a recognition of the existence of peoples who had been erased from the scene. As anthropologist

Anna J. Willow further expounded in relation to the Grassy Narrows blockade more specifically, this proves to be especially significant in the perspective of Indigenous activism.[71]

Beginning in the spring, the people of the Pines had maintained a camp where a fire always burned, "as an impromptu symbol of the resolve of the occupiers," as reported in a publication by the Tsi Niionkwarihò:ten Cultural Centre.[72] They set up a fishing hut over which they hung a large banner stating what was at stake in the occupation: "Our Land, Our Culture, Our Future." Family members, friends, and acquaintances regularly dropped by to get news, bring food, and stay for a while to talk, sitting in the middle of a stand of pines and hemlock planted by their ancestors in the early twentieth century to prevent soil erosion and landslides. Places come into being through praxis, not just through narrative, as Willow also pointed out, and using the communal lands and the pine grove renewed the living connection the Kanehsata'kehró'non maintain with a place where they had often gathered, including to play lacrosse, the Haudenosaunee sport that still attracts many enthusiasts. On political and legal levels, the occupation had the effect of granting legitimacy to occupancy of the place.

In a significant way, the initial occupation and the armed conflict that followed proceeded not in a parliament or court of law, but on the very territory that the protestors wanted to protect. Shortly before the armed conflict broke out, the protestors repeated that they were prepared to talk to the authorities, but on condition that these talks take place at Kanehsatà:ke; they considered it to be out of the question that they should go to Montreal or Quebec City to meet the governments' representatives.[73] In addition to insisting that the discussions and negotiations be conducted on their territory, the Mohawk activists would maintain their position in the face of the police operation, and they continued to do so until the Canadian Army intervened and eventually pushed them to the last ditch.

On the morning of 11 July 1990, the police officers who arrived at the site were met by Mohawk women, who negotiated that time be given to the occupiers in the Pines to conduct a morning ceremony prior to beginning discussion of the injunction. As mentioned in the journal *Karihwatàtie* that was published in Kanehsatà:ke after the event, the ceremony consisted of the *Ohén:ton Karihwatéhkwen* opening speech, or thanksgiving address,[74] which is regularly recited at the beginning of gatherings, often in the Mohawk language. That morning, it was the spiritual leader John Cree who delivered "the words which come first," a version of which can be found at the beginning of *At the Woods' Edge* (Gabriel-Doxtater and Van den Hende 1995, v–vii). This written version of the ceremony starts by alluding to a living and constantly renewed transmission of what is said: *"These words are recited before all gatherings of the People. These words end or close each gathering. It is up to each of us to know these words. This is one version. We have been instructed that whenever the People gather together for whatever reason, we are to remind each other of these words which have been given to us"* (v). The person presiding over the ceremony then gives thanks, referring to the close relationship between the people and the elements supporting their existence, as was done by John Cree on the morning of the police intervention in the Pines:

> We have been instructed that the first thing we should think of is our Mother Earth for she is the one we have come from and the one who sustains us and supports us all the time as we are walking about in this existence.
>
> So at this time, we gather our minds together as one mind and we extend our greetings and thanksgiving to Mother Earth for the support and sustenance she continues to provide us.
>
> *So be it in our minds.*
>
> As we look about, we take notice of the vegetation life all around us. There is the tall and the short vegetation who since the beginning of our creation have been carrying on with their duties. At this time we acknowledge the short vegetation whose leader is the strawberry. The short vegetation have agreed to provide us with foods, medicine, their beautiful fragrances and their colourful nature. We also acknowledge the tall vegetation whose leader is the maple tree. The tall vegetation has agreed that, from time to time, they would give up members of their families so that our families would have shelter or warmth or that we might have transport, utensils and all the other things they contribute to our existence.

So now it is that we gather our minds together as one and
extend our greetings and thanksgiving to all the vegetation life
who continue to support us in this existence.

So be it in our minds.

At this time we turn our attention to our relatives the four-
legged whose leader is the deer. Since the time of creation, the
four-legged have agreed that from time to time they would give
up members of their families to support our families with food,
clothing and other necessities.

So at this time we gather our minds together as one mind and
we extend our greetings and thanksgiving to our relatives, the
four-legged.

So be it in our minds. (v)

This recitation outlines the principles of Haudenosaunee environmental
ethics, foregrounding interrelatedness, respect, and reciprocity. It continues
with thanks to the birds, "our relatives the winged, whose leader is the eagle";
the fish, "our relatives who live in the waters, whose leader is the trout"; and the
rivers and oceans, those "many waters who support us" (vi). Having recognized
the role played by animals and water in maintaining human life, the recitation
outlines the elements of a Haudenosaunee cosmology by expressing gratitude
to the "lower sky world"; "to all our relatives"—that is, "to our Grandmother
the Moon, to our Elder Brother the Sun and our Grandfather the Thunderer";
to "all our ancestors who have journeyed in the sky road ahead of us" and "that
which has created everything" (vi–vii). The ceremony closes with the following
speech, which invites each person to give his or her own thanks, linking the
individual mind to the collective mind:

Now, it may be that I have left something out or it may be
that each of you may have something that you are especially
thankful for.

So now is the time for you to offer up your greetings and
thanksgiving as we gather our minds together as one mind to
offer our thanks and add them to all that has been said before.

So be it in our minds.

So it is now that we have done what is required of us.

We are now ready to begin what we have gathered here for. (vii)

When he pronounced the thanksgiving address in the presence of the
people assembled in the Pines, John Cree reanimated these particular connections to the land and the various elements of the world that surrounds and sus-
tains us. Significantly, he was doing it at the very moment when the officers
in the Sûreté du Québec's tactical intervention squad were preparing to force
the lifting of the barricades and throw tear gas canisters into the woods. The
call for shared thinking and its affirmation strongly evoked the collective action
behind the occupation. The last sentence, "We are now ready to begin what we
have gathered here for"—that is, to protect the land, as we can infer from the
context—expresses the spirit of the ceremony that Cree had brought to life that
morning. It takes on a special dimension in being recited at the same time that
the occupiers—women, men, and children—were preparing to resist an assault
by the Sûreté du Québec's tactical squad.

Many Mohawk people have reported being motivated by a sense of duty,
a feeling of responsibility, and the need to stay on the site and protect their
land, whatever the consequences. "One thing for sure, people here are never
going to give up the pines," declared one Kanehsata'kehró:non after the event
(Gabriel-Doxtater and Van den Hende 1995, 256). On this subject, Vernon W.
Neufeld Redekop observed that deep-rooted conflicts are characterized by "the
willingness of people to put at risk both the sense of order that follows from
compliance with authorities and the sense of security and physical well-being
associated with the status quo" to avoid compromising the satisfaction of a fundamental need.[75] For Oka's mayor and its town council, it might have been a
question of economic development and decision-making power. For the community of Kanehsatake, on the other hand, it was a matter of needing to protect
the little territory left to it, gain the political and economic means to control its

own destiny, and maintain a relationship with the land that is fundamental to an identity that had been damaged by centuries of colonization. In this regard, for the people of the Pines, complying with settler authorities and maintaining the status quo were not to be equated with any particular sense of order or security; in fact, in that context such a stance would have threatened to compromise some fundamental human needs such as connectedness, meaning in life, and belonging. The connections among the Pines, the cemetery, the history of the Mohawk people, and the relationship to the land as a source of pride and identity were made explicit by spiritual leader John Cree: "The pines is a sacred place for me, for all Mohawks. It's like a church. The pines is our sacred burial ground. We call it *Onen'to:kon*. It means 'under the pines.' We have been in this area for as long as we can remember. There's always been Mohawks here. It's part of our tradition. It is our sacred place. There's all kinds of medicines, and the trees are very old. It's our sacred land. It gives us pride, the pines give us pride. This land . . . it is who we are. Without it we would not be Mohawks."[76]

Today, the quiet, majestic presence of these tall pines marks the transition between Oka and Kanehsatake, along Route 344. Numerous symbolic references to the pine tree can be found in Haudenosaunee stories, ceremonies, and history. In addition to appearing in the story of creation and the speeches of Haudenosaunee chiefs to British or French colonizers, references to these sacred, symbolic trees are part of the Haudenosaunee Confederacy's wampum code. Seneca researcher Arthur C. Parker cites this excerpt as an example: "If any individual or any nation outside the Five Nations shall obey the laws of the Great Peace and make known their disposition to the Lords of the Confederacy, they may trace the Roots to the Tree, and if their minds are clean and obedient . . . they shall be welcome to take shelter beneath the Tree of the Long Leaves. We place in the top of the Tree of the Long Leaves an Eagle who is able to see afar; . . . he will warn the people."[77] The tree's roots lead any person or nation who intends to submit to the Great Law of Peace to the confederacy's centre, while its leaves provide a symbolic political and spiritual shelter. The tree's crown serves as a perch for the eagle that warns of any danger looming on the horizon. During Oka, media releases by the Mohawk negotiation team used the symbol of the eagle at the top of a great pine, which in the context can be read to signify the danger presented by the municipal development project and, more broadly, the infringement on the people's integrity and sovereignty.

The potential threat of desecration to the cemetery, the sacred place of rest for the ancestors, gave the occupation a symbolic dimension that held a powerful appeal for Indigenous peoples as well as the general public. Furthermore, it appears from various testimonials that the cemetery that is part of the lands threatened by the town's project is closely linked in the minds of the Kanehsata'kehró:non to the Pines, the land, and the community. The encampment set up in the Pines, the very physical barricades, the presence of people who supported the siege, and various personal accounts all signalled that an ultimate limit had been reached and retreat was inconceivable.

In the framework of the siege, the stance of the Mohawk protestors raises the issue of the Mohawk people's collective survival and, in a broader sense, that of Indigenous peoples in general. The burden of violent armed conflict was all the harder to bear because it caused painful historical wounds to resurface. Talking about 1990, one resident of Kanehsatake remarked, "A lot of people felt as though they were used, physically and mentally. A lot of times they went back to all the things that happened many years ago" (Gabriel-Doxtater and Van den Hende 1995, 255). The resistance that flared up in 1990 revived an idea of collective survival conceived and articulated in connection to the traumatic experiences undergone under the continued settler colonization process, whether the wounds were caused by being chased off the territory or by the physical and symbolic violence inflicted on community members. For that reason, the mere fact of surviving, its manifestation and invocation, also signifies a categorical refusal to disappear. Taiaiake Alfred addresses the collective aspect: "Our bodies may live without our languages, lands, or freedom, but they will be hollow shells. Even if we survive as individuals, we will no longer be what we Rotinohshonni call *Onkwehonwe*—the real and original people—because the communities that make us true indigenous people will have been lost. We will be nothing but echoes of proud nations floating across a landscape possessed by others."[78] Contrary to the settler push towards appropriation of Indigenous lands, the siege offered the shape and definition of a space in which the connection to the Mohawk and Iroquois land, history, and political and spiritual structures was affirmed. It was affirmed with still greater power because the act of surrounding the community with military and police forces rendered palpable the imminent danger of a violent confrontation during which lives could be destroyed.

During the conflict, and afterwards, the Mohawks spoke of the power to be found in spirituality, as demonstrated in this testimonial: "Their spirit was strong and the faith was there. A lot of people, although they weren't physically, were there in spirit. Their hearts were there, and all the sacred stuff was going on to make sure that it didn't happen any worse than it already was" (Gabriel-Doxtater and Van den Hende 1995, 255). Holding ceremonies in the besieged space took on an additional significance in an historical context in which the enactment of this spirituality, whether it be through belief, ritual ceremonies, or the political and spiritual structure represented by the longhouse, had been systematically denigrated, suppressed, and often outright forbidden and criminalized by the colonial authorities and successive Canadian regimes.

In 1990, spiritual leaders remained on the site of the siege and played a critical role all summer. In this regard, it is significant that in the agreement signed on 12 August 1990 by the Mohawk Nation with the federal and provincial governments, the second condition for negotiation should be couched in these terms: "The governments of Canada and Quebec will ensure unrestricted access to and from the Mohawk communities of Kanehsatake and Kahnawake of spiritual leaders, clan mothers, chiefs, advisors and attorneys as designated by the Mohawk Nation."[79] Such an experience of spirituality might be difficult to grasp and describe from an outside perspective, but this does not mean that it was not very present and active during the armed conflict, within the Mohawk communities and among the other Indigenous peoples. That can be understood from testimonials like the following in *At the Woods' Edge*, which relate territory to spirituality and identity:

> [The crisis] brought a lot of Indian nations together to fight
> for a common goal, the land issue. You saw how powerful the
> women were, spiritually and physically. It brought back our
> roots. Before women had many roles, they maintained the long
> house, they took care of other earth, they were mothers. Their
> connection to the earth was renewed. (Gabriel-Doxtater and
> Van den Hende 1995, 257)

> I seen a lot of good. At that moment, people got together for a
> common cause—the land. The people respected the land, the
> Creator, and themselves. The people became more aware of
> what was happening. Before that, they were in a kind of limbo.
> People started to become aware of who they are and they were

proud of themselves. What was hard to see was the extent the
government went to split the people up. (249)

It wasn't 'til 90, that I really learned who I am. I'm learning now
and I'm teaching my son. I'm gonna make sure that he knows
who he is. You see a lot of people now, going into the longhouse
and the traditional way, looking into the mirror and saying this
is who I am. (251)

The significance given to protecting the territory for the Indigenous peoples,
the key role played by women in the resistance, the power of affirming First Nations identity and politics during the siege, and the intrinsic duality of the conflict's dynamics strengthened a particular form of symbolization that was generated by the struggle to exist. By becoming the site for a reterritorialization of politics,
spirituality, and culture, the siege encouraged a movement of coming home and
opening up to the future. Further, the resistance played out on the siege site was
often conceived of and described as a struggle in the name of the generations
to come. The Great Law of Peace, on which the Iroquois constitution is based,
was often cited by the Mohawks who took a stance in 1990. This law suggests to
delegates engaged in deliberations to think first of the welfare of all the people,
and to "have always in view not only the present but also the coming generations,
even those whose faces are yet beneath the surface of the ground—the unborn of
the future Nation."[80] The representation of generations to come as faces emerging from the earth powerfully illustrates how destroying land associated with the
community's identity and survival becomes an act of extreme violence.

The painful and traumatic nature of the armed conflict is undeniable. Paradoxically, it produced a closing of ranks and a feeling of pride that resonated in
Indigenous communities across the country. Risking one's life and demanding
that a limit be set in the besieged space seem to serve as symbols that can help
to strengthen a damaged identity. French anthropologist David Le Breton made
the point that risking one's own life constitutes a "transgression that adds to the
power of the one who dared to do it." According to him, "the closeness of death"
is a "structure that generates meaning" insofar as a symbolic exchange with this
"major signifier" confirms the legitimacy of the survivor's existence.[81] In this perspective, it is possible to suggest that, in 1990, the armed conflict's violence and
the omnipresence of death paradoxically lent additional power to the stance of

the Mohawk protestors behind the barricades. Many of them, repeating what their ancestors had expressed in similar situations, pronounced themselves ready to die to protect the land. This assertion expresses a deep, powerful feeling often found in Indigenous literary narratives that mention the resistance at Kanehsatake. Other testimonials, couched in terms of Mohawk nationalism, speak of recovering a sense of identity, confirming one's existence, and becoming politicized. For example, as Randy Horne, a member of the Mohawk Warrior Society in Kahnawake, concluded after the crisis:

> I never gave much thought to the warriors, never considered
> myself to be a member before the golf course problem. When I
> saw them with no fear, standing up to Canada, I wanted to be
> part of that too. . . . They gave me a sense of knowing who I am, a
> stronger sense of cultural identity and meaning. They gave me a
> political purpose, the fight for Mohawk nationhood. They made
> me understand it was about more than a golf course. They made
> me understand it was about nationhood. Mohawk Nationhood.
>
> That political purpose was seen in "The Pines" in everyone's
> faces. For me, it started there, and it still continues today. As
> long as our territory continues to be taken away from us, I
> will have political purpose. As long as it's a matter of Mohawk
> nationhood, I will fight for that political purpose.[82]

Anthropologist Anna J. Willow observed that activism can transform a site into a politically charged vantage point from which the activists can comprehend, configure, and communicate their place in the world.[83] In the same way, the siege maintained at Kanehsatake and Kahnawake conveys the determination expressed by members of the Mohawk people to engage in collective reconstruction, give themselves the means for long-term action, and recentre their knowledges, stories, culture, and identity. The siege was one way to counter forced displacements that, according to Willow, may provoke a feeling of collective disorientation caused by "the inability of a people to answer fundamental cultural questions—Where are we? Who are we?—in clear terms."[84] The siege helped to define, formulate, and perform answers to these questions; it constituted a way to reaffirm, in the public space, a Mohawk identity positioned and conceived of as the centre. As a counter to the process of exile and its devastating effects, the siege became for many the venue for a reterritorialization: that is, for taking over a space in which we impose a discourse that tallies with the physical reality (McLeod 2001, 22).

CHAPTER 3

The Disputed Land: Performing Sovereignty

Whose land is this; whose nation is this; how is it that we are here if these people who were here first, who have this different constitution, are pushing back, refusing the encroachment, refusing the ongoing dispossession of their land? They did what they did because they were and are not Canadian citizens, indeed. They did what they did because of a responsibility to their territory, the bodies of their dead who were buried within that territory, and the fearful spectacle of that responsibility to the military arm of the state as it views Mohawk women, Iroquois women, fulfill their mandates to the territory, to act.

—*Audra Simpson*, Mohawk Interruptus

The spring occupation and the sustained siege that followed enacted a resistance that was expressed and performed on the very site of the territory selected for the municipal development project. The initial dispute became so poisonous that it degenerated into an armed conflict and reached national crisis proportions. It was able to do so specifically because it addressed fundamental issues intrinsic to settler-Indigenous relations in Canada and elsewhere on the continent. The territorial and political issues that came into play during the siege in action involved a colonial dynamic that set up a tension between legality and legitimacy, fragility and certitude, movement and enclosure.

THE MUNICIPALITY'S DEVELOPMENT PROJECT

As exemplified by the crisis, the spaces defined by disputed lands constitute sensitive zones in which promoters' projects can run up against particularly energetic resistance. In *Skyscrapers Hide the Heavens: A History of Indian-White Relations in Canada*, Canadian historian James R. Miller made the observation that, since the 1940s, economic development has tended to be the principal source of disputes between settlers and Indigenous peoples. That is exactly what transpired at Oka-Kanehsatake when the construction of the first private golf course in 1961, and the planned expansion thirty years later, became the source of open conflict. The development project that was the proximate cause of the 1990 crisis consisted in expanding a nine-hole course to eighteen holes and constructing fifty luxury homes alongside it. This plan was made public in 1989, without any consultation with the Kanehsatake Mohawks. The project was evaluated at $1,350,000 and promised attractive economic benefits for the investors and the municipality.[1] However, it was not to be carried out, because on 8 August 1990, in the middle of the Oka Crisis, the federal government bought up the disputed land for $3,840,000, and paid out $2,500,000 to the municipality in compensation for the loss of taxes and revenues. As for the little cemetery, it was purchased for the sum of one dollar.[2] During the crisis, the municipality initially refused to sell the land to the federal government until the Mohawk barricades had been taken down, but in the end it yielded before the government's threat simply to expropriate without compensation.

In the planners' vision, the project would transfer publicly owned land, a communal area, to non-Indigenous private parties. As the local history illustrates and confirms, successive sales of Mohawk land and its exploitation by private businesses strengthened settler occupancy of the territory by placing it, politically and legally, within a colonial framework. The Municipality of Oka was convinced of its right to the region's territory and its exploitation. It was therefore incensed to see a promising economic development project stymied by the Kanehsata'keró:non's actions, asserting their right to the land and sovereignty over it. The municipality felt compelled to cancel a symbolic tree-cutting ceremony planned for the summer of 1989 (Quebec 1995, 85), and was then obliged to put off starting the work by the declaration of a moratorium at Kanehsatake's request. The moratorium's intent was to allow for negotiations with the federal government regarding the unification of Mohawk land, a file that was competing with the project to expand the golf course. In March 1990, when the moratorium was lifted, members of the Mohawk community occupied a dirt road to deter the work threatening their land. The Municipality of Oka, which had grown increasingly irritated and wished to proceed, then appealed to the Superior Court, which acquiesced to its request by issuing injunctions ordering the protestors to open the road. Bolstered by the legality conferred by the courts, Oka's mayor invoked the municipality's legal right to make an appeal to the Sûreté du Québec, in order to force the dismantling of the barricades, and following the municipality's third request, the Sûreté intervened.

The municipality's legalistic attitude and the failed police operation were loudly criticized, and, as soon as the armed conflict broke out, voices were raised in condemnation. Stephen Lewis, Canada's former ambassador to the United Nations, expressed strong disapproval of the motivation behind the police intervention at Oka-Kanehsatake: "I find it indefensible and unreasonable. We do not do battle over a golf course. That is simply inconceivable."[3] Lieutenant-General Kent R. Foster, who was dispatched to the scene of the siege when the Canadian Armed Forces were asked to intervene, reflected a commonly held feeling when he declared unequivocally, "There's nothing in a golf course—a *nine-hole* golf course, fer Chris' sake—worth a human life."[4] Lieutenant-General Foster's reasoning cannot be denied; we don't kill people to build a golf course. However, it should be said that when the mayor asked for the Sûreté du Québec's intervention to bring down the barricades, he could not foresee its tragic consequences. The mayor and his council could no doubt imagine and even vindictively hope for the arrest of the Mohawk protestors, forcefully if possible, and the jailing of other actors; but they certainly didn't anticipate the exchange of fire and the death that would result. At that stage of the conflict, the municipality wanted to force a dismantling of the barricades, run off the protestors who were preventing the start of the construction work, and, with a strong sense of settler entitlement in this tense social atmosphere, send a clear signal that it intended to make its will prevail. It was the event, then ready to erupt, that would allow the entire country to see this blatantly colonial attitude exposed.

As demonstrated by the land dispute that would take place two decades later in Caledonia, Ontario, similar scenarios are regularly played out across the country. The settler colonial impatience and resentment on the part of Canadian authorities and a local populace who find their projects blocked and then resort to police repression to dislodge the demonstrators are all too common. Peter H. Russell demonstrated this clearly in his text on Indigenous flashpoint events from Oka to Ipperwash.[5] Interventions by the police do not always degenerate to the point of attracting widespread media attention. Nevertheless, the settlers' desire to proceed with economic development despite overt

Indigenous opposition and the use of force to sweep aside impediments to that desire are far from being unique to the Municipality of Oka. In 1995, before the Ipperwash crisis blew up, then Ontario premier Mike Harris also encouraged repressive action. At a meeting to determine how to end the occupation of the provincial park by First Nations protesters, he told his staff: "I want those fucking Indians out of the park!"[6] Eleven hours later, an Ontario Provincial Police officer shot and killed unarmed Anishinaabe protestor Dudley George. As expounded by Thomas King in *The Inconvenient Indian*, the sense of entitlement among settler societies generates attitudes that are closed and arrogant and never augur well. The forms this feeling will take in a crisis are the exaggerated manifestation of a settler agenda that is pursued every day in ways that are often much more insidious.

CONSOLIDATING PROPERTY RIGHTS

It would be easy, not to say comforting, to attribute all the wrongdoing in this case to the mayor of Oka and his municipal council. The acts they committed were real and reprehensible; the accusations directed at them, well founded. The municipal players made shocking, unacceptable declarations and many public displays of racism and denial; moreover, following the shooting, the mayor went so far as to tell the media that, if he had to do it all again, he would still call in the Sûreté du Québec. It might be easy to direct indignation at a figure who had become the cartoonish embodiment of all the settler faults at work in this event. However, this feeling could also provide a convenient way to overlook a more discreet complicity that, on a daily basis, endorses the structures of a colonial order battening up white privilege, which had rarely been challenged as it was in 1990. What was the connection between the Oka municipality's attitude and the grammar of settler colonialism that structures our everyday lives? Why did the Oka mayor and his municipal council, backed by the citizens' coalition of the Regroupement des citoyens d'Oka, feel that they had sufficient reason and authority to dismiss the Mohawks' objections and proceed, no matter what? What role did the history of settler colonialism, state structure, and nation stories of Quebec and Canada play in the siege?

The municipality's legalistic attitude is made clearer by the political and legal history that shaped the situation at Oka-Kanehsatake. Since the eighteenth century, in response to repeated petitions from the Kanehsata'keró:non demanding that their rights to the land be recognized, a series of government and court decisions had confirmed and strengthened the title of the Séminaire de Saint-Sulpice to the seigneury lands and, subsequently, the Oka municipality's title to the communal land. These decisions were key steps in the process of establishing title or, in other terms, appropriating the Indigenous land for the purpose of colonial settlement. Following are several examples. In 1787, a decision by the British colonial authorities established that the issue of property titles was in the purview of the courts (Gabriel-Doxtater and Van den Hende 1995, 61), rendering the agreements recorded in the wampums inoperative. In 1841, after the British conquest, the seminary's title to the seigneury land was confirmed by special order. Significantly, the explicit aim of this order was to eliminate all doubt regarding the Sulpicians' title to the property.[7] In 1912, London's Privy Council rejected the appeal by Mohawk Chief Angus Corinthe against the Séminaire de Saint-Sulpice and declared that the 1841 order had therefore accomplished its objective.[8]

The colonial project to consolidate rights to the land continued into the twentieth century. In 1959, when the Kanehsatà:ke Mohawks opposed Oka's first golf course, a law was passed to confirm the municipality's ownership of the communal lands and authorize their use for sports and commerce.[9] The propensity to invoke settler law in order to foil the Kanehsata'keró:non claims has been patent. In 1975, the federal government rejected a general land claim submitted jointly by the Mohawks of Kanehsatake, Kahnawake, and Akwesasne, based on two principles applied by the Department of Indian Affairs and Northern Development. The first was that ancestral rights could not be invoked, owing to a perceived lack of continuous occupation of the territory since time immemorial; the second considered that any existing ancestral title would in any case have been extinguished, first by the kings of France and then by the British Crown.[10] In 1986, a specific land claim submitted nearly ten years before by the Kanehsatake Mohawks would in its turn be rejected by the federal government, which concluded that the claim in question did not meet the criteria it had set out as part of its policy regarding specific claims.[11]

These unilateral decisions did not settle the dispute; just the opposite— they reinforced settler law by reiterating it. While they failed to convince the Mohawks to abandon the campaign to assert their rights to the land, the decisions strengthened the conviction of settler populations that their own rights were well founded, since they had been constantly reiterated and confirmed by the legal and governmental institutions defining their citizenship. When the

Municipality of Oka ran into opposition that threatened its recreational and housing development project, it spontaneously invoked the law in an attempt to use power relations to its benefit. In that, the municipality was completely in line with the logic of settlement.

In March 1989, then Grand Chief of Kanehsatake Clarence Simon wrote to the municipality and directed it to abandon the development project. In response, the Municipality of the County of Deux-Montagnes, presided over by warden Jean Ouellet, passed a motion "reasserting its rights in law and the infringement represented by the civil disobedience of certain citizens" (quoted in Quebec 1995, 84). Subsequent to passing the motion, which was intended to reassert its right to occupy and use the land, the Municipality of Oka sought the support of the Superior Court. On 29 June 1990, the court ordered the occupiers of the Pines "to refrain, under the penalty prescribed by law, from obstructing or barricading the Chemin du Mille, property of the Municipal Corporation of the Village of Oka" (quoted in Quebec 1995, 166). The injunction therefore confirmed the municipality's right to have the barricades dismantled and at the same time, by virtue of the terms it used, it confirmed the municipality's property rights. This is the context in which the mayor would invoke his right to call in the police to re-establish "public safety on the occupied territory" and to do so "without further delay or any further request from us" (quoted in Quebec 1995, 188–89).

THE FRAGILITY OF SETTLER SOCIETIES

Over the centuries, the decisions that reasserted, so as to strengthen, the Sulpicians' legal title and that of the Municipality of Oka could not completely conceal an insecurity that returned again and again to haunt North America's settler societies. In fact, argued Audra Simpson, "the greatest threat to settler state security and the economic, political and moral right to govern these entirely new spaces [has been posed by] Indigenous peoples, their governmental and philosophical systems, and most significantly, their lands."[12] The state of coexistence in which the Municipality of Oka and the community of Kanehsatake continue to live is a striking example of this interrelationship. This is what the Oka Crisis, or the Kanehsatake resistance, illustrated in concrete terms, and what is also, although in a less visible way, evidenced in the constant jurisdictional conflicts caused by a checkerboard distribution of territory in Oka-Kanehsatake.

This colonial dispute did not arise overnight. By itself, creation of the Municipality of Oka in the late nineteenth century—the direct result of a strong settler push that provoked an intense conflict between the Sulpicians and the Kanehsata'keró:non—made future clashes foreseeable. The Sulpicians, without respecting even "their own legalities,"[13] to use the phrasing of Québécois anthropologist Rémi Savard, were selling off large tracts of the seigneury to French Canadians, simultaneously dispossessing the Mohawks of their land.[14] As Savard wrote, "Since then, the devious Sulpician legalism has become the golden rule for dealing with the repeated suits of the Kanienkehakas of Kanehsatake."[15] As well as poisoning the social environment, the legally dubious transactions orchestrated by the Sulpicians weakened the legitimacy of settler occupation of the land, as the Mohawk protestors persisted in reminding us in 1990.

The court and government decisions that confirmed settler property rights by reiterating them were an attempt to sweep this nagging doubt under the rug. At the same time, the reservations expressed by certain government and legal agencies, in particular those that recognized grounds for the Kanehsatake Mohawk claims, had undermined the Municipality of Oka's position well before the crisis blew up. For example, the 1841 order that confirmed the Sulpicians' title to the property also set out certain obligations to the Indigenous people within the area. This derived in turn from the royal deeds of 1717 and 1735, in which the king of France ceded the land to the Sulpicians so that they could use it to establish a mission for the natives. In 1984, before refusing the special land claim by Kanehsatake, the federal minister of Indian Affairs and Northern Development recognized the Canadian government's moral obligation to establish a better territorial base for the "Oka Indians."[16] Finally, on the eve of the crisis, a court injunction ordered the demonstrators to allow access to the land, but the judge also notified the mayor of Oka that this judgement could not be used to promote the golf course expansion. He stated: "No golf project is valuable enough to necessitate the wiping out of an important forest, especially in the context of the evidence I've heard."[17]

The Mohawks' cause received support from environmentalists concerned about protecting this ancient forest and preventing landslides that might result from its destruction.[18] In comparison with the position of Québécois and Canadian environmentalists, that of the Mohawk demonstrators had the particular feature of referring to the very foundations of coexisting on a shared territory under settler colonialism. Consequently, it reminded a settler society of a presence that preceded it and questioned what it considered to be certainties. The municipal council's discourse refered to legality, while the Mohawk discourse placed the problem on the level of legitimacy. With regards to this tension, the coroner made the observation that "when legality confronts legitimacy, there can be no absolute certainty on either side" (Quebec 1995, 453). This fragility is what the event of summer 1990 would expose.

The police intervention on 11 July 1990 was intended to re-establish and reinforce legality, but it did not have the anticipated effect. On the contrary, it instead created a breach in the dominant structure, a fissure that exposed state fragility to the light of day. The report on the causes and circumstances of Corporal Marcel Lemay's death would conclude unequivocally that it was "an error to intervene at Oka on July 11" (Quebec 1995, 398). The coroner went on to say that the Sûreté du Québec should not have been the body to make that decision. He added that intervention was not justified, on the following three points: 1) the legal basis for the intervention; 2) the need to intervene; and 3) the situation's urgency (409). The coroner's report would not be published until five years after the crisis had ended. Nonetheless, the disquiet and confusion he noted were at work during the siege in 1990 and helped to erode the certainty of the Municipality of Oka regarding legality, as well as that of the settler societies of Canada and Quebec. As soon as the conflict broke out, Premier Robert Bourassa took the side of the Sûreté du Québec, but there was a feeling that all was not as it should be. This impression was strengthened by the federal government's refusal to intervene, on the pretext that the conflict fell under provincial jurisdiction.

COUNTER-PERFORMATIVITY AND MOHAWK SOVEREIGNTY

During the crisis, the Mohawks' protest actions and the assertion of their sovereignty stimulated a nagging uncertainty about state sovereignty. The resistance mounted by the Kanehsatà:ke community, the occupiers of the Pines, and the community of Kahnawà:ke in summer 1990 was a reminder that, as Audra Simpson explained, "the practice of state sovereignty is marred by an "uncertainty [that] is especially precarious and, in different ways, onerous in Indian country."[19] The relation between state sovereignty and Indigenous resistance operates on a number of levels. At Oka-Kanehsatake, the performativity of the law, whether municipal, provincial, or federal, first ran up against the actions of the Mohawks, who opposed the development project through legal channels. This performativity then met the counter-performativity of the people of the Pines and their civil disobedience, and, in a much more forceful way, that of the Mohawk activists brandishing firearms in the space of the highly publicized siege.

As soon as they got wind of the municipality's development project, the Kanehsatake Mohawks expressed their opposition clearly and directly. Grand Chief Clarence Simon responded to the municipality's legal measures with a letter addressed to Mayor Jean Ouellet stating the historical, legal, and legitimate grounds for the Mohawks' land claims in Kanehsatake (Quebec 1995, 84). The band council circulated this letter to all the municipalities, various ministers, Quebec's premier, and Canada's prime minister. In order to increase the pressure, Mohawk political actors organized public demonstrations, spoke out at Oka's council meetings, and approached the courts and the federal government. A year later, the golf course project was still going ahead.

Before the crisis blew up, the people of the Pines defied the injunction ordering them to "abstain from posting placards, signs or any other directional materials on the public land of the Corporation Municipale du Village d'Oka without prior permission" (quoted in Quebec 1995, 166). Hanging from a tree in the Pines, a bilingual banner interpellated passersby with the question written in capital letters: "ARE YOU AWARE THAT THIS IS MOHAWK TERRITORY / SAVEZ-VOUS QUE CECI EST TERRITOIRE MOHAWK?"[20] The banner was the companion piece to a large wooden sign nailed up at the edge of the Pines that read: "These lands are under the sovereignty of the Mohawk People of Kanehsatake so respect the natural beauty of the Land for the future."[21] These public reiterations of Mohawk sovereignty were produced despite the injunction and did have significance because, as American performance studies scholar Diana Taylor put it, "the performance of a claim contributes to its legality."[22]

The performativity of these discourses, which consists in making an event with speech, was enacted in a context in which the field of legitimate political struggle was being challenged on all sides. The negotiations raised questions about legitimate speech. The barricades, on their part, could be seen as a counter-performativity, since they constituted a refusal to obey the injunction ordering the Mohawk protesters to yield and allow passage. In early July, a sign was installed above the log barricades in anticipation of the Sûreté du Québec's intervention, announcing: "MOHAWK TERRITORY / NO TRESPASSING." Not only did this sign set the limit of dispossession, it also reversed the authority relation by forbidding entry to the Mohawk territory.

The barricades and signs on the siege site rendered visible the Mohawk protestors' refusal to respect the terms imposed by the settler state powers of Quebec and Canada. This refusal, which is part of a larger politics that was powerfully theorized by Audra Simpson in *Mohawk Interruptus: Political Life Across the Borders of Settler States*, was expressed with determination during the event in 1990 and became the affirmation of a sovereignty that has been constantly practised and reiterated by the Mohawks. The anthology *At the Woods' Edge* also expresses an explicit refusal on the part of the Kanehsata'keró:non to recognize the Canadian authorities' ability to extinguish ancestral rights (Gabriel-Doxtater and Van den Hende 1995, 218), and this deep conviction was still motivating the Mohawk protesters during the summer of 1990. Ellen Gabriel, a member of the Turtle Clan and Kanehsatà:ke Nation, explained that, in July, they had no intention of obeying an injunction whose legal basis they did not recognize: "We don't recognize the authority of the province over our land. We weren't about to let an injunction prevent us from defending our land. It didn't matter to me how many injunctions they had. We had no intention of obeying the court order. We were protesting to protect our land, our sacred land. Our people had to stand up to the encroachment, we just had to."[23] By refusing to obey a formal court order, the protestors enacted what the American feminist philosopher Judith Butler described as a "misappropriation of interpellative performatives." This way of resisting, Butler added, "is central to any project of the subversive territorialization and resignification of dominant social orders." Further, it can be "the very occasion for the exposure of prevailing forms of authority and the exclusions by which they proceed."[24] When the armed conflict broke out in summer 1990, the effects of this misappropriation were underscored. Despite having their legitimacy denied in the official discourse, the Mohawk protestors exposed the actuality of settler encroachment and drew attention to the fact that the state's power rested on resorting to force. In so doing, the protestors sought to throw the established foundations of state legitimacy into question, and simultaneously to assert and validate Haudenosaunee forms of legitimacy.

In an article in which she roundly denounces colonial violence, Audra Simpson observed, "While it is argued that indigenous sovereignty is unceded and inherent, it is also anxiety provoking, as it threatens state sovereignty, a sovereignty that owes itself to the dispossession and the death of Indigenous peoples."[25] In this context, Simpson added, "the politics for Indigenous peoples is to reveal that uncertainty, to point continuously to the contradictions of the colonial rule."[26] This is exactly what the besieged Mohawk communities were doing in 1990, causing guilt and unease in Quebec and Canadian settler societies. Their reiteration, on the site of the siege, of Mohawk land rights and sovereignty referred directly to assertions that had been made in Kanehsatake for over two centuries. On a larger scale, such reiteration recalled the history of relations between the people of the Haudenosaunee Confederacy and French and British settlers since the colony was founded. In August 1990, when the government decided to buy the land and give it back to the Kanehsatake Mohawks, they replied that the land was theirs by right and the government could not buy what already belonged to the Mohawk Nation.[27] Attesting to what Simpson described as "a deep sense of certainty about the sovereignty status of Indigenous nations,"[28] they would once again reaffirm the consistency of Mohawk discourse regarding the territory.

STRATEGIES AND TACTICS DURING THE SIEGE IN ACTION

In the realm of politics, as in that of the imagination, surrounding the Mohawk communities with police and military forces reactivated a settler movement that has exerted a constant pressure on the Indigenous peoples' lands and existences. While exposing boundaries of colonial structures that generally go unnoticed in daily life, the siege also drew attention to the points of contact and intertwining that relate these structures to elements that challenge them and are articulated according to other forms of legitimacy.

Following French philosopher and historian Michel de Certeau, the complexity of power relations can be understood schematically through tactics enacted "in the Other's place" and strategies operating in one's own place.[29] According to him, "a strategy postulates a *place* that can be delimited as its *own* and serve as the base from which an *exteriority* composed of threats (customers or competitors, enemies, the country surrounding the city, objectives and objects of research, etc.) can be managed." As for the tactic, it constitutes "a calculus which cannot count on a 'proper' (a spatial or institutional localization), nor thus on a borderline distinguishing the other as a visible totality. The place of a tactic belongs to the other."[30] In the framework of the Canadian state, Indigenous nations must present their claims in what de Certeau called the "Other's place." Canada recognizes those claims only insofar as they conform to the federal jurisdiction and Indian Act, and the Indigenous claimants are required to negotiate a legal system that has been conceived and implemented by—and for—settler governments. Regarding land claims, for example, the bizarre situation arises in which the judge is also one of the parties, which serves to illustrate the enormous control over place—territorial, political, and imagined—that the federal government and, by extension, the provincial and municipal governments arrogate to themselves. Similarly, where governance is concerned, the institution and control of band councils by the minister of Indian Affairs and Northern Development involves setting aside traditional Indigenous political structures, which are not recognized by the government, leading to a division of political power and allegiance within the communities and in dealing with the governments. Finally, "Indian status" imposes an exogenous and racialized definition of Indigenous identity, one conceived and inscribed in law within the Canadian state's geographical and historical boundaries; its effect is to contain Indigenous political action within the state framework. These different elements, which contribute to control over the territorial, political, and imagined place, are crucial to the strategies implemented by Quebec and Canadian authorities to restore the status quo during the Oka Crisis.

Again according to de Certeau, "strategies are actions which, thanks to the establishment of a place of power (the property of a proper), elaborate theoretical places (systems and totalizing discourses) capable of articulating an ensemble of physical places in which forces are distributed."[31] The Canadian government, proceeding from a political sovereignty established by means of colonization, developed a law that made it the guardian of the Indigenous nations, such that unrecognized political actions could be characterized as criminal and therefore legitimately suppressed. Some of the associated powers reside with provincial and municipal jurisdictions, so that in July 1990, it was officers of the provincial police force who arrived at Kanehsatake to order "the occupiers to leave the Pines, notifying them that they are there illegally and unless they comply, they will be arrested" (Quebec 1995, 275). To the Mohawk protestors, making their political and land claims in the siege space, the federal government retorted that it would refuse to negotiate as long as the barricades remained in place. It thus signalled its intention to hold negotiations in the "own place" represented by the Canadian state.

In the daily newspaper *La Presse* of 21 June 2010, Minister John Ciaccia addressed the government's fear that the crisis would spread across the country by directly interpellating and mobilizing Indigenous peoples Canada-wide. Concerning the government actors, he wrote: "They did not want to sign an agreement as long as there was a barricade. They looked over their shoulder, and there were 600 other Indian reserves in Canada, waiting to see what would happen in Oka. They were really afraid to set a precedent." All indications were that the precedent in question would be to negotiate with Indigenous groups acting outside the legal framework, which could invite other political assertions of this nature. Settling land claims in the courts reaffirms the existence of a common framework to which both parties subscribe, and it parallels Georg Simmel's interpretation of a court case as characterized by a "common submission to the law" and "the awareness that the entire procedure takes place within a social order and power, which alone give it meaning and endorse it."[32] This is not true of an armed conflict.

During the crisis at Oka, the governments' strategy, whose objective was to depoliticize the armed conflict so as to more easily impose the settler political framework, consisted in relocating the Mohawk protestors' legitimacy outside of that framework. Amelia Kalant explained that the federal government wanted to be sure to draw a distinction between the territorial conflict and the armed conflict, and to present the latter as an instance of violence and criminality like those involving casinos and the cigarette industry that had made the headlines as "smuggling" in recent years.[33] To restore the established political configuration, further specified by Kalant, the government made sure to create a difference between the "real" Mohawks—legitimate protestors—and the "warriors"—armed and masked imposters—gaining an advantage by publicly assigning them to the criminal element and thus more easily depoliticizing them. The presence on the siege site of Mohawk warriors from the United States posed a special difficulty, since their involvement fell outside the framework of the state and administrative territory of Quebec and Canada. In order to bring the conflict back inside the legal and state boundaries, the government therefore called these participants "foreigners." At the same time, it called them to order by directing them to put down their arms and submit to Canadian law. The federal government, according to Kalant, killed two birds with one stone by melding the image of the warrior with that of the American,[34] thus consigning them to a doubly external position.

According to de Certeau, tactics differ from strategies in that they "are procedures that gain validity to the pertinence they lend to time—to the circumstances which the precise instant of an intervention transforms into a favorable situation, to the rapidity of the movements that change the organization of a space, to the relations among successive moments in action."[35] Since their effectiveness depends upon taking judicious advantage of the circumstances, the tactics of the Mohawk protestors exploited the indeterminacy created by the political crisis. Therefore, on the morning of 11 July 1990, the protestors changed the spatial organization by blocking off the Honoré-Mercier Bridge so as to draw the city of Montreal and its suburbs into the conflict while expanding its scale exponentially. According to Richard Two Axe, a member of Kahnawake's Mohawk Warrior Society, the tactic consisted in blocking the bridge to gain political leverage:

> The police had to fight us on two fronts. They could not isolate
> us as a group of militants in the woods. They had to see us as
> a major political problem, a political force. . . . We had yet to
> decide on any long-term strategy. It was more of a spontaneous
> thing, a tactic that had worked for us in the past. We only knew
> that we had to do something, and we were counting on this.
> When you look at it, what else could we have done, it wasn't
> a choice to do it or not. To the outside we are Mohawks from
> Kahnawake, Mohawks from Kanehsatake, but we are more than
> that, we're all part of one Mohawk nation.[36]

At the same time as the Mohawk warriors were implementing tactics to change the spatial organization of the Other's place, the network of roads and the urban and suburban space of Montreal, Châteauguay, and Oka, they were marking out their own place, the Mohawk territory at Kanehsatake and Kahnawake; they were also affirming a Mohawk Nation conceived in terms other than those of the nation-state. The two parties—the settler state and the Mohawk Nation— both claimed to be exercising a sovereign political power over the disputed land. It therefore became at the very least complex to distinguish what, depending on the perspective, was a tactic or a strategy.

The siege of Kahnawake and Kanehsatake defined a space in which territorial rights were asserted and Mohawk sovereignty was uttered and exercised. During the event, that space seemed to define what Audra Simpson described as "Indian country": that is, one of those "spaces of Indigeneity that are framed by settler regimes."[37] The state's framing of these spaces of Indigeneity then shows up in an aggravated fashion in 1990, in the form of police and military perimeters that are physical manifestations within the space of a state power that exerts pressure on whatever contravenes the established legality.[38] This image spoke powerfully to Indigenous people throughout Canada, as demonstrated by the extent to which support for the Mohawks' claims was mobilized. For both sides, the siege thus became a venue for staging legitimacy, and while the soldiers were invested with the authority of the Canadian state's power, the Mohawk people and warriors invested their actions with the authority of the Mohawk Nation and the Iroquois Confederacy.

It was in the name of Aid to the Civil Power that the Canadian Army responded to the request made by the Government of Quebec, and through Operation Salon that it would lend its support to the Sûreté du Québec. As Lieutenant-Colonel Robin Gagnon explained in an interview, the soldiers recognized that resorting to the army's assistance was not the way to resolve such fundamental political problems as the territorial dispute that had been festering for over two centuries at Kanehsatake.[39] They nonetheless had to intervene when the political authorities appealed to the Canadian Armed Forces. During the Oka Crisis, Operation Salon was conducted and assessed in accordance with the Canadian Armed Forces' basic mandate, which is to protect Canada and defend its sovereignty, defend North America in cooperation with the United States, and help to contribute to peace and security on the international level.[40] In the context of this domestic operation, the Canadian Army saw the Mohawk protestors not as adversaries in a foreign country, but as Canadian citizens disrupting the public order and security that are the army's mandate to restore. In an interview, General John de Chastelain, Chief of Defence Staff responsible for the 1990 operation, remarked that when the Quebec government contacted him about the crisis, two other matters were competing for his attention: a possible Canadian military engagement to counter Iraq's invasion of Kuwait and a process to normalize relations between the North Atlantic Treaty Organization and its former Cold War antagonists.

Since it concerned a domestic event, Operation Salon was conceived of very differently from operations conducted overseas. According to General de Chastelain, the Canadian Army should not be seen as a force directed against the Indigenous peoples: "It must be understood that OP SALON was not the army confronting Canada's First Nations. A large number of First Nations members across Canada were totally opposed to what the Warriors were doing. They supported the need to address the cause of the dispute (the attempt by the mayor of Oka to build a golf course extension on native burial grounds), but not the armed blocking of bridges and highways, and the interference of Canadians going about their legitimate business."[41] Under the provisions of Aid to the Civil Power, the Canadian Army will intervene under a law enshrined in the state's framework to ensure the protection and stability of the state that defined it. The Canadian Army's intervention is therefore part of a legal and political framework that also defines the status of Canada's Indigenous peoples. From that viewpoint, the Mohawk protestors were breaking the law, and their actions were understood in terms of that transgression. General de Chastelain explained the parameters as follows: "The CF's role was specifically that of maintaining law and order in support of the police. The fact that the 'law-breakers' were First Nations members was not a factor. The CF would have acted the same way if the 'law-breakers' had been members of illegal groups or gangs."[42]

The Canadian Army's role, as a military institution, is clearly defined and delimited, as reflected in the four components of the army's strategic mission during the Oka Crisis, as described by Harry Swain in his book *Oka: A Political Crisis and Its Legacy*: "1) remove the barricades at Kanehsatake and Kahnawake; 2) restore freedom of movement on all roads and bridges; 3) remove all strong points; 4) restore normal conditions of public order and security."[43] Although this description outlines the situation in very rational terms, the military intervention at the scene in 1990 took place in an extremely charged political and emotional context. Lieutenant-Colonel Robin Gagnon explained that, from a philosophical and human perspective, in no instance does a soldier wish to fire on his fellow citizens. He added that it would involve a real aberration on the political level: "The last thing you want is to turn your army against your fellow citizens. That goes against all the principles of sovereignty, democracy, etc."[44] A soldier's actions are judged according to the values and principles enshrined in the Canadian state and recognized by the international community.

The representatives of the Canadian Armed Forces therefore placed the armed conflict within the state context that officially governs their actions, a context they recognize and to which they are beholden, but which is not necessarily accepted and recognized by the Mohawk communities. The army's mission was to restore law and order in accordance with Canadian law. To do so, it attempted to put down the Indigenous protest that was so forcefully enacted during the siege and contain it within parameters recognized by the state, in order to successfully reinstate the established power relationship. The Canadian

Army's intervention was met with mixed feelings; on the one hand, it was condemned, since the military action was experienced as violence and generated the persistent fear of a massacre; on the other, the army was welcomed with relief, since its presence, contrary to that of the police, was associated with restraint, expertise, and the possibility of creating grounds for agreement on the site of the confrontation. Further, it conferred a "nation to nation" dimension on the confrontation. This positive perception would be marred by an accumulation of incidents, but also strengthened by the fact that the armed conflict concluded without the much-dreaded violent assault that threatened to take numbers of lives. The mixed reception given to the Canadian Armed Forces' action was due to the army's status as the last defence against social disorder and, consequently, its capacity to expose and unleash the foundational state violence that normally goes unseen.

On their side, the Mohawk protestors under siege at Kanehsatà:ke and Kahnawà:ke drew on the political legitimacy conferred by the Great Law of Peace, on which the Haudenosaunee Confederacy is founded. During the siege, many protestors talked about the duty to protect of the warriors, the men, the *rotisken'raké:ta*. The Iroquois political tradition sees them as "carriers of the burden of peace." This political and philosophical thinking also values independence and free will, and throughout history, the guardians of the oral tradition have preserved and validated this tradition in public recitations and critiques that are constantly being renewed.[45] During the siege of summer 1990, members of the Mohawk Warrior Society were very present and active on the sites, which sparked debates and differences of opinion within the Haudenosaunee communities; nonetheless, they expressed a nationalist ideology and a warrior philosophy that put forward principles derived from the Kaianere'kó:wa, or Great Law of Peace,[46] and many of the debates were framed according to a specifically Haudenosaunee political perspective. Furthermore, contrary to representations of the Mohawk resistance as male, Iroquois women played a key political role thoughout the initial occupation and ensuing standoff.[47] In *Mohawk Interruptus*, Audra Simpson states that "the Oka Crisis illustrates the violent, vigorous defense of territory and the centrality of Mohawk women to this process." [48] Criticizing the abstract and romanticized ways in which Iroquois women can be represented as "caretakers of the land," Simpson adds: "With Oka we see the empirical face of that caretaking: women who called a peaceful protest and then an armed refusal against further dispossession."[49] It that sense, the siege becomes a space in which the impactful political authority of Mohawk women is enacted and made visible.

Throughout the siege, the Mohawk warrior flag flew above the barricades, a flag designed and produced by Kahnawà:ke writer and artist Louis Karoniakta-jeh Hall. Mohawk anthropologist Kahente Horn-Miller explained that this flag, which first appeared widely during the Oka Crisis and Lobster Dispute at Es-genoopetitj (Burnt Church), represents "the assertion of an Indigenous identity separate from the one imposed by the Canadian state," and one that "is charac-terized by a connectedness to one onother and to the land."[50] Horn-Miller went on to say that, after the crisis, the flag would be picked up and displayed in the struggles of Indigenous peoples as a symbol of unity and a beacon of hope ev-erywhere around the world.[51] This use of the flag in many of the public actions of the Idle No More movement initiated in 2012 is one of the many examples of this use and dissemination. Contrary to what was said by the governments and media in 1990, the discourse that promotes the warrior stance of protect-ing the nation is in line with a political philosophy practised in different ways in Mohawk communities. Kanatakta and Brian Deer explained that the Mohawk Warrior Society, to which the media made frequent reference during the sum-mer of 1990, occupies a less clearly defined place than would appear from the media representations and discourse of the time:

> We are all warriors, except those who hold official positions
> or are elected, such as traditional chiefs. The term used in our
> language means "he who carries the burden of peace." . . . The
> reorganization of this "Society" dates back to 1973. It was
> perhaps not necessary to do these things so formally in the
> past because, in our tradition, every able man would do all in
> his power to help the community, not only in a time of war
> but all the time. . . . In the 1970s, the people felt the need to
> come together more formally, and the term "society" came
> to be used. . . . But in our tradition, everyone has the right to
> gather in council around the fire, the women on their side and
> the men on theirs, with each clan also able to meet separately.
> The warriors are therefore simply men who exercise the right
> to meet and discuss the same topics as those we are talking
> about now, which is defending the jurisdictions, how to develop

the economy and educate our people, who will defend us if
something happens, and who is responsible for our well-being.[52]

Brian Deer went on to say that people of all kinds, whether they self-identi-
fied as warriors or not, were at the barricades in the summer of 1990. As Taiaiake
Alfred writes, the precepts of settler state order and their internalization conceal
"everything that is historically true and meaningful about Onkwehonwe—our
origins, languages, and name; our land, our heritage, and our rights."[53] Counter
to this, the Mohawk people under siege invoked the Great Law of Peace, undertook the process of deliberation by consensus it prescribes, and enacted on
the sites the authority of the longhouse, as a political and spiritual, physical and
conceptual entity; they also appealed to members of other Iroquois Confederacy nations for support. The Mohawk protestors revealed forms of cultural geography that had been obscured by the colonial project.[54] They made the siege
space the locus of forms of power derived from Indigenous political traditions.
By means of actions that were political and cultural performances, they made
struggles and practices visible that, far from having disappeared, continued to
convey their meaning to anxious observers who failed to grasp them.[55]

The siege thus showed up a contrast between Western and Indigenous perceptions of the nation and the interactions. To take Taiaiake Alfred's approach,
during the siege in action, there was a noticeable lack of congruence between
the Western forms of nationhood, "based on territorial boundaries and the nor-
malization of key Western values," and their non-Western equivalents, which
tend to refer instead to other bases, "such as religion, kinship and culture."[56] At
the same time, as the Mohawk resistance in 1990 also demonstrated, points at
which relationships intertwine make the interactions and conflicting positions
very complex. The issue of strategies and tactics, as well as that of recourse to
one or the other, can also be viewed from an anthropological perspective, so as
to include such intertwined relationships.

To this end, Audra Simpson noted that Indigenous peoples must deal in a
very concrete way with three layers of meaning: "one, the imposed structures of
the settler or colonizer societies such as Canada's Indian Act of 1876 and other
legal and governmental instruments; two, the ancestral Nations that predate the
settlement; and three, the daily lived experience that constantly navigates and
negotiates between them."[57] This constant shifting between different layers of
meaning intensified during the crisis, especially insofar as the conflict set up a

tension between legitimacy and legality and saw them overlapping. In *Mohawk Interruptus*, Simpson added: "Because [the Indigenous peoples] are recognized by and at the same time antagonistic to the state, this is a tight normative spot to be in."[58] Power relations therefore raise difficult questions. As Simpson further wrote with regards to Kahnawà:ke more specifically: "How does one assert sovereignty and independence when some of the power to define that sovereignty is bestowed from a foreign power?"[59] It was therefore a special way of exercising sovereignty and independence that was performed in the siege space at Kanehsatà:ke and Kahnawà:ke, but one that the governments attempted to bring back within the state framework so that protest activities could be better defined and controlled.

Although the antagonists did not succeed in reaching an understanding on the issue of legitimate authority, they were nonetheless forced to recognize the modalities of the conflict that gave rise to their opposition. In this way, as Georg Simmel explained, a conflict's unity resides in agreeing on the ground where the confrontation can take place.[60] It is also from this perspective that the interactions operating in the struggle for legitimacy, and rendered visible by the siege's scenography, made it easier to identify the conflict's dynamics.

PROTECTING THE COMMUNITY: TEKAKWITHA ISLAND

Once the Honoré-Mercier Bridge had been reopened to traffic, in early September, the Canadian Army helped the Sûreté du Québec to conduct searches on the territory of Kahnawake. These were perceived as invasions and sparked the ire of the community, all the more because the army had pledged not to enter the territory once the barricades had been removed from the bridge. To add to this, on 18 September, a little more than two weeks after the bridge was reopened, the Canadian Armed Forces landed in numbers on Tekakwitha Island at Kahnawake. The Kahnawa'kehró:non's reaction was instantaneous. Thanks to a highly efficient internal communications system, the entire community was immediately alerted and hundreds of people converged on the site.[61]

Donna K. Goodleaf, author of *Entering the War Zone: A Mohawk Perspective on Resisting Invasions,* was working at the Kanienkehaka Nation Office at the time, in charge of international relations and human rights violations. As a witness to that day, she reported that she and her colleagues learned that "3 Chinook and several Bell UH-1 helicopters had landed on the Island and dropped over 400 troops clad in riot gear, and 4 Huey gunboats surrounded the Island."[62]

She and her colleagues immediately rushed to the site, where they saw dozens and dozens of soldiers coming out of the woods, while others were attempting to cross the bridge that leads directly into the community's centre.

Refusing to let the Canadian Army make an incursion into their community, men, women, and young people pushed back the soldiers, stared them down, and ordered them to leave. Some pulled up the barbed wire that had been set down by the military, some went at the armed soldiers with their bare hands, and one person went as far as trying to tear the weapon right out of a soldier's grip. To cut off access, a dump truck flying the Mohawk flag deposited a load of dirt at the end of the little bridge leading to the main territory. In the midst of these heated skirmishes, soldiers fired warning shots into the air and threw tear gas canisters in the direction of the crowd. Disabled by the gas, many people took refuge under the bridge to catch their breath, shocked by the developing battle. In the confusion and gas fumes, some people jumped or fell from the bridge; community members rescued a woman who almost drowned. Mohawk residents and Canadian soldiers were wounded and many were sent to the hospital. Donna K. Goodleaf, who herself fell from the bridge, provided this description of what came next: "Several minutes later, in spite of the tear gas attacks, the Kahnawakeronon, more angry and defiant than ever, returned in full force, pelting soldiers with sticks and rocks which forced the army to retreat several hundred yards from the bridge. The troops were eventually forced into defensive positions."[63]

The soldiers were not equipped for crowd control. They reacted in keeping with the rule of minimal force that forbade opening fire, as they would have in certain situations in foreign wars. Some of them hit community members with their rifle butts, while others sought to protect themselves or fought back without using weapons. They all remained on alert and nervous, standing before a crowd that regarded them menacingly. The resistance was so fierce that they finally had to leave the site. Later on, the lieutenant-colonel responsible for the operation would say, "The strong resistance surprised us. It was amazing how they reacted, especially since we weren't at the Longhouse or sacred place."[64] Waiting for the military helicopters that were due to pick them up at nightfall, the soldiers had to remain on the spot for almost seven hours, facing community people who were awaiting their departure. Community members were simultaneously speaking to journalists who were covering the story live. A campfire was lit, and the crowd celebrated the soldiers' departure. The episode has remained branded on the memories of the Kahnawa'kehró:non, as demonstrated in particular by Peter Blue Cloud's account and Donna K. Goodleaf's poetry, which will be examined in the final chapter of this book.

The spontaneous, unarmed resistance to soldiers landing inside the perimeter gave the siege a community dimension that contrasted with images of the barricades, where armed, masked warriors confronted soldiers in full combat gear. On 18 September 1990, when the Canadian military landed on Tekakwitha Island, it seemed to threaten the living heart of the community. This is all the more striking because the helicopters carrying soldiers dropped from the sky just when all the defences had been installed. Timothy C. Winegard described the scene of the siege at Kahnawake as consisting not only of barricades on all roads leading into the community, but also of a "defensive perimeter designed in three concentric rings (consisting of 10 sectors) of field fortifications, from the outer edge of the Reserve back into the inner core."[65] Winegard's description evokes the image of a protective circle made concrete by the fortifications; it also reflects the general determination to protect the territory and community from incursion.

The image of the protective circle recalls the circular wampum that symbolizes the Haudenosaunee Confederacy and the relationships among its nations and clans. In the Mohawk language, the circular wampum or Teiotiokwaonhaston signifies exactly that "it circles the people." The strings that converge towards the wampum's centre represent the fifty confederacy chiefs, while the two strings that form its circumference symbolize those chiefs with their arms linked. In the wampum's symbol system, the chiefs have gathered around the Great Tree of Peace, as in their places in council, and they link their arms to prevent the symbol of the Kayaneren'kó:wa, the Great Law, from falling.[66] A display at the Kanien'kehá:ka Onkwawén:na Raotitióhkwa, Language and Cultural Centre in Kahnawake, explained that this representation of the chiefs refers to their "responsibility to oversee and protect both the political and spiritual ways of the Haudenosaunee." This representation delineates different national identities, since "within the protective domain of this circle exist the national characteristics that define the Haudenosaunee as a people." The description mentioned "a protective circle, a sovereign domain protected by the strength of unity and peace," two concepts that are central to the Haudenosaunee tradition. As underscored by ethnohistorian Kathryn V. Muller in "Holding Hands With Wampum," the Mohawks' determination to protect their community becomes clear when seen in the continuity of Iroquois political philosophy and thought, which were actualized in various forms in twentieth-century Mohawk political culture.

It can also be discerned in the words and gestures of many Kahnawa'kehró:non, recorded live on the scene by Alec G. MacLeod and portrayed in his documentary film *Acts of Defiance*. In response to a journalist asking what impelled the people to take on with their bare hands the soldiers who had landed on the island, a Mohawk man hotly exclaims, "Anger! They have no business here! They are under the jurisdiction of the provincial government. They have no business here whatsoever. . . . They are here under [Robert] Bourassa's orders. They have to get out!" The elected chief of the Mohawk Council of Kahnawake at that time, Joe Norton, can be seen in the documentary inserting himself between the Canadian military and the people from the community. He gives the media a similar response, saying about the federal and provincial authorities, "They don't give a damn about cigarettes, they don't give a damn about bingo. It's just an excuse for them. The politics of this community is that we are a sovereign people. We are Mohawk Nation people. This is our jurisdiction. We will patrol it. We will make our own laws over here and the government doesn't want that. The government says you have to obey, you have to obey provincial law, federal law, et cetera, et cetera. That's what's behind that!"

The defence of Tekakwitha Island against the Canadian Army's intrusion expresses this determination on the part of the Kahnawa'kehró:non to exercise their sovereignty on the community's territory, with a significance that goes beyond merely drawing boundaries. To the Canadian Army lieutenant-colonel and Canadians in general who expressed surprise at the fierce, steadfast resistance to the soldiers, Mohawk poet Peter Blue Cloud responds with a question: "Will you ever begin to understand the meaning of the soil beneath your very feet? From a grain of sand to a great mountain, all is sacred. Yesterday and tomorrow exist eternally upon this continent. We natives are the guardians of this sacred place."[67] This poetic answer may come from a spiritual and philosophical register that could seem removed from the contingencies of urban and suburban life, but it can nonetheless exist among extremely pragmatic political, economic, and administrative concerns.

The sovereignty defended during the resistance at Kanehsatà:ke and Kahnawà:ke can be symbolized by the invisible connections suggested by the Circle Wampum. The wampum represents the very strong relational connection binding each of the chiefs to the five nations composed of the various clans that founded the confederacy, and its two strands represent the inseparability of the spiritual and political aspects of Kaianere'kó:wa (Gabriel-Doxtater and Van den Hende 1995, 12). In 1990, the governments repeatedly drew a distinction between the Mohawks of Kanehsatake and those of Akwesasne, depending on whether they were included in the state framework of Canada or the United States. The Mohawk protestors, on their part, referred back to the network of clan and nation connections extending across the vast ancestral territory of Kanienkeh, or the Mohawk Valley. Loran Thompson, a member of the Akwesasne Mohawk Warrior Society, spoke of a relational network that became rooted in and ran through all the Mohawk territories, linking confederacy members. He added that these members "come from a culturally connected group of families . . . who all have the same commitment to Mohawk sovereignty."[68] During the resistance at Kanehsatà:ke and Kahnawà:ke, a drawing of the Circle Wampum, symbol of the confederacy and the political philosophy it embodies, appeared at the top of the media releases published by the Mohawk Nation Negotiating Team. In this form, the wampum circulated through the siege space, evoking the ideas of consultation, deliberation, and consensus that are held within it. In relation to the siege in action and what that represented, the Circle Wampum could symbolize a protective closing up against intrusion, but it could also evoke the circle that shelters and interconnects the constituents of the wide-ranging ancient confederacy.

THE HONORÉ-MERCIER BRIDGE AND THE ST. LAWRENCE SEAWAY

Throughout the 1990 siege, the representations of the state, Canadian Army, federal, and provincial police, and the Mohawk warriors and communities relied on images of encirclement and intrusion, concentration and unity. They also reflected images of barriers, limits, and delimitation. That is what was illustrated by the barricades built across the Honoré-Mercier Bridge to support the Kanehsatake protestors, who themselves blocked a side road and then a main road against the municipality's economic development project threatening Mohawk land. During the siege in action, these barricades came to stand for a deterrent to the mobility that is so much a part of the North American process of settlement and industrialization. The Honoré-Mercier Bridge, which connects and separates Montreal and Kahnawake, revived the tension generated by colonial borders; in the summer of 1990, it became a real symbol of power relations for the region and the entire country.

The Honoré-Mercier Bridge was named for a former Quebec premier. It has linked the Island of Montreal and the Mohawk territory of Kahnawake since 1934. Its original construction was financed by the government in the 1930s as a response to the Great Depression. The bridge significantly reduced the distance from Montreal to the state of New York,[69] thus promoting tourism as well as facilitating the transportation of agricultural products to the city and traffic flow between the urban centre and its southern suburbs. It was also occasionally used for completely different purposes. In 1988, to protest police intervention directed at cigarette vendors on the territory of Kahnawake, Mohawk protestors blocked the bridge. Two years later, when they learned that the Sûreté du Québec was conducting an assault on Kanehsatake, protestors again blocked it, for both political leverage and symbolic expression.

For fifty-five days, this direct action disrupted traffic in key zones of Montreal's urban and outlying regions. From a political point of view, the traffic disruption forced the governments to react. Symbolically, it turned a factor of mobility against itself, one that had for a long time worked to the detriment of Kahnawake and the other Indigenous communities in North America. In "When Bridges Become Barriers: Montreal and Kahnawake Mohawk Territory," Daniel Rueck identified various surveyors, enumerators, Indian agents, and other officials who had foreshadowed the many intrusions into Mohawk territory. In this regard, he added: "The accumulation of these incursions and disruptions destroyed Kahnawakehró:non trust in outside governments, and the memory of these offenses fuels a determination to recover what was lost. The blockade of the Mercier Bridge in 1990 only gave Montrealers a taste of the kind of interruption Kahnawake Mohawks have been living with for 150 years."[70] Powerlessness, rage, and isolation are the lot of those who find themselves confined to a forced immobility, whether physical or symbolic. Residents of the South Shore would have to live with it for fifty-five days, which is not much compared with a century and a half.

During Oka, members of the First Nations, as well as Métis and possibly also Inuit, organized demonstrations across the country in support of the Mohawks' land struggle. The Indigenous mobilization took a variety of forms—speeches, media releases, and public declarations; demonstrations in urban centres and the seats of power, such as parliaments; camping out in symbolic locations; marches expressing a political message through movement; the sending of runners to Kanehsatake and Kahnawake; logistical support; and, significantly, direct actions affecting strategic avenues of traffic. These axes of mobility and division were transformed into political leverage tokens by the Indigenous protestors, who thus made the effects of their opposition felt. Not only was it significant that much of the Indigenous protest operated as a deterrent to the mechanisms of settler mobility, but the fact that so many of these strategic axes were to be found in Indigenous territory points to the extent of encroachment as much as its methods.

As ethnohistorian Kathryn V. Muller reminded us, the early business of colonization was characterized by "attempts to control important waterways, strategic trading corridors, and relationships with far-off *Onkwehonwe* nations."[71] This business, which has continued, has involved conceiving of the anticipated territory as a "commodity to be conquered, appropriated and bought, and subdued."[72] Everywhere in North America, Indigenous peoples have felt increasing pressure from a colonial push that gradually distances them from the strategic centres. Without proper consultation or compensation, it eventually backs them into closed, cramped territories crossed and hemmed in by countless roads, bridges, railways, pylons, and waterways. According to Anna J. Willow, this encroachment continued into the industrial era and until today, systematically promoting the interests of industry at the expense of Indigenous concerns, because a "stark power differential" constantly tips the scales in favour of the industrialists.[73]

While the incursions gradually grew in number, the power differential to which Willow referred, for its part, made itself brutally felt at Kahnawake in the 1950s, when the St. Lawrence Seaway cut through the Mohawk village. Approximately two decades after the construction of the Honoré-Mercier Bridge, following the Great Depression and the Second World War, Canada and the United States agreed on the construction of a sea lane that would allow commercial navigation from the Gulf of the St. Lawrence to the western shore of Lake Superior, a distance of 3,700 kilometres into the land at the heart of the continent. As journalist and author D'Arcy Jenish further explained in *The St. Lawrence Seaway: Fifty Years and Counting*, this large-scale, publicly financed project consisted in making the St. Lawrence River an indispensable route for commerce and the profitable exploitation of mineral deposits, dams, and electrical power stations. In the atmosphere of euphoria typically surrounding major projects, the seaway was inaugurated with great pomp in 1959 on Montreal's South Shore, in the presence of Canada's prime minister John Diefenbaker, Her

Majesty Queen Elizabeth II, and the president of the United States of America, Dwight D. Eisenhower.[74] The seaway was a work of considerable engineering and economic might. It fulfilled the dreams and efforts of settlers who, from the early seventeenth century, had been working on a canal that would bypass the Lachine Rapids, dangerously fast-moving water that Mohawk navigators had long negotiated in various kinds of vessels, as recounted by Johnny Beauvais in *Kahnawake: A Mohawk Look at Canada and Adventures of Big John Canadian, 1840–1919.*

While the seaway's construction represented a big step forward for the governments of Canada and the United States, it was perceived as a real intrusion by the Mohawks of Kahnawake, who saw their way of life and community profoundly disrupted. From 1954 to 1959, the project involved the expropriation of nearly 511 hectares of their territory, or one-sixth of the community's land base, while at the same time cutting off the community's direct access to the river. The seaway ploughed a wide furrow through riparian land that had been the site of Mohawk economic and cultural activity, posing a genuine threat to the community's culture and identity.[75] Large sections of the territory were dynamited and then cleared with bulldozers; the old village was partially destroyed. Land was expropriated, and people's houses were moved or torn down, while those who refused to leave were arrested. Normal activities of swimming and fishing were replaced by the frequent passage of enormous cargo ships, causing pollution of the relatively stagnant water in the canal, in contrast to the formerly free-flowing rapids. This shift was ironically underlined by the place name, Kahnawà:ke, which means "beside the rapids."[76]

In the Mohawk discourses, the imposition of the seaway's construction illustrates the government's propensity to seize Indigenous land and make it its own, despite the people's presence and against their will. The loss of territory to the seaway in the 1950s was felt to be a form of failure. That is what we are given to understand by the protagonists of the film *Kahnawake Revisited: The St. Lawrence Seaway I & II* who report having wondered for a long time why their ancestors did not prevent this intrusion. In the same vein, Audra Simpson explained that the seaway saga led the Mohawks of Kahnawake to conclude that their own self-image did not coincide with that held by the state: "With the Seaway debacle *Kahnawakero:non* realized that their self perception as brave, heroic, river-taming people conflicted with their legally defined perception by the State—as status Indians who were under the jurisdiction of Ottawa and therefore subject to discretionary 'intrusions' by Canada. Hence their years as a relatively independent people were over."[77] The contrasting representations of the seaway adopted by the Canadian authorities and Kahnawake's Mohawks speak to a colonial tension that determines the dynamics of relations between the Canadian government and the Mohawk Nation, as was made apparent by the political crisis of 1990. The seaway's encroachment and intrusion seem to enter directly into the process of spatial and ideological exile discussed earlier in this book. In a letter to the Human Rights Commission dated 27 September 1960, Chief Matthew Lazore wrote: "The decision to confiscate Indian Reserve Land in connection with the St. Lawrence Seaway project is part and parcel of the plan to evict the Indians from their Reserve and force them to abandon their way of life, culture and traditions. The Canadian Government continues to infringe on our rights and to force their way into our midst."[78]

In the view of the Kahnawa'kehró:non, explained Mohawk scholar Stephanie Phillips in her thesis "The Kahnawake Mohawks and the St. Lawrence Seaway," "the seaway has become a metaphor for the intrusiveness of the Canadian government" and, consequently, it ended up symbolizing, like a daily reminder inscribed on the community's geographical and cultural landscape, "the necessity of resisting any encroachment on Kahnawake's autonomy."[79] Faced with a loss of political autonomy, land base, and resources, an attack on a way of life that depended on a close connection to the river, and "the feeling of being confined and ultimately controlled by outside forces," the community reacted by taking back control of the situation, so that in the years that followed, Mohawk nationalism grew stronger in Kahnawake.[80] In the documentary *Kahnawake Revisited,* many individuals report a determination never to let such a situation happen again, and talk about a "collective stance against losing another inch for the benefit of the outside." It was this "never again" that would be played out three decades later on the approach to the Honoré-Mercier Bridge, during Oka.

The documentary film brings a better understanding of how various key representations of the 1990 resistance are related—first, representations of the seaway construction as an incursion and the imposition of a colonial limitation; then the barricades across the Honoré-Mercier Bridge as a brake on the encroachment on Mohawk territory; and finally, the bare-fisted battle with the military who landed on Tekakwitha Island as protecting the community's centre against incursion. The accounts in *Kahnawake Revisited* address the methods used by the community to regain access to the river, but also to obtain compensation from the governments and from third parties, such as the railway and electricity companies that had installed their facilities on Mohawk territory. Interestingly, considering "the militancy and aggressiveness embedded in the character of [Kahnawake's] political culture" discussed by Taiaiake Alfred in *Heading the Voices of Our Ancestors: Kahnawake Mohawk Politics and the Rise of Native Nationalism*,[81] there is particular emphasis placed on cooperation and reciprocity, and thus on a cohabitation that duly respects the political and cultural autonomy of the Mohawk Nation. On 22 August 1990, during the crisis, a statement of the Mohawks' position regarding the negotiations affirms: "The Kanienkehaka approach these negotiations with the view and firm belief that there is and always has been a sovereign nation and that their relationship with the other governments in North America is defined by the tenets of the Two Row Wampum."[82] This wampum features the image of two boats sailing along the same watercourse without either attempting to impose its law on the other. By making reference to it, the Mohawks evoke a principle of non-interference that is central to Iroquois political thinking. While the kinship relations within the Haudenosaunee Confederacy are symbolized in the Circle Wampum, as described by Kathryn V. Muller in her PhD thesis "Holding Hands With Wampum," the relations with the European settlers and today's colonial state are symbolized by the Two Row Wampum. Going from a circle shape to that of two parallel lines signifies the nature of the confederacy's kinship links compared with that of relations with foreign nations. Muller explained that the Europeans' arrival led the Iroquois to enter into other forms of alliance. Among them, she mentioned the chain of alliances that rests on two fundamental principles, which are "mutual collaboration on issues of common importance but autonomy to regulate one's internal affairs, even if that meant frequently violating and remaking the alliance."[83]

Significantly for the dynamics of conflict that were underscored by the political crisis of summer 1990, Muller recalled that, over the centuries, the colonial authorities' and governments' appropriative and assimilationist policies caused the Haudenosaunee to close in on themselves and adopt a defensive attitude. Briefly, the intensification of domination drove the parties further and further apart, because one of them insisted on maintaining a grip to which the other refused to submit. In contrast to a chain of alliances that emphasizes the need to polish the links and thus maintain good relations, the Two Row Wampum displays at first glance a marked separation between the parties. Muller explains that the more Canada refused to recognize the *kaswentha* ethic, which encapsulates the core values of Haudenosaunee morality and political theory and is inherent in the wampum, the more the political discourse was dominated by "displays of Haudenosaunee sovereignty" that were "increasingly vocal—sometimes forceful."[84] Again, according to Muller, the stories on which the *kaswentha* ethic rests make it possible to understand the anger and discontent displayed at Oka in 1990 and then at Caledonia two decades later.[85] As with the imposition of the seaway in the 1950s, the threat of encroachment and the reluctance of the governments to negotiate nation-to-nation during Oka can be interpreted as a failure to respect the spirit of the Two Row Wampum.

According to Georg Simmel, a common element of relation will often become coloured by hostility.[86] While conflict magnifies the divisions between antagonistic parties, it tends to erase the borders separating groups that are united by a battle for the same object. By viewing conflict as a modulator of social relations, it is possible to see how interactions were structured and imaginative worlds transformed during the Oka Crisis or the resistance at Kanehsatake. As Québécois political analyst Daniel Salée observed, increasingly vehement Indigenous claims and political mobilization "unequivocally interpellate Canadians and force them to examine their conscience on the historical meaning of their relations with the First Peoples."[87] In this sense, the Oka Crisis does not properly constitute an "Indian crisis" or a "Mohawk crisis," as the conflict has often been called, but a genuine crisis involving Québécois, Canadian, and Indigenous peoples, one that encourages us to rethink the relations that oppose and unite us in a deeply unjust settler colonial context.

CHAPTER 4

From the Spectacular to the Documentary—*Okanada: Behind the Lines at Oka*

The armed conflict evolved around issues of territoriality, legitimacy, and sovereignty, but it was not limited to the siege space itself; it also entered the media space and the public space, where power relations came into play. The conflict's scenography illustrates how interactions were negotiated both on the siege site and in the public space, where the crisis was treated as a spectacle. In fact, the media were broadcasting what was happening on the site in real time, so that they themselves became an integral part of the event they were covering. Regarding the event that exploded in early July, communications researcher Lorna Roth spoke of it as the beginning of a "public relations war between First Nations and non-native communities in Canada."[1] She went on to say that, by concentrating the Mohawks' territorial and political claims on a single point, the siege in the communities of Kanehsatake and Kahnawake became the repository and focus of Indigenous peoples' historical and current recriminations against the governments.[2]

While the battle of images and representations in the public space helped to shape the collective imagination concerning the siege and to spawn the core figures in the confrontation, such as that of the Mohawk warrior and the Canadian soldier, it was basically waged over the definition of legitimacy. French historian Marc Ferro pointed out that, as the televised image's pretension to producing true discourse has come under fire, it has itself "become an issue, both culturally and politically."[3] Throughout the crisis, therefore, the parties involved made significant efforts to control or exploit the various media, including television, in order to manipulate the power relationship. Soldiers reported following the operations live on television, as did the demonstrators and other members of the Mohawk and other Indigenous communities. Reporters and journalists played an active, critical role throughout the siege, especially in the period from the day the event erupted to the day the last activists left the site. Some of the media material would later be included in documentary films about the event, among them *Okanada: Behind the Lines at Oka*. In his book *Cinéma et histoire* [Cinema and History], Ferro maintained that, "in terms of power, the televised image is catching up to the filmed image: it has in turn become an historical document and agent of History for the society that not only receives it but also, let's not forget, produces it."[4] At the crossroads of history, politics, and media strategy, documentary films lead us to question the reasons why certain narratives prevail while others ultimately disappear.

THE JOURNALIST'S CAMERA

At the very end of August, after fifty-five long days of siege, an agreement negotiated by the Canadian military and the Mohawk warriors led to a joint dismantling of the barricades on the Honoré-Mercier Bridge. Blocking the bridge had brought considerable political leverage, and for the remaining occupiers at Kanehsatake, the effect of lifting the barricades was moral isolation and deflation. Two days later, on 1 September, the Canadian Army took advantage of this strategic situation and launched a new push on Kanehsatake, creating an extremely tense atmosphere, and, as recounted by author Réginald Gagnon, it was as usual "in front of cameras filming all the action" on both sides, the army's and the protestors'.[5] At this juncture, the Canadian Army also captured the last Mohawk barricade to have been erected, the overturned police cars and large tree trunks put in place on the day of the fatal exchange of gunfire. The remaining Indigenous occupiers took refuge in the treatment centre, called Onen'to:kon or "under the pines," whose opening several years earlier had caused heavy friction between the communities.[6] To put pressure on the group remaining behind the barricades, the Canadian Armed Forces forbade entry into the area and cut off all communication. They then installed a telephone line that connected the protestors directly to the military post. There was a risk that the end of the siege would be covert, which raised the issue of surveillance of people's actions and live coverage of the conflict.

At that point, at the very end of the summer, the Canadian Broadcasting Corporation, fearing for its reporters' lives, ordered its remaining television crews to withdraw from the area surrounded by the Canadian Army. As recounted in the documentary film *Okanada*, after more than sixty days of siege, Canadian journalist Albert Nerenberg made his way through the woods and surreptitiously slipped under the army's barbed-wire fence, accompanied by Canadian photo-journalist Robert Galbraith. The two were determined that the event would not end in secrecy. Having been recognized as reporters by the people behind the barricades, they got the inside story on the final days of the siege. In 1991, using footage shot on the scene along with archival and news materials, Catherine Bainbridge and Albert Nerenberg produced the documentary *Okanada: Behind the Lines at Oka*. That same year, Robert Galbraith was a contributor to the book *This Land Is Our Land: The Mohawk Revolt at Oka*,[7] which contains photographs and interviews from behind the barricades at Kanehsatake; scenes from *Okanada* can be recognized in many of the photographs.

The film is rooted in a tension between mediation and direct experience, the recording of data and subjectivity, and it allows the viewer to live through the final days of the siege alongside the fifty men, women, and children who were pushed to the last ditch by the Canadian Army at Kanehsatake. To be noted is that the Mohawk warriors interviewed by Nerenberg are the same activists the governments and media had depicted as outlaws and explicitly linked to terrorism, organized crime, and cigarette smuggling. This discourse, based on the dominant ideology, of course had the effect of isolating the protestors further and further behind the barricades, not only physically but also symbolically. In this perspective, it is instructive to observe how the transformation of the event into spectacle and its cinematic mediation are treated in *Okanada*. One of the film's particular features is to borrow an aesthetic of witnessing to convey the experience as lived inside the besieged area. In a context of discredited speech, it also raises issues of judgement and speaking the truth in the public space.

THE PARADIGM OF THE VIEW

The event's abrupt advent on the morning of 11 July 1990 introduces the subject matter of *Okanada*. An initial title informs the viewer of some 2,000 unresolved land claims in Canada, including that of Kanehsatake. Images of the cemetery threatened by Oka's development project then move slowly across the screen, accompanied by a nostalgic, disquieting musical track. To signal the place's ties to ancestry and its continued use by the Mohawks, a shot shows tombstones scattered among the tall pines and tilted by the passage of time. Erosion of the stones and the names carved on them, along with the grasses and saplings reclaiming the space, confirm the cemetery's great age. Over this series of images we hear the voice of Susan Oke, a Mohawk woman who took part in the siege, describing the site and the community's relationship to the cemetery. Her face is seen in close-up, with the cemetery behind it, as she recalls the context of the police intervention on 11 July:

> My name is Susan Oke. I'm from Kanehsatake. This is our
> cemetery. We've been in this area for as long as we can remember.
> There has always been Mohawks here. The mayor of Oka, Jean
> Ouellet, wanted to expand the golf course from nine holes to
> eighteen holes. They were to go around our graveyard, which . . .
> they already have their parking lot next to the graveyard and golf
> balls have been found in the graveyard. It's not a large forest, but
> it's . . . it's the only forest that's around here. There is all kinds
> of medicine, and the trees are very old. And they would have
> destroyed all that for . . . a golf course. The Mohawks here had
> set up a peaceful blockade in our pines, in March. The mayor of
> Oka, Jean Ouellet, called in the police, the provincial police. On
> July 11th, the people here woke up to tear gas.

The images of Susan Oke outlining the land claim issues are intercut with images of golfers on Oka's course. The description of the initial peaceful occupation and the subsequent appeal to the police by the mayor is conveyed over visuals of archival photos showing the log barricades and the mayor making a gesture of categorical refusal with his hand. Oke winds up by describing how the residents of Kanehsatake woke up on the morning of the police intervention, and as soon as she finishes speaking, the film cuts to images of the grove's huge pines shrouded in clouds of tear gas.

We hear someone's ragged breathing, then the voice of Mohawk journalist Marie David making a live report on the arrival of the Sûreté du Québec's tactical squad. Having described the protestors' retreat into the woods ("The Mohawks are backing off!"), she anxiously reports the entry of the first police officers in the Pines, and then expresses her disbelief when the initial shots are heard: "Shit! This is real, folks . . . this ain't no movie." The scene is very real, even if it seems to be fictional. Images show Saint-Michel Hill, along with the sign reading "Mohawk Sovereign Lands!" that, nailed to a large pine, announces the stand taken by the occupiers. The journalist's voice then announces the police assault ("They're coming in! They're coming in! The cops are in!"). The sound of the exchange of fire that follows is accompanied by images of trees and clouds of tear gas. The scene of the firing remains invisible to the camera, hidden by the trees. These sequences provide a preamble and context for *Okanada: Behind the Lines at Oka*. They refer to the unforeseen, unexpected nature of the armed conflict that exploded in 1990, calling for a "declaration of the extreme"—a phrase used by Gad Soussana, Alexis Nouss, and Jacques Derrida in their book *Dire l'événement, est-ce possible?* [Is it possible to speak the event?][8]— and causing everyone to wonder what was happening.

Real-time coverage of the event made the armed confrontation visible from moment to moment, keeping the entire country in suspense. The Oka Crisis, as constructed by its mediation, placed the image at the heart of the tactics and strategies used by the Mohawks as well as the governments and the army. With a constant eye on the siege, the media machine interpreted, selected, and recorded what was happening at the barricades, thus "making" the event as much as telling it. In a situation in which the relative restraint displayed by the two camps was based on a bilateral promise not to fire the first shot, Albert Nerenberg's view is that television was seen as "a pacifying element, . . . keeping a close eye on the pledge made by both sides not to start firing."[9] The camera thus functioned as a surveillance device in the tense atmosphere of a much-covered armed conflict and as a factor that could possibly dissuade the parties from engaging in confrontation. Providing arbitration and constraint, the cameras aimed at the barricades reported on the event as much as they created it. From another point of view, the quest for exclusive images of the conflict was surely driven by a hunger for sensationalism that feeds and is fed by the media machine. Nevertheless, the documentary's construction allows for a certain subjectivity in the camerawork, and it thus manages to transform the voyeuristic device into one for bearing witness.

Nerenberg's stance is quite unusual. He witnessed the event and actively participated primarily as a journalist. His audiovisual recordings of the siege's final days are first of all media material, but they also become elements of evidence and historical traces. Later on, he would use them, this time as a documentarist and narrator, as an account of his experience at the epicentre of the event. In *Okanada,* what is shown therefore essentially represents what Nerenberg saw and also what he experienced with photojournalist Robert Galbraith among the Mohawk occupiers and their supporters, all of them uncertain about the conflict's outcome. The lack of visual polish in the sequences shot behind the barricades produces an effect of authenticity. The same is true of the abrupt, jumpy camera movements, which convey the vulnerability of a witness who has been projected into the thick of a dangerous armed conflict. The camera collects the testimonies of people who have been, as it has, thrown into this high-tension event. It helps to make the event that it is simultaneously recording.

The recordings were themselves under threat, as confirmed by the confiscation of media and film materials by the police and the military. The longer the conflict continued, the more uncertain it became that recorded content could be transmitted. The sketchy quality of shots in the heat of the action, which make up the core of the documentary, corresponds to the protagonists' experience of being tossed into the event's epicentre. Following the last protestors, who suddenly rise up and cross the barricades on 26 September 1990, the cameraman runs and trips, letting his camera shoot the ground and trees in imitation of an unsteady gaze, and then capture the arrests by the soldiers in the midst of chaos. Viewers are inevitably induced to identify with the camera-witness. Having themselves seen the images, they are prey to a kind of vertigo at the idea that the film will be seized and the evidence it contains will not be passed along—even if they know that this cannot be, since at that very moment they have access. The titles tell us that journalist Albert Nerenberg was arrested and beaten, but that he was able to save his video cassettes by passing them to a friend prior to his arrest. Crossing into the fenced perimeter in order to show what is happening, the camera becomes a witness and transmits the event as a third party. It was present throughout the crisis, and the determination to record the experience and preserve that record was reinforced by the fact that the camera was one of the last to be able to capture what was happening inside the perimeter, along with that of Abenaki filmmaker Alanis Obomsawin.

While being besieged is associated with an emergency or being shut in, it can also evoke openness and reciprocity. As it was, being surrounded limited one's sense of belonging to a single place, from which a whole network of relationships and interests could be called upon to mobilize support and build convergence. During the siege, appeals for help were made to the Six Nations of the Iroquois Confederacy, and the Mohawks requested the presence of international observers on the siege sites to document—and prevent—human rights violations. Two hundred Indigenous chiefs converged on Kahnawake in July for a meeting to discuss the conflict's issues. In support of Kanehsatake, between

1,500 and 2,000 demonstrators gathered at the peace camp in Oka, manifesting the support from First Nations and other sympathizers in physical space.

The siege's duration created a space for expression that the protestors used to their strategic benefit, mainly to win support on national and international levels. Operating simultaneously as public tribunals and instruments of strategy, the media played a key role in creating solidarity and mediating the experience. The Canadian Army realized that while the presence of journalists reduced the possibility that violence would erupt, it also helped to prolong the crisis. And while the continuing armed conflict increased the probability that a disastrous incident might occur, it also allowed Mohawk political actors to take advantage of the means of communication to promote their cause to institutions and the public.[10] Media centres and community radio stations were operating throughout the siege in both Kanehsatake and Kahnawake. Towards the end, when the protestors had retreated to the Kanehsatake treatment centre, they used a communications network that allowed them to stay in contact with Kahnawake and Akwesasne and thus with the world beyond the barricades.[11] They therefore maintained communications that would influence the conflict's outcome in various ways, whether through logistical support, strategic information, or public opinion.

As soon as the Canadian Army arrived on the site, it became obvious that the deployment of a larger force would bring the siege to a rapid halt. Nonetheless, since it would be inconceivable to launch a military assault that could very well involve further loss of life, the army's objective consisted in progressively taking possession of the area so as to force a surrender while limiting the violence. To exert greater pressure on the Mohawk people who were defending their positions physically and symbolically, the army developed a public relations strategy intended to have an official story of the event prevail. It simultaneously initiated a strategy of isolation that consisted in limiting entry, encouraging departures, and tightening control over communications.[12] The Canadian Army established media centres that every day relayed information to the media and, consequently, to Indigenous and non-Indigenous audiences, including the Mohawk communities and the people behind the barricades. About this, General John de Chastelain remarked: "To keep the media informed of what the CF was doing and to reassure the public that everything possible was being done to enforce law and order and to avoid further death or injury, I made the point in an early TV appearance that we would announce what we were doing before we did it, so there could be no surprises. That affirmation was held to, by and large."[13]

The Canadian Armed Forces were, therefore, concerned about the public perception of the conflict. That was also the case for the federal government, which was directly interpellated by the political issues the crisis raised. As pointed out by Amelia Kalant in *National Identity and the Conflict at Oka*, the crisis dramatized a territorial conflict, certainly, but also a battle over the significance of the conditions and imagining of identity and belonging. The government's ability to construct the event through the media was a determining factor. Representations in the media and cameras on the scene played a critical role in how the siege played out. It was relayed live in the media, sometimes even continuously, twenty-four hours a day. We must remember that in 1990, cellular telephones and digital cameras were far from common, lending still greater importance to the cameras of the media and filmmakers.

As the army tightened its grip, it instituted measures to put greater distance between members of the media and the perimeter of the siege site. At the same time as they physically displaced the outside journalists away from the barricades, the military and political authorities undertook to discursively discredit what was being said by both the Mohawk people and the journalists behind the barricades. These journalists were often accused by the authorities of making biased reports. As military historian Timothy C. Winegard explained, they were suspected of having fallen victim to the Stockholm syndrome, despite the fact that they were never taken hostage by the protestors, but were there of their own free will. Levelling this suspicion at the journalists implicitly discredited the speech of the Mohawks behind the barricades, since they then appeared to be the source of the bias. Frustrated by difficulties in communicating with the protestors, the Canadian Association of Journalists (CAJ) charged the army with censorship hindering freedom of speech and public information. Julian Sher, chair of the CAJ, deplored the fact that the press briefings held by the Canadian Armed Forces should ultimately constitute the only information available on what was happening behind the barricades, declaring:

> The fundamental issue in this crisis right now is who decides.
> Who decides if the journalists are biased? Who decides if the
> reports are balanced? Who decides what news gets out? Is it an
> army general, is it a federal cabinet minister, is it the editors and

the journalists working across the country, and ultimately, is it the readers and the viewers of television? Our position is very firm on this: there is censorship going on, and at a time when the government is talking, and the army is talking about the final sprint in this crisis, it is vital that Canadians across the country get all sides of the story, and right now a big part of that story is going on behind the barbed wire in that treatment center.[14]

This was the situation when Albert Nerenberg and Robert Galbraith slipped behind the barricades without the army's knowledge. In *Okanada*, the voice-over narration underscores the effectiveness of the isolation strategy that cut off the story of the siege from the inside: "Thus isolated from the outside world, the Mohawks sensed that public opinion had shifted." In *National Identity and the Conflict at Oka*, Amelia Kalant noted that as the conflict progressed, the governments tightened their control over media relations. This tightening up would have direct repercussions for media coverage and public opinion, which became less and less favourable to the Mohawk occupiers.

Paradoxically, journalist Albert Nerenberg, equipped with his camera, was determined to film the denouement of a siege the authorities were attempting to hide from view even as it was being widely shown around the world. Like other journalists who wanted to get to the heart of the event, Nerenberg did not want to cover it in its entirety, but intended to capture images and accounts of what happened behind the barricades. As a result, *Okanada* does not offer an overall analysis of the event, but shows essentially what went on within the besieged area. In so doing, it renders what was experienced on that site and not in the community of Kanehsatake as a whole, whose experience is conveyed only in the shared history of community members, the greater Mohawk Nation, and the Haudenosaunee Confederacy. The film's particular point of view, while necessarily partial, contributes to an overall understanding of the conflict.

The media and political objective of the journalistic and documentary process therefore consisted in bringing out the experience of those within the besieged area. Like the political conflict it recounts, the documentary helps to shed light on the hidden depths of the historical context that rise to the surface during the event itself.[15] In this sense, the event changes the relation between the visible and the invisible, regarding not just the historical facts but also the contemporary situation that proceeds directly from them. By shedding light on

the unseen violence perpetrated on Indigenous peoples by the colonizing nations, the breach opened by the event helps to alter the visible field for a time. In
that way, by circumscribing the territorial conflict, the highly publicized siege
caused a contemporary Indigenous presence to break into the very centre of the
dominant space, generating a range of configurations that depend on respective
points of view.

In her book *Indian Country: Essays on Contemporary Indian Culture*, Gail
Guthrie Valaskakis noted that, for Indigenous peoples, the siege at Oka in 1990
and the siege at Wounded Knee in 1973 constitute forms of resistance that are
"assertions of cultural persistence." From a non-Indigenous point of view, added
Valaskakis, these events are seen as "episodic explosions of political confrontation, which are ahistorical and unpredictable."[16] Stances taken up in the siege
space, like the various perspectives determining how they are represented, derive
from the paradigm of the view.

The siege renders visible a long-standing dispute. It also bears witness to
a history characterized by settler colonial mentalities and assimilation policies
inflicting violence on the Indigenous peoples by working towards their disappearance. These policies of erasure and appropriation were central to the
establishment of residential schools that were expressly designed to "civilize"
and "Christianize" Indigenous children, with the goal to "kill the Indian in the
child."[17] In the early twentieth century, a government official commonly believed to be Superintendent of Indian Affairs Duncan Campbell Scott uttered a
determination to find "a final solution to the Indian Problem," a statement that
today recalls many dark events. This government offical stated: "I want to get
rid of the Indian problem. I do not think as a matter of fact, that the country
ought to continuously protect a class of people who are able to stand alone. . . .
Our objective is to continue until there is not a single Indian in Canada that has
not been absorbed into the body politic, and there is no Indian question, and
no Indian Department."[18] For more than a century, more precisely from 1879 to
1996, approximately 150,000 Indigenous children were taken away from their
families to attend these federal institutions. As a result of the children's imposed
separation from their relatives and environment, the indoctrination and isolation, a prohibition against speaking Indigenous languages, sustained neglect,
and numerous and recurring instances of moral, physical, and sexual abuse, the
survivors and their children suffered serious trauma, which continue to affect
Indigenous families, communities, and peoples.[19] In 2008, in reaction to the

determined and courageous efforts of survivors and their communities to obtain reparation, the federal government issued a solemn apology to residential school survivors, and a Truth and Reconciliation Commission (TRC) was established in order to shed light on the history and ongoing repercussions of these colonial institutions. In its final report released in 2015, the TRC stated that Canada engaged in "cultural genocide" in its dealings with Aboriginal people, which included separating children from their parents in order "primarily to break their link to their culture and identity."[20] The report explicitly expounded:

> *Cultural genocide* is the destruction of those structures and
> practices that allow the group to continue as a group. States
> that engage in cultural genocide set out to destroy the political
> and social institutions of the targeted group. Land is seized,
> and populations are forcibly transferred and their movement
> is restricted. Languages are banned. Spiritual leaders are
> persecuted, spiritual practices are forbidden, and objects
> of spiritual value are confiscated and destroyed. And, most
> significantly to the issue at hand, families are disrupted to
> prevent the transmission of cultural values and identity from
> one generation to the next. In its dealing with Aboriginal
> people, Canada did all these things.[21]

The report specified that the residential schools were a cornerstone of that policy in Canada.

In this troubled historical context, the action of the Mohawk protestors and communities at the close of the twentieth century, putting up clear, unequivocal resistance on the siege sites, constituted a public rebuttal of the Canadian government's assimilationist projections. By making a forceful entry into the public space with Oka, the Mohawks provided evidence of a presence whose reality contrasted starkly with the imagined vision—and political practices—that reduced them to figures of absence and envisioned reciprocal relationships contingent on their supposed future disappearance. In this sense, the siege constituted a real declaration of their existence.

In addition to creating a venue for witnessing, the siege attested to a Mohawk presence that had maintained its position and survived despite the vagaries of history. This is what the documentary *Okanada* highlights by letting the last occupiers be heard. In one scene, Loran Thompson, a Mohawk man from Akwesasne, underscores his people's determination and stares fixedly into the camera with a gaze that drives home the failure of the identity assimilation campaign. "It's never going to end," he declares, clearly in response to a question from a journalist. Sitting on a lawn chair in the Pines, he goes on to speculate that some of the people, when they finally cross the barricades, will probably be put in prison for their participation in the conflict. They will perhaps spend a few years or a few days in jail, or else they will not be sent there at all. "We don't know," he concludes. In a calm, firm voice, over the roar of a helicopter flying overhead, he explains that the issues are not limited to the immediate time frame: "Many children have seen what is going on. A nation never dies, unless the people are willing to let it die." He reaffirms the continuous connection between the Mohawks and the territory: "There are no papers anywhere where Quebec or Canada can prove that the Mohawks sold their territory or have been conquered. Never! There's no document you can find anywhere. We've never sold this country. We never will." His insistence is not on the state of being dispossessed, but rather on the continued resistance of his people, as symbolized by the warrior flag shown in the following shot.

Okanada does not present the historical background to the conflict. It deals with time through the testimony of witnesses who reconstitute it and testify to who they are when they are in the siege space. Thompson reiterates the statements of the Kanehsata'kehró:non who had been tirelessly reasserting their rights to these lands as far back as the eighteenth century and the disputes with the Sulpicians, and emphasizes the importance of the act of vision in maintaining the will to resist among generations to come. He thus highlights the privileged position of the witness in relation to the event, especially concerning the children who will carry the legacy forward. If we rely on the people interviewed by Albert Nerenberg, we observe how eyewitnesses are expected to act as guardians of the experience's transmission and the preservation of a living memory trace, making them historical witnesses as well.

The film's production, by virtue of its motivation and content, fulfills the function of a testimony—showing a signal event that causes an historical dispute to resurface; recording narratives that are making the event as they tell it; and acting as the camera-witness to an encounter whose performative effect ultimately blurs the line between documentarizing and fictionalizing. The camera located itself at the epicentre of an armed conflict; one that arose out of an unusual coincidence of circumstances and that at that moment threatened to end in violence, hidden from sight. By introducing itself directly into an experiential space, the documentary is understood to be a presence, a performance; the witness is there because he resists and, at the same time, takes part in an act of performance.

THE SIEGE AS INTERPELLATION

The Oka Crisis, or the resistance at Kanehsatake, was constructed in accordance with its media coverage. It gave the issue of performance a central place among the concerns of the Indigenous protestors, as among those of the governments and the Canadian Army. In the image war that was waged through the summer of 1990, the Mohawk activists went after the Government of Canada while they mobilized support in this country and elsewhere in the world. By showing themselves to be unmoved by the tanks and soldiers in the course of a conflict that stained Canada's reputation as a peaceful country, the occupiers of the Pines and the bridge called Canadian society out to the point of making it no longer possible to ignore the Indigenous peoples. Mohawk anthropologist Kahente Horn-Miller wrote that the siege constituted both "a show of strength and a call for assistance from supporters."[22] The event's unreal, tragic nature prompted everyone to wonder what was happening and ask who exactly was confronting them. In one sequence from *Okanada*, the image of three masked warriors sitting side by side inside the barricades is accompanied by the voice of an anglophone television news announcer who asks mysteriously, "The Warriors. . . . Who are they? What are they? Why are they?" In a cinematic response, the announcer's voice reads the names of members as if their identity were a military secret, over scenes from daily life behind the barricades of children running and hopping forward with their feet in big corn bags. Their faces are intercut with the figure of the warrior constructed by the media, foregrounding the children's individuality instead of a fixed representation.

Faces are an important dimension of the film, confronting the viewer with the need to "face up" to the situation, this time from inside the barricades. By seeing the siege from the point of view of someone who is surrounded, the viewer can in turn feel what it is like to be besieged and watched—rather than protected—by the Canadian Army. The film exposes an exchange of gaze that is constantly in play between the members of the two camps, as well as between the Mohawk protestors and the camera-witness. We thus see the warriors filming the soldiers, usually from above, watching them with binoculars, photographing them, commenting on their operations, asking them questions, and challenging them, often from a subjective viewpoint that reinforces the viewer's feeling of identification. Put in the witness's place, the viewer meets the gaze of the soldiers who stare at the Indigenous people as they keep watch, which leads the viewer to see the event through the eyes of the besieged protestors rather than from the point of view of the Canadian soldiers confronting them. Through the mediation of such images, the camera-witness invites the viewer to question what happened during the siege and what he or she should think about it.

The barricades' materiality, the opaque physicality of the masked individuals guarding them, and the accounts collected from inside the siege site all speak to having reached a limit, a boundary from which retreat is simply unthinkable: "It just comes to the point, you can't be pushed in a corner anymore," an activist known as Boltpin explains to the camera. The limit referred to could be the Sûreté du Québec's assault on 11 July 1990, and, more generally, the process of spatial and ideological exile that has for a long time exerted pressure on all Indigenous peoples. In the context of the Oka-Kanehsatake territorial conflict, it could also refer to the Mohawk cemetery's part of the land coveted by the Municipality of Oka for its golf course expansion and housing development. The opposition between a profit-making place for recreation and a sacred place of rest for the ancestors only heightened the conflict's symbolic aspect. The images of the cemetery at the film's opening serve as a reminder that the siege represents a battle fought not only for the generations to come, since the loss of territory threatens the community's future, but also for generations past, with the potential harm to the cemetery creating fears that their memory will be obliterated. The prospect of seeing bones marking the ancestors' presence removed seems like a threat to transmission. This threat is particularly disturbing in the context in which it appears, shaped by an all-encompassing settler colonial project of "the elimination of the Native,"[23] and by a century of Canada's Aboriginal policy of "cultural genocide."[24] Whatever the municipality's principal aims might have been,[25] the land targeted for expansion was indisputably contiguous to the cemetery, and protecting this sacred place showed up as an important symbolic issue throughout the conflict.

In *Okanada*, the Mohawk people being interviewed deliver their testimony against the backdrop of the huge pines making up the forest at the heart of the dispute, representing both the conflict's deep roots and its object. The tree trunks' massive, imposing appearance echoes the resolve of the people standing up to bear witness, just as they stand before the forest they say they are determined to defend, even at the cost of their lives. At this point in the conflict, the issues included the broader questions of amnesty and the Mohawk Nation's sovereignty. Nevertheless, the land issue remained central and was viewed as being directly related to sovereignty. As seen in an archival photograph at the beginning of the film, the barricades built of tree trunks in the Pines and watched over by masked individuals constituted a sort of witness-place to be protected with one's body—they evoke the witness's vertical stance, which sets up an obstacle and directs the gaze even as it blocks it. Beyond the barricades, extending across the road, there are the voices, whose corporeal quality, as literary theorist and philosopher Roland Barthes understood it, can be seen as a rampart or an incarnated presence. The steady and tense voice of Mohawk spokesperson Ellen Gabriel, who is seen addressing the media, is a sign of the corporeality of speech and materiality of voice that operate as the voice operates in the body, and vice versa.[26] Through its power and invincible quality, the voice helps to reach and move the viewer.

THE IMAGE AS EVIDENCE AND HISTORICAL RECORD

Speech was included in the film as a form of historical artifact. Similarly, the images shot on the scene would not only circulate in the media, but also serve as evidence in a subsequent trial and cause the dominant version of history to be seen in a new light. It is to be noted that the video and audio recordings obtained from journalists who had covered the crisis served as "elements of proof that made a large contribution to shedding light on the causes and circumstances of Corporal Marcel Lemay's death" (Quebec 1995, 32). On the one hand, therefore, recordings of the event were used as elements of evidence, and, on the other, the speech registered on the siege site would help to foreground a history that had long been buried by the dominant society. This is probably the reason why the people behind the barricades welcomed Albert Nerenberg's camera-witness and made efforts to communicate their experience. While the protestors interviewed clearly wanted to see a documentary record created of the event, they perhaps also wanted the viewer to question his or her own responsibility. As part of the film's narrative, such questioning echoes the criticisms levelled at the federal government for, among other things, its inertia with regard to the crisis.

In *Okanada,* the Mohawks behind the barricades deliberately stage situations in which soldiers are questioned, with the specific aim of having them say on camera that they are unable to talk or are not responsible. For example, one sequence involves a telephone call made on the line connecting the last remaining occupiers to the military post. A Mohawk woman asks the soldier on the other end of the line if she can make a long-distance call, to which he replies that she can do it only if she crosses the barricades, in which case she would not be able to return to the site. In order to force the soldier to state the Canadian Army's position, the woman asks him what would happen to her if she chose that option, and he replies that the question falls outside his authority: "It's not for me to answer." As well as asking questions about third-party responsibility in the event, soliciting such admissions required the person addressed to take a clear position.

Quebec scholar and activist Alexa Conradi suggested looking at the Oka Crisis "as a place of non-identification where assumptions about the superiority of Canadian (or Québecois) values and norms became unsettled." During the event, she added, the norms were thrown into question, along with a certain ethnocentrism, so that members of the public, shaken by what was taking place before their very eyes, were "called upon to judge from a place of non-identification."[27] This interpellation is replayed in *Okanada* when it leads the viewer to compare the stereotypical image of the criminalized warrior circulating in the mass media with images of the people who are experiencing the reality of the armed conflict on a daily basis. From then on, the viewer is compelled to reflect on what happened at the siege sites and think about the issues arising from the political conflict that undermine the national configurations of Canada and Quebec.

In *Okanada,* the images of tanks, helicopters, and armed soldiers surrounding fifty men, women, and children are used to good advantage to reveal Canada's methods of dealing with Indigenous people. The film opens with the statement of a Mohawk speaker, who reasserts, on the very site of the Pines, that her community has lived on the territory from time immemorial. It ends eloquently with scenes of the brutal arrests of the occupiers who, after having burned their weapons and held a ceremony, started to cross the barricades without notice, thus ending the siege while refusing to give themselves up. A series of slow-motion images then follows, showing a row of soldiers with bayonets facing the protestors as they leave the woods and gain the road amid shouts, altercations, and arrests. As a unique commentary on this final sequence, we hear an Indigenous version of Canada's national anthem sung by Mi'gmaq singer and documentary filmmaker Willie Dunn. In *Okanada*, a documentary with an evocative title if ever there was one, the lyrics of this reappropriated anthem are used to provide the commentary for the scenes of the arrests:

> O Canada, our home and native land
> One hundred thousand years we've walked upon your sands
> With saddened hearts we've seen you robbed
> And stripped of everything you prized
> While they cut down the trees we were shunted aside
> To the jails and penitentiaries
> O Canada, once glorious and free
> O Canada, we sympathize with thee
> O Canada, we stand on guard for thee.

These lyrics are accompanied by images of a Mohawk woman with her arms held behind her back in a soldier's grip that looks very painful, while other occupiers have been thrown to the ground by soldiers who are handcuffing them. At the point when the song refers to the marginalization and imprisonment of the Indigenous peoples in penitentiaries, we see Robert Skidder, a Mohawk warrior nicknamed Mad Jap, in handcuffs, being escorted through the crowd by two soldiers. We then see shots of a man in camouflage brandishing the warrior flag that until then had been flying from a pole inside the barricades. Next to him, looking lost in the surrounding chaos, is one of the children who had been on the site. Another shot then shows an AK-47-style weapon left lying on the ground. The film ends with a scene showing the Canadian soldiers lined up across the road with their weapons trained on the crowd while the last line of the national anthem is playing: "O Canada, we stand on guard for thee." By associating the arrest of the Indigenous protestors as they leave the barricades with the image of the country's colonization, the film makes the viewer see Canada's national defence from a completely different angle. In addition, Dunn's voice recalls the film *The Ballad of Crowfoot*, produced by the National Film Board of Canada in 1968, in which Dunn reviews how the conquest of the continent has affected the situation of Indigenous peoples from yesterday until today, using archival images to recall the military repression that supported the campaign.

With the image tribunal it sets up, *Okanada* brings a documentary viewpoint to the event. Further, it lets the voices be heard of witnesses who were launching proceedings against the Quebec and Canadian authorities. For example, a television news clip included in the film shows Mohawk spokesperson Ellen Gabriel firmly telling the media: "They've turned a deaf ear. They've not listened to our requests. And it brought us to this point, where people's lives are at stake." In this case, the lack of recognition finds its place in the perspective of a historiography that the Mohawk protestors were putting forward on the siege sites and that was disseminated in the media. Rather than attempting to justify themselves in terms of the dominant political discourse, which required them to submit and criminalized them if they did not, they promoted their own discourse, which then became the authoritative version. Speaking to the camera, they reaffirmed the historical antecedents and continuity of the Mohawk Nation, anticipating the question of rights by basing their discourse on the Iroquois narrative of legitimacy. Having been projected into the event, they set their testimony in the present; at the same time, with a collective sense of belonging, they testified to an historical past. The people behind the barricades addressed the camera-witness, saying, "I'm here," knowing that the audiovisual recording would make that into "I was here." The duplication of performance was fully operative, superimposing a mediation by images on the event under construction. Just as cinema implies testimony because of the vision it presents,[28] the documentary, by mediating experience, itself produces the effect of presence.

The siege produced a presence in the centre of the public space, which the documentary then made visible by means of images and testimonies recorded on the site of the event. In his reflection on the political function of the witness as a device for producing factual truth in the public space, the French sociologist Renaud Dulong explained that the truth of an event also aligns with the experience of the individuals engaged in it.[29] Testimony, understood by Dulong as an act of speech oriented to the future,[30] thus underscores the idea of engagement, which derives from an ethical requirement that would be intrinsic. On this point, American literary critic Shoshana Felman wrote: "Witnessing is not just telling a story, but becoming engaged and engaging through a story told to others: making oneself responsible— through one's words—for the history or the truth of an event."[31] In *Okanada*, the witnesses explain that they are ready to die for the survival of the Mohawk Nation and express a feeling of belonging to all Indigenous peoples. While each of the witnesses provides visible and audible evidence of a unique experience, they all refuse to speak for themselves alone and insist that what is at stake for the community is bigger than they are.

While this position can be explained by the need to present a common front in order to exercise political strength, it also operates in another register. The testimonial function of witnessing is in fact a matter of passing on whatever goes beyond the individual life experience, thereby interpellating the Other by appealing to her or his sense of community. By speaking to the camera, the witness makes a connection with the person facing him, who listens and has not necessarily had this experience. It becomes not only a matter of transmitting the experience of the event itself, but, beyond that, of conveying the very reality of the Mohawk communities' existence and their uniqueness. The documentary does not encompass the complexity of the conflict's political issues. On the other hand, the unique experiences and stories it transmits bear witness to something that is larger, notably their inclusion in the history of Indigenous peoples. In this, the documentary helps to accomplish the dual historical task of countering invisibility and transforming imagination.

Although it is not a primary point in this analysis, it is interesting to note that the documentary film constitutes a memory of the event for the younger generations who experienced the conflict as children or who know it only through third parties. In 2010 in Kanahwake, at the international conference Revisioning the Americas through Indigenous Cinema, Mohawk actor Kaniehtiio Horn said that at the age of four, with her mother and sister, she had experienced the final days of the siege alongside the protagonists of *Okanada*. In the presence of journalist and filmmaker Albert Nerenberg, she stated that this documentary allowed her to make sense of a critical passage in her life: "That's how I pieced together a really big time in my life that's shaken me forever."[32] Her testimony refers to the necessity for the kind of expression that is made possible by a film such as this one, which depicts the daily life of people projected into an event that does them violence. We will come back to this point when we look at literary narratives.

THE DUPLICATION OF PERFORMANCE

By becoming the conflict's stage set, the siege embodied the kind of expressive, performative protest sought out by the media and, for that reason, it allowed the Indigenous peoples to speak out and assert themselves in the public space.[33] The documentary *Okanada* reflects both the speaking out and the asserted presence.

There is also a displacement, since the medium of film has been used to produce a duplication of the event's performance. In a combination of reportage and artistic production, the film connects what is taking place elsewhere to what is going on before our eyes, using strategies that give the work its artistic character, as explained by French philosopher Jacques Rancière in *Le destin des images* [The destiny of images]. The performance on the siege site underscores the distance from what is being conveyed in the dominant society, owing in part to the fact that the Mohawk protestors show themselves to be both 'contemporary' and 'traditional,' two characteristics that the colonial representations have sought to dissociate from one another. Further, the edited film, which is not a faithful copy but a certain (re)presentation of the event, leaves room to introduce differences: what is shown in the film is not exactly what happened on the site. A distance remains between the filmed reality and the documentary.

In *Okanada*, the Mohawk protagonists display great control when telling their story, which they deliver calmly and concisely. They speak in a relaxed, even tone, without becoming excited or gesticulating. The land issue that is central to the dispute is presented in simple, direct terms. For example, when asked by the interviewer how she felt on the last day of the siege, a Mohawk woman smiles and replies, "Glad to be alive," and immediately moves off. The concise testimonies and short statements leave us wanting to hear more. The witnesses' narrative authority gives what they say the ring of truth and, in particular, a repetition of the same statement across testimonies strengthens an essential relation of trust with the receiver. Moreover, on the political level, repeating a claim increases its intelligibility and legitimacy.[34] The Mohawks' ability to impose silence, tell stories, and make themselves heard is perhaps not foreign to the people's long oral tradition. About this, Kahente Horn-Miller has written: "The oral tradition used to communicate the treaties becomes part of us because each time a recitation occurs or a story is told, it is relived."[35] From one occasion to another, depending on the story, the tradition is evoked and experienced in a unique way. As for the documentary, it adds another dimension to orality by making reiteration possible through recording, thus transforming words into traces, or items of historical record.

In an article about the event, Alexa Conradi suggested that "by embodying a Mohawk political style embedded in an indigenous rhetorical culture, the protestors at Oka paved the way for the emergence of a rhetoric of listening in which *partialities became visible and the conditions for new forms of judgment arose.*"[36] By allowing them to hear and see the last remaining protestors speak out, the documentary reminds viewers of the partiality of viewpoints and consequently leads them to formulate new lines of questioning. For example, what would explain how individuals who were so thoroughly disparaged and criminalized, even by people from their own communities, could pronounce a political discourse that is not only coherent, but also motivated a very large number of Indigenous people all across the North American continent?

Since it tells the story of the last days of the Kanehsatà:ke resistance, *Okanada* more specifically engages the viewer in revisiting the sensationalist images circulated in daily reports by the mass media during the siege's endgame. While the Mohawk warriors were represented in the media and the authorities' discourses as outlaws and criminals who were holding their community hostage at gunpoint, the warriors we see in the film display restraint and dignity in their gestures and speech. Indignation can be detected in what they say, but not aggression. "We have controlled ourselves very well here. Native people have always controlled themselves," states the speaker nicknamed Boltpin, underlining the self-control that gave such credibility to the actions of the Mohawk people under siege.

In the film, the restraint of the Mohawk protagonists is contrasted with the hate-filled excesses of the crowd of local settlers, who are shown in the act of burning a warrior in effigy. These images were widely broadcast in television news bulletins in the summer of 1990. They reinforce what the Mohawk witnesses have to say and disquiet the viewer, leading her or him to side with a television news commentator who recalls the horror he felt several decades earlier on seeing effigies of African Americans burned by Ku Klux Klan members in Alabama. Later on, Boltpin calmly and imperturbably repeats the xenophobic epithets of the white demonstrators telling the Mohawks to go back where they came from. With a touch of humour, he expresses his astonishment at a spectacle that, aside from its disturbing racism, betrays an ignorance that strikes him as unreal: "When I watched the news and I saw these people saying about the Indians, 'Go back to where you came from.' . . . It's *unreal* that they don't realize that we were here before them! This is *our* land. This is our *home.*" Given the extreme nature of the situation, the witnesses themselves have a hard time believing what is happening to them, which does not make it easier to live through the experience or transmit it.

HUMOUR BEHIND THE BARRICADES

The events that took place at Oka seem almost unreal, owing to the extreme antagonism expressed and the absurdity of what triggered the armed conflict—a golf course. "All that for a golf course," observes Susan Oke laconically as the film begins. How could a small, rural Indigenous community find itself surrounded by an imposing number of Canadian soldiers, in the middle of an event that had projected it to the forefront of the international scene? How could a local dispute have degenerated to that point? How could the settler sense of entitlement within the local populations have persisted so unquestioned? How could the contemporary settlers show themselves to be so openly racist and xenophobic, and, even more unbelievably, how could they fail to realize that Indigenous people do not come from somewhere else? More fundamentally, how to make sense of what was happening?

Italian philosopher Giorgio Agamben observed that the impossibility of accounting for experience can be overcome by channelling it into performance. During the siege, the Mohawk protestors and community members often fell back on humour, among other things, to deal with the event and give themselves the means to make sense of an inconceivable reality. Similarly, the producers of *Okanada* opted for a humorous approach midway between reportage and the documentary. The conflict's tragic aspect is relieved by touches of humour in the film, in both the material that was shot and how it was edited. In one sequence, the scene of the fatal shootout is followed by the shot of a large sign reading: "Oka welcomes you. Watch out for our children. [Signed] The Oka Optimists Club." This word of welcome is accompanied by images of tanks moving along the town's streets, one of them going in the direction indicated by a red arrow with the word "inn" written on it, which, under the circumstances, suggests an odd form of hospitality. As we have seen earlier, the situation on the siege site was extremely tense. A threat hung over the daily life of the Mohawk protestors and their supporters behind the barricades, and also over that of the entire communities of Kanehsatake and Kahnawake close to the perimeter. The documentary conveys the equally sombre and incongruous nature of the situation with images that underline the strangeness of the siege site—damaged boxes of food; a warrior wearing a gas mask, seated on a log to read the paper, against a backdrop of barbed wire; a young protestor pretending to play guitar with his rifle; soldiers waiting in front of the barbed wire; and more soldiers floating large red and white balloons above the perimeter, over a soundtrack of suspenseful music.

Twenty years after Oka, in Kanahwake, Albert Nerenberg related how, like the Mohawk demonstrators and communities that experienced this event up close, he was traumatized by the armed conflict and his brutal arrest.[37] He explained that it was his experience behind the barricades that not only led him to the cinema, his first film being *Okanada*, but also inspired him to turn to laughter and humour in his filmmaking practice. Regarding humour, a Mohawk woman who had been present during the confrontation recounted: "When we were in Oka, our lives were on the line and the only way we could face it and deal with it was through humour. Humour was always something very truthful. Looking at the situation and seeing how ridiculous it was, and everybody would laugh because they saw the truth of it."[38] Finding herself in this extreme situation, the speaker had no choice but to face up to it, take stock, and react in a way that would get her through the ordeal, so that she could then communicate her experience as a third party.

Humour provided a means for people to deal with the unreal aspect of the confrontation and stay calm in a high-tension zone, while distancing themselves from the danger. In the Mohawk language, the idea of humour, *tehoteriwak-wenten*, according to Kahente Horn-Miller "more literally means 'a balanced mind which has taken a matter to the ridiculous extreme,'"[39] and it asks us to see what such a situation can yield in terms of humour. Recalling that reality can sometimes be stranger than fiction, Boltpin exclaims with a cheerful perplexity, "It's like *The Twilight Zone*! You can't believe this is going on!" (His comment refers to Rod Serling's television series, in which ordinary people suddenly find themselves in extraordinary and often supernatural circumstances.) Since the analysis of the situation inevitably tends to the humorous, the viewers are led to think that things could not be otherwise; after all, if they laugh, it's because the situation must indeed contain an element of absurdity. In the same way, humour reveals a certain truth through the distance it always creates and a shared sensibility by the fact that everyone is laughing together.

In *Okanada,* the intercutting of archival documents with images shot during the last days of the siege displays this humorous touch, as do the witnesses who get into the act to parody their current experience. In one scene, the cameraman is teasing one of the warriors by playing with both typical questions from journalists and the self-image that some of the warriors involved in many acts of resistance might have developed. He is quizzing the late Mi'gmaq warrior Tom Paul, nicknamed The General. Paul is quietly sitting in a lawn chair, dressed in camouflage, when the cameraman asks him if he has ever cried during the crisis, whether out of fear for his family or himself. Incredulous, Paul asks him to say it again, then quickly looks at the young man sitting beside him before exclaiming, in mock disgust and outrage, "Cried?!! Fuck!! What kind of fucking foolish question to ask!" At that point, we see him getting up and going off, followed by the young warrior, who is smiling, amused, while we hear the cameraman and other people off camera gently laughing. As noted by writers and scholars like Drew Hayden Taylor and Kristina Fagan, humour is a very common survival mechanism in Indigenous societies.[40] Similarly, *Okanada* does not portray the Indigenous protestors as victims, but rather as people who find themselves pushed into an absurd situation by the stubbornness of those who put them there. They present themselves as reasonable people who have been forced to defend themselves by the circumstances but sincerely want to see an end to the absurdity. By doing so, they directly contradict government statements describing their political demands as unreasonable.

THE MASKED WARRIOR: PLAYING
BETWEEN MEDIA SPECTACLE AND LIVE EXPERIENCE

At work in *Okanada* is a significant tension between a documentary treatment and a fictionalized one—if only due to the minimal structure of the witnessing in the narrative—as well as between making a spectacle of the event and mediating the lived experience. This results from contrasting the media image with the reality of the besieged Mohawk warriors. According to Lorna Roth, the immediacy of the media coverage and the media's display of images of Mohawk warriors during Oka was in contrast to the usual absence of Indigenous issues and journalists in the mass media.[41] In a text she co-wrote with Beverly Nelson and Kasennahawi Marie David, "Three Women, a Mouse, a Microphone, and a Telephone: Information (Mis)Management during the Mohawk/ Canadian Governments' Conflict of 1990," Roth underscored the effectiveness of the Mohawk protestors' "sophisticated media strategy" in putting powerful, evocative symbols to work for their cause. She noted that "the form of the confrontation fit into a sensationalist media format," partaking of a duality commonly seen in the well-known scenario of cowboys and Indians[42]—something that Manitoban Anishinaabe writer Wab Kinew would explore from the perspective of Indigenous youth of the time in the text "Cowboys and Indians," published in the 2010 anthology *This Is an Honor Song: Twenty Years Since the Blockades*.[43] Making a spectacle of the resistance was precisely what allowed the protestors to appropriate the language of television so as to achieve their political ends. Roth parses it in the following terms: "Here were masked Indian Warriors wearing camouflage, using pseudonyms, uttering perfect sound bytes in a confrontational manner, feeling free behind disguises to construct brand new personae along the flat lines of the television cartoon caricature. The Mohawks had figured out within a few months how to capture the imaginations and the attention of the Canadian public by appropriating television's own vernacular and using it to serve their political ends."[44] About the particular way in which the Mohawk activists played with the mediatization of past and present events during the armed conflict, Amelia Kalant wrote that, in 1990, "the warriors could be regarded as partial parody and partial street theater, a necessary means of gaining attention and creating fear."[45]

The film *Okanada* exploits the play of representations that went on during the event. However, in this instance, the journalist and photograph connived with the warriors, who deliberately joined in the game. The camera-witness presents a staged scene with Ronald Cross, well known to the media by his nickname Lasagne. The sequence of shots would be reworked in the editing and an appropriate soundtrack added. Cross, who was undoubtedly the most mediatized of the besieged warriors, has since then often been identified (incorrectly) as the one in the emblematic face-to-face photograph with a Canadian Army soldier by Shaney Komulainen. (Many such photographs were taken during the siege; in this case, we are referring to that published by Komulainen of the Canadian Press in 1990.) A steelworker from New York State, Cross found himself in the middle of the event somewhat by accident, having been visiting his mother in Kanehsatake when the crisis broke out. He joined the besieged occupiers and then stirred up a controversy within the group and also in Quebec's public space, where he was portrayed in an especially negative light, his legitimacy voided because, as anthropologist Pierre Trudel wrote, he was "supposedly American of Italian origin, rather than Mohawk."[46] Cross had a strong presence at the barricades, and through his performances and the representations made of him, he embodied the media's myth of the Mohawk warrior.

In *Okanada,* to the famous theme music of Sergio Leone's Western *The Good, the Bad and the Ugly*, a slow-motion close-up shows the massive trunk of a man sitting in a lawn chair, dressed in jeans and a camouflage jacket, his gloved hands holding a pistol, pretending to get ready to fire. The camera then frames

Canadian soldier Patrick Cloutier and Brad Laroque, a.k.a. "Freddy Kruger,"
come face to face in a tense standoff at the Kahnesatake reserve in Oka, Quebec, 1 September 1990. Canadian Press/Shaney Komulainen.

the gaze of a masked man with black outlining his eyes, before cutting to his
tattooed arms and hard-looking face, with a cigarette between his lips. We hear
the voice of the interviewer-narrator presenting, with a drum roll, "Lasagne, the
media's gun-toting, outlaw Indian," the one who had left his mark on the popular imagination during the Oka Crisis. The character remains silent throughout
this scene, but in the following one is seen berating the soldiers posted on the
other side of the barbed wire. Wearing a hat decorated with a skeleton figurine
and a serious air that is not entirely sincere, he shouts at, calls out, and defies the
soldiers facing him across the wire, who cannot be seen by the viewer. A little
later in the film, we watch this same warrior continuing to provoke the soldiers,
ordering them to move aside and let the Sûreté du Québec come and settle its

account. After this speech, he turns and disappears behind the flaps of a white tarpaulin put up by the protestors to cut off the soldiers' vantage, like an actor exiting the stage and disappearing behind the curtain.

Playing up the myth of the warrior broadcast by the media, the narrator (erroneously) describes Cross as the "leader of a heavily armed faction of Warriors." Next on screen is a photograph taken from the middle of a horde of journalists, one of the famous face-to-face shots of a masked warrior and a Canadian soldier that peppered the news during the armed conflict. The narrator goes on to announce a scoop regarding this protagonist: "One day he took off his mask to give a single interview." In a staged interview granted to the camera-witness behind the barricades, Ronald Cross / Lasagne goes from subjectification to desubjectification—he plays himself and then adopts the mediatized warrior persona, and he alternates between the two, consciously constructing his testimony in accordance with his media image.

By engaging in self-mockery, despite the statement's seriousness, the witness performs counter to expectations, playing in particular with the projections forced on him. With a slightly ironic air, Cross later tells the interviewer that, yes, he is of course ready to die for the cause, that all those who support the siege are, and he then adds with a wry smile and a rhetorical flourish, "Of course, we're all willing to die for the cause. Like Chief Dan George said, it's always a good day to die." By making jokes drawn from Indigenous politics and a Hollywood film, he's winking at the viewers, with whom he has engaged in connivance and complicity, thus helping to establish a relationship of trust and intersubjective communication. At the end of the interview, we see a shot of the protagonist resting his weapon on his shoulder and facing the camera with a winning smile. This sequence is immediately followed by another showing a black-and-white photograph of Cross, arrested and handcuffed, with black eyes and a bruised face, looking sadly at the camera. In contrast to the image of bravado he projects, here the fearsome warrior is shown from another angle that takes in the hard realities of the siege and its aftermath.

The masks worn by the warriors in the summer of 1990 hid their faces, as if to put greater emphasis on their gaze. The masks played into the game of the visible and invisible that proved to be so telling in terms of symbolism and media representations. The image of masked warriors engaged in negotiations was no doubt so shocking because of the significance of someone wearing a mask, an image that carries an immediate charge on the level of historiography and also on that of the event's configuration in images. If we parse the paradigm of this configuration in the context of Oka, the image of the masked individual refered to widely reported events from the past in which we had seen many images of hooded terrorists. The aim of wearing a mask is to create a diversion and avert the possibility of being identified, while being seen everywhere; in 1990, it evoked, in particular, the hostage taking at the Olympic Games in Munich in 1972, when the victims were Israeli athletes. It would later be associated with the uprising of the Zapatistas in Chiapas, Mexico, in 1994. In the popular imagination, the kerchief hiding the nose and mouth is also associated with robbers in the Old West and cartoon characters. During the siege, a short-circuiting of these two images gave rise to the masked *warrior* in the public space. Amelia Kalant noted the effectiveness of the accessory that was such an annoyance to the Canadian and Quebec authorities, who were convinced that those who wore it were trying to disguise their "true" intentions: "Ironically, during that long summer, it was the warriors' masks—which drew government ire because they 'hid' the true purpose and intention of the warriors—that had made the protesters visible. For only in hiding themselves and refusing to look the part, could the protesters move beyond the fantasies of Indianness that had been projected onto them by Canadianness."[47]

Thanks to a function similar to that of the baton in a relay race, the mask is the opaque object that obscures and, because of its opacity, allows for the signs and images to be further transmitted and circulated. In the particular context of Quebec, the term "warrior" itself eloquently resists a linguistic transfer into French, and entices the francophone settler audience with its "foreign" quality.[48] Exposing this tension between language and non-language, the face-to-face of the warrior and the soldier in the summer of 1990 at first defied understanding, and then became an inexhaustible source of discourse and representation. Paradoxically, it was through this ostentatious form of camouflage that the Mohawk protestors and communities were able to step out of the shadow cast on their existence by a figure of disappearance and absence.

THE REAL, THE UNIQUE, THE FEATURE OF PRESENCE

As I mentioned, the documentary film *Okanada* does not offer an in-depth analysis of the political conflict and the attendant political issues. Rather, it presents unique experiences that stand out for singular features of presence. Albert Nerenberg has been quick to explain that he is not an historian but only

In a scene from *Okanada*, warriors and friends gather for last time before exiting the barricades in Kanehsatake, at the end of September 1990. Used by permission of Albert Nerenberg.

a journalist who intended to tell a good story.[49] The stance he deliberately adopted effectively dodged the thorny issue of choosing spokespersons who would respond to the mass media. Further, it allowed him to ask questions, through the device of the documentary narrative, about justice and dignity, notably regarding the dehumanization generated by false, melodramatic images of the warriors and, by extension, all of the Mohawk communities. With reference to a completely different context, Shoshana Felman noted that mediating the trivial has the effect of desanctifying events and allowing for an historicization that would otherwise be impossible. By paying increased attention to small details and discreet action in expression, *Okanada* helps to dismantle the mythic figure of Jean-Jacques Rousseau's 'noble savage', as well as that of the criminalized warrior. It thus makes it possible to inscribe the event in a historiography to which the film contributes as an archive and a document. By making heard what Felman calls the "single uniqueness of an act of telling"[50] expressed in the voice of the witness, the film finds ways to reach an audience that is prepared to listen.

Okanada is studded with reality fragments that cannot be completely stripped of their evocative power. In that, it takes advantage of the cinema's "language of reality," which, as film scholar Pascal Houba argued, does not have the normative grammar that oral or written languages do.[51] Towards the end of Bainbridge and Nerenberg's film, we see Mohawk children posing for a group photograph before leaving the siege area. Behind them, in the middle, a boy waves a large Mohawk flag, and then all the children raise their fists as a sign of triumph. In the foreground, in the middle, a small girl can be seen, unmoving, apart from the other children's action. Apparently lost in thought, she stares straight ahead. It is only after a long while that she looks to either side and, as if noticing the presence of a community around her, suddenly lifts her clenched fist very high, with determination. After resting fixed on the small group for several seconds, the camera moves on to another take before coming back to the children. We then see that they have all lowered their arms except the little girl, whose small closed fist can be seen in the lower frame. The camera resists the temptation to focus on her face and instead, as if duty-bound, shoots the symbol of the Mohawk warrior flag. If the raised fists of the children convey an obvious meaning, being a synonym for resistance and victory, that of the little girl conveys an additional expressiveness akin to the obtuse meaning described by Roland Barthes. The lengthy pause for reflection and the conviction in her gesture lead us to speculate about the serious, obstinate nature of this child, who with a simple gesture reveals a moving mixture of strength, determination, and vulnerability. By capturing the image of a penetrant trait that stubbornly persists, the camera cedes to the filmic aspect, which represents nothing but can speak nonetheless. The shot showing the group adopting a pose for the camera harks back to the photograph's ambiguous and uncertain status. In fact, according to what follows, this group photo could very well signify victory, as the people behind the barricades assert, or be the equivalent of a visual legacy that will fix in time the final moments on the siege site. By making a connection among the siege's nature as an event, the circulation of images, and the experience, the film encourages viewers to assemble the elements they need to arrive at a new judgement about a situation that has now been shown to them from a different point of view.

In the summer of 1990, the siege endured by the Mohawk communities made visible an Indigenous presence that the societies of Quebec and Canada believed had faded away, to which the documentary film *Okanada* bears witness.

Because the film is constructed out of the geographical and cognitive position of the Canadian journalist and the Mohawk protagonists who deliver their testimony to the camera-witness, it provides a special perspective on the siege's denouement. This inside perspective, necessarily partial, itself contributes to an overall understanding of the event. As distinct from the political crisis's media treatment, which is primarily conveyed as information, *Okanada* exploits the advantages offered by the film medium to create a place for narrative of the experience lived through by the people behind the barricades. In addition to staging the conflict, these people registered their action in the Mohawk historiography, such that the siege appears in the film to be the site not only of eyewitnessing but also of historical witnessing.

The film sheds light on partialities, the appeal to a third party, and the need to formulate lines of questioning that are not developed solely with reference to the mass media. Similarly, material shot for purposes of journalistic coverage was put to use in a documentary film that gives a voice to unique narratives and plays in a humorous way with the tension between making a documentary and making a fictionalized account. Although its subject is an event that inflamed antagonisms, *Okanada* interpellates non-Indigenous viewers in a manner that does not lock them into a defensive position. By not trying to represent the Mohawks in their supposed authenticity, but rather conveying the uniqueness of each person, the film goes beyond prepackaged representations in reaching the viewer. Since simply knowing is not sufficiently powerful and effective as an act of revelation,[52] *Okanada*, with its artistic, humorous qualities, makes it possible to gain a more perceptive understanding of the experience of a group of Indigenous witness-actors surrounded by the Canadian Army.

CHAPTER 5

"A Record We Made Ourselves"—*Kanehsatake: 270 Years of Resistance*

In the documentary film *Kanehsatake: 270 Years of Resistance*, Abenaki filmmaker Alanis Obomsawin tells the story of the lengthy siege that propelled the contemporary and historical struggles of the Mohawks and other Indigenous peoples across Turtle Island into the spotlight. The film, which was produced by the National Film Board of Canada three years after the Oka Crisis, in part duplicates the account to be found in *Okanada*. However, the respective positions of the directors regarding the territorial conflict, as well as how the two films were actually produced, differ on a number of points. As a journalist, Albert Nerenberg slipped behind the barricades only towards the very end of the siege, with the intention of recording its denouement, and the shots taken on the site were originally meant to be media reportage. The documentary he subsequently co-directed based on this footage in essence retells what he saw and experienced alongside the Mohawk occupiers and their sympathizers. His filmed account is therefore constructed around the siege space, and, since the film deals first with the immediate issue of the conflict, the history is perceived only through the accounts of the protestors delivering their testimony to the camera. In this sense, *Okanada* is based, on the one hand, on a simultaneous relation to the event in which the camera participates as it records it, and, on the other, on a relation of otherness between the protestors and the third party represented by the journalist. The journalist explicitly takes up an external stance relative to the territorial conflict.

In *Kanehsatake: 270 Years of Resistance*, the director's stance is very different from Nerenberg's. Obomsawin had rushed to the site of the conflict in Kanehsatake on the morning of the shootout. Like Nerenberg, she offers an account of the event, but she puts the emphasis on how the conflict proceeded rather than its denouement. In this case, the filmmaker does not position herself as a third party, but rather locates herself among the members of the Mohawk communities on the siege sites. With her production crew, she circulates on both sides of the barricades, so that the siege appears to be less of a retrenching and more of a generalized situation of conflict, marked by the incursion of the police and the army into Mohawk territory and more specifically into the disturbed daily life of the communities the conflict affected. Finally, the filmed account was based on footage shot on the siege sites, supplemented with an in-depth historical reconstruction and interviews from after the event that place the conflict in its broader context.

Alanis Obomsawin is a pluridisciplinary artist and one of Canada's pre-eminent documentary filmmakers. This is indicated by the many awards for *Kanehsatake: 270 Years of Resistance* and various tributes for her body of work, such as the major retrospective organized by New York's Museum of Modern Art in 2008 and the several honoraris causa doctorates she was awarded. As stated by Randolph Lewis in his 1996 book *Alanis Obomsawin: The Vision of a Native Filmmaker*, she is a leading figure in the development of North American Indigenous media. Obomsawin is a model and an inspiration, especially for young Indigenous people. Like many other Indigenous film professionals, she is very politically and socially engaged with Indigenous peoples.[1] Her commitment is reflected in her film work, including her more recent documentaries *The People of the Kattawapiskat River* (2012), *Trick or Treaty?* (2014), and *Our People Will Be Healed* (2017), the fiftieth in fifty years as a filmmaker.[2]

Obomsawin's career in documentary film has been closely tied to her personal history. She was born in Abenaki territory in New Hampshire, in the United States. She grew up in the community of Odanak, Quebec, where she immersed herself in Abenaki songs, stories, language, and culture, especially at the side of her uncle, Théophile Panadis. When she was nine, she moved with her family to Trois-Rivières, Quebec, where she was suddenly cut off from her roots and exposed to incidents of racism, which very early on led her to demand and fight to win respect and follow her own course in life. In the 1950s and 1960s, according to Lewis, she moved in Montreal's bohemian circles with such artists as sculptor Morton Rosengarten, filmmaker Derek May, and singer-songwriter Leonard Cohen. She then launched a career as a singer that led to appearances across the country.[3] In 1967, she started working at the National Film Board of Canada (NFB) as a consultant, and over the years went on to produce numerous documentary films on the social realities and political struggles of Indigenous peoples.

National Film Board producer Robert Verral realized that Obomsawin's commitment to her people would keep stardom at bay: "She could have been a jet setter. There's no doubt, if she had wanted to go in that direction, she would have found the support for it [based on her talents and charm]. But her commitment to her people was so real and so genuine."[4] This stance speaks to an honourable social and political commitment, as well as a strong sense of belonging. It must be said that it also bears witness, less happily, to the precarious situation of Canada's Indigenous peoples and their unceasing struggle to survive, reclaim lands and history, and to win respect, dignity, and recognition. Today, Obomsawin continues to be engaged in Indigenous communities, whether through her presence, her documentary films, or her work as a mentor. In 1990, less than ten years after having directed the documentary *Incident at Restigouche*, which reconstructs the 1981 intervention of 550 Sûreté du Québec officers in a protest of salmon fishing regulations on a Mi'gmaq reserve, this commitment to Indigenous struggles led her to spend seventy-eight days in the middle of a dangerous armed conflict, which would result in production of the documentary *Kanehsatake: 270 Years of Resistance*, along with three other films.

THE DOCUMENTARIST'S STANCE

On 11 July 1990, as soon as she heard about the Sûreté du Québec's intervention, Alanis Obomsawin went straight to Kanehsatake to see what had happened. She immediately told the NFB that she was postponing shooting on her current project and returning to the site of the conflict with a skeleton crew,[5] impelled by anxiety over what would be said about the Mohawks and a feeling of responsibility for covering the event from an Indigenous point of view. She later explained: "We had to have a record we made ourselves, . . . it was crucial."[6] As the film's voice-over narration contends, the Mohawks ran the risk of being cast as the guilty party in the eyes of the public and the governments of Canada and Quebec: "They knew they would be blamed, no matter where the bullet came from." Although the Kanehsatake Mohawks' land struggle at first received considerable support, that support was gradually whittled away as the authorities implemented a media strategy through which negative discourses, images, and representations concerning the Mohawk warriors were imposed upon the public.

Under the circumstances, the footage the Abenaki filmmaker shot on the site of the standoff would later be regarded as real-time documentation and evidence for a subsequent trial. Like Nerenberg's, but in a less spectacular fashion, the cameras wielded by Obomsawin and her crew played an active role in the conflict. By providing constant surveillance and gathering evidence, they acted as a deterrent for the actors on the scene, and thus became an integral part of the event that was taking place as they recorded it. On this point, Obomsawin reported that she has often been told that her presence on the site, armed with a camera, and especially as an Indigenous person, had a restraining effect on the police and the army.[7] It seems that on the siege site, the documentary work was in a very practical sense part of the activist engagement. Unlike a surveillance device parked on the ledge of a building with a panoramic point of view, the filmmaker's camera made an assertive activist gesture in moving around the site. This gesture also made a display of recording what was happening in the moment, often deliberately intended to protect Indigenous protestors and community members from incidents of violence at the hands of police officers and soldiers.

As the conflict progressed, the Canadian Army imposed greater and greater restrictions on gathering images and testimony about the siege, with the aim of depriving the protestors of a public platform they could use for strategic purposes. The documentary notes the increasingly diminished media presence and the threat created by a lack of surveillance. It also criticizes the subsequent imposition of a dominant narrative about the political crisis. However, rather than having this criticism expressed by the Mohawk protestors, the film shows the reporters and journalists expressing their anger at infringement of the freedom of the press and a growing difficulty in having their basic needs met on the siege site. Towards the end of the armed conflict, the camera followed Geoffrey York, a reporter for the *Globe and Mail* and also co-author of *People of the Pines,* as he left the barbed-wire perimeter and made the following declaration to the media, looking very concerned and stressing every word: "There's only two reporters left from mainstream newspapers. There's no CBC reporters left. There's no broadcast reporters at all. I think the thing that is the most unbelievable, is that in a country like Canada, we're allowing the army to tell us what can be published in a newspaper and what can be put on the nightly news." The restriction York was addressing took a physical form, with the media limited to spaces set aside for them in the siege area. A sequence from the film shows Obomsawin and perhaps ten journalists at a distance, lined up behind the barbed wire that served as the military perimeter. On the other side, at a remove from the outer barricade, members of the media are confined to an area designated by the Canadian Army. This is where a journalist denounces the seizure of exposed film

to the assembled media, which the documentary confirms in footage of a soldier
with his hands full of photographic and film materials.

Okanada, which launched Albert Nerenberg's career as a documentary
filmmaker, runs for some forty minutes and is essentially a documentary reportage. By contrast, the production by seasoned filmmaker Alanis Obomsawin, at
more than two hours in length, constitutes an archival document and a major
historical document. In 2008, during the conference Paroles et pratiques artistiques autochtones au Québec aujourd'hui [Indigenous speech and artistic practices in Quebec today] at the University of Quebec at Montreal, Obomsawin
recalled that she started with some 200 hours of 16 mm film and video footage,
produced an initial edit that was twelve hours long, and then cut that down
to approximately two hours for the final version of *Kanehsatake: 270 Years of
Resistance.* She went on to discuss the need to transmit the experience and story

of a political event that was as significant as it was traumatic, and towards the end of the editing process "it was like pulling teeth because everything was so important." She added that she could not feel free until she had produced three other films about the conflict, because she was absolutely determined that "the story of what happened there," which had not been told by the major media outlets, should at last be understood:

> That's why I ended up making three other films. Because I didn't feel free . . . until I had made *Rocks at Whiskey Trench*. It was always there . . . we hadn't heard from the people in the cars and I couldn't live with that. After I'd made that last film, I felt that I was free where that topic was concerned, but it took a long time . . . to make myself clearly understood . . . there were so many things being shown on television, but people didn't understand what it was, the history that was being made there. I didn't want to make a film that would be like that, and to me, the historical background was very important.[8]

The event's historical context and the importance of witnesses' accounts were imperatives that impelled Obomsawin to produce a series of four films on the conflict.

A boxed set titled *Alanis Obomsawin—270 Years of Resistance* was produced by the NFB to present the four documentary films together. In addition to the historic feature-length film, there are shorter pieces featuring the experience of an individual or an important episode from the event. *My Name Is Kahentiiosta,* produced in 1995, features the political gesture of a Mohawk woman from Kahnawake who, at the trial following the armed conflict, insisted on identifying herself by her Mohawk name, without adding a Western version requested by the court. Made two years later, the documentary *Spudwrench: Kahnawake Man* deals with the life of Randy Horne, a steelworker from Kahnawake who, in the summer of 1990, was brutally beaten by soldiers who had crossed the perimeter. The last film, which was produced ten years after Oka, was *Rocks at Whiskey Trench*, mentioned above. It uses the verbal accounts of Mohawk speakers to convey the tragic incident in which a convoy of cars evacuating Kahnawake was pelted with rocks. In this sense, the four films appear to constitute a political project that is both personal and collective. Obomsawin was compelled not only to set up a tension with the dominant historiography, but also to transmit the direct experience of a signal political event that was traumatic for many reasons. The project's objective seems to have been to contribute to the ongoing development of an Indigenous historiography that has been discredited in various ways. *Kanehsatake: 270 Years of Resistance* was precisely made, as Obomsawin put it, "for memory and posterity."[9]

KANEHSATAKE AND OTHER FILMS ON THE EVENT

Several films were later produced about Oka, including by Kanien'kehà:ka. In 2006, Kanehsatà:ke filmmaker Sonia Bonspille-Boileau released *Qui suis-je?* [Who am I?]. In this documentary, she explored the painful tensions she experienced within herself and her Mohawk and Québécois families because of the standoff and colonial violence of 1990. A decade later, Bonspille-Boileau directed the documentary *The Oka Legacy*, in which she examined "how the Oka Crisis has transformed contemporary Indigenous identity in Canada,"[10] notably through the standpoint of people such as Kanehsatà:ke activist Clifton Nicholas, Kahnawà:ke Olympic athlete Waneek Horn-Miller, Innu activist Melissa Mollen Dupuis, and Francine Lemay, the sister of Corporal Marcel Lemay and translator of *At the Woods' Edge*. Recent cultural and political developments are called upon to better contextualize the Oka event and its lasting impacts. Bonspille-Boileau concludes: "If the residential school system tried to 'kill the Indian' in me, the Oka Crisis breathed new life into it."[11] Her understanding of the generative impacts of the Oka event is present in several other Indigenous film and literary narratives, as we will further see in this book.

From Kahnawà:ke, Mohawk artist Skawennati directed and produced a futuristic episode on the resistance at Oka as part of TimeTraveller™, a multiplatform project presenting a nine-episode, historical, animated film series in the "machinima" mode (2008 to 2013).[12] The episode on 1990 revisits the event by bringing the viewer alongside the men, women, and children taking a last stand at the treatment centre in Kanehsatake, and discussing their action and political motivations. This displacement to fictionalized representations of the event points to a certain creative distantiation that can also be observed in the short dramatic film *Legend of the Storm* (2015), written, directed, and produced by Kahnawà:ke media artist Roxann Whitebean. In her film, Whitebean revisits the siege from the perspective of a nine-year-old girl, Otsí:tsa, who experiences the standoff in her community and refuses to be defeated.

Whitebean worked on the series *Mohawk Girls* by Kahnawake filmmaker Tracey Deer, who has also tackled the Oka event in her film work. In *Club Native* (2008), we hear Waneek Horn-Miller recounting to Deer's camera how she was stabbed by a soldier, at the age of fourteen, when she exited the barricades the very last day of the siege in Kanehsatake. We learn how she thought and acted in the following years in order to redirect the traumatic impacts of the standoff on her life, notably through her outstanding sports career.[13] Horn-Miller's account is situated in the larger discussion of Kahnawake identity politics taken on by Deer in *Club Native*, and the significance of Oka is important in that regard as well. At the conference "Je suis île / I Am Turtle" held at Université de Montréal in 2017, Tracey Deer told the audience about two films she is now preparing in direct relation to Oka.[14] In a later correspondance, she specified: "My first feature will be a coming-of-age story of a 12-year-old Mohawk girl during the Oka crisis, inspired by my own experience. It is tentatively titled *Beans* (this is the girl's nickname) and is being produced by Ema Films. The second is in its early stages and it will examine forgiveness as it relates to the concept of reconciliation. I want to revisit the most traumatic event of my life, when our cars were pelted with rocks by Quebecers as we left the community during the Oka Crisis." These two productions are promising in terms of a continuing reflection on the event and its impacts on the lives of Mohawk people and communities, but also in terms of the nation-wide discussions on reconciliation foregrounded by the TRC and critically interrogated in the field of Indigenous studies.

The communities of Kanehsatake and Kahnawake found themselves at the core of the siege in summer 1990. However, as can be seen in the related film production, they were not the only ones to be affected by the event. In *We Share Our Matters: Two Centuries of Writing and Resistance at Six Nations of the Grand River*, Mohawk scholar Rick Monture explored a "less reported on and studied" element: "the significance of this event within Haudenosaunee communities and the important role that Haudenosaunee women played at this time."[15] Not only did the community of Grand River "bec[o]me heavily involved with organizing demonstrations and raising funds," explained Monture, but in the years following the event, writers, filmmakers, and artists from the community addressed in their works issues raised up by 1990. It is, for instance, in response to the Oka Crisis and to the first Gulf War that Mohawk artist and filmmaker Shelley Niro created the popular series of photos *Mohawks in Beehives* (1991). Furthermore, Niro and co-director Anna Gronau alluded to the event in their film *It Starts with a Whisper* (1993). As Rick Monture further specified: "Although Oka is never mentioned explicitly in the film, it is still a large presence in the story because it is the event that provoked thousands of young people like Shanna [the main protagonist] to want to learn about their history and cultural past, making them more politically aware and often angry as a result." In that examination of the effects of the Kanehsatake resistance on other communities and nations, Niro's film work bears witness to the mobilizing force of the event, its power to generate Indigenous pride, and its decolonizing capacity.

Beyond Haudenosaunee communities, films that focused specifically on the siege in summer 1990 include the feature-length documentary *Acts of Defiance* (1992) by non-Indigenous filmmaker Alec G. MacLeod, as well as the two-part historical fiction miniseries *Indian Summer: The Oka Crisis* (2006) by late Métis director Gil Cardinal. Films that alluded to the event include the feature film *Windigo* (1994) by Québécois filmmaker Robert Morin, as well as the feature film *Mesnak* (2011) directed by Huron-Wendat playwright and filmmaker Yves Sioui Durand. Of note, Sioui Durand co-wrote *Mesnak*'s screenplay with Morin and Louis Hamelin, who have both creatively contributed to the conversation on the event. More recently, the documentary film *Québékoisie* (2013) by non-Indigenous filmmakers Mélanie Carrier and Olivier Higgins featured the story of Francine Lemay, the sister of the corporal who died on 11 July 1990.

Among all these films, *Kanehsatake: 270 Years of Resistance* undoubtedly remains one of the most significant and widely seen. Aside from the awards it received, its regular screening at universities and in activist circles, as well as in Mohawk communities and Indigenous film festivals, demonstrates the extent of its circulation and the interest it attracts for political, historical, and educational reasons. In 2010, twenty years after the event, at a conference in Kahnawake, Mohawk political journalist and activist Kenneth Deer paid homage to Obomsawin's unique work in documentary film in an address to the filmmaker who has just spoken at a panel discussion on Oka and its cinematic accounts. With particular reference to Oka, he said to Obomsawin, "Without you there would be no record. *Kanehsatake* is the seminal record of what happened in 1990."[16] Joe Deom, who also took part in the siege and appears in the documentary, underlined the accuracy of the film's political statement and its contribution to understanding this significant historical event: "I just want to say to Alanis that your film *270 Years of Resistance* is the only film that I've seen that embodies what happened. You had a full understanding of our position, and of the position of the government at the time. That film should be shown in every classroom in Québec for sure."[17] In this regard, the film's mission has become to raise awareness so as to make the conflict's issues better understood by the non-Indigenous population.

Underscoring the contrast between the reality of the experience in her community and the representations circulating in the major media outlets in the summer of 1990, Mohawk documentary filmmaker Sonia Bonspille-Boileau remarked that for her, Obomsawin's documentary represents a way to gain access to what really happened during the conflict:

> Coming from Kanehsatake, I have to say that *Kanehsatake: 270 Years of Resistance* is for me one of the most significant pieces of documentary work that I've seen . . . because I lived through the Oka crisis and what I saw on TV and what I saw with my own eyes were obviously two very different things. I'm sure a lot of people here [in Kahnawake] lived through the same thing. If it wasn't for the cameras from the inside, from the documentary, there's a lot of images that the rest of the world wouldn't have seen and they wouldn't know . . . and they would only base what they know on what they saw on the media. This is a very important thing about archival material within documentary filmmaking.[18]

The documentary has a media-countering value that has proved to be crucial for this highly mediatized political crisis, regarding both the images of the armed conflict and how the event was interpreted in the media. Many of the testimonies published in *At the Woods' Edge* report a clear difference between the images on television and what the people saw with their own eyes in their community, as if the crisis had created a rift between the two worlds. Oka sparked a violence in media representations that had repercussions for all of the Mohawk communities; it also had an effect on the Quebec and Canadian populations, where racism towards Indigenous peoples was seen to intensify. These representations produced an even greater impact because they circulated in a context in which the Indigenous peoples, when not completely absent from media coverage, had usually been depicted in a negative way.

THE CONCEPT OF VISUAL SOVEREIGNTY

During the event, the media's representations, and the authorities' discourse that helped to fuel them, promoted a figure of the warrior associated with a violent, criminal context and, opposed to it, a figure of the stolid soldier associated with a national army ensuring law and order. This opposition became focused in a photograph by Shaney Komulainen that made the first page in media across the country, that of a face-to-face encounter between an imperturbable Canadian soldier and a masked Mohawk warrior who is cursing him. Significantly, this is not the representation that comes out of the film *Kanehsatake: 270 Years of Resistance*. In fact, instead of underscoring the duality embodied in this confrontation, Obomsawin's documentary puts the emphasis on the experiences and expressions of numerous actors in the conflict. As has argued Randolph Lewis, "her cinematic vision reflects an indigenous sovereign gaze, a practice of looking that comes out of Native experience and shapes the nature of the film itself. . . . The gaze is sovereign, when it is rooted in the particular ways of knowing and being that inform distinct nationhoods."[19] In that perspective, *Kanehsatake: 270 Years of Resistance* can be understood as embodying an Indigenous aesthetic and enacting a form of self-determination in creation.[20]

As discussed earlier, the study of the Oka Crisis, or Kanehsatake resistance, raises epistemological questions that cut across the siege in action, documentary films, and literary accounts, especially in a context where relations between the peoples involved are deeply intertwined and shaped by a lengthy colonization process whose machinations are ongoing. In his 2015 book, *La "chose indienne": cinéma et politiques de la représentation autochtone dans la colonie de peuplement libérale* [The "Indian thing": cinema and the politics of Indigenous representation in the liberal settler colony], film and settler studies scholar Bruno Cornellier reminded us that the act of reading and the act of interpreting are never neutral.[21] He added that we cannot "underestimate the capacity of liberal discourse to hijack dissident expression in the service of the campaign for citizens' education adopted by the nation, regarding the production, distribution and funding of documentary 'realities.'"[22] Drawing attention to "the discursive context in which the act of reception is carried out,"[23] Cornellier argued that the NFB hijacked Obomsawin's documentary work to put it at the service of a nation that sees itself as having the power to subsume its Indigenous citizens and define their identity, specifically the set of elements that he called the "Indian thing." He contended that by promoting reception that values the filmmaker's "feminity," the NFB kills two birds with one stone: ultimately, the NFB restores relations with a conciliatory Indianness that is crying out to be "saved," while it dissociates itself from the ostentatious "masculinity" of the warrior who caused a communications breakdown during Oka.[24] Therefore, while dissident expression cannot ignore the structural nature of power relations that tends to hijack documentary production in the act of interpretation, as Cornellier explained, we nonetheless cannot take away Alanis Obomsawin's agency, or deprive the power of reception of its ability to situate a work in a given field.

In this regard, research in the field of Indigenous film studies has put forward interpretive tools developed in relation to the contexts, practices, and communities of Indigenous filmmakers. The concept of "visual sovereignty" cited by Haudenosaunee researchers Jolene Rickard[25] and Michelle Raheja[26] has much hermeneutic potential, especially regarding this particular film, since the film deals with a political event that placed the issue of sovereignty at the forefront. The same is true of the concepts of rhetorical or literary sovereignty to be found in the work of Indigenous film and literature scholars such as Beverly R. Singer, Steven Leuthold, Randolph Lewis, Scott Richard Lyons, Craig S. Womack, and Daniel Heath Justice, as well as in the reflection on the modes of interpreting Indigenous arts outlined by Wendat curator and sociologist Guy Sioui Durand. In a discussion on "Indigenous visual culture" and theory, Rickard envisions sovereignty "as an overarching concept for interpreting the interconnected space of the colonial gaze, deconstruction of the colonizing image or text, and Indigeneity."[27] Similarly, Raheja defines visual sovereignty as both a cinematic and a reading practice, understanding "visual sovereignty as a way of reimagining Native-centered articulations of self-representation and autonomy that engage the powerful ideologies of mass media, but that do not rely solely on the texts and contexts of Western jurisprudence."[28] Visual sovereignty thus operates on two levels—on the one hand, it provides "the possibility of engaging and deconstructing representations of Indigenous peoples generated by the Whites"; on the other, "it intervenes in larger discussions of Native American sovereignty by locating and advocating for indigenous cultural and political power both within and outside of Western legal jurisprudence."[29] In this, the concept of sovereignty as discussed by Raheja coincides with that developed by Mohawk anthropologist Audra Simpson, who suggested three layers of meaning that Indigenous peoples must constantly negotiate: the structures imposed by settler colonial governments; the ancestral nations that preceded the arrival

of the settlers; and the daily life of Indigenous people who must constantly function on these two other levels, which intersect in different ways.[30]

Obomsawin's film actualizes the concept of visual sovereignty in a very interesting way. It features images and discourses from the Mohawk communities
that refer to and deconstruct the representations of the armed conflict and the
outlaw warrior figure conveyed by the mass media in the summer of 1990. It
also conveys the event using Indigenous words and experiences, both contemporary and historical, in such a way as to give a central place in the narrative to
the cultural and political power of the Mohawk, Haudenosaunee, and Indigenous peoples in general, a power that operates both within and outside the settler state framework of law and the courts, without nonetheless being reduced
by or measured against it.

THE STORY YOU WILL SEE TAKES PLACE . . .

The sustained siege at Kanehsatake and Kahnawake was an affirmation that
broke with the invisibility and silence of Indigenous peoples to which the dominant society had become accustomed by the early 1990s. *Kanehsatake: 270
Years of Resistance* assumes a point of view that is in line with the director's cinematic process of listening to and presenting multiple voices. Obomsawin gives
primacy of place to history, especially that of the Indigenous peoples, which
nonetheless does not prevent her from rejecting any pretense to objectivity. She
has explicitly refused to accede to the expectations of the critics, who charged
her with producing a biased view rather than a balanced account of the Oka
Crisis.[31] In 2010, in Kahnawake, she responded to a question about the difference between a documentary and a propaganda film by stating that her films
communicate a point of view, and she went on to explain that any filmed story
necessarily implies choices,[32] involving the inevitable partiality we discussed earlier. Despite this admission of inevitable partiality, and probably also because of
it, the filmmaker takes pains to grasp the situation experienced by her protagonists as accurately as possible and to describe, from this perspective, the historical context for the political struggles of Indigenous peoples. In this sense, the
point of view she adopts bears witness to a heightened awareness of the power
relations at work in a history's construction and particularly in the history of
Kanehsatake, which was brought abruptly to the surface by the event.

Art historian Steven Leuthold wrote that Indigenous peoples often see the
documentary film as "a form of statement of historical truth speaking . . . a way

of accurately recording and presenting both history and contemporary lives in contrast to the fictitious world portrayed in popular imagery [like Hollywood movies]."[33] Obomsawin's documentary seems to proceed from this attitude, showing a reality of the siege that was not seen in the mass media outlets. In contrast to the spectacular images and stereotypical figures circulated by the media, the film offers a perceptive version of the real-life experience of the protestors and the Mohawk communities, who, surrounded by police and military forces, persisted in asserting their sovereignty and their determination to continue the struggle. At the beginning of his book *Peace, Power, Righteousness*, Taiaiake Alfred wrote that he made a great effort to "grasp and convey a knowledge situated in and respectful of the shared experiences of our peoples."[34] It seems that is also what Obomsawin wants to do by producing a film on the political conflict, based on a methodology that engages multiple Indigenous voices and perspectives. According to Randolph Lewis, "her cinematic vision reflects an Indigenous sovereign gaze, a practice of looking that comes out of Native experience and shapes the nature of the film itself."[35]

In the way that it grants importance to listening to people speak and to a collective creation of the diegesis, in many respects Obomsawin's cinematic process resembles that of Québécois filmmaker Pierre Perrault.[36] Like Perrault, Obomsawin is very definitely a "filmmaker of speech." According to Randolph Lewis, she also draws on the Abenaki oral tradition, which gives a central role to listening, understanding, and transmitting knowledge orally. In talking about her documentary process, she insists on the fundamental role of speech, or word, and the collective nature of the account being constructed: "It's not the image. It's the word that's important. It's what people are saying. . . . It's the people themselves who tell me what they are and what the story is. And . . . if it means listening for 15 hours with one person, I'll do it."[37]

In the case of the 1990 crisis, not only does the filmmaker begin her documentary project without a script, but she is, like everyone else, completely uncertain of the siege's outcome. Having projected herself into the event, she collects verbal accounts and shots that dictate the story of the armed conflict she will then relate in a documentary film. *Kanehsatake: 270 Years of Resistance* makes a place for the voices of the people directly engaged in the conflict, including that of the filmmaker, who provides the voice-over narration. The film becomes a real site for speech, like the armed siege that takes Indigenous speech into the centre of the public space. In the style of her ancestors, who transmitted through storytelling the massacre of the Odanak village by General Roger in 1759, Obomsawin, as Lewis says, "zooms in on one moment of extreme crisis to provide a marginalized perspective on a critical historical event."[38]

The film does not present an argument in order to justify an Indigenous point of view to dominant settler institutions, and neither does it set out to dismantle their legal and institutional framework. As indicated by the first words of the voice-over narration, it rather intends to relate the events as if in a story developed and delivered in the oral tradition: "The story you will see takes place near Montreal, in Kanehsatake, a Mohawk village near the town of Oka, and in Kahnawake, a Mohawk reserve, south of the city, at the Mercier bridge." After having located the site of the action with the visual of a map of the region, the narrator, off-screen, informs the viewer of the immediate cause of the conflict—the project to expand the golf course—which threatens to extend the encroachment initiated with the construction of the first nine holes in the 1950s. Shots showing golfers on the land next to the pine woods are followed by a scene of Mayor Ouellet summarily telling the media that he refuses to abandon the golf course project. The next people to speak are two individuals who have spent the summer behind the barricades: first, Kahentiiosta, a Mohawk woman who is also the protagonist in another film in the four-part series; second, Ellen Gabriel, an activist and artist from Kanehsatake who was one of the spokespersons for the Mohawk negotiation team during the crisis.

The two women, one of them sitting in the Pines, the other in what seems to be an artist's studio, tell the camera what happened on the morning of 11 July 1990. Refering to the political role of women in the Haudenosaunee Confederacy and contemporary Mohawk communities, Gabriel explains that on noticing the arrival of the police, she and several other women instinctively went to meet them, because it is their obligation "to protect the land . . . to protect our mother." The two speakers provide details about the scene, and it is only after they have finished speaking that we see images of the exchange of fire marking the eruption of the event. The film plays on the contrast between the police violence and the peaceful location. First there is a sequence showing the fog of tear gas, the police entry into the Pines, and chaotic images of trees taken during the shootout. We then see a shot of the pine woods with quiet, contemplative music under it, as the narrator gravely summarizes what has just happened. The event's sudden eruption is thus framed by the voices of Mohawk women that give it meaning and place it in the context of their respective communities.

Notably, the film does not rely on the commentary of a detached expert or some other authority who would pronounce on the facts at a remove. Just as the Mohawks who are interviewed are speaking from the siege site, the government representatives, when expressing themselves in this film, are shown as being active parties in the conflict. They are most often seen in the middle of a crowd, especially when addressing the media. Obomsawin constructs her argument by juxtaposing words and images that support or contradict one another, depending on the topic. In this way, she presents her perspective very clearly without actually stating it, allowing the viewers to draw their own conclusions from the succession of shots and sequences in the film. The chaos resulting from the event's sudden breach is brought out by numerous scenes shot in the larger space of the conflict. These scenes include roadblocks with lines of police vehicles next to the barricades, media conferences given by various political actors surrounded by journalists, and many locations where people gathered to talk, argue, comfort, or confront one another, express their anger, or shout out their indignation.

The settler viewpoint is rarely present in the film, except in declarations by political and military figures that are exposed as lies by juxtaposed images and succeeding shots presenting contradictory evidence. For example, a sequence in which Albert Nerenberg tells the camera how he managed to sneak onto the siege site is intercut with the shot of an embarrassed soldier answering a volley of questions from reporters by flatly denying that a journalist could have crossed the Canadian Army's perimeter. The discrediting of Mohawk protestors' statements by the authorities during the crisis gives way, in the film, to the lies, betrayals, and broken promises of political figures from the Quebec and Canadian governments, whether during the event or in the larger historical context.

The film shows disturbing images of the crowds from neighbouring suburbs who physically attack police officers, threaten to cross the perimeter to attack the Mohawks as well, and, with tremendous symbolic violence, burn an Indigenous warrior in effigy. These images are taken up by the narration, which frames the white mob's disorderly violence by using a calm, even tone. Further, the scenes of settler violence are often contrasted with peaceful shots from inside the perimeter. Lewis explained that, in this way, the insults aimed at the Mohawks are turned back against their speakers. The film marginalizes and denounces the dominant forces that move against the assertive Indigenous presence at the siege site. Conversely, it recruits to its cause the Québécois and Canadian groups and individuals who supported the Kanehsatake Mohawks' struggle. An example is a sequence in which Québécois demonstrators march through Châteauguay holding up a red banner reading "Regroupement de solidarité avec les autochtones [Association in solidarity with the Indigenous peoples]."

Michelle Raheja explained that in the silent film *Nanook of the North* by Robert Flaherty, the Inuit protagonists were making signs to the camera that an audience made up of non-Indigenous people or people from other Indigenous nations would not necessarily understand. However, they sent a clear message to Inuit viewers that they found the film very funny. Raheja highlights the effectiveness of a visual sovereignty tactic that consists in "laughing at the camera," which can mean mocking it or laughing into it. Whether they were appearing in ethnographic or Hollywood films, Indigenous actors often used this tactic to "confront the spectator with the often absurd assumptions that circulate around visual representations of Native Americans, while also flagging their involvement and, to some degree, complicity in these often disempowering structures of cinematic dominance and stereotypes."[39] This tactic is demonstrated in action in the documentary film *Reel Injun,* directed by Catherine Bainbridge, Neil Diamond, and Jeremiah Hayes. The film includes a sequence from a Hollywood movie in which a character says something very solemnly in an Indigenous language, and the actual translation can be read in subtitles.[40] In a humorous way, this sequence illustrates the contrast between the representation the U.S. producers were after and the impertinent dialogue the Indigenous actor inserts into that representation, without the producers being aware of the ploy. In a similar fashion, in the film *Okanada,* Ronald Cross, known as Lasagne, parodies his own role by drawing on images from Hollywood Westerns.

The film *Kanehsatake: 270 Years of Resistance* also includes numerous comical scenes made up of shots taken on the siege site. Unlike Flaherty's protagonists and the actors in Hollywood films who were laughing at the camera, however, the people filmed by Obomsawin are the camera's accomplices, as very clearly indicated by some glances at the lens. On the site, jokes were often made without the knowledge, or at the expense, of the targets, especially if they were police officers or soldiers. For example, one scene shows an outraged soldier accusing the Mohawk demonstrators behind the barricades of having thrown eggs at the military. When one of the warriors assures him that his men have done no such thing, the soldier, still extremely offended, points out where one of the eggs was smashed against a tank. We can sense the irony and amusement in the way warrior Robert Skidder, known as Mad Jap, responds to the ire of the soldier, who is apparently too angry to catch on. This humorous skit played out before the camera underlines the absurdity of the scene and the incongruity of the offence, since in the final analysis an egg seems rather harmless compared to a tank. The scene ends when the soldier proposes to film the damage with the very camera that is being used to shoot the exchange from inside the barricades. This is followed by Obomsawin's reaction, obviously refusing to let the Canadian Army get its hands on her camera. Humour is featured in many of the film's scenes as a way to dedramatize the situation and ease the narrative while bringing out forms of resistance that, especially in the context of the armed conflict, are located, in Raheja's words, "along a spectrum of political and social efficacy."[41]

UNITED FRONT IN THE PINES

The film counters key representations of settlement by locating the issues of the territorial conflict on the site from which they sprang. In a context where "imperialism and capitalism, whether in the consumer society or in the neocolonized country, veil everything behind a screen of images and appearances," argued Latin-American film directors Fernando Solanas and Octavio Getino, "the restitution of things to their real place and meaning is an eminently subversive act."[42] In the summer of 1990, the event broke into the visible realm and actualized power relations in the siege space. In a situation in which Indigenous peoples had been systematically erased or sidelined, the film resorts to a consistent media strategy of highlighting what is meant to be obliterated.

The land, the Pines, and the cemetery remain central to the film, representing both an issue in the dispute and a place of habitation to which members of the Kanehsatake community are closely connected. From the film's outset, the narration locates the story inside Mohawk territory ("the story you will see takes place . . . "), and then describes the municipal project to expand the golf course, over images of golfers on the course. When the planned encroachment is mentioned, the camera gradually pulls back, slowly revealing the pine woods and headstones. The camera's movement locates the filmmaker on the threatened site. Further, it seems to imitate the movement of the town's projected encroachment on land that, as the narration unequivocally states, belongs to the Mohawks. With these words, there is a close-up of the sign nailed to one of the trees, marking in capital letters the boundary that is not to be crossed: "MOHAWK TERRITORY! NO TRESPASSING!" The narrator continues by saying that the notice, which is at the entrance to the territory targeted by the town, has gone unheeded, and this prompted a peaceful occupation of the site in March. We then see images of several casually dressed Mohawk men and women quietly seated on logs set up in a circle at the edge of the woods.

Once the issues involved in the land dispute have been outlined, the film's title appears on the screen, over an Indigenous song. The title is superimposed on an image of the pine woods and the headstones in the cemetery marking the place where the ancestors are buried on the site. Inscriptions carved in Mohawk in the stone show how deeply rooted the community is in the territory and the language. Having recorded the siege's setting, the scene shifts a short distance to the barricades built of Sûreté du Québec vehicles newly tipped up across the road, this time to the accompaniment of lively music. The camera again sweeps past the trees in the Pines, while the narrator mentions the sense of unity that followed the failed police assault: "The Mohawks now present a united front despite the tensions among different factions in Kanehsatake." In this way, the film highlights the forces focused on the site in the Pines that the community is determined to protect.

The strong presence of the pine woods throughout the film refers to the territorial conflict behind the Oka Crisis, or Kanehsatake resistance. It also recalls the sacred aspect of the land in which the forest, like the community, has its roots. Steven Leuthold noted that the Indigenous aesthetic is characterized by a profound sense of place that comes out of a close connection between spirituality and what he described as "nature,"[43] a concept better understood in terms of world or environment. In the film, the land becomes the backdrop against which the features of the story are drawn, all the more forcefully because it is what is at stake in the armed conflict. The film eloquently ends with the words of the two women who began the documentary narrative. In conclusion, they reassert a relation to the world and the earth that takes its meaning from a world view not categorically defined in terms of administrative territorial limits, and not separating nature from culture, as in the Western tradition. Speaking about the grove of great pines, Kahentiiosta states, "That's a part of us, that's a part of me." And about the people who had actively defended the Pines, Ellen Gabriel observes, "They were a small number of people, but the quality of the people that were there was just outstanding." The very last image in the film appears after these words are spoken. It shows a mask set on a stick planted in the earth, with the setting sun shining through its eyes, as if to signal the spiritual power of the resistance. The film sees the land threatened by development in relation to the people who live there, and imposing limits on encroachment as a matter of their collective survival.

270 YEARS OF RESISTANCE: THE HISTORICAL RECONSTRUCTION

By rooting the Mohawk protestors and communities in the land they are defending, *Kanehsatake: 270 Years of Resistance* helps to uncover the hidden depths of the non-event brought to the surface by the event. As mentioned at the beginning of this book, imposing Western forms of legitimacy and legality resulted in a territorial dispossession of which the details have often been erased. Alanis Obomsawin considers it essential that the Indigenous youth of today and tomorrow should be able to understand the territory and the history of its loss. She explained that this understanding, which she seeks to instill through documentary filmmaking, is made more crucial by the fact that the land and its natural resources remain the fundamental issue in most of the conflicts involving Indigenous peoples.[44] For this reason, it seems imperative that the encroachment process and the sense of territory be understood by future generations, and that current struggles be linked to the struggles of previous generations. This is pointed up in the film's title, *Kanehsatake: 270 Years of Resistance*, and continues to be evoked in the current struggles for the protection of Indigenous lands and waters, and the honouring of treaties.

To underline the historical continuity of the resistance, the film identifies the siege undergone by the Mohawk communities as a direct sequel to what their ancestors lived through. Since individuals and societies perceive the injustices of centuries past more easily than those taking place today, this way of connecting the resistance of the previous century to that of the Oka Crisis transfers the legitimacy of past struggles to the actions of the Mohawk protestors in 1990. In a sequence with the trees in the background, a Kanehsatà:ke Elder, Muriel Nicholas, tells the camera: "My great-grandfather, my grandfather and my father have been fighting over this, and I never thought that I'm going to see it, myself, come up like this." This statement is followed by a sequence of white rioters preventing the delivery of food supplies to people behind the barricades and in the Mohawk communities, with some of the rioters attacking the police. We then see images of tanks driving through the village of Oka. When helicopters are shown landing on the shore of the Lake of Two Mountains, the narrator points out the irony that the army is landing on the same spot where the colonial conflict had begun over two centuries before.

The living testimony of Kanehsatà:ke protagonists is supported by an historical reconstruction that includes models, photographs, and archival documents. The reconstruction features the occupation of the territory since time immemorial, Iroquois political and spiritual structures, the Two Dog or Two Wolf Wampum, and the words of famous Mohawk chiefs. The voice-over pronounced by Obomsawin emphasizes the Mohawk people's lengthy history in the territory of the St. Lawrence Valley, while the screen shows a model of fifty longhouses surrounded by a palisade. Outside it, a cornfield surrounds the Iroquois village at the foot of Mount Royal, this at the time of Jacques Cartier's first visit. The following sequence relates the forced departures that accompanied the settlers' appropriation of the Island of Montreal and the establishment at Kanehsatà:ke of a group of Mohawks, on land described in the voice-over as part of ancient Mohawk hunting grounds. By basing the historical reconstruction on the Mohawk historiography, the film implicitly supports the grounds for the Mohawk land claims and the assertions of sovereignty on the siege site. The filmmaker has clearly taken a position, which is inevitable when a person is faced by a colonial conflict that has never been resolved. We must keep in mind that a filmed account from the federal government's point of view would also take a stance, but would probably seem more "objective" to settler viewers because it relays the dominant position.

In *The Archive and the Repertoire: Performing Cultural Memory in the Americas*, Diana Taylor reminded us that "part of the colonizing project throughout the Americas consisted in discrediting autochtonous ways of preserving and communicating historical understanding,"[45] for example, by refuting the validity of oral history and significant cultural performances. By eloquently opposing these accounts, the historical reconstruction provided by Obomsawin reverses the colonial campaign that was—and still is—conducted by Canada. Giving full value to the wampum, the film account reiterates the words of Chief Aghneeta when he presented Sir William Johnson with a wampum belt in order to have the Mohawks' territorial rights protected by the British Crown. In contradiction, the voice-over narration explains that royal transfer had been granted to the Sulpicians in the name of the king of France, who was then only six years old, which highlights the symbolic basis of royal power as well as the incongruous nature of certain Western practices. Regarding Obomsawin's documentary work, Randolph Lewis observed that it expresses a concern for putting the policies of the various Indigenous nations "on an equal footing with non-Indigenous policies in the public imagination, the political process, and the law within Canada and the international community."[46] This process takes on an explicitly political dimension in a documentary on the Oka Crisis or resistance at Kanehsatake.

The reconstruction makes a place in history for Joseph Onasakenrat, a Mohawk chief who markedly influenced Kanehsatà:ke's history in the nineteenth century. The voice-over informs us that, having learned to read and write, Onasakenrat discovered that the Séminaire de Saint-Sulpice had transferred the title to the seigneury of the Lake of Two Mountains to its own name without informing the Mohawks, who were thus dispossessed of their land without their knowledge. Chief Onasakenrat, accompanied by men from the community, then presented himself with weapons in hand to the Sulpicians and ordered them to clear out, a determined gesture if ever there was one, no doubt more radical than the defensive posture adopted by the protestors in the summer of 1990. Taking up a Mohawk discourse that had been repeated over the generations, Chief Onasakenrat reasserted the connection to the land as he spoke out against a colonial movement that sought to uproot and relocate the community: "This land is ours. Ours as a heritage given to us as a sacred legacy. It is a place where our fathers lie beneath those trees, our mothers sang our lullaby. And you would tear it from us and leave us wanderers at the mercy of fate?" Despite being threatened with life imprisonment, adds the voice-over, Chief Onasakenrat refused to obey the Sulpicians, who were urging him to move to Ontario with his community. He replied: "We will never go there. We will die on the soil of our fathers and our bleaching skeletons shall be a witness to nations yet unborn of Rome's injustice and greed." While these words are being recited, archival photographs of families and chiefs from Kanehsatà:ke fill the screen, rendering concrete the historical presence of the ancestors who had refused to leave their land, like the protestors and community members in 1990.

The historical reconstruction concludes with an archival photograph showing police officers in uniform, while the narrator comments: "In response, the priests asked Quebec to send police, who imprisoned Chief Joseph and many of the people of Kanehsatà:ke. In July 1990, this sad legacy continues." The arrests mentioned in the reconstruction foreshadow the arrests of Mohawk protestors that we see at the end of the film. They also recall the statement of a Mohawk woman in Alec G. MacLeod's documentary film *Acts of Defiance*, who exclaims in anger and exasperation during the siege at Kahnawà:ke, "Every time we stand up for our rights, we get arrested!" Because it is described as resistance to a colonial push in *Kanehsatake: 270 Years of Resistance*, the siege does not appear to be a legal infraction, but rather resistance that had been made necessary by ongoing encroachment.

At the commemoration of the event's twenty years, in 2010, Alanis Obomsawin said with emotion that she almost always includes archival materials in her films for the express purpose of reappropriating a history that the First Nations have been denied. It has been denied and stolen to such a point that "a lot of our people didn't know who they were anymore. They were forced to be invisible."[47] The filmmaker explained that this forced invisibility, when internalized, is the source of an individual and collective alienation that she tries to counteract with her documentaries. Speaking about what film historian Marc Ferro describes as the "rivalries, conflicts and battles for influence" at work in film production,[48] she reported that in the final editing stages for *Kanehsatake: 270 Years of Resistance,* one of her producers wanted to see the historical reconstruction withdrawn, but she refused to distribute the film without that section, considering it to be crucial. About the First Nations, she explained, "For me, for us, history is *very* important. There is not a film I will make without the historical context . . . because our history, they've *stolen* it from us!"[49] While this can seem distanced from a non-Indigenous stance, her preoccupation takes on its full meaning when seen from the perspective of the First Nations, Métis, and Inuit who have been dispossessed of their history, regarding both their dealings with settler societies and their own concerns.

In *Peace, Power, Righteousness: An Indigenous Manifesto,* Taiaiake Alfred promotes the development of an intellectual, social, and political movement that would reinvigorate traditional values and cultural elements and integrate them into the contemporary political reality. His idea consists in counteracting a dual suppression of Indigenous voices: "Not only has the indigenous voice been excluded from the larger social and political discourse, but even within our own communities it has been supplanted by other voices."[50] To counter this silence, Obomsawin sees the documentary as a place for speaking in which Indigenous people can express and define their experiences and struggles. The medium helps to make Indigenous voices heard by a large and diverse audience, and, in an essential way, make them present and alive within the communities themselves.

Rather than relying on the norms and discourse of the established order, Obomsawin offers a filmed account of the Kanehsatà:ke resistance that develops and takes its shape from the Mohawk experiences and speech that then become the real authority. In writing about "rhetorical sovereignty," Ojibwe literary scholar Scott Richard Lyons insisted on the fact that, despite repeated attempts to erase it, the "discourses of resistance and renewal have never ceased in Indian country, and these marginalized narratives of the continuing struggle for Indian sovereignty are making themselves more and more visible in public representations and talk."[51] The siege that was sustained at Kanehsatà:ke and Kahnawà:ke clearly contributes to this movement by renewing and making visible the persistent, determined assertion and exercise of Mohawk sovereignty.

As well as equating the discourses expressed on the siege site to the community's and confederacy's historical discourses of resistance, the documentary aligns the Mohawks' struggle with the struggles of Indigenous peoples everywhere on the continent. Over sequences featuring the peace camp at Oka, close to the Kanehsatake barricades, the narration states that some 2,500 protestors[52] gathered to express their support for the Mohawks. A large, colourful crowd is shown, with men singing to the beat of a large drum in the centre of their circle and speeches by influential political figures, illustrating the spirit that suffused the camp. Other shots intercut with these images show Ovide Mercredi, then the regional vice-chief of Manitoba's Assembly of First Nations, making a solemn address to the crowd. Speaking slowly and firmly, pausing after each phrase, he asks:

> Why is it
> that we live in a country
> where the police never come
> to the aid of the Aboriginal people?
> And yet we see them
> across this country
> being utilized by provincial governments
> to suppress the rights
> of the Aboriginal people of this country.

Mercredi's points are confirmed by the historical reconstruction describing the arrest of Chief Joseph Onasakenrat and his men, once again linking resistance to oppression, past to present. In the same sequence we can see Elijah Harper, the Indigenous member of the Legislative Assembly of Manitoba who had refused to ratify the Meech Lake Accord, speaking out to declare that it is neither the Indigenous peoples nor the people of Quebec who represent the greatest threat to the country's unity, as so often heard in the media, but rather the lack of leadership on the part of the Canadian government.

These addresses by Indigenous leaders are shot on the very site of the gathering, emphasizing the effect of presence and centrality of Indigenous mobilization. Conversely, the public speeches of Canada's prime minister Brian Mulroney and Quebec's premier Robert Bourassa are shown in the documentary only on televisions the Mohawk protestors have set up behind the barricades. They are conveyed to the viewer exclusively from inside the siege area, alongside the warriors and journalists who are watching the news, which creates an effect of distancing from the government authorities in power. The editing thus frames a subtle but sustained criticism regarding the governments' lack of engagement in the territorial conflict. This criticism is added to the recriminations that are heard throughout the siege concerning what is perceived as a failure on the Canadian government's part to fulfill its responsibilities. It also coincides with the coroner's report on the inquest, which concluded that the decision to intervene in the situation at Oka on 11 July 1990 was an error, adding that the Sûreté du Québec should not have to shoulder the blame, since "faced by the Oka Crisis, of which the police intervention was a part, the Québécois simply lacked government" (Quebec 1995, 398).

The film also devotes attention to the various forms of solidarity that were active on the siege site. In doing so, it counters the strategy of isolation implemented by the authorities as the conflict progressed, as well as the process of exile that cut off the Indigenous peoples from their stories and what binds them to their families, communities, land, and language. During the crisis, the governments set out to dissociate the territorial conflict at Kanehsatake from what was going on in the other Mohawk communities. By contrast, the film brings out the connections that existed between the communities. For example, it showed the strong reactions of the Kanehsatake last occupiers when they learned that the police and military had invaded Tekakwitha Island and the longhouse in Kahnawake. Further, the film makes visible the presence of people from other Canadian provinces, the United States, and Mexico who were sympathetic to the Mohawk cause. It shows newspaper clippings of protests across Canada supporting the Mohawks, and a spiritual leader from Mexico carrying out ceremonies around an army tank and soldiers at Kanehsatake. By doing so, the film includes the struggles of the Kanehsata'kehró:non in Indigenous struggles on the national and continental levels.

Obomsawin uses various devices to render more palpable the solidarity that developed and was manifest on the siege site. The continuity and extent of Indigenous resistance were expressed through individuals, objects, and the media. Among the shots taken during the siege, there is one of Mi'gmaq spiritual leader Tom Paul, known as The General, sitting at the foot of a tree in camouflage and talking about the importance of a return to spiritual ways, because "that way everybody will be strong." In a tribute to Paul, who died two years after the crisis at the age of forty-nine, the narrator says that, in his lifetime, Paul had participated in many acts of resistance, at Wounded Knee, Ganienkeh, Restigouche, Akwesasne, and Kanehsatake. By tracing the personal history of this Mi'gmaq activist, the film links the actions of the Mohawk protestors and their sympathizers to other political protests in contemporary Indigenous history, in which Mohawk political actors often played a key role.

The connections between the Indigenous protestors inside and outside the barricades were also conveyed through the media. In another sequence, it is noted that a speech given by Lakota-Oglala activist Russell Means at Oka's peace camp is heard live on the radio by both the warriors behind the barricades and a woman at a community radio station. By itself, this sequence shows an act of solidarity being carried out across the greater area of the siege—in the peace camp, at the barricades, and at the radio station. It thus makes connections among the gestures and presence of various political actors. While they have their attention focused on this event, the sequence connects them to several other signal events in Indigenous political struggles from the recent history of Turtle Island, such as the occupation of Alcatraz Island in 1969, the occupation of the Bureau of Indian Affairs in Washington by the American Indian Movement in 1972, and the siege at Wounded Knee in 1973. As well, in a scene taking place at the peace camp, the continuity of resistance is expressed through a sacred object. We see an Indigenous protestor who tries, in front of the camera, to convince the police officers to let him join the people behind the barricades, explaining that his small group is holding a calumet, a ceremonial pipe, that had been used during negotiations at Wounded Knee nearly twenty years before.

According to Randolph Lewis, the cinema of sovereignty practised by Obomsawin consists precisely in recognizing and highlighting the gestures and symbols that would go unnoticed by someone who is outside the community of belonging. Unlike certain ethnographic films, hers do not attempt to record moments the community intends to hide from the camera, or, as Lewis also noted, to expose any kind of exoticism or primitivism.[53] Further, as Steven Leuthold observed, Indigenous cinema helps to maintain and create a sense of identity among Indigenous peoples, while ensuring continuity with ancient objects and such concepts as place, sacred elements, and natural cycles. A feature of this film is its ability to bring out how these concepts are expressed in the siege space, at the event's centre.

Obomsawin steers away from the stereotypes that were reproduced or generated by the media representations of Mohawk warriors during the crisis. In her documentary narrative, she places emphasis on the embodied politics that are lived out in a unique, perceptible way within the siege space. In one scene, after the voice-over narration has announced the advance of the Canadian Army, we see Obomsawin herself in conversation on a park bench with a masked warrior, whose eyes are hidden behind dark glasses, an AK-47-type weapon in his lap, with trees and the lake in the background. While she listens attentively, leaning slightly in his direction, the warrior identified by the pseudonym "Wizard" softly explains that, as a traditionalist, he follows the Haudenosaunee Constitution that was given to his people by the Creator. He then clarifies the meaning and role of the warriors, *rotisken'raké:ta*, a term that in the Mohawk language essentially means "the men." According to the constitution, he continues, it is the men's responsibility to protect the people within the circle of the confederacy. Each of his sentences is intercut with shots of Canadian soldiers being trained to fire rocket launchers from tanks lined up in a row. Unlike the conversation on the bench, which is shot at head height, the tanks are often seen from below. Juxtaposing this intimate conversation with the images of the military preparing to put an end to the siege sets up a telling contrast that confirms the relevance of the duty to protect being described, not to mention deconstructing the settlers' mythical image of the warriors as "monstrous beings."[54]

Altogether, *Kanehsatake: 270 Years of Resistance* shows us men who are very concerned about the future of their nation and who base their resistance on the Haudenosaunee version of legitimacy. Further, the film gives great importance to the individuality and humanity of the Mohawk warriors and Indigenous protesters from other nations, as well as to their community relationships, in particular by showing that they stand alongside the women and children who are taking part in the political action. To be noted is that Obomsawin focuses on the issues of territory and sovereignty without addressing the contentious matter of the Mohawk Warrior Society or the divisions between different factions within the communities. It seems that she is trying instead to lay the foundation for unity and, to this end, bringing out fundamental issues and shared feelings.

RETERRITORIALIZING MOHAWK POLITICS

By shaking up the norms and values of the Canadian and Québécois populace, the Oka Crisis generated "new forms of judgement" among them, to use Alexa Conradi's phrase.[55] The event also interpellated the First Nations, but in a very different way. The siege became a real space of identification for the Indigenous peoples, who saw their existence and their pursuits confirmed there, all the more forcefully because the protestors were confronting the foundational violence of a state that had been established at great cost to them. In that regard, the siege generated a renewed certainty that was reinforced by the sight of tanks in the streets of Kanehsatake, since they represented that same settler state.

One episode that exposed the deep-rooted conflict of legitimacies that lay at the centre of the Oka Crisis, or the resistance at Kanehsatà:ke, was the signing of an agreement on three prerequisites to be met before negotiations could begin. The signing ceremony took place on 12 August 1990, when the siege had already stretched on for a month. The agreement was drawn up by the parties at the conclusion of intense negotiations conducted before Justice Alan B. Gold, the mediator named by the federal government. Under its terms, the governments of Canada and Quebec pledged to ensure free access to medications, food, and clothing; free passage for spiritual leaders, clan mothers, chiefs, council members, and lawyers identified by the Mohawks; and the presence of foreign observers during the negotiation process.[56] As agreed, the ceremony took place behind the barricades at Kanehsatà:ke in the presence of mediator Gold, the two representatives of the Quebec and Canadian governments, John Ciaccia and Tom Siddon, and five representatives of the Mohawk nation, including Water David Sr. and Walter David Jr.[57] At the last minute, a masked warrior sat down at the table in the seat of one of the designated representatives. He signed his Mohawk name at the bottom of the document, in front of cameras that recorded and immediately transmitted the scene to all the media outlets in the country. He then ceremoniously handed a Mohawk flag to one of the government representatives, who had no choice but to accept it.[58]

In his book *Oka: A Political Crisis and Its Legacy*, Harry Swain, the deputy minister of Indian Affairs and Northern Development at that time, observed that signing this agreement cost the governments dearly, since they saw their representatives publicly ridiculed and humiliated: "After all the promises of not negotiating with armed and masked men, or at the point of a gun, or while the barricades were up, the governments had allowed their most senior representatives to be manipulated into a Mohawk photo op. Never mind that the document was an innocuous statement of bland principles and understandings long reached. The Quebec media went nuts. Châteauguay rioted. Former Kanesatake grand chief Clarence Simon belatedly denounced the agreement as 'void and non-existent,' objecting to a lack of Kanesatake representation on the committee that signed it."[59] To appease those who were outraged, the federal government pointed out that it was only a procedural agreement. However, this argument was weakened when it was learned, as Swain reported, that a document in the Mohawk language, whose text was different from those in English and French, had been slipped into the pile as a translation, and that this document, which in fact laid out the Mohawk activists' sovereignty objectives, was signed by the ministers of Indian Affairs from Quebec and Canada.[60] This episode, which so outraged the Québécois, is described in detail in the film, but in a completely different light.

In Obomsawin's documentary, the episode is depicted as a solemn and very serious moment bringing hope, as the narrator's introduction indicates: "There is a feeling of hope and reverence as John Cree leads Mohawk negotiators and representatives of both governments across the original barricade." The film shows the negotiators walking two abreast towards the Pines, guided by spiritual leader John Cree, who is dressed in ceremonial regalia with the traditional headdress and staff. He is followed in the prescribed order by two Mohawk women and the five Mohawk representatives, all dressed in traditional shirts, and then the two government representatives and the mediator in suits. A young man carrying a Mohawk flag completes the procession. In the scene that shows a boundary being crossed, the Mohawk activists lead the participants as they all climb over the low earthen berm making up the original barricade. They enter the woods and are clearly in Mohawk territory, as announced in capital letters by a bilingual banner that had been hanging right above this boundary since the occupation in the spring: "ARE YOU AWARE THAT THIS IS MOHAWK TERRITORY? / SAVEZ-VOUS QUE CECI EST TERRITOIRE MOHAWK?" The next shot shows a Mohawk woman, Konwaitanonha, reciting the prayer of thanks to the Creator in the Mohawk language. We then see one of the Mohawk negotiators, Joe Deom, declaring that the barricades will come down when the parties reach an agreement. He reminds the assembled audience that "these barricades are just a physical manifestation of the barricades that have existed between our nations since contact occurred in the Western hemisphere almost 500 years ago."

While these representatives deliver their presentations on their feet in the gathering, the negotiators are shown seated at the table, with the governments' representatives to one side and the Mohawks' to the other. Media sound recorders have been set down in the middle of the table, which is covered by a highly symbolic Hudson's Bay Company blanket. Behind it, in a semi-circle, stand fifty people in attendance, and behind them, between two tall pines, we can see hanging next to each other a Quebec flag, a Mohawk flag, the Hiawatha flag of the Six Nations, and a Canadian flag. While the voice-over lists the prerequisites for the negotiations, the representatives are shown signing the documents, and, in the crowd, there is jubilation over this significant event. Once the agreement has been signed, we hear a speech by the eloquent Mohawk spokesperson Ellen Gabriel that is received seriously and solemnly. First, in Mohawk, with the translation provided in subtitles, she says, "Today, I am proud to be an Indian." She waits a beat before continuing in English, seriously and with dignity, punctuating each phrase: with a pause:

> I am proud to state that
> I am a Mohawk
> within the Mohawk nation
> of the Six Nations Iroquois Confederacy.

> When we started this blockade
> something had to come out of it
> that would progress our cause
> and unite our people.

> This agreement is something that
> our nation has been searching for
> for many years:
> recognition
> of who we are as a people
> not just as Mohawk people
> but as the first people
> of this continent.

> The struggle is not over.

as we say in Mohawk:
Skennen
which means peace.

Her speech, performed as part of this official ceremony, is followed by cheers and applause from the gathering, before other representatives are invited to speak.

With this pronouncement, Gabriel executes a reterritorialization of Mohawk identity and political power on the siege site. Standing in the middle of the Pines, she expresses her pride in her Mohawk identity, states her position within the nation, and connects it to the political and spiritual structure represented by the Six Nations Iroquois Confederacy. In so doing, she defines the political relationships that shape the confederacy. Making the initial occupation, the cause being defended, and the need for unity all elements of a single destiny, she explains that the agreement grants the Mohawks the recognition they have been seeking for many years. In pronouncing the word "recognition," she lifts her arm, with a ceremonial feather in her hand, and accompanies her statement with a ritual gesture. She then emphasizes that it is recognition obtained as a nation, and also as the continent's first peoples. What she is saying is endorsed by the armed conflict in the midst of which the ceremony is taking place, as she notes with emotion that the battle is not yet over. She concludes her speech with an appeal for peace, *skennen*, as it is understood in the Iroquois political philosophy. The filmmaker relates this episode as it was conceived by the Mohawk activists who staged it. She thus assigns a place to a Mohawk concept of sovereignty that comes into conflict with the settler state's concept but is nonetheless strongly held by the people who were present in the Pines that day. Like other films by Obomsawin, *Kanehsatake: 270 Years of Resistance* attests to a sovereign gaze that, according to Randolph Lewis, "is imbued with the self-respect and unique ambitions of a self-defined sovereign people, even if this sovereignty carries with it a complex and contested legal status."[61]

Contrary to the federal government's parlance about a simple procedural agreement, during a public talk held at Beaconsfield's Centennial Hall in 2012, Mohawk lawyer Martha Montour maintained that this ceremonial signing amounted to a treaty. Like the various treaties made between Indigenous peoples and settler governments since the initial contact, she added, the occasion of its signature in the Pines included significant elements of protocol, such as the presence of representatives from different governments, formal speeches, and the exchange of gifts. In this regard, anthropologist Rémi Savard also explained that the Europeans of earlier colonial times dealt with the Indigenous peoples nation-to-nation and that, by the very fact of participating in the Indigenous diplomatic protocol, they were confirming their recognition of Indigenous institutions.[62] In the summer of 1990, the signing of the agreement on the prerequisites to negotiation was indicative of the power relations operating during the siege. The government representatives were led onto Mohawk territory, where they participated with a certain nervosity in a formal ceremony conceived and conducted by the protesters. This political performance asserted a nation-to-nation relationship. Further, it recalled the political intertwining during the eighteenth century according to which, as Kathryn V. Muller explained, the participation of non-Indigenous governments in the Haudenosaunee political protocol demonstrated and confirmed a relationship of reciprocity rather than one of domination.[63] That is what comes out of this sequence showing the government representatives submitting to a formal ceremony conducted by the Mohawks. The same can be said of the sequence in the historical reconstruction showing the Haudenosaunee Confederacy chiefs gathered in a grand council in the presence of the British colonial authorities to discuss political negotiations relating to the transition from French to British rule.

In *The Archive and the Repertoire*, Diana Taylor speculated about what studying such performances could bring to light that the historical and literary documents leave obscure: "If, to study social memory and identity in the Americas, instead of disciplinary emphasis on literary and historical documents, we were to look through the lens of performed, embodied behaviors, what would we know that we do not know now? Whose stories, memories, and struggles might become visible? What tensions might performance behaviors show that would not be recognized in texts and documents?"[64] Harry Swain's description of this episode made no mention of the meaning and impact of the Indigenous political performances, if not to note that the Mohawk representatives were dressed rather casually. As a result, what comes out of his account differs in significant ways from what the ceremony details presented in the film allow us to take away from the scene.

The enactment of these political and cultural performances on the siege site, and their evident presence in Obomsawin's film, are that much more significant because such performances were directly targeted, forbidden, and erased by the colonial and settler state authorities. The siege therefore very clearly demonstrates the points at which the threads of history, politics, performance, and story came together. The suppression of the Haudenosaunee government, at times at gunpoint, and its forced replacement by the band council designed and run by the federal government did not put an end to government by the longhouse. On the contrary, this form of government persisted, and in 1990 it remained a real political force. This is what was demonstrated by the high-profile conflict, which was of course played out with weapons but was also an engagement of fundamental political and spiritual principles. By exposing the tension that was central to the issue of territory and the grounds for its legitimacy, the siege again shone the spotlight on the structural political stakes involved in the relationships between Indigenous peoples and settler societies in this country, and similarly on questions of sovereignty over land that have never been completely resolved. Because the film can create a space that is less constrained, forceful, and immediate in political terms than an armed conflict or negotiations between the parties, it has the advantage of being able to present more fully the significant, symbolic nature of a formal ceremony. It is also for this reason that it moves in the direction of visual sovereignty.

Further, by seeking to rally the parties around certain points of agreement, Obomsawin's documentary exercises a diplomacy that operates not only within the Indigenous communities concerned, but also within the greater public. It contains recordings of Indigenous speech that tally with the common claims of the First Peoples as well as non-Indigenous expressions of solidarity, but it does not put emphasis on the conflictual aspects of the signing ceremony in the Pines. The sequence thus shows the representatives in the process of signing the documents. But only briefly, among the others, do we see the masked warrior at the end of the table also signing. The director did not highlight the participation of this disputed signatory, or edit him out. As well, indicating a conciliatory intent, she did not include the sequence in which the warrior handed a Mohawk flag to a federal government representative who was forced to accept it, fully aware that he was being publicly and politically manipulated.

According to Michelle Raheja, "under visual sovereignty, filmmakers can deploy individual and community assertions of what sovereignty and self-representation mean and, through new media technologies, frame more imaginative renderings of Native American intellectual and cultural paradigms, such as the presentation of the spiritual and dream world, than are often possible in official political contexts."[65] The notion of visual sovereignty is that much more relevant when it concerns a documentary based on images shot during a siege that explicitly addressed the sovereignty of the Mohawk Nation and the Haudenosaunee Confederacy of which it is part. The film brings to the screen the cohesive, strategic, and uncompromising political stance of the Mohawk protestors, who forcefully asserted their sovereignty over the siege site. The documentary also lends visibility to the position of other Indigenous peoples whose survival is threatened, their constant struggle against ongoing encroachment, and their determined quest for justice, dignity, and redress.

Kanehsatake: 270 Years of Resistance does not look back at Oka by casting an outsider's eye on the armed conflict; it conveys the experience of the people behind the barricades from the standpoint of a shared experience of the conflict and its aftermath, including the siege's traumatic nature. Lewis quoted Ellen Gabriel as saying, "You would never be able to even describe—or people wouldn't believe—that this happened unless a documentary like Alanis' had come out."[66] In a very particular way, the Abenaki filmmaker set out to listen to the Indigenous protestors and communities, and then recount the armed conflict so as to transmit, diplomatically, the underlying issues that played out during the event. With her on-the-ground process and her cinematic creativity, Obomsawin uses the power of the documentary film to support Indigenous struggles that are generations old. In that, her work dovetails with the epistemological bases of Indigenous film, which, according to Randolph Lewis, consist in attentively listening and respecting the Indigenous forms of knowledge and history. In 2010, in Kahnawake, Obomsawin spoke about it as a means for Indigenous peoples to regain control of their existence collectively: "Documentary filmmaking is something that permits us to have a hold on our history, who we are, our traditions, our ways of thinking, our ways of living."[67] It seems that, based on experiences of the territorial conflict at Kanehsatake, the film has created what Cree researcher Neal McLeod calls an "ideological home." This home constitutes an interpretative place that "provides people with an Indigenous location to begin discourse, to tell stories and to live life on their own terms" (McLeod 2001, 19). It is the "layering of generations of stories, and the culmination of storyteller after storyteller, in a long chain of transmission" (19). This is precisely what the documentary establishes, laying the foundation for a shared discourse about the event by connecting the battles of the summer of 1990 with the struggles of past generations and the people of Kanehsatake with First Peoples elsewhere in the country.

By speaking out on the siege sites and in the public space during the event, the Mohawk and other Indigenous peoples affirmed a contemporary presence understood and expressed to be in a close relationship to the land and the stories and cultures of their respective nations. By doing so, they initiated what Jo-Ann Episkenew, drawing on the work of sociolinguist Charlotte Linde, described as a "relational act" that makes it possible to move from isolation to shared narratives, thus summoning an audience or, to put it otherwise, a community.[68] In this sense, the siege, as seen from an Indigenous perspective, encourages us to move from a paradigm of the view to a relational paradigm. It is precisely this relational paradigm that Alanis Obomsawin's documentary gives a shape to and amplifies, whether through the film's shooting, its editing, or its distribution.

CHAPTER 6

Settler Literary Narratives

In the decades since it occurred, the Oka crisis, or the resistance at Kanehsatà:ke, has inspired representations in several novels, short stories, poems, plays, personal accounts, and testimonies. While the literary narratives, like the documentary films, respond to a need to make stories, their way of addressing the issue of how we relate to reality is not the same. Unlike the recordings of voices and images on the siege site, these narratives are not expected to serve as evidence in court or historical materials in the strict sense of the term, and neither did they have a direct impact on political negotiations in the summer of 1990 or on ongoing land claims and struggles. First and foremost, they summon up the experiential and imaginative aspects of the event, without necessarily having concern for accuracy, political strategy, or facticity regarding the event. For this reason, they open up a free space in which the outline of the Oka Crisis, or the resistance at Kanehsatà:ke, can be redrawn.

This free expression is not without weight where the political crisis is concerned. In fact, while the siege effectively became a site of expression, the post-traumatic stress and the extreme political and social tension that it caused— which are still active today—can make speaking out difficult, since such speech is still directly engaged with and attached to very practical issues. Regarding the conflict's repercussions and how difficult it was, literature seems to be a way to free up speech precisely because it relieves it to a certain extent of a heavy burden of consequence. The figures drawn from the siege's scenography, for example, have been inscribed in a fictional world that creates distance from practical realities. Cherokee novelist Thomas King expresses his appreciation of the creative freedom literature offers in these terms: "Truth be known, I prefer fiction. I dislike the way facts try to thrust themselves upon me. I'd rather make up my own world. Fictions are less unruly than histories. The beginnings are more engaging, the characters more co-operative, the endings more in line with expectations of morality and justice."[1] This is the perspective adopted in the last two chapters of this book to look at how settler and Indigenous writers have reworked Oka in works of fiction. What changes have they imagined? To what extent have they shaped the event according to their place of utterance? This book studies the connection among literary narrative, the political event, and their context in the Oka Crisis, specifically exposed by an examination of literary narratives concerning the event. The narratives, despite all, maintain a close relation to the event's political dimension and its historical context, and this is especially clear in the works of Indigenous writers. French scholar Michel de Certeau maintained that fiction, like the media, advertising, and political representations, defines the status, objects, and field of vision.[2] In this way, literature and its interpretation ask questions similar to those raised by the event and its study. Who is speaking? What relations of visibility and invisibility are at issue? Which configurations of the siege become lodged in the imagination? How do the power relations play out in writing about and fictionalizing the event?

Across the board, the siege's representations arouse memories shaped by colonial history, divergent concepts of territoriality, and imaginary worlds marked by diverse, often antagonistic experiences. As a form of speaking out, the representations convey multiple trajectories that transmit cultures in motion and participate fully in a redefinition of power relations in the cultural, social, and political spaces. At the same time, this study of literary representations of Oka in the settler and Indigenous corpus takes into account the fact that the very practice of writing brings into play power relations analogous to those that evolved during the siege in action. Depending on their place of utterance, literary narratives mentioning the event can at times introduce figures from the margins or places of exclusion, and, at other times, figures associated with concentricity and the community.

In the literary corpus of Quebec and Canada, we see the emergence of an Indigenous figure who breaks into the centre after having been confined to the periphery for a long time. In the Indigenous corpus, the siege site is described more in terms of a central space that allows the collective expression of a resistance made necessary by the threat of encroachment. The differences in representation that arise from the place of utterance can be attributed to the deep-rooted nature of the conflict that came into focus in the public space during the summer of 1990. This chapter presents a reading of literary narratives from Quebec and Canada I have made by adopting an analytical approach that is deliberately Western. In the next chapter, it is my intention to give the reader a concrete, palpable sense of the difference that will become evident when Indigenous literary narratives are examined using a critical approach derived from Indigenous literary studies.

MYSTERIOUS REALMS

The literary narratives from Quebec and Canada often take up powerful images that circulated through the public space during the highly mediatized event. Notably, non-Indigenous accounts do not seem to attempt to translate the Indigenous experience so much as to express, represent, and trace the outlines of an event that rocked and interpellated the Quebec and Canadian societies. These narratives often refer to the siege's staging, but from an external point of view that betrays a lack of understanding of the suddenly erupting event. Some pieces place the Oka Crisis at the narrative's centre, while others merely use the siege as a transitional element. In *Les étranges et édifiantes aventures d'un oniromane* [The strange and edifying adventures of a lover of dreams], Québécois novelist Louis Hamelin refers to that "unworthy Oka" we might prefer to forget. The event that caused such confusion and perplexity appears periodically in Nicolas Dickner's *Nikolski*. The novel features the intertwined trajectories of a narrator and two characters on a lengthy migration that starts in Montreal and involves overwritten scraps of paper, traditional territories, activism, research, and fake IDs. The narrator's reflection on the television coverage of the Oka Crisis concludes with an observation on the unprecedented nature of what is happening: "And that's the trouble with inexplicable events—you're inevitably left with predestination, magic realism or a government conspiracy."[3] Combining ancient stories replete with mystery and the bizarre circumstances of his own account, he wonders, "Is it a coincidence, or is there an invisible connection between the internal politics of Kanesatake and a tattered old book of pirate stories?" (Dickner 2005, 178). How do the images of the barricades on television relate to the enigmatic stranger from the bookstore glimpsed in a crush of reporters? In similar fashion, the trajectory of a mysterious, elusive character is retraced in the novel *The Obituary* by anglo-Quebec writer Gail Scott. The novel's action takes place in a Montreal haunted by ghosts, conflicts between linguistic communities, memories of Indigenous ancestors, and the return of colonial history. It is towards the end of this enigmatic, fragmented narrative that the event erupts: "Before Ipperwash, Burnt Church, Port Radium James Bay, Kanehsatake, where a handful of armed Mohawks stopping Caucasians from The Outers. Backed by th' army + provincial police. From destroying sacred burial ground for golf. Course."[4] Fragments of the emerging event become associated with these mysterious realms, attesting to the confusion it generated.

THE FIGURE OF THE WARRIOR

Representations of the event tend to feature Indigenous characters who make their actions felt in the contemporary world, sometimes even in a fictional future. The armed conflict and the figure of the warrior fuel a literary imagination that sees Indigenous characters as having marginal or underworld associations that elicit admiration and fascination. The literary representations both alter and nurture an imaginary realm of Indigenous otherness that is peculiar to the Oka Crisis. As anthropologist Pierre Trudel explained, the racist calumnies circulating in Quebec about Indigenous people had for a long time developed around the issue of poaching, but beginning in 1990, they moved into another arena, that of smuggling.[5]

John Farrow's detective novel *Ice Lake* thus revives notions of the frontier imagination, the foreign warrior (that is, "American"), and the smuggling referred to in the Canadian media discourse of summer 1990. The novel begins with the finding of a murdered, drowned corpse beneath a fishing hut at Lake of Two Mountains, and its plot requires the collaboration of Mohawk warriors to cross the U.S.–Canada border.[6] The experience of a local police investigator in territory that is clearly identified as "Indian land" (Farrow 2001, 202) is bound up with memories of Oka, recalling the antagonism experienced by the character in what was unknown territory. A Mohawk character named Lucy Gabriel intercedes with Akwesasne warriors to get trucks carrying merchandise across the border. At first believing that she is helping HIV sufferers, the young woman eventually realizes that she has unwittingly become involved in a dangerous scheme driven by pharmaceutical companies, and in the end this brings her back on the detective's side and, at the same time, the side of the law.

While generally respected for her active participation in the armed conflict, the Mohawk character perplexes her employer. He wrestles with the contrast between the young woman he works with every day at the office and the woman he sees on the evening news: "During the Oka crisis we lost her services for weeks. I'd go home at night and there she'd be—my employee— on the evening news, taunting soldiers along the barricades. . . . Can you imagine? Instead of being at her station collecting a salary, she was behaving like a renegade" (273–74). Offering such insights as "one side's crisis was another side's war" (205), *Ice Lake* involves an event that leads to a redefinition of the relation to the Other. As the Oka Crisis is opening a breach that throws the settler society into question, the siege of Mohawk protestors facing down the Canadian Army starts to look very

much like a colonial war. And in the lyrics of the song "Oka Everywhere" by
punk-rock group Propagandhi, the siege often appears to be the manifestation
of a will to resist that commands respect. Similarly, the figure of the Indigenous subject battling the dominant order often becomes the reflection of a social
or political minority whose marginality has been exacerbated. In *Ice Lake*, the
Mohawk character of Lucy Gabriel is able to win the trust of the destitute who
come to the pharmaceutical laboratory to serve as experimental guinea pigs in
exchange for money: "Being native didn't hurt. The poor suspected that she
had known hard times herself, which eased their embarrassment at being there.
Those who recognized her as an activist for Indian rights, someone who had
spent time on the barricades during an explosive period in the history of her
reserve, believed that they had placed themselves in good hands" (36). In this
scene, the character is seen as a defender of precarious, minority subjects, whose
fate she in some ways shares. She is also the figure of a generous but misguided
smuggler. John Farrow dramatizes the internal tensions of a Mohawk community located in the border zone. Recalling the violence and uprooting she has experienced, Lucy talks about how her childhood home was burned down by the
Mohawk warriors and she was adopted by a white family as a result. Through
the device of this character, the novel depicts both internal dissension and a zone
of contact among Indigenous and non-Indigenous people, police detectives and
criminals, the good and the bad, whose paths cross and intertwine around an
odious scheme perpetrated by the pharmaceutical companies. The spatial configuration is made up of a situation under siege and one of exile through which
the character of the young Mohawk woman moves.

The genre of the detective novel itself reanimates the imaginary realm of
the shady world of Mohawk warriors. Benoît Bouthillette's novel *La trace de l'escargot* [The snail's trail] features an Indigenous police officer assigned to track
down a dangerous psychopath, the perpetrator of ritualistic murders, through
the murky streets of Montreal. The same imaginary universe can be found in
Wajdi Mouawad's novel *Anima*, in which the event lurks surreptitiously in the
background of a police investigation. Mouawad's novel, which is told through a
variety of animal voices, shows a husband, who has been devastated by the rape
and bloody murder of his wife, embarking on a quest that will put distance between him and his grief. It leads him to shadow the presumed murderer's movements and visit various Indigenous communities that serve as a haven. Similar
motives can be found in Québécois writer François Barcelo's road novel *Ailleurs*

en Arizona: Les aventures de Benjamin Tardif, II [The Adventures of Benjamin Tardif, II] which features, among others, a former sheriff and mysterious disappearances. In the novel, Oka erupts when an Indigenous character who is the owner of a service station in Arizona, abruptly interrupts his rescuing of a traveller's Westfalia upon hearing that the white driver is from Montreal, near Kanehsatake and Kahnawake. This gesture is described as an act of solidarity with the character's Indigenous brothers and sisters. It points at the issue of inherent settler complicity within the ongoing colonial context made manifest by the Mohawk resistance in 1990. In settler literary narratives, numerous stereotypes are either confirmed or exploded, amid concepts of inquest and interrogation, the quest and lines of questioning.

EVENT AND IDENTITY QUEST

In the novel *Sept lacs plus au nord* [Seven lakes further north] by novelist Robert Lalonde, who is from Québécois and Mohawk ancestry,[7] the main character sees himself regularly interpellated by the event in a sort of daily ritual: "The crisis, on TV, called out to him at the appointed hour, abyss promised, abyss delivered."[8] The event, which seems as terrifying as it is hopeful, shows him a deep, painful divide: "Something unhoped for, life-altering, something new was starting. He felt afraid and, mysteriously, resolute" (Lalonde 1993, 17). The 1993 novel has the character's ways of relating to the event, both mediatized and personal, converging in a glimpse on the television news of a lover from the character's teen years, a young Mohawk man from Kanehsatà:ke. The protagonist remembers it in this way: "And then there was the Indian, of course. Just once he'd seen him, on the news, on television—leaning against the trunk of a huge pine, he was crying, without covering his face, as in the past. The image flashed by, and right away, they again showed the masked warriors, the barbed wire, the blond, heroic, tidy soldier standing up to his black enemy, the Mohawk, the bloodthirsty warrior, a confrontation between cowboys and Indians from the old movies, that weird war day after day, in the pine grove" (15; translation).

Even as they revive scenarios from Hollywood westerns, the televised images of the duality of two worlds in confrontation at the barricades seem to be the continuation and exacerbation of an old local conflict between white settlers and Indigenous people. This conflict was hinted at as far back as 1982 in *Le dernier été des Indiens* [The last Indian summer], another novel by Lalonde, set in the same village some thirty years before the Oka Crisis, to which *Sept lacs plus au nord* appears to be a sequel. In her article "L'image de l'Indien chez Robert Lalonde: avant et après la crise d'Oka [The image of the Indian in Robert Lalonde's work: before and after the Oka Crisis]," Paola Ruggeri quotes the lead character in *Le dernier été des Indiens* as, perplexed, he wonders about the growing divide in his love relationship: "How is it that we should once again end up, tonight, on the edge of the same abyss, the great gulf that is so old and yet still gaping, making our heads spin? Why on this night of August 29, 1959, a dark night, lost in time, do we once again find ourselves, the Indian and I, on the edge of a deep chasm of misunderstanding?"[9] To be noted, although the author makes no mention of it, is that the novel is set in the same year that the town of Oka built the first golf course on communal lands, over the stated objections of the Kanehsatake Mohawks. Altogether, the novel underscores the conservative nature of the Catholic village's residents, called "the clan" by the writer, and the systematic stigmatization of their Mohawk neighbours up the hill.

In *Sept lacs plus au nord*, the Oka Crisis breaks out against all expectations, although it was foreseeable. Evoking the event's repetition and the latent conflict in times of peace, the protagonist remembers how "the Indian" had a premonition about the armed conflict years before, when he was drawing "Karihwas" in the sand by the Lake of Two Mountains' large bay. The "drawn writing" on the ground prefigured "an attack by two hundred enemies" and the positions of the opposed parties represented by "the two groups of arrows aimed at each other" (Lalonde 1993, 56). Tears in his eyes, the Mohawk character, "with the outsized gestures of a drowning man" (57), predicts the coming of vengeance and asks his lover with mixed ancestry to accept the violence of his people when it arrives: "I know you can't understand this, but it must be understood! You must recognize our violence, their violence, when it comes! You must know that I will be with them, even if I don't want to, because . . . because it's stronger than we are, stronger than I am! Because it's our law, our strength and also our sickness—revenge! [In English, italics in the original text] *And be sure, please, be sure that it won't be for you, I mean against you . . .!*" (57; translation). Referring to the polarization inherent in the conflict's dynamic and the vengeful motive often attributed by settlers to Indigenous people, the character of the Indian asks his lover to understand and accept the law of a community with which he is in solidarity. He then disappears into the pine grove that connects and separates the two villages, like "a sorcerer erased by the branches" (56). The premonition makes it possible to imagine how the land dispute at Oka-Kanehsatake could oblige individuals, against their will, to carry the weight of an historical dispute that for centuries had shaped the relationships between settlers and Indigenous peoples.

In *Sept lacs plus au nord*, the Oka Crisis triggers a quest for love and identity. This quest forces the protagonist, an "estranged half-Métis" (47), to reconcile himself to his mixed origins by making contact with the Mohawk lover of his teenage years, from whom he had been separated by "the village," an entity portrayed in the novel as a conservative, white, Catholic community. This distanciation of the young Mohawk lover was because, as his mother then explains, referring to 1990, "it would always have been like last summer, the war, the tearing apart that killed your father" (90). In fact, the siege appears in the novel alongside the trajectory of this character, whose Québécois and Mohawk roots have come into conflict. On arriving in the village shortly after the crisis, the protagonist notes that traces of the armed conflict can still be seen: "Opening his eyes, he saw neither the lake nor the pines but, on the ruined road, the last tanks blocking his view, desolate sentinels near the first of the houses" (12). Remembering his Mohawk grandfather, "chief of a clan that is now badly dismantled, like the barricades" (13), the character named Michel meditates on "this rift that underlay and decided everything about him, from always and for ever" (Lalonde 1993, 13). The internal rift experienced by people who embodied the antagonistic identities was played out in real space in the armed conflict. It is precisely the topic of Sonia Bonspille-Boileau's previously discussed documentary film *Qui suis-je?* [Who am I?].

Lalonde's character of Michel is possessed by the settler colonial drama, so that instead of living in a creative, harmonious state of convergence, as noted by Emmanuelle Tremblay, he inhabits a space in which "the differences are maintained in a relationship of conflict."[10] He can feel in his flesh the inextricable, profoundly conflicted tangle of Indigenous-settler relationships that the Oka Crisis had just brought to light and galvanized; the narrator says, "Double life. Polarities that are irreconcilable and yet joined, brought together, stuck together by the body's most deeply buried force."[11] At the same time, it is the quest triggered by the event that will lead Michel, the character with Mohawk and French-Canadian ancestry, to recognize and move beyond this crisis by integrating its elements. During the crisis, the character of the "Indian" presents himself at Michel's mother's door, "the upper and lower parts of his face covered with scarves, and two eyes that could have been imploring or murderous" (Lalonde 1993, 86). He brings her a letter in which he has sketched for Michel the route to his hideaway. The mother and son then make the long journey northward by car on what is, for Michel, an urgent quest to find "the Indian, his guide, his protector" (95). He is heading for "that body that had saved, defended and redeemed him" (43); he is moving towards "a hero, or a mentor, if you like, a hypothesis of god, the Indian's body, mixed together with his own muscles, his own intelligence, his heart" (43). The journey that will take him to his former lover ends by his yielding, as Michel gradually realizes, to an internal reconciliation that will detach him from the presence and body of his teenage lover, which for decades have haunted him like an obsession. The reconciliation also evokes a visibility and recognition that affect the Indigenous character as much as Michel himself. While approaching the place where his former lover waits, Michel goes back to a promise he had made to stir up his memories and exhume, in writing, "the old dream so that they could finally see it and recognize it" (155). The character of "the Indian" in this case becomes the figure of the guide, reviving the role often played by Indigenous people during early colonial times.[12] However, this time, the figure helps to trace a trajectory that brings a character with mixed ancestry back to himself, or back home.

The figure of the guide and protector also appears in the literary narratives of migrant writers. Examples are *Anima*, the novel by Lebanese-Québécois writer Wajdi Mouawad, and *Out of My Skin* by Guyanese-Canadian novelist Tessa McWatt. *Out of My Skin* is set in Montreal during the Oka Crisis. It features a Mohawk character who acts as a mediator between the Mohawk community at the heart of the siege and the character of a young black woman from Toronto named Daphne, who has recently moved to Montreal. Daphne was adopted as a young child and at the time of the event is in the middle of an existential crisis. At first, she follows the progress of the siege from a distance, through her colleagues and the media, and then gradually draws closer through her connection to the character of Surefoot. This Mohawk woman, whose name connotes certainty and stability, inspires Daphne in a quest for identity that leads her to discover the history of her biological parents and find herself. Nonetheless, as Michèle Lacombe noted, "Daphne's wounded, self-preoccupied perception of and reliance on Surefoot's 'motherly' psychological insights, cultural knowledge, and spiritual wisdom occur at the expense and in the absence of any personal and political support for 'the other woman.'"[13] Lacombe's analysis echoes that of Mohawk writer Joe David's on the passive, disengaged expressions of settler solidarity. Overall, the issue of the identity we create for ourselves often shows up at the centre of an identity quest sparked by the event.

In a poem titled "Oka Nada," Asian-Canadian poet Kaushalya Bannerji evokes the dream that connects migrant and Indigenous subjects. At the same time, she speaks of the misunderstanding and contempt underpinning the conquest and colonization of the Americas: "I am from the country / Columbus dreamt of. / You, the country / Columbus conquered."[14] Talking about a "silenced film" that is watched in a "Clear Quebec sky," then the army and police who "destroy dignity and land," the poem's migrant subject invokes the protection of the Indigenous subject: "Protect me with your brazen passion / for history is my truth, / Earth, my witness, my home, / this native land."[15] In the literary narratives, culturally marginalized characters tend to identify with the Mohawk protestors and communities. The narratives feature a quest leading the subject to make peace with immigrant or Indigenous origins. They also often make reference to a polarization of belonging, as well as to the violent reactions of hostility and racism among non-Indigenous residents of Montreal's southern suburbs.

SETTLER BACKLASH

Tessa McWatt's novel *Out of My Skin* stages a settler assembly of agitators and angry, frustrated residents who mobilize against the "Indians," whose actions they depoliticize in order to denigrate them more easily. Adopting as her themes the law and the bridge, she recalls in her fiction the demeaning statements so often heard during the crisis: "These Indians think they're above the law. . . . This has nothing to do with a graveyard. . . . They can't take the goddamn bridge every time they're mad about something."[16] The characters at the assembly loudly criticize the government's inaction and express a determination to take justice into their own hands. One of them makes an incendiary racist speech that stirs up the residents' hatred and incites them to take action. The narrator comments: "His speech was greeted by a chorus of grunted agreements punctuated by approving whistles and a smattering of obscenities. This was the fuel the group needed. Vengeance shined [*sic*] in their faces" (54). The theme of revenge recurs here, not on the part of Indigenous characters, as so often is the case in non-Indigenous discourses and representations, but rather in the ragged breathing and twisted faces of white residents carried away by resentment. The character of Daniel, Daphne's boss, follows the speeches, perplexed and confused, without joining in the general fury. In an involuntary movement, he rises to his feet by leaning on his chair with both hands, "as if he was about to lose his balance" (55). His instability is a sign of the atmosphere's volatility.

While the crisis engenders an identity quest among adopted or mixed-ancestry characters in the novels of Tessa McWatt and Robert Lalonde, it causes some confusion in the non-Indigenous populations featured in the fictions. These populations appear to be disturbed by the colonial backlash and the racist violence coursing through their ranks; they seem to have a poor grasp of the crisis's political and historical aspects. The narrator in Nicolas Dickner's novel *Nikolski*, whose hometown is just minutes away from Kahnawake, notes the unseemly nature of the local displays of resentment, which in the end are turned not only on the Indigenous people behind the barricades, but also on the forces of law and order surrounding them: "From time to time, I would see on the screen a former neighbour busily cursing out the police or the Indians, and even both at once" (Dickner 2005, 177). The narrator of Québécois writer Francine Noël's novel *Nous avons tous découvert l'Amérique* [We all discovered America] questions the effectiveness of barricades that hindered the flow of traffic all summer, and laconically observes: "The Mohawks removed the barricades without having gained anything, except perhaps a vague promise to negotiate territorial self-government."[17] In this, her sentiment is similar to that of Yves Boisvert in his poetry collection *Voleurs de cause* [Cause robbers], which refers to "an odd kind of war / lost ahead of time / won in a void / pitting the Iroquois against the rest of the world."[18]

Quebec and Canadian narratives of the Oka Crisis demonstrate the entrance of an Indigenous otherness that had been both ignored and right next door, whose suddenly visible presence caused a shift in perspective paired with a large element of indecision. In this connection, the event's representations in non-Indigenous literary narratives refer to the breach that opened up and the suddenly exposed fragility of the settler state. They encourage us to consider and question the violent colonial resentment that was expressed during the event.

THE DISRUPTIVE POWER OF THE
OKA CRISIS IN *VOLEURS DE CAUSE*

Heterogeneity means getting at what is essential using a
multilateral approach.

—Yves Boisvert, "Écritures des territoires de l'écriture"

The disruptive power, discord, and violent impact of the Oka Crisis are conveyed
with close attention to detail and great intensity in *Voleurs de cause* by late Québécois poet Yves Boisvert. This irreverent collection is a genuine epic, with many
characters inspired by the Oka Crisis transforming the chaotic space of the event
even as they intervene in it. While the poems describe the revolt against the established order with some consideration for aesthetics, they also display the violence
and destabilization typical of Boisvert's writing. In the literary correspondence
of *Aimititau ! Parlons-nous !* [Let's talk!], addressing the question of "rebellion
and the role of art," Boisvert wrote to Wendat writer, curator, and sociologist Guy
Sioui Durand the following about *Voleurs de cause*: "This book deals with the Oka
Crisis—the Pines, the golf course, the media, the whole thing. The Iroquois are
not Hurons. They first burned the Jesuits, which was not a great start; they then
made pacts with the French, which bears examination. The globalized version of
Voleurs de cause is titled *Bang!* It deals with September 11 in Washington and NYC.
The Muslims are hopeless at landing. They see the world as vertical. And there's
no turtle to hold up the planet."[19] Boisvert opposes an imperilled vertical architecture to a living, horizontal pedestal supporting life on the earth, as reflected on in
the Haudenosaunee and other Indigenous creation stories. Boisvert emphasizes
his interest in current events, especially those that cause a violent break and reveal
deep-seated conflicts between peoples and societies bound to each other through
complex sets of antagonistic relationships. His poetic endeavour in relation to the
Oka Crisis summons the literary endeavour carried on by Louis Hamelin in his
novel *October 1970*, in relation to the October Crisis, a political event that foregrounded the Front de libération du Québec and the intervention of the Canadian Armed Forces under the War Measures Act. In *Fabrications*, his book-long essay discussing what he calls "the hermeneutic novel,"[20] Hamelin explained how he
used the literary genre of the novel in an effort to elucidate an historical event that
is still affected by numerous, contradictory, and often nebulous interpretations,

more specifically in relation to the kidnapping of James Richard Cross and the subsequent death of Pierre Laporte. Dissatisfied with the generally accepted version of the events, Hamelin concluded that "the official fiction must be fought by fiction,"[21] and it is through his novel *October 1970* that he searched for a truth to the crisis. It is to be noted that defining moments and conflicting historical events such as the ones in 1970 and 1990 persistently question our relation to reality in the light of diverging discourses and different expressive forms.

In 1990, the Oka Crisis sheds light on the settler violence at the basis of Quebec and Canada. It clearly reveals an ambiguity between the history that makes us, befalling us without warning, and the history we make, which we fashion from discourses, ideologies, and schools of political thought that contradict, conflict, reassert themselves, and combine. By redoubling the play of fiction that is a fixture in our relation to reality, literary fiction intervenes in the eventalization by favouring another mode of eruption. Society generally attempts to exorcise the event's constituent disruption by making the event an element of information. The poetic attempt produces its effects centrally within the conflict, in a clash of antagonistic identities, certainly, but also in the colliding of two modes of symbolic representation: on the one hand, how human beings, at a given time, represent their world to themselves; and, on the other, how the poetic text intersects with conceptualized language and brings forth suggestions of what is real.

With little concern for being politically correct or adhering to any particular factual version of the event, Boisvert plumbs the various assorted images, discourses, and performances that marked the Oka Crisis. In the eighty-odd pages making up his collection, he presents a succession of scenes that revive the event's violent impact. The book opens up a polyphonic space in which the event's discordant voices can be heard and verbal insults degenerate into violent confrontations and muddled brawls. The poet foregrounds the presence of an Indigenous otherness that meets a corrupt and dysfunctional established order with nobility and dignity. By means of reversals, distortions, and exaggerations that are often insulting and uncalled for, he ultimately scrambles the bearings of the reader he has transported into the brutal, chaotic scrimmage. If the collection at first seems shocking, profane, and disrespectful of the tragic, traumatic nature of the armed conflict, it is because it has fairly rendered, through poetic freedom and licence, and with a focus on the Quebec society, all the virulence, harshness, and intensity of the crisis that shook up the self-image settler societies had created for themselves.

SURVIVAL AS COUNTER-PERFORMATIVITY

Voleurs de cause taps into the hidden depths of non-event that surfaced during the conflict. It features the settler ambitions to assimilate the Indigenous peoples, as well as the dispossession of territory and simultaneous erasure brought back into view by the event. The land dispute at Oka-Kanehsatake may have been a repetition of past events for the Mohawks and the other First Nations, but it had a completely different effect for the Quebec and Canadian societies. They suddenly saw the emergence of very real political actors in the stead of a figure that, in their imagination, was associated with some faraway place. Recalling the figure of the Indian that is central to the project of dispossessing the Indigenous peoples of their lands and political power, the collection opens with a statement by a Québécois subject about an Other who had been maintained in a position of absolute marginalization. The referential order of this subject's community, which is identified as "we," seems to have been conceived by dispensing with any reference to the Indigenous Other:

> Before it didn't touch us
> didn't mean anything at all
> didn't interest us
> it wasn't *trendy*
> not our thing
> to each their own thing
> crowding—disconnection—rejection
>
> missing piece dug up from schoolbooks
> next to the Conquistadors, Colonists and Negroes
> you're coming from the wrong end of a scrunched-up map
> (Boisvert 1992, 9)

The Indigenous Other in these lines has been relegated to the outer limit of a colony that is associated with a bygone age. At first, it seems that it neither affects nor concerns the narrator's community. Nonetheless, as the preposition "before" and the past tense tell us, the situation has now changed. The sudden appearance of Indigenous otherness, which the speaker suddenly recognizes with the use of the second person, reveals the missing piece; it exposes to the light of day the colonial devices behind the dispossession.

In *Voleurs de cause*, the municipality's project to expand the golf course on land belonging to the Mohawks finds a place in the long line of generalized expropriation that represents the colonial and capitalist enterprise, historically and currently. "Golf as leisure sport entertainment" for the "pleasure of Mr. Mrs. So-and-so / to arrange their berth in the élite" (14) is directly related to "the trickery" of the authorities "since the Colony began" (18). In addition, "three white demons / each taking his turn at / humiliation / invasion / assimilation" (54) are the figures who represent the settlers' repeated attempts to achieve their dark designs by passing "a growing number of thousands of laws" that "cornered us and killed us one by one," as an Indigenous voice describes it (16).

In the collection, the proliferation of laws sets up many spaces for a deadly confinement of the Indigenous peoples. Legislation therefore appears to be an instrument of domination that the authorities continually use in favour of their own ends and against those of the peoples indigenous to the land. Referring to the colonial anxiety the authorities seek to cover up, along with the white privilege that underlies it, Boisvert writes that during the event, "the lovers of genocide did their best to control / the milky fear of thinning out a usurped comfort" (34). As indicated by the titles of the collection's four sections—"Oppression," "Repression," "Depression," and "Suppression"—the authorities managing the crisis keep replaying the unequal power relations consecrated and maintained by an established order that leans on minority subjects with all its weight. The legal machine seems to be engineered to dismiss the Indigenous Other and his or her objections: "blinded by the Law, the magistrate decides to issue / an injunction" (12), the poet exclaims, and continues ironically, "what a great word for an epic poem *injunction* / what a dazzling image *decide to issue*" (12). As they criticize the law's performativity, the poems also denounce the logic behind private property and the elitist nature of a development project for recreation and luxury housing. It thus condemns the "legalistic fanaticism of golfing minorities / quick to decide the fate of the margins / of taverns in private clubs" (17). The established order depicted in the poems constantly does violence to the Indigenous subject, who in turn speaks of a fierce determination to thwart all forms of elitism, authoritarianism, and colonial encroachment.

The initial occupation and subsequent siege put a brake on colonial movement in the space. Addressing the resister's figure, the poetic voice states: "You say no to those who said yes on your behalf" (9). In this instance, Boisvert is alluding to the statement by the Mohawk subject, who refuses to make way and backs it up by taking a stance in the space. In the poems, speaking out and putting up barricades are part of the same determined objection to obeying the dominant society's court orders and letting settler history go quietly on its way: "this Iroquois evicted from the Narrative / nothing will make him take even one step back" (34). By occupying the territory he intends to protect, the character of the Iroquois signals a stubborn refusal to be erased; he is committed, facing the Other. Standing behind the barricades, he resists encroachment, and, in doing so, breaks the law confining him and defies the dominant settler society's plans:

> rooted in his integrity
> a guy chose to gainsay the race
> live another day
> wrong, right, by accident, in principle
> to do what was not said
> settling his score with local history
> to make it resound throughout America
> from 1492 to this day. (24)

Evoking a counter-performativity articulated in the colonial context, this stanza describes the presence of an Indigenous subject who decides to thwart "the race." By asserting himself very specifically in his integrity as a survivor, he counters the dark colonial forecasts that since the first contact have been hoping for, plotting, and projecting his imminent disappearance. It is therefore precisely his survival, with the evidence of continued presence it provides, that enables him to demand that his usurped territory be returned. In *Voleurs de cause*, the gesture of protest that consists of settling the account with local history resounds to the historical depths of the continent. This gesture brings to the surface the disputes generated by a meeting of two worlds at a decisive moment the Europeans call the "discovery" of the continent, an encounter that set the stage for the settler colonialism under which we continue to live.

Voleurs de cause was released two years after the Oka Crisis, in the year where the 500th anniversary of the Americas was underlined. The latter event brought the problematic issue of coexistence after 1492 back into the public space. Québécois scholar Claudine Cyr has observed that the multiple commemorations and demonstrations that took place in 1992 reanimated "a foundational scenario of America that has been endlessly repeated and performed for

500 years, and still acts on America's current state and its future."[22] According to the various performances that reassert or contest this scenario, Christopher Columbus, the lead character, is at times viewed as a national hero and at others as the initiator of genocide. In 1992, Indigenous protests of the 500th anniversary celebrations made a contemporary Indigenous presence and discourse manifest in the public space. Like the Oka Crisis two years earlier, this groundswell replayed the failure of the projected assimilation and disappearance of the Indigenous peoples. It also brought to the forefront colonial violence and the need for a structural redrafting of the relations between settlers and Indigenous peoples. The deeply entrenched assumptions deriving from this colonial scenario were to be contested once again around the celebrations of the 150th anniversary of Canada and the 375th anniversary of Montreal in 2017. In response to the confederation's anniversary, for instance, numerous Indigenous artists, educators, political actors, and communities either refused to take part in the official celebrations, or accepted to do so on the condition that they be reframed in order to acknowledge the continuing presence and stories of Indigenous peoples on this continent, as well as the ongoing impacts of colonialism and settler colonial history.[23]

Whether the scenario of discovery is reaffirmed, subverted, or refuted, its multiple performances and (re)interpretations can reiterate the origins of the America that we know today "through negotiations and power relations that, taken together, can recast the dominant version of America's history and can also, over time, change some of its basic elements."[24] In a similar way, the Oka Crisis, or the resistance at Kanehsatà:ke, has influenced the national narratives of Quebec and Canada. The political event, like a scenario, can be reanimated and reinterpreted in different ways, so that it remains open to change and negotiation for as long as it is expressed and replayed. This is precisely what its literary representations are doing, among them Yves Boisvert's poetry collection. Rather than drawing a clear, obvious figuration, it muddies the picture so as to keep the event's indeterminacy active.

"THE STATE OF SIEGE IN THE LAND OF THE CAUSE ROBBERS"

"The Redskins have the land heavy on their heart / this weight resists the police invasion / the most costly in History" (Boisvert 1992, 17), wrote Yves Boisvert to sum up the armed siege's most fundamental issue. In *Voleurs de cause*, the conflict's scenography takes shape in the style of a resistance. Right away, it locates the actors in the deep-rooted colonial conflict: "The guys have resolved to hold a Siege / as an affront to the effrontery / that knows no bounds" (22). In order to counter the looming territorial encroachment, they decide to "block off the bridge connecting the metropolis to the Americas," and to "invest it instead of investing in it" (22). In a few hours, in an unforeseen and tragic reversal, a police officer lost his life, the suburban traffic came to a standstill, and the two armed camps faced each other from opposite sides of the improvised barricades. All of a sudden, "it is a State of Siege in the land of the cause robbers" (17).

Unlike the 500th anniversary celebrations and protests, which reanimated the foundational scenario of the "discovery," the Oka Crisis revives scenarios of colonial wars in which troops were deployed against the Indigenous peoples. At the same time, it evokes the scripts of the Hollywood Western in which cowboys and Indians have violent confrontations, generally in the territories associated with conquest of the Western frontier. The borderline between reality and fiction sometimes proves to be thin where this political event is concerned. In early May 1990, shortly before the crisis exploded, the scenario of Western wars was evoked in all seriousness by Quebec's minister of Public Safety Sam Elkas. In reaction to the request by Oka's mayor for the provincial police's help in dismantling the barricades, Elkas attempted to reassure the public by saying, with reference to the police force: "I don't want to send in anyone to play cowboy in the matter of a golf course."[25] With these words, the minister hinted at a prediction that in the end he himself would help to come true. Using the same tone, regarding the people in the Pines and the injunction ordering them to free up the roadways by 10 July 1990, he went on to issue threats that the coroner would later characterize as insolent, namely: "They have until the 9th, and after that it all comes down"[26] (quoted in Quebec 1995, 416). Recalling the failed police intervention that followed, *Voleurs de cause* attributes the event's eruption to the unfortunate actions of a fragile, inconsistent government that was having a rude encounter with reality: "this diamond in the mud echoes / the shock of reality in the puppet's strutting / John Wayne's body falling / lower than the heels of his cowboy boots" (Boisvert 1992, 25). The fate of this emblematic figure from the Hollywood Western who suddenly and disgracefully loses his footing is used to illustrate the tumble taken by the settler authorities. When Boisvert remounts the event as a poem, he makes everything explode; but, by rendering the multiple elements of the Oka Crisis in detail, he gives his poetry collection power and displays an in-depth understanding of the siege and its context.

The staging of the shootout in *Voleurs de cause* is based on components of the event we have already examined in various ways in the previous chapters: for instance, the role of Mohawk women in the occupation; the recitation of the thanksgiving address on the morning of the police intervention; and the death of a police officer who was struck by a bullet during the shooting. The poetic scenography of the event's eruption takes the form of an imagistic anecdote:

> as it turns out the police attack the girls
> during a religious ceremony
>   worse than savages
> a target of living flesh topples
> a cop trips over a lung in the mud
> the little orb impaled on a hemlock snag (13)

These lines reopen a breach that presents the fatal police intervention in another way. As described, the scene may be shocking, but it can also be said that it uses poetic distancing to create detachment from the real-world constraints and violence. In the style of the carnivalesque, which lets no one take the high ground, the poem deconsecrates the death at the event's centre by returning the scene to a raw, natural setting. The armed assault fails, and the police officer, who has become a target, suffocates in the mud, his eye ironically impaled on a hemlock in the contested woods, as if that fatal tree was defending Mohawk land. Suddenly, the roles have been reversed.

Faced with a spectacular, violent death broadcast live, "the world cannot contain its morbid stupefaction" (14). The event attests to a form of resistance that elicits what is clearly astonishment in the dominant society—it has the effect of a "shout that bites" (9). Because it is what is stumbled over, the event is often what can never be talked about. Its verticality cuts off the daily flow of time, and it is disconcerting, astounding: "the man with the camera can't get over it / the script is denying his profession / nothing works any more / what will we say on State TV?" (13) The settler's scenario is skewed, it falls apart and runs off the road; against all expectations, the police operation turns back on itself, so that where a restored public order and security ought to be, there is a yawning void that leaves us open-mouthed. And out of this suddenly created void comes the vengeful, cynical speech of the last Indigenous survivor, who will write the script from now on: "*You will say what we will let you translate: / a good corporal is a dead corporal* / so said the last of the Mohicans" (13). With this reply, which resounds like an insult, the poem opposes the figure of the Indigenous survivor to that of the corporal of the U.S. Army. This opposition is reinforced by the reversal of the genocidal watchwords "The only good Indian is a dead Indian," which, in the colonial history of the United States, tied the undisturbed occupation of the territory by settlers from Europe to the disappearance of the peoples indigenous to it.

THE EVENT'S POLYPHONY

In the summer of 1990, political performances and public speech modified the event even as they caused it to happen, in close collaboration with media representations. In *Voleurs de cause*, Yves Boisvert goes after the media strategy orchestrated by "the land army [that] had therefore all foreseen / how to draft the releases in advance / eliminate all sensitive information / contradict the last one" (87). In raising the question of complicity, he is also unsparing of the public's credulous passivity, observing with disgust that "people swallowed it all without blinking" (87). His work delivers a critique of how a given interpretation of the event is imposed on the spectator, who is the target of media and political strategies. It also features a control over the media that is used to twist the facts of the event in favour of white privilege: "the Whites have again succeeded in belittling things / making a travesty of collecting evidence / distorting the facts and misleading" (51). In this way, an act that is intrinsic to the colonial project is played out again in the siege's media space. It is what Diana Taylor described, in her book *The Archive and the Repertoire*, as a form of "percepticide" that consists in promoting certain points of view while working to make others disappear.[27]

During the Oka Crisis, the images circulating in the public space tended to relegate the Mohawk protestors' siege to a context of illegality, thus dissociating it from, among other things, the land struggle of the Kanehsatake community as a whole. In answer to these representations, *Voleurs de cause* repeats the discourse of the governments, which were seeking to marginalize the Mohawk protestors' actions. For example, Boisvert reproduces this divisive speech by a well-meaning female politician and puts it in italics: "*We must not confuse the Iroquois acts of war / with the legitimate claims of Natives in general*" (Boisvert 1992, 46). The poet immediately disqualifies this statement, which was widely circulated during the crisis, by viciously describing the speaker as "Ms. Democrat, a hair-splitter parachuted onto the scene" (46), and, after having described her in rather sexist terms, specifiying that she "had never set foot on a Reserve" (46). During the crisis, the stereotyped discourse of the governments was immediately picked up, blown up, and dramatized by the media and public rumour, and now it is reworked in poetry. In Boisvert's collection, a voice repeats the discriminatory and stereotyped accusations of imposture and illegality:

> *They're bandits like the others*
> *reselling cigarettes with the left hand*
> *Mafia guys from the northern States*
> *they hold back 1500 per week*
> *you never see their faces*
> *maybe not even Indians!* (12)

This stanza evoked widely circulated terms like "criminals," "smugglers," "Americans," and "masked warriors," and, in conclusion, a persistent settler suspicion directed at the Mohawk warriors during the crisis: that is, "maybe not even Indians!" In sum, they appear in these discourses like foreigners and delinquents on all points who, as a result, do not have a legitimate claim to the land. Taken from the list of neo-colonial stereotypes, the accusations of banditry are intended to discredit the Indigenous identity so as to deny it and along with it the grounds for Indigenous land claims in the courts. They reiterate a received idea while misappropriating it: the idea that there can only be an Indigenous identity that falls within the limits of state law and conforms to it. These are the accusations the poem challenges.[28]

To explode them, Boisvert makes an effort in his poetry to dislodge the mind-numbing stereotypes associated with Oka. Regarding the stereotype applied to Ronald Cross, the Mohawk protestor publicly known as Lasagne, anthropologist Pierre Trudel remarked that this fixed representation had the effect of "efficiently destabilizing efforts to understand Indigenous political claims."[29] In the context of the Oka Crisis, Boisvert identifies various expressions of what he calls "idiotic thinking," and which he conceives of, according to writer Janie Handfield, as a "state of mind that makes us categorize everything in order to assign meaning to what is around us, for fear of being caught in the void."[30] In this case, the void could be the equivalent of the settlers' fragility, which had just been exposed by the Mohawk land struggle and the sovereignty being asserted so forcefully on the siege site. This fragility becomes accentuated in the presence of a publicly asserted Indigenous certainty during an event that reanimates "the high tension of centuries-old resilience" (Boisvert 1992, 74). At the same time that they destabilize the effort to understand Indigenous land claims, the stereotypes and received ideas have the effect of convincing and reassuring the contemporary settler societies of their perceived rights, especially concerning their legitimate entitlement to occupy the territory and the probity of their relations with Indigenous peoples, both of which are rightfully and openly challenged by Oka, or the Kanehsatake resistance. In this connection, we can perhaps presume that the rate at which such stereotypes accumulated during the event was directly proportional to the intensity of the settlers' anxiety, then breaking the surface.

As Janie Handfield explained, *Voleurs de cause* is the continuation of a creation process by which Yves Boisvert "grasps the entire society." She added that he "works on, displaces, transgresses its discourses, conduct, icons and ideologies to produce new realities, to render visible and manifest the void that weighs on the world."[31] The poetry collection recuperates and reshapes the various elements that fashioned this distressing event, while preserving all the confusion it generated. Addressing the *"malaise of conquest"* (Boisvert 1992, 67), the poems juxtapose the ideas, political positions, and conceptions of the world that opposed, denied, confirmed, and did violence to one another throughout the crisis. In this, they do not provide a representation of a "world of objects, illuminated and ordered by his monologic thought," as semiotician Mikhail Bakhtin wrote in his discussion of Dostoevsky's poetics. Rather, they stage "a world of consciousnesses mutually illuminating one another, a world of yoked-together semantic human orientations."[32] Boisvert connects the disparate, tangled, conflicting elements that make up the event, which itself reflects and exacerbates a conflict that is deep rooted and extremely complex.[33] In fact, the Oka Crisis, or the resistance at Kanehsatake, involved differentiated, mutually antagonistic, and intertwined concepts of history, politics, and territory in a head-on collision, which led to confrontations between legality and legitimacy as well as between nations and forms of sovereignty. *Voleurs de cause* presents the latency of the deep-rooted conflict, asking a question without an answer: "when will this boxing match end / that is never over?" (Boisvert 1992, 81)

Like the many processes and discordant voices that make up the conflict, everything is in confrontation in the collection's polyphonic space, starting with the official political actors in the event. Boisvert describes them in very unflattering terms. Replicating the siege's scenography and its political makeup, he attacks the "clan of Impossible Affairs" (48) and denounces the "municipal blunder" (19) that started the crisis. In the same vein, he calls Aid to the Civil Power a "military regime" (61), depicting the Canadian soldiers as "mercenaries" (18) and later as "a wheezing trooplet" (Boisvert 1992, 15). The civil servant is not spared, making an appearance as "a puffing little White man / —future assistant" when not as an "executant" (58), a follower of orders who would be "tamed with stories of cowardice / a bit light in the shorts / petrified with discomfort" (58). As for the political characters, they become "champions of ignorance" (47), and the negotiators, void of substance, are *"jabberjaws with mandates"* (40).

Voleurs de cause does not present the attempt to erase and control the Indigenous peoples as a logical, rational, or targeted enterprise that is legitimized and organized according to a rationale of settler colonialism or a hegemonic structure. In fact, while the collection certainly presents an image of institutional hegemony, the predominant theme is that of a malfunctioning machine that runs on greed, corruption, lies, and repudiations. Contrary to the representations summoned up in the government discourse, the imposters in this case are not the Mohawk warriors but the politicians and government representatives, so many "faces-with-two-sides" (57) busy plotting various machinations in the fictive space of the crisis. *Voleurs de cause* criticizes the idea of a caring universalism embodied in democratic institutions by speaking in terms of "democracy on parade," "terrifying neutrality" (47), and people from the UN who are "necessarily neutral and tenants in New York" (51). It contrasts a pacifying discourse with a brutal reality that blatantly contradicts it.

The hate-filled gestures of the local settler populace represented in the poems reinforce this image of a brutal reality, while at the same time denying the image of a caring democracy as portrayed by the governments. The poems thus report that "on the occasion of crossing the bridge of two worlds / condemned by the Great Spirits" (54), the residents being evacuated from Kahnawake were caught in a trap. As it was, "a long convoy of cars full of Iroquois / old people, women, children / mothers sad and miserable at having to flee / comes in midcourse to the bridge's apron" (52). That is where, as during the event, they are shouted at and violently pelted with rocks by a crowd of non-Indigenous residents gathered on the sides of the road, in plain sight of police officers who do not intervene: "complacent, lethargic, as if hit with an interdiction / the police looked on with turbid eyes" (53). Boisvert speaks out against a scandalous impunity when describing the act of aggression towards the Mohawk families perpetrated by the "pale faces above all suspicion" (52). He describes the violent manifestation of racial prejudice by observing that "each idea being a rock / they slung their ideas with a vengeance" (52).

The attack reveals to a non-Indigenous public an unsuspected, disturbing element that had been hidden and yet was all too real: "not London Bridge where your love rains down / not Mirabeau Bridge where your sorrows weep / here we are on the approach to Mercier Bridge / in the elect land of America" (Boisvert 1992, back cover). The event's rupturing power makes itself harshly felt: "something in the corners of the space breaks apart / and flies off in pieces / the dismayed faces take cover from the hail" (Boisvert 1992, 52). Neither a point of passage nor a boundary line, the bridge suddenly becomes a gaping hole through which the genocidal intentions re-emerge, exposed to broad daylight. The event's breach is associated with the disintegration of an institution that is unable to hold back the violence it helped to arouse—"the Machine-perse breaks down in its dementia" (14)—to such an extent that the society itself loses its bearings and is troubled: "the relatives are in a bad way / the incontrovertible truth is brought out in front of the whole world" (18). Amid this stupefaction, the army's arrival is seen to re-establish the familiar order: "suddenly, a modicum of primal truth / something that can be seen on screen / heavy, hard, big and dangerous / finally, the tanks!" (37). Boisvert thus portrays in his poetry the transgression of a social limit that revealed the settler state's violence by exposing the violence of some of its citizens.

Yves Boisvert recycles, confuses, and reverses points of view. He takes in everything—from the politicians' speeches to public rumours, by way of the Indigenous protestors' speech, not to mention the narrative configurations that come to predominate during the crisis. Multiple antagonistic voices accuse, curse, and interpellate one another in the book's dialogue. The conflict's political issues and popular clichés are at once repeated, reshaped, and denounced, so that the reader detects a bias without ever quite managing to grasp the argument in detail. The voices making themselves heard in the poems constitute a dialogue about politics, but conflictual politics. It is definitely at a remove from the rational debate in the public sphere theorized by sociologist Jürgen Habermas, all the more because the antagonisms are manifested in the flesh. In fact, in the poems, people do not limit themselves to words—they take up arms, call out the tanks, come to blows. In contrast to the passage depicting the one-way current of the crowd attacking defenceless Mohawk elderly people, women, and children by throwing rocks, other sections feature raw scrimmages in which Indigenous characters, "an inflammable Indigenous person" (44) and "the authentic rebel" (45), vigorously defend themselves against attacks perpetrated by the colonial aggressors, among them a "Canadian Tire soldier" (63), a "repulsive footsoldier" (14), and a "mob" (19) that includes in its ranks the "leader of Montreal's Ku Klux Klan" (54).

Transposing the painful events of the Oka Crisis into scenes of bizarre brawls, the poems invite the reader to side with the figure of the warrior heroically defending his community against violence and intrusion. Nevertheless, the perspective is constantly shifting, which keeps the reader wondering where the blows are coming from and on which side the hero is to be found, destabilizing identification with the character. In the end, while the Mohawk warrior is made out to be the figure of the authentic rebel who takes a dignified stand against what is low and petty, the author shows himself to be just as ungracious towards this hero, whom he describes in terms foreign to any political correctness. Ironically, although not unproblematically, adopting the settlers' paternalistic, racist terms, he describes Indigenous characters as "our little savage" (49) and "our heroes" (51), creating ambiguities that detract from certainty in his statements even as they convey deference towards the Indigenous subject who stands up to the established order.

CHAOS AS A SITE OF EMERGENCE

Regarding the "ensavaging of Quebec poetry," scholar and poet Jonathan Lamy-Beaupré reported a "vast symbolic construction that may not be related to Indigenous cultures." According to him, "l'ensauvagement" ["ensavaging"] is characterized by various traits whose manifestation is always unique, including

> a movement that is deliberately perpendicular to domesticity, so
> as to favour a rebellious freedom; a logic that proceeds on the
> basis of diversion and inversion, especially between positively
> and negatively connoted representations, such as the good
> and bad "Savage"; a manifestation that favours cunning, the
> unexpected, eruption, even fury, and that can make use of
> violence; a certain return to nature, which does not necessarily
> develop in an idyllic manner and can take the form of an attempt

at osmosis with chaos, or "chaosmosis," as Félix Guattari would put it; and finally, a certain way of acting or writing marked by the presence of the instincts, spontaneity or rebellion.[34]

Ensavaging is present in *Voleurs de cause*, but not related to any particular character; in fact, it is the entire event that is virulent, full of fury, rebellious, and chaotic. Playing with archetypes and clichés, Boisvert takes apart the representations in order to more effectively replay the breach caused by the event. He writes, "Tekakwitha / that name echoes like a plaster crucifix / point-blank in the windshield of a police car" (61), invoking imagery laden with meaning on the symbolic level. Like the conflict's elements, the resonance produced by the name Tekakwitha is multilayered and shattering—images of the Mohawk saint and the Christian iconography, of the police forces and the colonial enterprise, of civil engineering and the army's incursion fly into pieces all at once. In the space of fiction, the iconoclastic resonance registers a failure and says that, when the event suddenly erupted, the words were missing. The multiplicity of elements packed into this image brings out all the intensity and complexity of the conflictual weight that was so emphatically manifest with Oka and its representations. At the same time, out of the event's chaos is born the image of a freedom that is like an explosion: "your freedom in the public scrap-heap shines / among the carcasses of police cars" (78). Here, the poet is describing the breach opened up by the gesture of the Indigenous subject divesting himself of oppression's legal shackles. With the line "Born to be wild, my Wâbo, born to be" (78), Boisvert projects an ensavaged destiny inspired by Hollywood movies and the very popular Quebec television series *Les belles histoires des pays d'en haut* [Tales of the high country].

In the following passage, the Mohawk warrior under siege is like a sudden apparition of otherness that imposes itself, throws everything into question, and generates a decided fascination:

> unknown, foreign, restive, pirate
> entrenched concentrationist of history
> a masked warrior
> rises majestically among the Coke ads
> the soot-covered face in the midst of bloody ferns
> the marvellous mug of indocility
> that we guess at through the dirty kerchief (Boisvert 1992, 16)

Coming out of an unknown elsewhere, an underworld, an ahistorical time, the figure of the masked warrior solemnly emerges from among the advertisements when we thought he had disappeared. The non-Indigenous societies, blindsided by a resistance they had not thought possible and which, very often, they cannot understand, tend to experience the event as the emergence of a disturbing difference in a palpable political order that they had assumed was inviolable.

The apparition of this contemporary figure from the beginnings undermines the fixed representation that confines Indigenous peoples to an immutable past, as if they were cut off from the contemporary public space by an unbridgeable gulf. This subversion is underlined by the poetic voice of an Indigenous community asserting its antecedence and its survival: *"first to arrive never having left / never very far away always elsewhere / fashioned by wind, cold and sun / anaphoras of continuity / our anteriority does not set us back in advance / we are not the type to sink into the beginning"* (Boisvert 1992, 65). By warning the Other that it is still there, ancient and contemporary, not at all ready to erase itself in an ahistorical time, this voice evokes the contemporary political action of the Mohawk people who actualize their ways of being and acting without dismantling the foundations of their society. Further, the images of this passage render visible various interlocking levels of meaning, as well as exploded constellations drawn from the general emotion. Thus, the figure of the glorious rebel who stands, intractable, in the middle of the fronds of blood, with a blackened face camouflaged by a dirty scarf, possesses the "noble gravity" of one who sees his existence imperilled, just as it is a unique reiteration of the figure of the "noble savage." While the siege the Mohawk people maintained against the Canadian Army means a hovering danger of more violent deaths, it paradoxically constitutes a limit that in some way allows the protestors and their communities to make themselves exist, although often traumatically. This is precisely the image summoned up by the figure of the Indigenous rebel, the "torso on the brow of a cliff facing the sunset / under the unfailing blue of a sky overloaded with helicopters" (48).

In Yves Boisvert's poetry, the figure of the Mohawk—"the Iroquois, the opposite of the tenants" (Boisvert 1992, 42), "the rebel, the one who is banished, loathed, not ordinary / not easy to tell to sit / not easy to control" (58)—becomes the object of an open admiration, precisely because of his perceived insubordination. The figure of the oppressed Indigenous subject who defies a settler society that seeks to crush him recalls the universal nature of the gesture of rejecting established power. As a setting and venue for speech, the siege replays a dynamic of marginality that Franco-Ontarian scholar François Paré found in the writings of Québécois poets Claude Gauvreau and Patrick Straram, who, like Boisvert, opposed the dominant social forces. Regarding writing's political function, Paré explained that "minority writers remain articulators of collective conscience, and, in language, exponents of the transformation of that conscience into dramatic action."[35] He added that the minority writers who express themselves today in the name of all are precisely "the marginal writers, because their very marginality, unflinching and unyielding, plays out the drama of our collective exclusion from power."[36] Québécois poet Yves Boisvert's expression comes out of just such a marginalized position. In his representation of the Oka Crisis, it is precisely the marginality of the Mohawk warriors and their affirmed exclusion from the seats of settler institutional power that make up the motif of unity, the element of stability in the midst of the event's infernal chaos. Through their marginal yet ostentatious stance behind the barricades, the characters of the "Iroquois" in the poetic space, like the Mohawk protestors in the siege space, replay the drama of the exclusion of all minorities from wielding power.

In a certain way, the Mohawk activists behind the barricades come to speak in the name of us all, without necessarily claiming or wanting to, but by the fact that the role of spokesperson falls to them. In this role, they speak for the collective consciousness of the minority, the opposition to the dominant order, the Indigenous subject fighting for the survival of her people and the protection of her territory. It is perhaps the unique nature of the armed resistance and the exercise of Mohawk sovereignty on the siege site, being both central and marginal, that gives this drama of exclusion all its power. The drama is present in Boisvert's poetry collection, and also in Indigenous literary representations of the resistance at Kanehsatake. It is behind the novel *Bottle Rocket Hearts* by anglo-Québécois writer Zoe Whittall, among others. Set in a politicized scene of Montreal Island, five years after the Oka Crisis and in the months before the 1995 referendum, this coming-of-age story brings the reader on the radical path of a young queer woman who ends up locating her decision-making power through Riot Grrl politics and tumultuous, non-monogamous romance. The resistance at Kanehsatake was also taken up by anarchist, punk, and metal bands, including Rhythm Activism, a Montreal-based, "rock 'n roll cabaret" ensemble, and Iskra, a crust punk band with heavy black-metal influence. They illustrate how the criticism of empire at the core of such formations brought about an identification and feeling of solidarity with the criticism of settler colonialism inherent to the Mohawk and larger Indigenous protest in 1990.

SOVEREIGNTIES IN CONFLICT

"Minority within your minority / my one-seventeenth of your two percent of America" (Boisvert 1992, 10), an Indigenous voice observes in *Voleurs de cause*, addressing the Québécois subject. This voice raises two especially sensitive points: on the one hand, the North American francophone minority's insecurity about language and identity; and, on the other, Quebec society's uneasiness at being confronted with its own status of colonizer by the Indigenous presence, when it had for a long time—and still does in some ways—defined itself as colonized.[37] The collection's title—in English, *Cause Robbers*—makes humorous reference to the conflict of sovereignties at work in the siege space and at the heart of the epic poem. Note that the Oka Crisis is distinct from other similar disputes because Quebec and Canada were then themselves engaged in a power struggle and a confrontation, making half-hearted attempts to achieve reconciliation following the traumatic 1980 Quebec referendum on whether Quebec should pursue a path towards sovereignty. The political crisis that blew up ten years later in Quebec following the failure of the Meech Lake negotiations reminded us all that the two so-called founding peoples were not alone and that others were there before them. This forced them to rethink their respective stories in light of Indigenous narratives that cast them both in the colonizer's role. *Voleurs de cause* depicts in poetry a well-established colonizer confronting an Indigenous subject who not only demands restitution, but also clearly rejects the state's influence in favour of his own sovereignty: "your government doesn't interest me" (47), replies a "beaver trapper" (47) to a settler politician.

Canada hardly appears in the poem, other than in the guise of Canadian Army tanks; it is rather the political and cultural sovereignties and marginalities of the Mohawks and the Québécois that slug it out in the poetic space of the crisis. More specifically, as the title suggests, *Voleurs de cause* plays with the idea that the Mohawk Nation's struggles would come to compete with those of the Québécois, so much so that the Mohawk sovereignists, those "concentrationists / insurgents / reality-driven autonomists / libertarians of consequence / wicked, shameless, offensive people" (74), would rob the Québécois sovereignists of their cause. The community represented by the Québécois narrator sees itself destabilized by a disturbing element that is stealing its aura as an oppressed people bearing up under the majority. It is all the more upset because this element is also turning the tables by putting it in the position of the colonizer. As if that were not enough, "the defensive offended / the people we hate for being less loved than we are" (74), these "libertarians of consequence" (74) with the courage of their convictions, maliciously mock the Québécois' feeble pretensions to sovereignty. "So, still independent in stages?" (59) an Iroquois voice taunts the Québécois interlocutor, in a situation in which relations between the two parties are strained. The relation outlined in the poems is therefore lukewarm towards the Other, who is viewed as both a rival and a hero. Tainted with admiration and jealousy, fascination and rancour, this relation harks back to the very peculiar expression of a colonial stance in a minority situation.

Yves Boisvert intervenes in eventalization. While staging the Oka Crisis, he does not report the facts as they followed in sequence or suggest that the narrative order imitates pure eventalization; rather, he brings out what is left over, what has been forgotten and repeats itself. In so doing, he displays a determination to take the place of the media and possibly also the historian, to offer a poetic historiography that can express the event's power without confining it to the unity of dogma or ideology. By repeating the event's emergence in poetry, he exposes a gap; but he does so in another mode, that of poetry, which participates in the explosion of meaning and representation and also in the birth of a contemporary Indigenous figure.

Boisvert perhaps becomes something of a robber of the Mohawks' cause himself: in his poems, he depicts a figure of the Mohawk rebel who serves indirectly to make a sharp criticism of Quebec's entire society and government. At the same time, he establishes a relationship of complicity and sympathy with the Indigenous subject who resists, asserting against all opposition his ancestry, persistence, and sovereignty. The poet does not so much counter the fixed representations as play with them and break them up, reanimating the event's indeterminacy in the space of fiction. In what ways are the images of the crisis that appear in literary narratives like or unlike the usual representations of Indigenous otherness in the literatures of Quebec and Canada? This is a question that the Oka Crisis certainly encourages us to ask ourselves. As has been observed by many writers, among them Thomas King, Margaret Atwood, and Amaryll Chanady, Indigenous characters in these literatures most often seem to be solitary beings who are inevitably destined to disappear. These literary representations refer back to the figure of the Indian in social discourse and political ideology just as much as they detach themselves from it and reshape it. Jonathan Lamy-Beaupré has observed a progressive change in the representations of Indigenous cultures in contemporary Quebec poetry: "Given that until the first half of the

Yves Boisvert's *Voleurs de cause*, published by Écrits des Forges, 1992.

twentieth century, Québécois poetry had symbolically killed off all the Native American characters that it could, contemporary poetry was able to begin a different relationship with their cultures. The Indigenous presence in poetry then became more episodic and rare, and showed up as scattered images and traces."[38]

Voleurs de cause is especially interesting on this score, because it represents marginal beings by locating them at the very centre of the poetic space. Far from appearing detached or unperturbed, in Boisvert's vision, Quebec society is thrown into the scrimmage, commits unexpected acts of violence, and comes away from the conflict flayed and shaken. The Indigenous presence in his poems asserts itself through its refusal to be compromised, assimilated, or supervised. Echoing the way in which the Oka Crisis confirms that the Indigenous peoples are not about to disappear, a settler voice in the poem states in perplexity, "Decidedly the assimilation of these exotics is hard work" (Boisvert 1992, 80). In the book, the representation conveyed is the figure of the Iroquois who survives and resists, risks his life and confronts a hostile world, sets his limits and plays with power relations. By substituting a figure of resistance and rebellion for one of disappearance, does the figure of the warrior offer an image associated with rebirth, or does it rather partake in other forms of erasure? That question is certainly worthy of study.

While attesting to an Indigenous presence in the contemporary public space, the figure sketched in the literature nonetheless remains a representation generated by the imaginations of non-Indigenous writers. Some narratives, such as the poetry collection *Voleurs de cause*, partake of a postcolonial process insofar as they throw the dominant historiography into question and explode the received identities. Demonstrably, a distance has been created from the old representations of Indigenous otherness. A recent example of these transforming representations is the 2017 novel *Taqawan* by Bordeaux-based Québécois writer Éric Plamondon. *Taqawan* is set in Gaspésie in 1981, at a time marked by the armed assault conducted by the Sûreté du Québec to seize the nets of the Mi'gmaq fishermen asserting their fishing rights in Listiguj. On the cover flap, we can read: "*Taqawan* is a story of fishing and confrontations. A story of crimes and contacts, of injustices and rights violated. *Taqawan* is a story of encounters and new beginnings, of survival and resistance."[39] On the one hand, the novel evokes the 1990 Mohawk resistance through elements of its scenography and allusions to Alanis Obomsawin, whose film on the resistance at Listiguj was used by Plamondon as a documentary source. On the other hand, the novel frames the Mi'gmaq resistance in the context of Indigenous history, and situates the violent police assault in that of a settler colonial occupation driven by abuses of power through law and corruption. While imagery related to criminal realms is present, this fictive narrative is based on historical facts that re-establish Indigenous narratives, thereby contributing to renewed representations of Indigenous peoples. Nonetheless, the relation to the imagined Indigenous referent in settler literary narratives is rooted in part in the writer's place of utterance, such that the representations of Indigenous otherness in Quebec and Canadian literature constitute first and foremost a reflection of the societies from which they arise.[40]

In this regard, studying the representations of the Oka Crisis in the literary narratives of Québécois and Canadian authors makes it possible to question what kind of mark the conflict left on the settler societies and how the societies now envisage their relationship to Indigenous peoples. To attempt to grasp the crisis in all its complexity, it is therefore essential to make room as well for the words of Indigenous writers, poets, storytellers, and novelists.

CHAPTER 7

Mohawk and Other Indigenous Literary Narratives

Indigenous writers, certainly, also wrote about the watershed Oka event, addressing its representations and significance, and its impacts on Indigenous peoples. Their work can be situated in a larger post-Oka literary movement, in which, as noted by Métis writer and scholar Warren Cariou in the *Oxford Handbook of Indigenous American Literature*, "Indigenous writers took up Lee Maracle's challenge to step into the discursive arena and provide the world with their own representations of Indigenous cultures."[1] Indigenous literary narratives that mention the Mohawk resistance at Oka are generally closely linked to its political aspect. In an historical context in which colonial discursive constructions have long condemned Indigenous peoples to silence and dehumanized them, it cannot be denied that speaking out becomes a patently political act, even when it takes an artistic form.[2] The crisis had an effect for both settlers and First Nations. Similarly, literary representations function on two levels: on the one hand, they challenge settler representations of the Oka Crisis; and, on the other, they give voice to Indigenous experiences and accounts of the resistance at Kanehsatake and Kahnawake. Indigenous writers often take up the very charged political issues that were played out on the siege site and in the public space in the summer of 1990, notably that of territory. When they place the event in the context of its emergence in their own discourse, they address a structural and representational violence directed against Indigenous people on a daily basis.

Ojibway writer and scholar Armand Garnet Ruffo observed that the narratives of Indigenous writers often thwart or frustrate the expectations of non-Indigenous readers, scholars, and literary critics. They also encounter resistance on the part of dominant societies, which tend to give them a mixed reception. In the 2001 book *(Ad)dressing Our Words*, Ruffo added that Indigenous writers "must contend with the issue of writing from Aboriginal perspectives in countries that consider it too confrontational and offensive to raise and address the myth of Discovery and the horrific legacy of Colonialism."[3] Despite the transformations that have occurred since in that respect, including with the influence of the Truth and Reconciliation Commission of Canada and the growing field of Indigenous studies, similar considerations often determine which narratives will be received or not by non-Indigenous audiences. With regards to Oka, Indigenous writers often present harsh criticisms of colonial history and the state structures established at the expense of the peoples indigenous to the land. When they expose unmentionable injustices, their critical stance may cause a certain malaise among the non-Indigenous audiences from Quebec and Canada targeted by these "wordarrows." In fact, this concept from Gerald Vizenor refers to words that "are like arrows that can be shot at the narratives of the colonial power" (quoted in McLeod 2001, 31). In relation to 1990, the poem "I Know Who I Am" by Mohawk writer Donna K. Goodleaf features the speech of an Indigenous subject who exposes her settler interlocutor to the dark side of his history:

> colonial history, full of lies
> history of tyranny, massacres, disease, theft, state terrorism
> history of genocide
> that is your history[4]

Goodleaf's poetry and narratives from other writers take a colonial relationship that is defined from an Indigenous perspective and expose it in the fictional space. In doing so, they force non-Indigenous societies to take up the demanding task of reviewing and rewriting their histories and their myths in light of the narrative configurations that now emerge.[5] At the same time, they express and demonstrate how, as Jeannette C. Armstrong expounded in her text "Land Speaking," "Realization of the power in speaking is in the realization that words can change the future and in the realization that we each have that power."[6] The armed siege in summer of 1990 was indeed a very vocal, impactful form of resistance that has continued to act through literary narratives.

Stories of the crisis that fractured Canada's national myth in summer 1990 help to foreground the voices and thoughts that arose out of the breach created by the event. Like the siege, these stories acquire a particular meaning from the fact that their telling often works counter to the process of dual spatial and ideological exile discussed earlier. Their telling is all the more important because, as Cree scholar Neal McLeod put it, "Every time a story is told, every time one word of an Indigenous language is spoken, we are resisting the destruction of our collective memory" (McLeod 2001, 31). In her poem "I Know Who I Am," whose title clearly points to a certainty about her identity, Goodleaf attacks the colonizer, of course, but she does not limit herself to that. She also associates histories of resistance and survival with the spirit of the Haudenosaunee Constitution and the Great Law of Peace:

Indigenous Nations, histories of resistance
we are clans, Nations, ever so strong
our roots, one with mother earth
this land, Turtle Island
Kaianerakowa, Great Law of Peace
ancient constitution of Haudenosaunee people
history of survival, this is my history
I know who I am.[7]

The poem's themes illustrate the close relation between politics and poetry that often appears in Indigenous literature and criticism. Unlike the narratives of their non-Indigenous counterparts, those of Indigenous writers do not celebrate the warriors' stance for reasons of marginality or the accusations they level against the established order. Rather, the Indigenous narratives tend to present images of the communities and families who became caught up in the event and of warrior men and women who risked their lives to defend the territory and ensure their people's survival. These narratives speak to the will of Indigenous peoples to engage in a collective reconstruction, a determination frequently expressed by Indigenous writers that finds reinforcement in their practice. Cherokee scholar Daniel Heath Justice observed that most Indigenous artists, including writers, "are creating art not only for themselves, but also for the survival and enduring presence of Native people."[8] In the summer of 1990, a strengthening of the relation between the physical survival of individuals and the collective survival of their people made the connection between writing and the practical realities of Indigenous peoples very visible. This was magnified by the trauma caused and reawakened by the siege.

Donna K. Goodleaf's
*Entering the War Zone:
A Mohawk Perspective
on Resisting Invasions*,
published by Theytus
Books, 1995.

NARRATIVES OF OKA IN INDIGENOUS LITERATURE FROM QUEBEC

In this respect, it is telling that Quebec's Indigenous writers, with the exception
of the Mohawks, made almost no mention of the Oka Crisis in their narratives
in the two decades following the event. The difficult conflict's immediacy, with
its epicentre in Quebec, no doubt serves to explain a nearly total silence that is
only now being broken. In "Mediating Identity: Kashtin, the Media, and the
Oka Crisis," sociologist Val Morrison recalls the silence imposed on the Innu
music group in 1990, at a moment when Kashtin had just been declared Quebec's musical success of the year, with the larger Québécois public singing along
with their folk songs in Innu-aimun. When they performed in the province
that summer, the duo of Florent Vollant and Claude Mackenzie suddenly saw
the security reinforced, and their recordings were even boycotted by leading

French-language radio stations in the Montreal region.[9] Although he would have preferred to avoid political issues that summer, singer-songwriter Florent Vollant told the media that doing so was impossible because, in that situation, "just being an Indian is already political."[10] The backlash experienced by Kashtin also affected the Indigenous artistic scene across the province in the aftermath of the Oka Crisis. Innu André Dudemaine, director of the First Peoples Festival Présence autochtone in Montreal, remembered co-founding the Indigenous cultural organization Terres en vues / Land InSights the same year as the event, and having to work "in a context that was difficult, and even hostile,"[11] notably in terms of funding, or absence thereof. Similarly, Huron-Wendat playwright Yves Sioui Durand denounced at different venues the major cutbacks in funding that affected the theatre company Ondinnok in the aftermath of Oka, something he described as "administrative repression."[12]

Today, nearly thirty years later, young poets, writers, playwrights, and composers who are active in Quebec's Indigenous literary and arts scene do make reference to the crisis in their creations. Some of them talk about feeling dissociated from, and yet identifying with, a political event most of them experienced as children, and that they still find compelling. In the piece "Injustice," from his album *Face à soi-même* [Facing oneself], popular Anishinaabe rapper Samian distances himself from the crisis by declaring, "The Oka Crisis has nothing to do with my case." He nonetheless resolutely continues, "But I'll fight to the end to defend our rights! I want to follow the path of my ancestors, be the voice of my people! A disappearing language, I want to rebuild the nation!" This distanciation can be understood as a will to dissociate from the negative representations of Oka that circulated in Quebec during and after the event. At the same time, this evocation of the Indigenous peoples' struggles on behalf of the planet and the nation, dignity and justice, pride and survival continues to define the core issues in the resistance at Kanehsatake. In a similar way, in the poem serving as epigraph to this book, Innu poet Natasha Kanapé Fontaine forcefully proclaims, "I will not just be an Oka Crisis" and later goes on to say, "and when they look at me / they'll be looking at a people united and standing straight with the power of thunder! / my songs of peace will be the sap of my proud survival!" The Mohawk resistance clearly continues to motivate and inspire the contemporary political struggles of young Indigenous rappers, slam poets, and artists.

In her poetry anthology *Assi Manifesto*, Kanapé Fontaine relates the resistance of 1990 to other past and present struggles for Indigenous lands and lives across Turtle Island: "I back burst in the grass/ the grass of ancient songs in tons on the wheat/ the fields/ Wounded Knee my heart Athapaskan/ my Romaine soul/ Oka/ Nitassinan."[13] The poem places the sieges of Wounded Knee and Kanehsatake side to side with contemporary protest against extractive industries, from the Athabasca region to Nitassinan—land of the Innu people, foregrounding "discourses, aesthetics, and knowledges that are emerging at the intersections of public protest, artistic expression, and environmental ethics."[14]

In 2016, Atikamekw playwright Véronique Hébert published in *Inter, art actuel*, the first act of a stage play she has been developing based on the event, with a focus on Indigenous women and resistance across the Americas. Through the perspective of a young Atikamekw character named Wabana, "Oka" connects three landmark events of the last decade of the twentieth century: the deadly shooting of fourteen women by an antifeminist at the Polytechnique Montreal on 6 December 1989; the resistance and indignation of the Mohawk "matriarchal society" that made the headlines in summer 1990; and the struggle of the masked Zapatistas defending "Mother Earth and the oppressed" in Chiapas, Mexico, in 1994. Upon remembering the defence of "the pine forest at Oka, with its ancestral cemetery," Wabana states with emotion in relation to the summer of 1990: "We, Amerindians, even without knowing it, started to wake up. In our viscera there was like a great Plumed Serpent which began to rumble. Quetzalcóatl, the Quetzalcóatl, the Toltec god . . . or Aztec . . . I do not remember anymore, but the Quetzalcóatl, with its large Plumed Serpent body, coiled itself all along our backbones. Indians across the world felt something."[15] In the play, the event deeply affects Indigenous peoples, generates a new consciousness, and makes its impact felt across the hemisphere through an embodied relationship with Quetzalcóatl. The resistance at Oka marks a turning point at the personal and community levels, as well as in terms of reviving what Chadwick Allen described as "trans-indigenous"[16] connections.

Other configurations that are very close to the political crisis emphasized the settler backlash and its violent impact on Indigenous people in 1990. Innu writer Mélissa Picard has been working on a novel featuring the trajectory of a young Indigenous woman who, as a teenager, resented the Mohawks, holding them responsible for a difficult political situation; however, as her understanding increases, she gradually redirects her anger to the agents of racism and oppression. In his 2017 short story "Hannibalo-God-Mozilla contre le grand vide cosmique" [Hannibalo-God-Mozilla against the great cosmic void], Wendat poet, writer, and performer Louis-Karl Picard-Sioui evokes the disruptive character of the event in an opening scene featuring a reminiscence of a car accident, in which the violent collision with a moose creates a chaos that is at once destructive and generative. Oka directly comes into play through the eyes of the young narrator who is watching reruns of *The Dog Who Stopped the War* (in French original, *La guerre des tuques*) interspersed with flashes of spectacular media clips of the Oka Crisis. The siege's scenography is ironically depicted. The narrator observes: "Native hoodies equipped with Chinese imitations of Russian automatic weapons sow terror in the south of Montreal. The populace wants bread and games, and the wicked Indians refuse to share their cemetery for the extension of a golf course. Again, the city is besieged by the bloodthirsty barbarians of history books. The grand return of the Iroquois, those ghosts of another age who refuse to disappear in front of the Sacrosanct Francomontrealian empire. Kahnawake, an irreducible village surrounded by the Gallic colony of Bourrassix" (translation).[17] Picard-Sioui's use of eclectic stereotypes stirs into the standoff the international mafias, the Roman Empire, the *Asterix* series of French comics, and the colonial history that pitted the Iroquois against the French. In this story, Picard-Sioui takes up some of the same imagery used by Yves Boisvert, bringing to mind the extremely negative and racist representations of the Iroquois that prevailed until not too long ago in French-Canadian history books. He reverses the common representation of the surrounded francophone minority to put forward that of the besieged Iroquois. The Wendat writer also unsettles the contemporary settler evocations of historical French and Huron allyship, against the Iroquois and the British, by portraying an event in which both the Iroquois and the Wendat become targets of settler aggressions. The narrator concludes with a sight of the settlers of the South Shore who are watching the same children's movie as he is, but who go out and pelt Kahnawake elders, women, and children, not with snowballs, but with stones. The insult "Kawish" shouted at them resonates with how it was shouted at the narrator years earlier, a memory that links the violence of the event to that of the racism experienced on a personal, daily basis. In many respects, these representations dovetail with those produced by Indigenous writers elsewhere in Canada, but they also bring out several aspects peculiar to the Quebec situation and its specific colonial history.

NARRATIVES FROM THE SIEGE SITES IN
KANEHSATÀ:KE AND KAHNAWÀ:KE

Narratives by Mohawk authors illuminate the event from the perspective of the communities that were directly affected by the police and army presence, the heightened political tension produced by the armed conflict, and ensuing post-traumatic stress. Regarding the 1973 siege at Wounded Knee on the Pine Ridge Reservation in the United States, Gerald Vizenor concluded that "Wounded Knee has had post-traumatic effects on several generations [of Indigenous people] because the stories of the survivors were seldom honoured in the literature and histories of dominance."[18] Like the sixty-one-day siege that stood for Indigenous militancy in the 1970s, the armed resistance in Kanehsatà:ke and Kahnawà:ke retains an inaccessible, unexpressed core of feeling that is not easily addressed.

Mohawk writer and artist Joe David of Kanehsatà:ke treated the issue with evident bitterness in the story "How to Become an Activist in One Easy Lesson." The title itself makes an ironic reference to his becoming involved in the peaceful occupation and then, against his will, in the subsequent armed siege. Lamenting a certain voyeuristic quality in the media spectacle, he observes that when he is invited to speak about his Oka experience in churches, at universities, and in meeting halls, it seems to be taken as mere "entertainment."[19] Shocked by the lack of engagement of the people who come to hear him, he writes: "It's as if they're watching me spill my guts in front of them. They seem detached, untouchable, like they're watching something on TV" (David 1994, 161). This lack of compassion, solidarity, and ability to relate, he notes, is also reflected in confessions of culpability that are essentially seeking his absolution. Other examples are provided by the words of encouragement telling him to "keep fighting the battles and never give up" (161), battles that invariably fail to result in concrete action.

David mentions the exhausting legal battle he must wage in a courtroom, "a much less honorable place to fight for our rights than in the pines" (161), and one waged without the necessary support. Raising the issue of settler complicity, he says about the well-intentioned, "I want them to take responsibility, individually and collectively" (161). His narrative encourages readers to take political action that will change the larger social situation, but it is also intended to raise awareness about the colonial structure that is doing violence to Indigenous peoples.

Joe David's narrative is marked by bitterness, anger, and sadness. The writer concludes that the harsh armed conflict and its long-term effects have made a cynical, exhausted, radicalized person out of someone who had always led a life that was "fairly quiet and uncomplicated in Kanehsatake" (162). He remarks that history repeats itself, recalling his great-grandfather's participation in 1909 in the armed confrontation to prevent Canadian Northern Railway tracks from crossing Mohawk territory. Joe David concludes his story by encouraging the non-Indigenous people to speak out, because "as long as nobody says anything against the policies except the Indians, it will just stay as it is" (164). The author is referring to the structural nature of injustice and the deep-rooted colonial conflict in which people become engaged despite themselves, and in which they are ethically bound to act. Joe David does not elaborate on the "underbelly of the resistance"—that is, in Kiera Ladner's and Leanne Simpson's words, "stories of a community divided and stories which serve to divide a community"[20]—but he clearly identifies the external pressures that serve to amplify it. His narrative also renders tangible the pain and sacrifice endured by the people and community of Kanehsatà:ke in 1990 that Ladner and Simpson wanted to acknowledge and honour by co-editing the 2010 *This Is an Honour Song: Twenty Years Since the Blockades*. Their anthology expresses how the Mohawk resistance affected, unsettled, and inspired settler and Indigenous peoples across the country.

In the personal account "Razorwire Dreams" he published in 1992 in *Voices: Being Native in Canada*, Kanehsata'kehró:non writer Dan David, Joe David's brother, discusses a traumatic aspect of the armed conflict that makes it hard to symbolize in writing. He explains that it took him a long time to be able to speak about what he saw behind the barricades, and even longer to be able to describe what he felt there. Two years after the crisis's denouement, he reports that his writing is still hampered by the intensity of his emotions: "The words are tied up by a mass of twisted emotions. I'm still too angry, too full of hate at what they did and keep doing to the people back home. I know I can't make sense of what really happened back there until I can make sense of the way I feel."[21] The failure to make sense of the event and his emotional confusion are accompanied by disturbing dreams: "I wake up sometimes in the middle of the night, or in that quiet time just before dawn, feeling displaced and disoriented" (David 1992, 20). The narrator further describes how he awakes feeling completely destabilized, with sweat on his forehead, damp palms, and his stomach knotted with fear, from anxiety-producing dreams that feature images of the barbed wire strung out by the soldiers. The dreams bring back contrasting memories from the summer of 1990: "Some of my memories are stark and ugly and full of threat; of guns of all shapes and sizes, of barricades and razor wire and of the hatred in people's eyes.

This Is an Honour Song: Twenty Years Since the Blockades, edited by Leanne Betasamosake Simpson and Kiera L. Ladner, published by Arbeiter Ring Publishing, 2010.

Strangely, confusingly, some of these same images are tinged with an almost surreal beauty: of helicopter searchlights dancing across distant hills; of people dancing to a Mexican drum between barbed wire; and of a Mohawk bunker glowing eerily under a full moon. These images repel me. But they fascinate me at the same time" (20). These contrasting images, both fascinating and repellent, echo the feeling of unreality reported by protagonists in the documentary films examined in previous chapters. Admitting ruefully that the duty of remembrance is not a pleasant one, the narrator in David's account explains that while he hopes that the nightmares will fade away, "even these dreams force me to confront some things I know I must never forget" (20). The author's post-event reflections on the conflict's fallout are intercut with scenes from the summer that occasionally surface: his mother courageously respecting his brother's decision to go to the barricades; children shouting and waving to chase away the army helicopters hovering over the community; police officers driving slowly by in their vehicles to intimidate the women and children, who reply with humorous signs carrying messages like "15 MORE MILES TO FREE DONUTS" (29).

The narrator describes an atmosphere in the Pines that is both friendly and uncertain on a full-moon night when the people are keeping watch over the site, anxiously anticipating an imminent attack by the police. In this scene, he sees shadows slipping into the dark, alerted by a suspicious noise, "like cats on a prowl. Their rifles ready, they hop over a log and disappear into the woods" (21). He remembers a feeling of time standing still, silence descending, the signal being passed from bunker to bunker, and then, when the threat has passed, a release of tension and the "jokes and good natured chatter" starting up again (21). Unlike the media's representations of the siege, this narrative describes a spirit of mutual help and protection among the people in the Pines. The "protestors," as they are conveniently refered to, are not depicted as avowed warriors, but as people who in only a few days accustomed themselves to the situation of an armed conflict, aware that they were putting their lives in danger: "We stand in little knots behind the bunker, stretching ourselves. We all understand, without saying, that they'll probably wind up dead or wounded if the police attack" (21). Notably, the narrator locates himself among the people ambushed in the pine grove ("we") while drawing a distinction ("they") seemingly between those who conducted the siege and those who lived in the community and moved freely across the barricades until the perimeter shut them out.

In Dan David's narrative, the violence directed at the community is represented by the infernal rhythm of the drums: "Kill, kill, kill" (25). The author's sister Linda points it out to him, noting that the rhythm has been growing more intense for weeks. He fails to understand at first, but after a moment grasps what his sister is trying to get him to perceive: "I realized then that I'd been hearing those drums all along. I'd heard the drumming coming from the rock-throwing mobs in LaSalle and Chateauguay and from some blood-thirsty commentators in the media. And even from some Mohawks. The choppers had picked up the rhythm. So had the tanks rolling by. The police were chanting incessantly to that beat. Everywhere the drums were calling for death" (25). The violence embodied in the army tanks and police presence and the racist aggression in social discourses that turned into attacks with rocks come to seem, in Dan David's account, like a murderous movement directed against the community. Having heard the drums' fatal rhythm, the narrator can see what only seems to be a possibility becoming a violent reality. At Kanehsatà:ke's emergency department, David witnesses the distress registered by Margaret, one of the staff, on seeing the medical equipment supplied by the Red Cross: "I saw her reel back in shock as the back-boards started coming in" (27). The narrator reflects on the rift between a rational approach to the unthinkable and the sudden realization that members of his family stationed in the Pines are under threat of meeting a brutal end: "Thinking the unthinkable was one thing. Intellectually, we could deal with it. But coming face to face with the awful possibility that we might have to go in and pull out their bodies was almost more than we could accept" (27).

The siege clearly seems to be a threatened space. It also becomes a community configuration in which connections among the Indigenous people are reactivated, in contrast to how the situation is perceived by the outside world. Rather than creating the image of a Mohawk warrior standing alone against all comers, "Razorwire Dreams" reveals a network of solidarity converging on Kanehsatà:ke. For example, the narrator recounts how an Ojibway Elder approached the barricades to transmit words of hope and encouragement in person, and that "runners came from all over with similar messages" (28). The narrator paints a unique, humane portrait of the people occupying the Pines and living in Kanehsatà:ke. This is apparent when he conveys what these actions mean to the people in the community, repeats the words and gestures of his family members, or remembers the people who distributed food and kept an eye on houses that had been vacated. Given this perspective, the discourse of the authorities and the media describing the protestors as "warriors" and "terrorists" motivated by the desire to expand an "international criminal empire" based on bingo and smuggled cigarettes sounds to the narrator like "an insult and a smear" (24). Dan David's account expresses a conscious determination to unveil and contest the discursive manifestations around Oka of what the co-editors of *Fragile Settlements* have described as the "transcolonial historical processes associated with the subjugation of Indigenous peoples through law."[22]

According to Dan David, the protestors in the Pines found themselves "trapped in the cross-fire of guns and propaganda" (25), to such an extent that the issues behind the conflict became obscured: "Lost in the war of words in the media was the simple plea from the Mohawk people of the Pines for survival, for their land and for the right to live with dignity" (25). The members of his family and his friends in the Pines, he explains, are people who fight to defend ideas and hold ceremonies and who, basically, refuse to see carried out the mayor of Oka's vow to "take the land and erase the Mohawk presence" (24). The siege becomes a matter of resistance to a project of elimination whose correlative is a definite, not-to-be-contested appropriation of the Mohawk territory. The return to the status quo desired by the mayor, who says that he wants to "put things back the way they were" (24), represents to the Mohawk protestors "a sure and steady slide down a one-way street to an oblivion called assimilation" (24). David explains that, in addition to opposing this disappearance with their presence, the small group makes a "simple but dangerous" statement: "This is Mohawk territory and it always has been" (24). David repeats the words of the people of the Pines, who declared that it was not a reserve, not Crown land, but definitely a Mohawk territory belonging "to the Mohawk people and to their Mohawk government" (24). Like the siege, this narrative traces a threatened space in which the Mohawk people's sovereignty is stated and practised. Its author is replicating, in the space defined by the writing, how the Mohawk protestors and communities took a stand in 1990.

The David brothers' narratives recall the physical and symbolic violence directed at their people, but also an ancestral resistance—that of parents, grandparents, and great-grandparents—that was transmitted from generation to generation. In this respect, they resemble the stories of late Mohawk writer Myra Cree, who is well known in Quebec, principally as the first woman anchorperson for Radio-Canada's flagship television news program *Téléjournal*. Cree is one of the founding members of the Mouvement pour la justice et la paix à Oka-Kanehsatake [Movement for peace and justice at Oka-Kanehsatake], which was created during the 1990 crisis. In the story "Miroir, miroir, dis-moi . . . [Mirror, mirror, tell me . . .]," which she published only a few months after the siege's denouement, this self-described "daughter and granddaughter of Chiefs"[23] brought critical insight to the event as viewed from personal experience. She writes that at the end of the nineteenth century, when the Canadian government decided, "following a lengthy dispute between the Sulpicians and the Mohawks of Oka," to move the community to Ontario, the refusal was clear and effective: "My grandfather, Iroquois Grand Chief Timothy Arirhon, objected to this decision, and he remained at Oka, with the great majority of his people" (Cree 1990, 304). By emphasizing the unilateral nature of this initial attempt at delocalization and encroachment, Cree implicitly demonstrates that the expropriation planned a century later by the Municipality of Oka is its repetition. At the same time, she exposes the role played by the federal government in the appropriation of Indigenous peoples' territories over the centuries. Citing her family tie to the grand chief who opposed the settler government's desire to uproot her community, she confers additional legitimacy on the Mohawks' opposition to a repeated attempt at encroachment, this one at the end of the twentieth century.

Myra Cree is highly critical of the dramatic exaggeration establishing a media image of the Mohawks that is "distorted to the point of caricature." In this text addressed to a large audience, she maintains that the hasty judgements expressed by the Québécois majority during the crisis demonstrate "a crass ignorance of the habits and customs of the Iroquois, who include the Mohawk Nation" (304). By locating the event from the perspective of a Mohawk historiography, Cree outlines the timeline of the crisis in no uncertain terms: "For us, the Mohawks of Oka-Kanehsatake, the crisis is not over, far from it" (304). She firmly maintains that before relations between the communities of Oka and the Mohawks can be resumed, "peace would have to rhyme with justice, and legality with legitimacy" (304), and, to conclude, she endorses this imperative by saying, "because we are *Onkweón:we*" (304), and provides the following translation in a footnote: "those who are and always were" (304).

The poem "Mon pays rêvé ou la PAX KANATA [My ideal country or the Pax Kanata]," which Myra Cree published five years later, depicts an idyllic country free of the tensions exposed to the light of day by the failure of the Meech Lake Accord and the Oka Crisis, in the context of the 1995 Quebec Referendum. In this poetic space, historical agreements are respected, so that "we are very well *treatied*," and furthermore, the First Nations enjoy a fully recognized sovereignty: "We are assured of our autonomy, / we have our own Parliament, / from now on there will be three visions of this country."[24] In the poem, the reason for the territorial dispute has vanished to clear the way for a coexistence that is the reverse of the strained relations between the Québécois and Mohawks during the Oka Crisis: "In Kanesatake, where I live, / there's birch and pine enough for everyone, / the golf course has disappeared / and everyone, Whites and Redskins (I dream in Technicolor) / can, as in the past, enjoy this enchanting place" (Cree 1995, 23). In this space where peace has been restored, political and cultural exchanges are respectful and egalitarian. Some illustrative examples are reserves that "have become summer camps," a translation of "Marguerite Duras'

novel *L'amant* into Inuktitut," and Québécois film director Denys Arcand preparing "a musical comedy with a score by Pierre Létourneau on the life of Ovide
Mercredi, / who has agreed to play himself" (23). The waking dream, which
ends when the dreamer "pinches herself to make sure she can believe it" (23),
projects exchanges carried out in a spirit of recognition and reciprocity rather
than settler domination and confrontation.

Mohawk writers also provide accounts of the event as it was experienced in
Kahnawà:ke. The fight against the army's incursion onto Tekakwitha Island, which
is very strong symbolically, is depicted in various stories and poems. The speaker
in Donna K. Goodleaf's poem "Remember This!" addresses the figure of the Canadian soldier, instructing him not to forget the resistance of the "Grandmothers,
Clan mothers, Mothers, Aunties / Nieces and Daughters"[25] at Tekakwitha Island:

> Remember the day of Sept. 18th?
>> the day you invaded and occupied Tekakwitha Island
>> and we, the Women,
>> ripped away your razor wires with our bare hands
>
>> the day you tear gassed women, men and children
>> tear gas that fueled our fighting spirit
>> and forced you to retreat   stunned
>> stunned by the resistance of Kahnawakeronon
>> the people who kicked your ass
>>> Remember?
> We do. (Goodleaf 1995, 98)

The poem inscribes the episode in the community's collective memory. It show-
cases the political role of women in Haudenosaunee society and celebrates the
aggressive response to the invader. An ancient collective spiritual link to the
land they live on and protect is reaffirmed:

> We are the People
> who love our land, our mother
> and will continue to fiercely resist you
> to protect and defend always
> this spirit of the land

land of the Flint
ancient and continuous (98)

The poem directly echoes the discourse about the land and sovereignty heard during the siege, with still greater power because it was published as part of Goodleaf's non-fiction book *Entering the War Zone: A Mohawk Perspective on Resisting Invasions.*

Mohawk poet Peter Blue Cloud also recalls this fighting episode in an account he published in the anthology *Native American Testimony: A Chronicle of Indian-White Relations from Prophecy to the Present, 1492–1992.*[26] As Vine Deloria Jr. explains in the preface, the anthology makes every effort to shore up North America's historical knowledge by making a place for "the informality of human experience, which colors all our decisions and plays an intimate and influential role in the historical experiences of our species" (xvii). Ironically, Blue Cloud's "Resistance at Oka," describing an armed confrontation that has Indigenous protestors opposed to the Canadian Army, is included in a section of the anthology devoted to modern Indigenous history, that is, editor Peter Nabokov pinpointed in his introduction, "as tribes leave the frontier spotlight to fend for themselves with dwindling resources, many regulations, and words and symbols as their weapons" (xxiii). Contrary to this trend, the siege of summer 1990 summons up the image of colonial wars that many believed had passed into history.

In the first part of his narrative, before relating his direct experience of the Kahnawà:ke siege, Blue Cloud places the event in its broader historical context and recalls the armed conflict's immediate issues. In the second section, he provides a poetic testimony to the community's resistance to the military incursion on Tekakwitha Island. Before beginning this testimony, Blue Cloud specifies that he is writing exclusively "from my own observations and thoughts" (432), and then adds, insisting on the personal nature of his account, "I speak for no one else" (432). Immediately at the outset, he recalls the immensity of the land occupied by the Six Nations Iroquois Confederacy, territories that "were ours long before the coming of the Europeans" (432). Having established the Mohawks' continuous occupation of the land, he explains that, at Kanehsatà:ke, the Sulpicians obtained "lands to hold in trusteeship for the natives, to remain their property until natives left them or died out" (432). He concludes that, under the terms of this agreement, the Sulpicians' sales and leasing of the land were illegal, "since the Mohawks never left Kanehsatake" (432). Like Dan David, Blue Cloud underscores the correlation between the settlers' appropriation of territory and the project to eliminate the Mohawk people.

Blue Cloud describes the protestors' stand in the Pines as a last resort that consisted in declaring and exercising sovereignty over the land: "The Mohawks tried to fight the expansion of the golf course by legal means, but they lost and the lands were declared no longer theirs. There was no other recourse but to declare it Indian Land" (432). More than a counter-performativity, occupying the pine grove here appears to be an exercise of Mohawk sovereignty and the recourse to weapons to be part of defending the territory. With reference to traditional forms of government and significant family relations, the narrator explains that, when the community learned that the police had begun an assault on the pine grove, it took action: "Our traditional clan mothers ordered our Warriors to blockade the highways going through our lands, to support our relatives at Kanesatake" (432). Regarding Kahnawà:ke, he states that "most of us stayed because it was our home" (432). In his text, Blue Cloud then reports on the lack of medical personnel, food rationing, supplies being brought in by boat, and attacks that he and others witnessed. He recalls one disturbing moment in particular, "as caravans of our children, elders, women, fearing an invasion and trying to leave, were stoned by a mob while police stood by" (432). The impunity granted to these extremely disturbing acts of racial violence is thus clearly and soberly denounced.

It is in this context that Peter Blue Cloud sets his account of the seventieth day of the siege, 18 September 1990, which brought the Canadian Army's incursion onto Tekakwitha Island. It occurs as Blue Cloud is sitting quietly on his balcony, trying to think about faraway things "unrelated to the presence of the Canadian Army surrounding our lands" (434), and recalling memories of childhood, "when violence and death were dreamlike happenings in a World War far away" (434). His melancholy musing is rudely interrupted by "the sudden whacking, roaring sounds of a huge helicopter directly over my house" (434). The sounds are accompanied by the sight of troops climbing out of helicopters and rolls of barbed wire being set down, along with "other equipment to accompany whatever demonic drama was unfolding before my eyes" (434). It is only the rapid arrival of Mohawk men, women, and teenagers, incensed by the military incursion, that dispels the impression of unreality inspired by the scene: "The reality of this bizarre scene became evident with the immediate arrival of honking cars from all over town. Mohawks—men, women, and young people—poured onto the bridge, in outrage and anger that our sacred territory was being invaded by an armed force of the military" (434). This memory of the poet was also echoed in the memoirs of late Karonhiaion Annie Cecilia Charlie, a respected Kahnawà:ke Elder and fluent Kanien'keha speaker, who had remained at home throughout the standoff in 1990.[27] In his text, Peter Blue Cloud salutes the bold, courageous actions of the people who went after the soldiers with their bare hands to chase them off the territory: "There was no fear on the faces of our Mohawk people, only anger" (Blue Cloud 1995, 434). He also reports feeling a sense of serenity, standing in the middle of the fighting and the tear gas: "I stood at the center of the bridge when the third barrage of tear gas fell. I stood at the center of myself and my people" (435). The impression of being centred harks back to the connections uniting community members and, in a way, the symbolism of the Circle Wampum joining the nations in the confederacy.

Unlike Yves Boisvert's irreverent, raucous poems, Peter Blue Cloud's account of the crowds, the fights, and the general scrimmage is steeped in a profound respect for his people, the Mohawks. He remembers these people bravely battling the soldiers and forcing them to beat a retreat, signifying the army's defeat and the assembled crowd's victory: "When the last of the soldiers finally left in darkness, a great cheer went up from the crowd" (435). Evoking a conception of the world that we mentioned earlier, Blue Cloud concludes his narrative with a reaffirmation of the sacred nature of each of the earth's elements and, as he explains it in reference to Indigenous environmental ethics, the role of the earth's guardians to be played by the Indigenous peoples.

The constant reiteration, on the siege site and in the literary narratives, of Mohawk sovereignty and the people's connection to the land is linked to the Mohawk people's continued resistance to a process of spatial and ideological exile that is equally insistent. The book *Basic Call to Consciousness,* edited by *Akwesasne Notes,* speaks of a persistent state of siege: "For over three hundred years, our people (Haudenosaunee) have been under a virtual state of siege. During this entire time we have never once given up our struggle. Our strategies have, of necessity, changed, but the will and determination to continue on remains the same."[28] In this context, the Mohawk literary narratives partake of the affirmation and reinforcement of this determination to carry on the struggle. While remaining as close as is possible to the political realities of the siege, as directly experienced and seen from a Mohawk perspective, the narratives of writers such as Myra Cree, Dan David, and Peter Blue Cloud[29] also allow us, as we will see, to gain a better grasp of the way in which Indigenous authors from other nations represent the conflict in writing.

THE LITERARY NARRATIVES OF CANADA'S FIRST NATIONS

Writers from other First Nations in Canada have made reference to Oka in various novels, plays, short stories, tales, poems, and testimonies.[30] Whereas the Mohawk poetry and literary narratives speak out of a very close relationship to the siege's realities and political issues, the others describe relating to the event both at a distance, generally through the media, and up close, by virtue of a strong identification with the Mohawks and a personal and political engagement in the resistance. And, unlike the representations to be found in the Quebec and Canadian corpus, these works do not feature themes of smuggling, criminal activity, or illegality, but rather those of colonial history, political battles, and the feeling of individual and collective alienation that constituted the context for the event's occurrence. The stance of the Mohawk protestors, endangering their lives to protect their land in the face of the Canadian Army's deployment in their communities, constitutes a major symbolic element.

In many literary narratives, the event brings to light a structural racism that does violence to Indigenous characters on a daily basis. At the same time that the crisis emphasizes the separation between the settler and Indigenous worlds, it brings a realization that the Canadian society can no longer make the First Nations disappear. In the narratives, the mobilization in support of the Mohawks inspires feelings of pride and anger as well as political exchanges and debates. The narratives present words that are spoken and heard, a reversal of perspective, and a sense of coming home that shows itself in the process of discovering connections in shared stories, familial ties, and experiences generated by the event. In the context of the armed resistance at Kanehsatake, they demonstrate the ways in which, as Tonawanda Seneca scholar Mishuana Goeman explained in her book *Mark My Words: Native Women Mapping Other Nations*, "Native stories speak to a storied land and storied peoples, connecting generations to particular locales and in a web of relationships."[31]

THE POLITICAL EVENT

The event that exploded on 11 July 1990 shocked, worried, and directly interpellated Indigenous peoples across the country. This was clearly reflected in

Indigenous literary narratives. In her novel *Daughters Are Forever*, set during the conflict at Ipperwash in 1995, Stó:lo writer Lee Maracle summons up Oka as a memory. A particular feature of this memory is that it orients the actions of Indigenous characters involved in the new territorial conflict at Ipperwash, during which a police officer shoots and kills a protestor, Dudley George. Describing the police intervention at Oka in terms of an invasion and the stance of the Mohawk protestors as a refusal to abandon their position, one of the female characters remembers "the day the Quebec police invaded Oka and no one retreated."[32] The aspect of a tense game being played immediately arises from the recollection of the parties on both sides standing their ground. The narration goes on to recall the gravity of the conflict, as signalled by the army's intervention:

> The army had replaced the Quebec police. "Well, now we've finally gone and done it," she said to Catherine, who was sitting at the table with her. "Now there is going to be a war."
>
> "Done what?"
>
> "A cop is dead and they have called in the army and no one is retreating."
>
> "What are we going to do?" Catherine had asked. The assumption between them was that they, two Salish women who knew nothing about the issue between Quebec and Kanehsatake, had to do something. (Maracle 2002, 134)

Instead of leaving the characters perplexed and uncertain, like oftentimes in settler literary representations, the event immediately aroused an urgent need to act. This is found in many Indigenous literary narratives, even when the action is set hundreds of kilometres from the siege site. In the stage play "The Crisis in Oka, Manitoba," published by Saulteaux playwright Douglas Raymond Nepinak in the anthology *This Is an Honour Song*, a young male character, Isaiah, who is unsure about his future, expresses this strong sense of having to take action. Speaking to his mother, who, given the great danger, is trying to dissuade him from going to Oka, he exclaims fervently that he cannot remain a passive spectator of the event: "I'm not going to sit here on my ass and watch it on TV when I oughta be doing something about it, not just watch."[33] Similarly, the homeless from Vancouver's Hastings Street, who served as the inspiration for the characters in Shuswap playwright Darrell Dennis's *Tales of an Urban Indian*, interpellated one another in 1990, expressing their own determination to take action. Dennis explained in an interview that, while this determination did not result in concrete action, "the idea was they had to show support to their Native brothers and do something political. So it was really quite strange."[34] The history of the event, according to historian Pierre Grégoire, shows that the "'historical' event is often affected by a mobilizing value because it represents a sort of Gordian Knot involving a tangle of symbolic productions, discourses, collective attitudes and so on."[35] In the same way, Indigenous literary narratives that mention the 1990 crisis make it easier to discern the mobilizing value inherent in an event that, as we have seen, arose from a colonial conflict that was deep-rooted and therefore complicated in terms of settler-Indigenous relationships but also very clear in its expression of Indigenous refusal of encroachment.

In the Indigenous literary narratives, deploying the forces of law and order to remove the Indigenous protestors from the Pines is generally represented as a relentless campaign waged by white settler society to appropriate and destroy the Indigenous peoples' land. In Nepinak's play, the character of Isaiah clearly associates the golf courses, "plowed over sacred burial grounds" (Nepinak 2010, 142), with other forms of encroachment, such as the "villages evacuated because of a hydro project" and "logging companies in sacred forests" (142). The criticism that Indigenous peoples are never considered or heeded by Canadian society is often heard in the narratives, as illustrated by references to the fruitless political negotiations that require them to "talk, talk, talk until we're blue in the face" (142). This critical refrain regarding the settlers' failure to listen harks back to a long-standing dynamic that was aggravated by the political crisis. In the summer of 1990, the Indigenous movements of solidarity with the Mohawks in the Pines and against the governments' colonialist policies were motivated by interpretations of the event based on a context that existed from one end of the country to the other. As demonstrated in their political discourse and literary narratives, the Indigenous peoples could generally see themselves in the resistance mounted by the Mohawk protestors.

Regarding Kahnawake's internal politics during Oka, Gerald Taiaiake Alfred explained that, although the initial confrontations had been initiated by a specific group and not by the majority of community members or the elected council, once facing "the *fait accompli* of barricades and armed Mohawks face-to-face with non-Indian police forces, all Mohawks were compelled to accept the Warrior Longhouse's actions and move forward."[36] He drew attention to the shared consciousness and sensibility behind the solidarity manifested at that time of crisis in Kahnawake: "This 'crisis solidarity,' while temporary, rests on the commonality in all self-conceptions of Mohawk identity: the keen awareness of the difference between Mohawks and non-Indians, and a shared sensitivity towards territorial issues arising out of the common historical experience with non-Indian governments and their consistent effort to eliminate the Mohawk land base."[37] The difference in identity, territorial issues, and historical experience of troubled relations with settler governments were common points that encouraged the people of Kahnawake to feel compelled to support the actions of the protestors at the barricades, rather than falling into line with the police, military, and government authorities. In the same way, it seems that it is because the Indigenous peoples share with the Mohawks a similar consciousness and sensibility of this difference that they tend to see themselves in the political struggle that was actualized on the siege site by members of that nation. And this is precisely the solidarity evoked by Manitoban Anishinaabe writer Wab Kinew when he discusses the heightened polarization of the summer of 1990: "The 'Oka Crisis' was an event that forced people to choose sides, and we did not have to think twice about which side we were on. We were with the warriors" (Kinew 2010, 48).

POLARIZATION

Oka provoked a polarization that can be viewed, on the one hand, as the apparition of two poles in a single structure: for example, the settlers and Indigenous peoples. On the other hand, in relation to the event and, more practically, the siege in action, polarization can be seen as a focusing of attention, activity, influence, and feelings on a single point.[38] In the Indigenous literary narratives, the polarization caused by the event is sometimes compared to the failure of mixed marriages or the questioning they engender. This is the central theme of one short story in particular, "A Blurry Image on the Six O'Clock News" in the 2004 anthology *Our Story: Aboriginal Voices on Canada's Past* by Ojibway writer Drew Hayden Taylor.[39] In his story, the event does not summon up Canada's historical past, but rather the married life of the protagonist, Lisa, a white woman who has recently divorced an Ojibway man. When she sees an image of her former husband, Richard, behind the barricades at Kanehsatake, Lisa then avidly watches the television reports on the crisis while recalling the episodes from her married life that eventually led to separation and divorce. A parallel is set up between the mixed marriage's failure and the poor state of relations between the two peoples, a state emphatically worsened by the Oka Crisis.

Tellingly, the love relationship starts to deteriorate following the death of Donnelly, her former husband's brother. The grieving process leads Richard to gradually take over the role of his brother, who was very active in his community and on the Indigenous scene. Richard eventually quits his job at a bank to devote himself to the Indigenous political cause and reconnect with tradition and his community of Otter Lake. Finally, he begins to feel colonized by his wife: "Sometimes I feel like I'm on a reserve in my head, and every time you ask me what's going on, it feels like you're trying to colonize me. Again."[40] This is his response when she confronts him about his distant attitude. Lisa, who is a stranger to the structural nature of her white settler privilege, considers the accusation to be completely irrational, because she has no such intention: "They were married. Bonded. Sharing each other's lives. There were no 'mind reserves' or 'intellectual colonization'" (232). In the short story, the cultural distance that little by little leads to the couple's breakup is reflected in the relation set up between the two by Oka, an event that one follows with perplexity in the media while the other lives out with certainty on the siege site.

Lisa feels strongly interpellated by an event that occurs during a period she describes as the "marital hangover" (233). The image of her former husband on the siege site puzzles her: "What was he doing there?" (235). The armed conflict is inconsistent with her personal perception of Canada, especially since the army was sent in: "This was Canada, these things weren't supposed to happen here! Tanks on streets, rows and rows of guns facing one another, barricades" (238). As well, her former husband's involvement in the armed siege at Kanehsatake does not match up with her perception of him from their life together: "This was definitely not the Richard she had married" (235). In an attempt to make sense of the event, she spends hours in front of the television, trying to place the man who looks to her like "a displaced Ojibway in an increasingly bitter Mohawk war" (225). The contrast between her feeling of uncertainty and Richard's assertive assurance reflects the polarization caused by the event. As we have seen, while the Oka Crisis constitutes a breaking point for a shaken Canadian society, at the same time, the resistance at Kanehsatake expresses a profound conviction, a certainty on the part of the Indigenous peoples regarding land, history, and the absolute need for political struggle.

When Lisa implores Richard to leave this dangerous place, he tells her over the deafening roar of the helicopters that she shouldn't worry, because he is convinced that what he is doing is right: "I'm exactly where I want to be. I want to make a difference. Recently I've had trouble convincing myself that I can do that in a bank" (240). The two separations, the divorce on the personal level and the armed conflict on the political, meld into a single image when Lisa sees on television a shot of her former husband, still behind the barricades, walking hand in hand with another woman: "Then, just as quickly as Richard's phone call had ended, she saw him once again. He was walking in the distance, towards the general direction of the camera. But somebody was with him, walking beside him. A woman. A Native woman. And he was holding hands with her. She used the last of the energy in the battery to turn the television off" (243).

The story ends on this image, which signals the definitive breakdown of the love relationship that had united the woman, a white settler, with her former husband, Indigenous. It confirms the narrator's observation, both dark and funny, from the beginning of the story: "Another mixed marriage had bitten the dust" (225). In addition, by showing the new couple, Indigenous, that had just come into being among the Mohawk occupiers, the televised image illustrates the logical course of the trajectory taking Richard further away from his Canadian wife as much as it speaks to the coming together of Indigenous peoples and individuals symbolized by the siege. With a single action, having understood her former husband's motivation, Lisa turns off the television and cuts the connection to her past life and to the event, which reflects the intertwining of the personal and political crises presented by the story's author. The breakdown of relations caused by the crisis or occurring in its context leads the Indigenous characters to step back or detach themselves from the settler society and, conversely, to focus their attention and energy on a siege grounded in a long history of resistance to encroachment.

HISTORY REPEATS ITSELF

The 1990 crisis underlines the repetitive nature of history as it is experienced by individuals. In her text "After Oka—How Has Canada Changed?" Chippewa writer and storyteller Lenore Keeshig-Tobias explained: "The summer for First Nations peoples has been a review of history, a history we know so well, and a reality we have lived through generation after generation."[41] While exposing a long history of territorial appropriation and erasure, the event marks a breakdown in the colonially inspired scenario. This is what comes out of another of her texts, the poem and tale titled "From Trickster Beyond 1992: Our Relationship," in which Keeshig-Tobias inscribes the event in an oral history and instructs the reader in getting rid of the colonizer.

"From Trickster Beyond 1992" begins with a poem about the coming of the white settlers to the Indigenous world. The colonial business comes under the aegis of erasing, whitening, and assimilating: "White Out,"[42] "White Wash" (Keeshig-Tobias 2005b, 264 and 265), "White Paper/1969" (266). Obliteration is not total, since there is a bright period that represents the reappropriation of a power and freedom of action embodied in the Trickster. The tale with the very evocative title "How to Catch a White Man (Oops) I Mean Trickster" (267) replicates the breach caused by the event in the fictional space. Trapping the white man is taught as a method for provoking a reversal of the situation. The narrator's voice describes the figure of a stupid, crude, greedy white man, whose propensity for encroaching on Indigenous land is equalled only by his obsession with appropriating the voices and stories of Indigenous peoples. Patriarchy and colonialism are united in his actions: "In that pack he carries the voices of his women and the voices of other people he has walked over with his long legs. 'I'm going to tell those stories for you,' he'll say. 'You're far too primitive to tell them yourself. I'm going to let the world know what you think. I'm going to let the world know how you think when you think. And I'm going to build a golf course here, too. These trees are so old, and besides you're not using them trees'" (267).

To make her points, the storyteller herself appropriates the voice of the White Man. She angrily depicts this character as a usurper of identities, stories, and land, and a colonizer who imposes and dictates his own definition of things, completely lacking in respect and otherwise absolutely without any regard for Indigenous peoples. In a mocking tone that creates distance, the tale encourages its reader to use the character's own predictability in laying a trap for him. The trap consists in arousing his cupidity with glowing descriptions of "better stories and a better place for a golf course, perhaps even a h-y-d-r-o-e-l-e-c-t-r-i-c dam, or two" (267), and why not also "a super fantasyland golf course" (267)? Anticipating that the White Man will thus be well and truly lured, the tale instructs the reader to dig a hole—in a forest that bears a close resemblance to the Pines at Kanehsatake—that will serve to trap this vile character: "Find another forest and dig a big big hole in the middle of it, beside a pine tree" (267). When the

White Man heads into the forest, it will simply be a matter of frustrating his desire for appropriation by telling him: "These stories are not for you, and you can't build your golf course either" (267). In her tale, Keeshig-Tobias picks up several themes from the Oka-Kanehsatake land dispute, among them the Mohawk protestors' refusal to allow the town to expand a golf course at the expense of the pine grove, the occupation of the Pines following the failure of legal measures, and the subsequent recourse to the police and military to dislodge the occupiers.

Lenore Keeshig-Tobias inscribes the event in a repetitive history by describing the completely foreseeable reaction of the White Man: "It won't be long and he'll come by with that great pack and this time with his guns and tanks, too—ready to take those stories—ready to build his golf course" (267). Now is the moment to catch him in the trap. All it takes is to tell him to close his eyes and listen to the trees and grass, and he will attain the promised vision, a procedure that will flaunt his inability to perceive in his face and arouse his uneasiness and impatience. Once again, alluding to the cultural blindness and deafness the Indigenous people often attribute to the whites, the narrator explains: "Of course, that man won't see anything. Never did. And he certainly won't hear anything. Never has" (268). In front of all the people who have been brought together in the forest to watch the awaited scene, "he'll cock his gun and open his eyes" (268), which is to say that he will get ready to shoot before even having looked to see what is before him. Then he will flail about in a rage and fall into the hole at the foot of the tree. Now the time has come to set free the voices tied up in the big bag he carries on his back, and to tell the children "the history of this land, the real history, before 1492 and since" (268), to guide them through the five centuries to come. Of course, it will be necessary to discourage them from imitating the White Man, and instead to encourage them to "listen to the trees and grass. The trees and the grass hold on to heaven for us" (268). The story then makes way for a poem that offers a new perspective on the future, a "New Angle" (269) under the sign of Indigenous autonomy, as in the slogan: "Let's be our own tricksters" (269). Keeshig-Tobias presents the loss of land and the relegation to silence as going together, so that the reappropriation of land can be envisioned in concert with that of a voice. She brings out the importance of stories that, growing out of a close connection to the land, convey a particular conception of the world.

REACHING THE LIMIT

Like the story and poem by Lenore Keeshig-Tobias, other Indigenous literary narratives frequently refer to the blindness, failure to listen, and irrepressible covetousness of the dominant society, which is often represented by the figure of the white man. In the poem "Let's Not Negotiate!!" by writer and activist Edee O'Meara in *Entering the War Zone: A Mohawk Perspective on Resisting Invasions*, this figure is associated with the laws and legal documents used by the settlers to cheat and dispossess the Indigenous peoples, while giving (themselves) the impression that they are acting in a completely legitimate way. The poem's subject right away announces a refusal to negotiate within the established framework; asserting a sovereign stance, she encourages the character of the white man to come instead onto her territory: "Come to my fire / white man / I have a few words / for your ears."[43] She orders the white man to show up with his hands empty, warning him that his documents and fancy wording will be of no use:

> Leave behind
> your lawyers
> history books
> legal documents
> and what have you
> NO!
> I don't want
> to negotiate.
> So don't bring
> your fancy words
> contract papers or bullshit treaties.
> (O'Meara 1995, 115)

In the end, the Indigenous subject grows weary and plans to escape the grip of a society that sets up a negotiation framework protecting settler privilege. As we have seen, unlike the political debates in parliamentary institutions or cases in court, with hundreds of land claims pending in 1990, Oka represents an armed conflict taking place outside the legal framework. It summons the image of armed resistance, a resistance that sets aside the conventional framework for discussion and, by doing so, plays upon power relations that force the governments to react. The poem reflects this idea in the space of fiction, and its subject, fed up with her interactions with the dominant institutions, declares that the time has come to take up arms:

It's time
Time...
for a showdown
shootout
bloodshed
nitty-gritty
reality-slapping
no-more-games
Fuck.
(115)

Even if it means bloodshed, sings the poet, the time has come for confrontation, to butt up against reality and stop pretending. These violent images echo the raw shock of reality represented by the event in *Voleurs de cause*, the collection by Québécois poet Yves Boisvert. Here, however, the imagery has a determined, politicized tone that bespeaks a strong feeling of belonging to the Indigenous peoples. In her poem "Post-Oka Kinda Woman," Cree poet Beth Cuthand conveys a similarly pronounced affirmation: "Post-Oka woman, she's cheeky. / She's bold. She's cold. / And she don't take no shit! / No shit."[44] The resistance at Kanehsatake thus clearly speaks of colonial excesses that cannot be further tolerated.

The representation of the siege as a refusal to be trampled on is articulated in various ways in these literary narratives. In Drew Hayden Taylor's short story "A Blurry Image on the Six O'Clock News," the limit that has been reached, and beyond which it would be inconceivable to retreat, is actualized in the power relations at the siege sites: "There was a palpable tension in the air, like a bad smell; a rumour that at some point, the Mohawks and their allies would try to push that line back. After all, one spokesperson said, that's what this whole thing is about. 'Being pushed beyond a reasonable limit'" (Taylor 2004, 237–38). The aspect of setting boundaries, which carries a freight of meaning, has an obvious association with the idea of a reasonable limit. This of course concerns the territory, but it also takes in many other irritants in the relationship to Canadian society. Justice, respect, and dignity are also recurring themes in Indigenous literary narratives.

In Douglas Raymond Nepinak's stage play "The Crisis in Oka, Manitoba," the young brother, Isaiah, reports feeling contempt for negotiation and being fed up with seeing the Indigenous communities manipulated by outside interests.

He expresses disgust with government practices that make them eternal losers, and he strongly disapproves of the betrayals he perceives within Indigenous circles. Inspired by the Mohawks' stand and the solidarity movement that is taking shape, he makes a fervent appeal for the Indigenous people to seize power: "Our people are getting together, you know. We're not going to take it anymore, and I'm going to be part of it. We're rising from the ashes. No more getting screwed in negotiations. No more caving in to outside interests. No more stabbing each other in the back. Red Power!" (Nepinak 2010, 149). Isaiah's inflamed rhetoric is immediately reined in by his sister, with her pragmatic comments. She critically assesses his small group of friends and, as if to bring him back to earth, asks him how he will pay for his bus ticket to Oka. However, she never questions his attacks on the dominant society.

In these literary narratives, Oka is associated with the lack of respect of an inconsiderate settler society, acting in bad faith, that has taken everything and still wants more. In this regard, the stance of the Mohawk protestors and communities opposing the police and the military to protect their land rekindles and underscores a feeling of being up against the wall. Isaiah, who is trying to impress on his sister the political necessity of choosing an Indigenous boyfriend, heatedly maintains: "We've lost just about everything, Martha. The land, our language, our culture. There's practically nothing left. We keep getting pushed back, until we got our backs to the wall. Until all we got left is this one square of land. This last stand. Like Oka. Like the warriors at the treatment center" (153). The Mohawk activists who have been pushed back to the last ditch in Kanehsatake here represent resistance to the ultimate dispossession, the one that would take from the Indigenous peoples their remaining land, and, with it, their very existence. In this sense, the siege introduces the issue of the Indigenous peoples' individual and collective survival, in a very concrete way, in the face of a settler colonial project that has been scheming for the ultimate dispossession of the peoples indigenous to the land of this continent.

INDIVIDUAL AND COLLECTIVE LIFE/SURVIVAL

The shootout, the blocked bridge, the Mohawk communities being surrounded by police cordons, and the Canadian Army being sent in—all these elements set the stage for an extremely tense armed conflict that aroused powerful anxieties in Indigenous communities across the country. In his personal account "Indians Have a Right to Be Happy Too," Mississauga Justice Harry S. LaForme writes of "the heart-wrenching drama and fear all Indians experienced during the Oka crisis, where some Indian people prepared to die."[45] Powerful symbolic themes often found in the Indigenous literary narratives are the fear that people would be killed in an armed confrontation, and the Mohawk protestors' stance of being ready to put their lives on the line to protect their land.

In Drew Hayden Taylor's short story, Lisa cautions her former husband that he could end up like the warrior called Spudwrench, whom she had seen, badly beaten, on television.[46] Richard replies by recognizing the man behind the name, and adds that he has fully accepted the danger: "I know. His real name is Randy Horne and he's a good guy. He didn't deserve what happened to him. None of these people do. Most of the people here are expecting to die here, Lisa. You can feel the fear here, and the anger. I can't walk out" (Taylor 2004, 241). The mix of fear and anger felt by this character on the siege site is also to be found among characters who experienced the event through the media.

Sitting in front of a television showing live coverage of the armed conflict, the mother of the lead character in Lee Maracle's novel *Sundogs* feels an inexpressible dread and sadness. The narrator and lead character, Marianne, describes her mother's feelings in these terms: "Momma cries in front of the television each night, powerless to express the horror and deep sadness she feels. No one believes this is happening to us."[47] The character's entire family is deeply shocked by the crisis. It reminds them of their own unresolved land claims, their continued land struggles, and, in a broader sense, of a life hampered by settler colonial violence that is manifested in various forms, as well as an historical trauma that still causes suffering. The event has generated a strong sense of threat: "There is a desperate tension in the air. We put everything on hold. Behind the crisis lies the threat of annihilation and we all feel it" (Maracle 1992, 127).

In *Sundogs*, Lee Maracle undertakes a detailed, in-depth exploration of how the event reopens deep wounds inflicted by settler colonialism. The fact that the event involves a territorial conflict that pits Indigenous peoples against the governments and the forces of law and order is critical. Following the analysis of scholars Eduardo Duran and Bonnie Duran, Métis scholar Jo-Ann Episkenew explained that the sufferings of Indigenous peoples today result from a wound to their soul from the attack on their territories during colonization. Here, the soul is defined in terms of a connection to the land as viewed from an Indigenous perspective: that is, as a connection to the various elements of the world around us.[48] As we have seen earlier, the Haudenosaunee thanksgiving address speaks to the earth, plants, animals, humans, the ancestors, and the world of spirits, which are seen to be closely interconnected and interdependent. Similarly, to describe an Indigenous conception of the land, Cree scholar Shawn Wilson borrowed the following from a colleague: "The land is paramount for all Indigenous societies. Their relationship to that land, their experience on that land shapes everything that is around them." He further added that "land is another word for place, environment, your reality, the space you're in."[49] It is in this sense that Duran and Duran considered that a blow against territory reaches the core essence of Indigenous consciousness. As they are quoted in Episkenew's *Taking Back Our Sprits*, "The core essence is the fabric of the soul and it is from this essence that mythology, dreams, and culture emerge. Once the core from which the soul emerges is wounded, then all the emerging mythology and dreams of a people reflect the wound. The manifestations of such a wound are then embodied by the tremendous suffering that people have undergone since the collective soul wound was inflicted half a millennium ago." Episkenew went on to explain that this wound is part of a heavy colonial legacy that is passed down from generation to generation among "Indigenous people who face the continual pressure to acculturate into settler society—the same society that created the genocidal policies and practices that continue to affect them today."[50] In that regard, Sam McKegney contends that the residential schools, a core element of Canada's genocidal policies and practices, were designed to sever Indigenous children from the land, but also to "isolate the individual student as discrete, disembodied, and deterritorialized." McKegney expounds: "To be clear, I contend that the bodies of Indigenous youth have been deliberately targeted for violence and humiliation within (and beyond) residential schools for the primary purpose of suppressing embodied experiences of the land and of kinship. And the denial of these embodied experiences was calculated to extinguish Indigenous modes of social formation and territoriality. To dispossess Indigenous youth of their capacity for integrated, embodied experience has been to dispossess Indigenous nations of land and sovereignty."[51] Although the focus of Maracle's *Sundogs* is not residential schools, the novel thoroughly addresses the loss of these "Indigenous modes of social formation and territoriality," their disintegration under settler colonialism and their reappropriation through a politicized, embodied action in 1990, namely the main character's involvement in the Peace Run from the Okanagan region towards Kanehsatake in support of the Mohawk warriors.

In *Sundogs*, the context in which the Oka Crisis erupted is characterized by a spatial and social marginalization, as well as denigration, alienation, poverty, alcoholism, and spousal abuse. They constitute the various concrete manifestations of the "postcolonial traumatic stress response" referred to by Episkenew. The event also summons up a wound to the soul sustained more recently, which directly influences how the siege is interpreted and experienced by these characters. In fact, in the novel, the fate of Indigenous peoples decimated by illness and famine is reflected in the mother's life experience. She is the only survivor of an epidemic that took her entire family, leaving her orphaned at the age of nine. The novel presents the loss of land, uprooting, and grief experienced by the inhabitants of numerous Indigenous villages that were destroyed in the early twentieth century, less than 100 years before the 1990 crisis. It draws an actual death map: "A map comes into focus. 1906: 1,800 small extinct tribes in B.C. It took only seventy-five years of settlement to destroy one thousand eight hundred villages by this process. Statistics become faces, relatives, friends. Every single one of these villages was constructed of families and relatives in other villages. Rivers of tears must have been shed. Death must have been so commonplace that we ceased to grieve. No, grief became so constant we ceased to want to live" (Maracle 1992, 156). The narrator imagines the deep sadness felt by the grieving, displaced families. She talks about their vulnerability and subsequent territorial dispossession, which the Canadian government justified by the fact that the Indigenous population in these villages no longer reached the required level: "Land. Land. We are landless. The land dribbled through our hands in moments when disease and hunger rendered us impotent" (156). The survivors' feelings of dispossession, exhaustion, and torment are symptoms of a grief that stops them in their tracks and takes away their desire to live.

Sundogs represents the Indigenous peoples as stripped of their land; torn from their families, way of life, and conception of the world; grieving, struggling, and persistently excluded from the dominant settler society. The people thus represented see themselves relegated to a kind of non-place or dead end, which gives rise to a deep anxiety concerning their very lives and continuance: "Disease and encroachment killed our future. We were not merely impoverished, but futureless. Prohibited from pursuing life as we knew it and excluded from the life they created we came to understand that our lives had no value" (156). Encroachment and impoverishment are associated with a devaluation of existence and an attack on the dignity of Indigenous people, who see themselves bullied out of a future. The dead end represented in *Sundogs* appears to be "the result of besiegement, encroachment, small neglect, impoverishment, and mass deaths" (161). In this context of pain, Oka erupts, immediately following Elijah Harper's refusal to consent to the Meech Lake Accord. The narrator explains that, before all of Canada, Harper "articulates, documents and advances the most obnoxious and despicable thing a Nation can do—attempt genocide on a people" (68).[52]

In such a context, the projected encroachment on land bordering a cemetery in Kanehsatake takes on a strong symbolic aspect, like the resistance of Mohawk protestors who are opposing both the erasure of memory and an attempt on their people's future. The *Sundogs* narrator opposes the figure of the insensitive white profiteer to that of the courageous Indigenous warrior and his integrity, and she expresses anger at "the ease with which men in power brokering positions in Quebec can play golf on land housing our eternal grief" (163). Conversely, she honours the warriors' resistance and how they "know the attack on their grandmother's graves" (163). Very clearly, the novel depicts men who took up weapons not to support criminal activity, as certain forms of discourse claim, but to protect their dead. Their action refers back to a break in transmission and a profound, paralyzing grief that the crisis exhorts them to feel and then move beyond: "No wonder those men at Kanesatake have armed themselves, armed themselves for our dead. Our dead constitute the lost potential of our lost race. They evidence our genocide. They represent the remnants of what might have been and never was—in their eternal sleep lies our grief, the grief that killed our will to live and love" (159).

The siege represents a battle waged in the name of disappeared Indigenous ancestors, and the resistance becomes associated with the question of survivance. According to French-Armenian writer and translator Janine Altounian, survivance would point to "having to live life backwards, aiming not to repair the ancestors—which is naturally impossible—but to give them a symbolic in-kind gift of the conditions for psychic parenting after the fact, when any way to engage in it had been taken from them."[53] While protecting the deceased, the warriors dramatically assert, in the public space, a serious determination to live that is radically different from the current representations of the warriors in government and media discourses: "They take up arms, not to deprive anyone of their life, but to show the world they are dead serious about living" (Maracle 1992, 163). For Maracle, as for other Indigenous writers, the siege is shown as the dramatic materialization of a will to survive, and also a desire to live that is so much stronger because it is visibly assailed on all sides.

A poem by Anishinaabe writer Kateri Damm published in *Entering the War Zone* makes the connection among land claims, gambling with life, and the siege's spatial configuration:

> what is it to be perched on the edge of the world
> camping under the stars while soldiers creep around your claim
> what is it to be one of those left to take a stand
> caught between honour and death
> fighting for peace.[54]

The warrior is represented in many narratives as a resister fighting for a just, honourable, and necessary cause, and this perception is reinforced by the presence of the army around the Mohawk communities. This represented warrior evokes the idea of survivance that, as Gerald Vizenor put it in *Survivance: Narratives of Native Presence*, is intended to denote an "active sense of presence" of the Indigenous people, one that will transcend the historical absence, uprooting, and oblivion that characterize the settlers' representations.

THE CANADIAN ARMY AND INDIGENOUS COMMUNITIES

During the 1990 crisis, the siege space became the site where issues were focused and consolidated, issues concerning the physical survival of individuals and the collective survival of a people, which took on even greater intensity because the Canadian Army was deployed in the vicinity. The event involves two aspects of the territorial conflict: first, the imminence of death at the heart of an armed conflict in which the Indigenous people defend their land; and second, reopening the wounds caused by the settlers' assaults on Indigenous territory and federal assimilation policies. In Drew Hayden Taylor's short story "A Blurry Image on the Six O'Clock News," the siege's configuration looks like a snare or noose that tightens ruthlessly around the community, threatening its physical and symbolic existence: "The army now encircled the whole community, severely restricting anybody and anything that wanted to cross yet another imaginary line imposed on the Native people by representatives of the government. And that imaginary circle kept getting smaller and smaller, gradually choking the life out of the community, like a noose" (Taylor 2004, 237–38).

This passage simultaneously suggests a shrinking of the territory, restriction of movement, and the community's being choked. Huron-Wendat playwright Yves Sioui Durand interpreted the resistance in this perspective when he explained to the daily newspaper *La Presse*, on 18 July 1990, that "the Indians can no longer stand to be smothered physically and culturally. It is a state of despair." In the same way, Mohawk writers Peter Blue Cloud and Donna K. Goodleaf describe the Canadian Army explicitly in terms of a force invading their territory. Writers from other Indigenous nations associate the army's intervention in a more general way with violence that is waged by the state on the Indigenous peoples and is completely counter to their interests. In this respect, the subject of writer Todd Baskin's poem "In the Spirit of" observes that the armed forces "didn't protect my people so well," then says that he "would rather have the land back."[55] According to Shuswap playwright Darrell Dennis, the different perceptions of Canada and the Canadian Armed Forces illustrate different relations to this country and its history. For the Indigenous peoples, in the end, the Canadian Army represents the country responsible for their dispossession:

> Native people don't look at Canada the same way that most
> English-Canadians do, like "Oh, we gotta be proud of this
> country," because Canada was the country that put them down,
> that took away the land, that took away the language, that beat
> them, molested them, put them in residential schools, took
> their culture. So it's a whole different relationship that Native
> people have with Canada. And so when you have something
> like an army coming in, that represents Canada, it's just an
> even bigger sort of slap in the face, about like "Oh, an army
> is supposed to go outside of Canada and defend, you know,
> Canada from outside intruders." It was like the army was
> putting the Indians as enemies to Canada. It just added to that
> whole animosity that Native people already had with Canada
> and the police and the army and that sort of thing.[56]

Representations of the Canadian Army also appear in a number of different ways in the Indigenous literary narratives. In Darrell Dennis's stage play *Tales of an Urban Indian*, Simon, a seventeen-year-old Indigenous youth, has left his community and finds himself "completely alone" in an urban environment that is mostly white, where he leads a double life—at times, he blends into the dominant society by denying his Indigenous background, day after day; at other times, he gets drunk and takes drugs with the marginalized Indigenous people on Hastings Street in Vancouver, trying to forget his grief over Nick, his best friend from childhood who became a "recent statistic" by dying from alcohol abuse.[57] In both of his lives, Simon remains invisible and disoriented, caught between despair and assimilation. This is his situation at the beginning of the 1990s, an era the play describes as being marked by such things and people as films like *Dances with Wolves,* Cree singer-songwriter Buffy Sainte-Marie, Ojibway-Cree politician Elijah Harper, and, finally, the Mohawk resistance at Oka. The narrator therefore observes, "I started to feel something I hadn't felt in some time—Native pride. Or was it anger? Is there a difference?" (Dennis 2005, 35). This change is also affected by the event's powerful resonance in the media: "To add to the confusion, we became the lead story on all the news channels" (35).

The event, whose setting is then described by the narrator, generates enthusiasm and anxiety among the Indigenous characters in Vancouver. They watch the news "with bated breath as the standoff became more and more volatile" (35). Solidarity movements spring up everywhere, even in the city's underbelly on Hastings Street, while white racism is also on the rise. It is at this moment that one of Simon's classmates, "a military brat who spent all his spare time in the Canadian Army reserves" (36), makes these hate-filled declarations to the class: "I'm serious guys! The army should go in to Oka, mow down all the Mohawk men, and send all the women and children back to whatever country they came from. Then everybody in that platoon should get a medal of honour for standing up to those ungrateful whiners" (36).

The play generally uses parody and caricature to condemn the veiled insults, contempt, and condescension normally camouflaged under political correctness or ethnographic fascination. In this scene, however, the classmate's open, frontal attack is used to expose in broad daylight a deep-rooted racism at the core of Canadian society. This momentary overt racism, a schoolboy affront in a highly politicized context, has a much greater impact on Simon than the insidious racism he experiences day in, day out. Identifying with the Oka Mohawks being attacked by his classmate, he feels that his integrity has been directly impugned, and it is as if this assault brings out years of pent-up anger. When his friends have finally started to think he is "just well-tanned" (35) because he plays the role of a white person so well, he suddenly comes out with this furious reply: "Your army's ready to kill women and children so a bunch of assholes can play golf. You think that deserves a medal? Go tell your army buddies to get the fuck out of Oka and go do what they do best: hazing rituals in Somalia! And tell those Indian soldiers that helped with that shit to turn on the news and see what it means to be a real warrior" (36). This reply from the character of Simon stops the other short, defining the perspectives and altering power relations in the classroom. Now the brave warrior is no longer the Canadian soldier, whom Simon denigrates by exposing the horrors perpetrated by the military in Somalia, but the Mohawk protestors fighting to defend his community's land.

In this scene, titled "Red Power," Simon's speech sounds like a moment of truth heralded by "the crack of thunder" (36). When he takes up his confrontational stance, the character of Simon produces a shocked silence and uneasiness among the students, who suddenly see him from another angle: "They all knew there was a hostile in their midst" (37). His classmates quickly turn their backs on him, moving on to a radical erasure of his presence, which had become disruptive when it revealed both his Indigenous identity and a perennially active colonial brutality. Simon's reply is followed by a break in the relationship between the protagonists, a break that paradoxically proves to be positive for the Indigenous character. With no going back, he has to change direction. From that moment on, Simon no longer hides his accent and he walks with his head high, like a "born-again heathen filled with zealous love for my people" (37). Having externalized his anger, he decides to reorient himself by taking over the dominant cultural space: "So, with my newfound Native pride—slash—fury, I decided to represent the Indian race by becoming a movie star" (37).

As in this scene from *Tales of an Urban Indian*, representations of the Canadian Army's deployment in the land dispute at Oka-Kanehsatake evoke the idea of antagonistic military forces, but very different ones. In the work of Lenore Keeshig-Tobias, the projected expansion of the golf course on Indigenous land appears as an unacceptable affront, representing the dominant society's callous cupidity. It is embodied in the figure of the White Man, who, when his desires for appropriation are frustrated, comes back "with his guns and tanks, too" in order to force the imposition of the projected golf course onto Indigenous land (Keeshig-Tobias 2005b, 267). In *Sundogs*, Lee Maracle presents the image of an Indigenous military force made up of family members engaged in political action to support the Mohawk protestors: "My family geared up and went into action as a block. A great tank of lineage rolling out across Canada's golf greens"

(Maracle 1992, 206). Such comparisons with the military in this case summon up the idea of an Indigenous political power that is embodied not in metal tanks but in the living bodies of a family that had survived "the most unspoken holocaust in history" (Maracle 1992, 206). Similarly, the short story "A Blurry Image on the Six O'Clock News" uses the image of fingers brought together in a fist to represent the mobilization of Indigenous peoples who have put aside their rivalries for a time. "Like the proverbial squabbling fingers, it was OK to fight among yourselves, but when a single digit was threatened, all the fingers came together as a fist" (Taylor 2004, 235). The siege summons images of both a people in danger and a people strongly united to defend their land. In Douglas Raymond Nepinak's play, it is this lesson of unity that Isaiah has drawn from the event, exclaiming, "We have come together as a people. We have to be strong. That's what the people at Oka are telling us" (Nepinak 2010, 155).

The representations of the warriors elicit very different interpretations, depending on whether they are seen from an Indigenous or non-Indigenous perspective. Wab Kinew observes that, for Indigenous youth, the warriors became "role models that were fighting for something bigger than themselves, role models that were fearless and role models that were proud to be Native" (Kinew 2010, 48). As well as inspiring feelings of admiration and pride, these new role models encourage the youth to look around for examples of other kinds to emulate. This is especially meaningful in a context in which the residential schools have caused a significant intergenerational breakdown and, as Jo-Ann Episkenew observed, "effectively removed children from their role models of culturally appropriate emotional expression."[58] Of note, the resistance of Mohawk women also proved to be a source of inspiration to many, especially as it was enacted on the siege's site, under the media spotlights, by the young spokesperson Ellen Gabriel. Michi Saagiig Nishnaabeg scholar, writer, and artist Leanne Simpson recounted the memories that came to her mind after a chance encounter with Gabriel in Montreal, years after the standoff: "As I looked into her blue eyes, I remembered. I remembered being a 19-year-old Anishinaabekwe. I remembered seeing her on TV, and I remembered what that image had taught me and why I carried it through the next twenty years. I remembered that this was the woman responsible for waking me up. For sending me on a path that led me to learn my culture, my language, my political traditions. This was the woman that challenged me to find my voice and to use it."[59]

The vocal assertion of Mohawk sovereignty in front of police and military forces became an impetus for Indigenous peoples across the country to engage in new conversations. In "Cowboys and Indians," Kinew relates how the crisis led him to discuss Indigenous rights with his parents and other members of his family, who then told him stories of community engagement, political action, armed occupations, and battles led by the American Indian Movement. The event was the occasion for the transmission of previously unheard accounts: "These were stories we had never heard before, and I do not know if our parents would have ever told us about them if it had not been for the stand that the people of Kanehsatà:ke made" (Kinew 2010, 49). By relating the event of summer 1990 to past struggles, these accounts reinforced connections between the generations and contributed to the process of "coming home through stories" we have been discussing throughout this book (McLeod 2001). In the novel *A Quality of Light* by Ojibway writer Richard Wagamese, an Ojibwe character, Joshua Kane, who was adopted at a young age by a white family, gradually returns to his roots during the 1990 crisis. It is the intervention of a childhood friend, an Indigenous-friendly, Indigenous-fascinated white boy affected by a troubled past, that brings Joshua onto this path. During the event, indeed, he is impelled to intervene in a critical way as a mediator when his former white friend stages a hostage taking, a performance designed to prompt reflection on the fate imposed on Indigenous people under settler colonialism. Joshua's path of reconciliation with his Indigenous heritage appears to be intertwined with the settler-Indigenous tensions that culminate with Oka in this novel that "creates a metaphor for Canada's treatment of its aboriginal inhabitants."[60]

In the stage play "The Crisis in Oka, Manitoba," young Isaiah's family gives his decision to go to Oka lengthy consideration. It is only towards the play's end that his father finally tells his children that, over his wife's objections, he himself attempted to join the siege at Wounded Knee in the 1970s, to support those he calls "our people" (Nepinak 2010, 161). As he explains, he was never able to reach his destination because he was arrested and thrown in jail on the way. His son is instantly impressed and listens as his father recalls not only the expected police repression but also the resistance he put up until the last minute before losing consciousness, badly beaten by the police officers who were interrogating him at the detention centre: "I fell down. The talker started laughing, he says, 'Now that's the way I like to see Indians, on their knees.' Sure enough, I was on my knees. I didn't have much strength left, but with the last I had I got back on my feet, I wouldn't give the sons of bitches the satisfaction of seeing me like that. They beat me until I passed out" (162).

This account of resistance to police brutality echoes those of Mohawk protagonists in *Kanehsatake: 270 Years of Resistance,* when they comment after the fact on images of their own arrests, emphasizing how they resisted and kept their pride and dignity despite the beatings and mistreatment. The character of Isaiah's father, who from the beginning of the play had only very discreetly expressed his opinion of the political issues and his son's determination to go to Oka, suddenly delivers this account of his experience of Wounded Knee and police brutality. At this moment, Isaiah understands his mother's anxiety over his departure for Oka. His father's account, with which he identifies, strengthens his resolve to go, despite the risks. The siege is seen as a mobilizing force, providing the occasion for expressing and connecting the present and past experiences of Indigenous peoples. It also causes a reactivation of kinship relations and shared narratives that, like Indigenous literature, make it possible to break out of the silence and isolation and join a larger community of shared stories.[61]

A similar scenario is outlined in Lee Maracle's novel *Sundogs.* Again in the context of Oka, the principal character, Marianne, a young Indigenous woman from British Columbia, joins a group of Indigenous youth who are undertaking a Peace Run to Kanehsatake—an action that clearly evokes the Peace Run to Oka organized by the Okanaga in 1990. In *Sundogs,* the young protagonist recounts her participation in a run of thousands of kilometres, "heading down a highway to stop the army from killing people we have never seen" (170). In Maracle's novel, the run is more than a political act: it is a spiritual quest that allows the young people to experience other forms of knowledge, restore connections damaged by settler violence, and (re)constitute their community as the centre. Along the way, the protagonist explores a sensitive, intelligent relation to the land the young participants are reappropriating as they march: "We had sunk little webs of roots into the vast soil of our homeland. The run re-created each of us. We're-imagined [*sic*] in every step of the run ourselves and acquired a vision of a different world" (197–98). It is a world of peace, where no form of oppression is tolerated. As another character remarks, "This is just the beginning . . . Oka is just a beginning" (200). The most telling change, the narrator assures us, is associated with a way of knowing that is intimately bound up with being and experiential, embodied ways of knowing: "Another kind of sight is born; that sight, that way of looking at my self is who I am. Words cannot describe this process. It is felt knowledge" (194). The run across the territory at the sides of other Indigenous youth, with stops in welcoming Indigenous communities, throws the alienating precepts of Western sociology into question in favour of Indigenous epistemologies that empower Marianne.

As well as drawing the character of Marianne out of her social alienation, the experience of the run leads her to reconnect with her mother and her ancestors, a connection she thinks of as an ancient, organic, loving force: "Spider weaves its web inside my soul. In the center stands my mother, her mother, her mother's mother—infinite lines of grandmothers who spiral out, gain numbers and accumulate strength in their numbers. The simplicity of their love, the greatness of it spins a web of ancient power in places inside me I have never tread. The omnipotence of my grandmothers spins a thread tied to their center, their original being and adds my own being into its magical construction—family is a spider's web of continuum" (Maracle 1992, 172).

Marianne regains an Indigenous balance by re-establishing a spiritual knowledge of her ancestry and kinship relations. She changes her bearings so as to establish her own centre, which becomes defined in the course of her movements, encounters, and reflections. When she returns to her family, she feels that the distance separating her from its members has disappeared. The resistance enacted and expressed during the political crisis identifies the sources of oppression and consequently also provides the grounds for a major reversal: "The crisis at Kanehsatake and Elijah's 'no' persuaded us to stop inflicting hell of the outside world on the corridors of our own private universe. The Warriors turned us all around and made us reconsider ourselves" (207). By inciting political mobilization and by giving a voice and validation to collective experience that is often denied and delegitimized, the event of summer 1990, with its subsequent representations in literature, help to strengthen connections within Indigenous communities and, at the same time, to register a contemporary Indigenous presence in the public space. Through the character of Marianne's mother, *Sundogs* presents a passage from speaking with no interlocutor to speaking out in the public space. The mother's launching of vitriolic criticisms at governments, journalists, and commentators as they flit past on the television screen in the security of her own home is replaced, later in the novel, by her active participation in a public assembly organized during the event. In the context of Oka, the mother spontaneously climbs onto a platform and, to everyone's surprise, takes hold of the microphone with steely determination: "She meant to speak, right in the heart of white urban Canada—this little bush Momma" (214). The political engagement of the event entails a necessary redefinition of relations between peoples. The novel's narrator concludes by saying, "We feel like this country will never be able to erase us again" (192).

However, this new feeling of presence, pride, and unity rises like an impossible hope. This is what the novel's title of *Sundogs* suggests, since it signifies "impossible images reflected in extraordinary circumstances" (184). The title *Sundogs* refers to the unexpected, unpredictable, and indeterminate nature of the Oka event and the opening up of possibilities that accompanies it. The extraordinary quality of the euphoric feeling aroused by solidarity with Kanehsatake can be explained by the context of the event's emergence. In 1992, Indigenous Justice Harry S. LaForme angrily observed that, in a context characterized by the Canadian settler society's indifference, contempt, and rejection concerning the Indigenous people, but also by the shame, anger, and sense of inferiority felt in return, the Indigenous people are "forced to find joy in victories that invariably result from tragedies," as was the case in the summer of 1990.[62] As he further noted, "the celebrations are short-lived." While the Oka event certainly brings about positive changes and a certain feeling of victory, it also bears witness to structural predicaments that remain unresolved. Looking at the armed siege at Kanehsatà:ke and Kahnawà:ke in the light of the critical insights drawn from Patrick Wolfe and Australian historian Lorenzo Veracini, it still can be said that "it is resistance and survival that make certain that colonialism and settler colonialism are never ultimately triumphant."[63]

CONCLUSION

If the residential school system tried to "kill the Indian" in me, the
Oka Crisis breathed new life into it. It wasn't just about taking a
stance for a forest and a burial ground. It was and it is still about
getting rid of the shame, about retelling our story, and about
fighting for what's right.

—*Sonia Bonspille-Boileau*, The Oka Legacy

We recall what we need to know to travel in the direction we choose
or do not choose. This is the work of conscious remembering.

—*Lee Maracle*, Memory Serves

Who are we? Who are we when we meet the other? Who do we become in our
relations to others? What are we to do about the colonial project revealed by the
event? These are some of the questions that arise when we take another look at
the siege in action, documentary films, and literary narratives of the Oka Crisis
or the resistance at Kanehsatà:ke and Kahnawà:ke. By replaying, in this book,
the epistemological conflict that was played out in the summer of 1990, I wanted
to make manifest the power relations operating in the research. I also wanted to
have readers feel and experience the event for themselves and thus gain a better
understanding of it. I hope that, on moving through the chapters of this book,
the reader could, like I could during the writing process, get a sense of the gap
between Indigenous and non-Indigenous perspectives, as they are expressed, located, and imagined in relation to a political crisis in summer 1990 that shocked
Canadians, Québécois, First Nations, Métis, and Inuit. This book looked at
the event from several different angles, contrasting and conflicting, that began
to take on meaning in themselves and in relation to one another. Rather than
sorting out an extremely complex armed conflict, I attempted to generate new

avenues of understanding and new approaches to the event and the context out of which it emerged. This dynamic form of interpretation proved to be beneficial in studying an event that, by virtue of what it shook up and split open, is primarily what raised questions and made us see things differently.

Pondering the idea of literary sovereignty, Craig S. Womack noted that, by considering the context for the expression of literary narratives, we put the focus on political questions that the dominant society generally prefers to set aside. He stated in that respect: "America loves Indian culture. America is much less enthusiastic about Indian land title."[1] The drastically serious nature of the political issues raised by the Oka Crisis or Kanehsatà:ke resistance militated against limiting reflection to its literary and cinematic representations. That is why this book also looks at media representations, social discourses, and political performances associated with the siege's scenography. Conversely, I have emphasized the relevance of using literary expression to address the unresolved political questions associated with the deep-rooted colonial conflict that flared up in 1990. The event, while ephemeral and elusive, momentarily revealed the institutional structures, narrative bases, and imaginary representations underlying the relationships between Indigenous peoples and settlers, and so opened a window on the state of those relationships.

The political crisis of summer 1990 marked a point when relations between First Nations and settlers across Canada broke down. Following on the failure of negotiations towards the Meech Lake constitutional accord, it made visible an Indigenous presence that the Quebec and Canadian societies had imagined had faded away, for all practical purposes, and its apparition shook the status quo. The siege within the Mohawk communities, for its part, reactivated and exposed a long history of resistance to the settler colonial project of appropriating Indigenous land and eliminating Indigenous peoples. It also generated a sense of pride and a spirit of resurgence that inspired Indigenous people to speak up in the public space and reconnect with their respective cultures, languages, stories, and political traditions. During the event, all could feel and were affected by the colonial violence at work in the entanglement of Indigenous and settler existences and in the polarization of their belonging that the event accentuated. The contradictory tensions that drove and shaped the conflict, and lent it strategic and symbolic power, showed up in a variety of ways in the scenography of a siege that had the entire country on edge for over two months.

THE EVENT'S SCENOGRAPHY

In the event's uniqueness, we rediscover power relations that have suddenly come back into play. The initial peaceful occupation and subsequent siege were carried on to counter a municipal development project whose planning proceeded without Kanehsatà:ke's consent. Significantly, both actions demonstrated a living Mohawk presence on the targeted land. In an atmosphere of imminent danger, the occupiers effected a reterritorialization of Mohawk political and cultural identity that worked against the process of spatial and ideological exile treated earlier in this book. The land dispute at Oka-Kanehsatake degenerated to the point of causing an armed conflict and reached the proportions of a national crisis, a sign that it raised fundamental issues that remain unresolved and are inherent in relations between Indigenous peoples and settlers. Nearly three decades later, these issues continue to be actual and disturbing, as has been evidenced by the Idle No More movement's numerous actions "to honour Indigenous sovereignty, and to protect the land and water"[2] in the face of troublesome modifications to state legislation; the massive mobilization against the Dakota Access Pipeline and for the protection of crucial water sources and sacred sites at Standing Rock, in North Dakota against resource development projects; as well as the final report of the Truth and Reconciliation Commission of Canada, which explicitly qualifies this country's Aboriginal policy of "cultural genocide." The current unfolding of the National Inquiry into Missing and Murdered Indigenous Women and Girls as well as the recent acquittal of two white men in relation to the murders of Tina Fontaine and Colten Boushie, respectively, foregrounds both a persistent colonial impunity and lack of justice for Indigenous people. Finally, the fact that as we speak the Kanehsata'kehró:non are still actively defending their land in the face of yet another land development "at the edge of the Pines area on traditional Kanien'kehá:ka territory, commonly referred to as Les Collines d'Oka,"[3] as well as against oil and gas developments, without receiving a responsive hearing by governments, brings once more into view the sustained and relentless character of settler colonialism.

This book has illustrated more specifically how the colonial issue was summoned up and took on a shape in the summer of 1990. It has demonstrated that the local land dispute that triggered the event is characterized by a tension between a performativity of the law invoked by the state and a counter-performativity enacted by the Mohawk protestors and communities. However, in addition to being a refusal to submit to the law, the occupation of the Pines constitutes an affirmation of Mohawk rights and sovereignty. The siege sets up a tension between legality and legitimacy; at the same time, it reveals settler fragility, which was especially evident at Oka, and an Indigenous certainty that has constantly and steadily been reaffirmed in the discourse of the Kanien'kehà:ka. During the event, in that space, the police and army perimeters rendered concrete and visible a state violence that was closing in dramatically on the Mohawk communities. For both sides, the siege became the site for staging political legitimacy, in such a way that breaking points, fault lines, and lines of conflict suddenly showed themselves as visible, magnified, and inflammatory.

Rather than providing a linear history of the territorial dispute, I chose, in this book, to examine given aspects of the siege's scenography in order to unpack what was concentrated in the event. In Kahnawà:ke, the discourse around sovereignty and protecting the territory was distinctly actualized in defending Tekakwitha Island from the military incursion. Against a state discourse that robs the warriors' political action of meaning, this discourse takes its own power and meaning from Iroquois political and philosophical thought, with roots that reach far into the continent. The Kahnawa'kehró:non's engagement in the resistance of summer 1990 can also be viewed in the light of recent history, which was marked by the construction of the St. Lawrence Seaway through the village of Kahnawà:ke. Considering the colonial dynamic of occupying and appropriating the land, the barricades across the Honoré-Mercier Bridge provided political leverage and, on the symbolic level, turned a mobility that had for a long time worked against the Indigenous peoples back on itself. The same is true of road- and rail blocks put up in other Indigenous territories across Canada, while the marches and runs in support of the Mohawks enacted and embodied a mobility that reactivated, and can be traced back to, ancient Indigenous pathways across this continent.

The crisis exposes the settler colonial societies' dark side to the light of day. In August, when the Canadian Army was preparing to intervene, the Quebec and Canadian authorities delegitimized the protest activities by criminalizing the Mohawk warriors. The discourses of the goverments, police, and military were rephrased and relayed in various forms by the television, radio, and print media, then immediately and consistently taken up by large segments of the white population. This dreadfully illustrated how, as Brisith-Australian scholar Sara Ahmed expounded in *The Cultural Politics of Emotions*, "the more signs circulate, the more affective they become."[4] In 1990, the racist hate speech was backed up by physical aggression, which at its nadir became a stoning of the Mohawk families being evacuated from Kahnawà:ke in the face of what seemed like an imminent entrance of the military into the community. The speed and virulence with which this violence surfaced and the impunity it received also show how deeply rooted in the populace and the state of Quebec and Canada is the dehumanization of Indigenous peoples that is central to the settler colonial project. In *Wasáse: Indigenous Pathways of Action and Freedom*, Taiaiake Alfred underlined the predictable nature of such reactions to Indigenous liberation, noting their "personal, visceral, and emotional" character.[5] In 1990, at the point when the Canadian Armed Forces were called in, the feeling of having reached a limit was mentioned by both the Mohawk protestors and the Canadian Army leaders. The former reported a need to take action, given the threat to their collective existence, and the latter conceived of their intervention as a last resort when the social order was threatened. While the Québécois populace felt increasingly uneasy and confused, the armed conflict's threat of danger and of taking more lives raised the question of the survival of Indigenous individuals and peoples in a traumatic way.

THE MEDIA AND THE DOCUMENTARY

The territorial conflict was played out on the siege site. It was also enacted in the broader public space, in a veritable war of images and representations. At a crossroads of politics, history, and media, the documentary films studied in this book present narratives of the conflict relating to different historical perspectives. The words and images captured during the event were not only fated to circulate in the media space, but also to fulfill two other functions: to serve as evidence in an upcoming court case and to make us see the event's historical context from another angle. With their inclusion in the documentaries, they also helped to determine a certain future for the event.

In the final days, Canadian journalist Albert Nerenberg attempted to document the denouement of a siege that military strategy was trying to conceal even as the world was watching. While the Mohawks' speech was being discredited in the media and government discourses, Nerenberg recorded what the last Indigenous protestors on the site had to say. Then, going from media spectacle to testimonial, he presented with co-director Catherine Bainbridge a documentary narrative from the siege space itself as *Okanada: Behind the Lines at Oka*. The film right away locates the conflict's immediate issue. However, the viewer has access to its history only through the accounts delivered to the camera by the Mohawk occupiers. Becoming both eyewitnesses and historical witnesses, the protagonists report what they are experiencing while in the siege space. They speak to the camera, reiterating their sovereignty and their right to the land, re-affirming the antecedence and continuity of the Mohawk nation, and question-ing who is responsible for the event and its larger context. Essentially, *Okanada* recounts what Nerenberg saw and experienced behind the barricades in the final days of the siege. It attempts to transmit the occupants' experience and, more broadly, the very existence of the Mohawk nation. This particular point of view, while necessarily partial, contributes to an overall understanding of the conflict. In fact, as French sociologist Renaud Dulong explained, the truth of an event is also to be found on the side of experience.[6] In the tribunal of images it sets up, *Okanada* encourages us to problematize the issue of judgement, given the injus-tices that have been revealed in the breach caused by the event. It invites more specifically the non-Indigenous Canadian and Québécois people among us to ask, as Paulette Regan suggested in *Unsettling the Settler Within: Indian Resi-dential Schools, Truth Telling, and Reconciliation in Canada*, "How do settlers bear witness? That is, how do we listen and respond authentically and ethically to testimonies—stories of colonial violence, not with colonial empathy but as a testimonial practice, shared truth telling?"[7] Accordingly, as Regan added, it is also time to ask how to "get past denial and moral indifference" and "take on the responsibility for our own decolonization."[8] In that line of thought, if we are to further understand that, as argued scholars Eve Tuck and K. Wayne Yang, "what is unsettling about decolonization, [is that it] brings about the repatriation of Indigenous land and life,"[9] we are incited to interrogate what actions this direc-tion requires of us, either settlers or Indigenous people, in the aftermath of Oka.

This is something that Alanis Obomsawin seemingly envisioned when di-recting *Kanehsatake: 270 Years of Resistance*, her documentary that relates the history of the long siege that propelled the contemporary and historical strug-gles of the Mohawks and other Indigenous peoples across Turtle Island into the spotlight. Motivated by a determination to document the event from an In-digenous perspective, Obomsawin spent the seventy-eight days of the siege with the Mohawk communities, surrounded by the police and the army. In the spirit of visual sovereignty proposed by Jolene Rickard and Michelle Raheja, as well as of the cinema of sovereignty elaborated by Randolph Lewis, Obomsawin pro-vides a film narrative of the event that is developed and shaped by Indigenous experiences and voices, both contemporary and historical, which in the film come to be regarded as authoritative. With undeniable counter-media value, the film deconstructs the dominant representations of the event, including the figure of the outlaw warrior propagated in the media and social discourses. Contrary to colonial representations of disappearance, the documentary presents the land, the pine grove, and the cemetery as being at stake in the struggle and as an inhabited area with which the residents of Kanehsatà:ke have a close relationship. The living words of the protestors and community members recalling similar struggles by their ancestors actualize the continuity of the Mohawks' resistance, past and present. These connections are reinforced by a detailed historical reconstruction that foregrounds the ancestral occupation of the territory and the political agreements made between the Haudenosaunee Confederacy and the British colonial authorities.

By relying upon Indigenous methods of recording history, the documentary narrative supports the grounds for land rights and struggles being defended by the Mohawk protestors in 1990. The political and cultural performances are staged on the siege site, and their presence is manifested in the documentary film. *Kanehsatake: 270 Years of Resistance* reappropriates and transmits the history as much as it does individual and collective political speech. The film has been regularly shown to both Indigenous and non-Indigenous audiences, and plays an important part in ongoing recollection and redefinition of the event. By countering the colonial falsehoods and erasures, it has become what Steven Leuthold described as "a form of historical truth speaking,"[10] an endeavour central to the long-standing career of Obomsawin at the National Film Board of Canada.

LITERARY NARRATIVES

The latter part of this book concentrates on literary representations of the event. Unlike the documentary filmmakers, the writers, poets, and playwrights do not reconstruct the event from fragments of the "real," and neither are they compelled to strictly conform to the facts, which multiplies the possibilities for expression. The literary fiction, by adding to the play of fiction that is always present in our relation to reality, nonetheless intervenes in the event by adopting another way of seeing and experiencing it. Despite the unique nature of each piece, the representations, which differ according to their place of utterance, all make reference to the political dimension of the narratives.

On the whole, the settler literary narratives from Quebec and Canada approach the siege's scenography from an outsider's point of view. They admit perplexity about the emerging event but also a fascination with and admiration for the figure of the Mohawk warrior who defies the established order. In these narratives, the Mohawk resistance is often associated with such marginal realms as piracy and criminality, which replay, as they displace it, a colonial literary imagination that opposes the primitive to the civilized. Unlike the representations of Indigenous characters as being doomed to disappear that prevailed for so long in Quebec and Canadian literature, representations of the Oka Crisis feature Indigenous characters who make their actions felt in the contemporary world. In these narratives, the indeterminacy of the event is linked to the fragility of the settler state that was suddenly exposed during the crisis. The conflict's polarization of belonging is also frequently featured, as are the disturbing manifestations of settler hostility. For these minority, migrating, or marginalized characters, such as the main character of Tessa McWatt's novel *Out of My Skin*, the event sometimes becomes the trigger for an identity quest, in which a Mohawk character acts as a guide, protector, and initiator. In the novel *Sept lacs plus au nord*, for example, Robert Lalonde describes the trajectory of a man of mixed Québécois and Mohawk heritage who, in the context of Oka, reconnects with a Mohawk lover from his teen years in Oka-Kanehsatake. Through this character, whom he has seen on the televised image from the siege site, the protagonist finally makes peace with the mixed ancestry that has set up a colonial conflict within him that is both ancient and actual. That said, Lalonde's narrative is unique in that it could also be approached as a Mohawk-authored text, tying into the movement of return as represented in many Indigenous literary narratives of the 1990 standoff.

The poetry collection *Voleurs de cause*, by Québécois poet Yves Boisvert, is the literary work that best conveys all the disruptive power, discordant affects, and violent repercussions of the Oka Crisis. Drawing on the diverse and divergent images, discourses, and performances that marked the crisis, Boisvert uses the event to create a chaotic epic, in the course of which dark colonial intentions are challenged and countered in all their forms. The collection features an Indigenous figure, both ancient and contemporary, who stands tall with nobility and dignity in the middle of a corrupt, violent, dysfunctional established order. At the same time, the perspective is constantly shifting, which keeps the reader wondering where the blows are coming from and on which side the hero is to be found, and destabilizes identification with the character. Recreating the feelings of uneasiness, hurt, and confusion, the poems rework the relations of fragility and certainty exposed during the event by repeating its colonial stereotypes and racist discourses.

In *Voleurs de cause*, it is precisely the warriors' marginality and confirmed exclusion from dominant power that provide the one stable element in the event's infernal chaos. The poems' Iroquois subjects, like the Mohawk protestors on the siege site, replay what François Paré described as a drama of exclusion from power for all members of minorities. According to this drama, expounded Paré, the minorities recognize themselves in struggles with the dominant order.[11] Notably, the Indigenous resistance enacted during the siege is often featured in the work of poets and writers who, like Boisvert and Gail Scott with their uncompromising anti-establishment stances, are in some way marginalized. The Mohawk warrior therefore appears as a figure of resistance through which Québécois and Canadian writers express criticism of their own society. By reanimating and reinterpreting the event, they replay, in the space of fiction, relations of conflict as understood and experienced from a non-Indigenous viewpoint. These representations of Indigenous otherness seem to constitute, first and foremost, a reflection of the settler societies from which they come, and for that reason they are worthy of study. In this connection, a further stage of research could consist in undertaking a critical examination of these literary narratives in light of postcolonial or decolonization theory, or settler colonial studies, to uncover the presuppositions and dynamics they contain. In-depth analyses of novels such as *Anima* by Wajdi Mouawad, *Taqawan* by Éric Plamondon, or *Bottle Rocket Hearts* by Zoe Whittall would no doubt be productive starting points, as would be extended analyses of other settler literary works examined in that chapter.[12]

I conclude the book with an analysis of the event's representations in the Indigenous literary corpus. The literary narratives of Indigenous writers, poets, and playwrights foreground the voices, images, and perspectives that emerged out of the breach created by the event. Generally, they describe the resistance at Kanehsatà:ke as an event that touched Indigenous communities deeply and directly. By contrast with non-Indigenous representations, they underscore the forms of encroachment that occurred throughout history, and they treat the besieged Mohawks' protest as a gesture of political resistance. To be noted is that it is not the mediatized figure of the warrior standing alone against all comers that appears here, but rather that of Mohawk community members who risked their lives to protect their land.

The narratives of Mohawk writers Myra Cree, Joe David, Dan David, Donna K. Goodleaf, and Peter Blue Cloud display a close relation to the event's political aspect and shed light on the unique experience of people who saw the police and soldiers deployed in their communities. The writers recall the connections uniting the members and clans of the Haudenosaunee Confederacy and reiterate, in the narrative or poetic space, the Mohawk rights and sovereignty declared on the siege site in summer 1990. If they emphasize a direct relationship between appropriation of the territory and the elimination of their people, they then reaffirm their people's determination to resist these joint colonial movements.

The more recent mentions of Oka in the literary narratives of a new generation of francophone Indigenous writers in Quebec speak to the difficult aftermath of the event in the province, and continuing Indigenous solidarity across the Americas. Their voices are especially significant after a long silence on the part of their predecessors in the province. Elsewhere in Canada, the narratives of writers from other Indigenous nations speak of relating to an event that is experienced from a distance, often through the media, but also up close because of a strong identification with the Mohawks and a personal and political engagement in the conflict. In these narratives, the Mohawk protestors and communities represent both a threatened people and an example of concerted action, strength, and determination. The project to expand the golf course that is the immediate cause of the conflict represents the settler society's obsession to appropriate the Indigenous peoples' land and eliminate the peoples themselves. The deterioration of colonial relations is sometimes represented by the breakup of a mixed marriage or the quest of an Indigenous child adopted by a white family, as in works by Drew Hayden Taylor and Richard Wagamese. Accounts of the armed conflict feature the figure of the White Man, who is characterized by blindness, an inability to listen, and cupidity, and who, by his intolerable actions, makes the resistance, even armed resistance, necessary. As presented in these literary narratives, the limit that is reached of course refers to the territory, but it takes in many other irritants in the relation to the settler society, notably with regard to justice, respect, and dignity. In this perspective, it is clearly a matter of resisting a process of exile, fighting to protect the land, but also of enacting resurgences, affirming culture, identity, spirituality, and political legitimacies.

As represented in these narratives, the siege stands in for smothering the Indigenous peoples, and very often the issue of individual and collective survival is explicitly mentioned. Relying on powerful symbolism, the narratives rework in fiction the imminence of death that was central to the armed conflict, in which Mohawk communities faced down the police and military to defend their land. As can be seen in Lee Maracle's novel *Sundogs,* the siege depicted in these narratives brings with it a reopening of wounds caused by the colonial assaults on Indigenous land and lives. To counter silence and invisibility, Indigenous literary narratives feature speech being expressed and heard. They set up a reversal of perspective, inaugurating a passage from shame to pride and from an internalized colonial violence to a political battle conducted in the public space. In these narratives, the event makes way for a movement of coming home that proceeds by linking up shared histories, families, and experiences, and, like the Mohawk protestors' resistance, they help to bring about a reterritorialization of Indigenous politics and identity. At the same time, against the virulent racism that emerged during the conflict, the narratives speak of a change in relating to a Canada that can no longer allow itself to ignore the Indigenous peoples. As in the case of the crisis itself, the Quebec and Canadian literary narratives bring out a superficial relation to the event, seen and experienced according to the paradigm of the view. The Indigenous literary narratives, on the other hand, speak of an in-depth relation to an event that is perceived and experienced in accordance with a relational paradigm. They convey how various sets of experiences and relations were mobilized in 1990 and continue to be so through their multiple retellings. This in turn reminds us of how, as James H. Cox and Daniel Heath Justice explained in *The Oxford Handbook of Indigenous American Literature,* "In the early 1990s, following the highly publicized Mohawk resistance in Oka, Québec, and the subsequent report of the Royal Commission on Aboriginal Peoples (1991–1996)," Indigenous writers "demonstrated that Indigenous arts could transform the lives and relationships of everyone, Indigenous peoples and settler Canadians alike, although such transformation required an honest assessment of Canadian colonialism and its enduring force."[13] This assesement continues to be a major task today.

Whether with reference to territory, cinema, or literature, the tension between the 1990 event and the context of its emergence accounts for the shock that is felt at numerous points of contact. The breach created by the event opens up many possibilities for the Indigenous peoples, generating solidarity, pride, and hope. The context of emergence, however, remains marked by deep-seated structural inequities that do violence to Indigenous individuals and communities on a daily basis. Conversely, while Oka profoundly shook the Quebec and Canadian societies, the context of emergence for these societies includes maintaining a white privilege that is inscribed in colonial and state constructs, dominant institutions, and social structures. Thus, a return to normalcy tends to restore the settlers' power to define the ground rules and, at the same time, to maintain structural inequality; this is apparent on the political, cinematic, and literary levels.

KARIHWATÀTIE, "THE CONTINUING STORIES OR EVENTS"

This book was not intended to elucidate what happened during the event. However, upon my reflection, core consistencies became clearly visible, particularly concerning the issue of representations and their impact on the occupation of the territory and on relations among the peoples who share it, whether willingly or by force. A fundamental aspect of the book's content has to do with a powerful representation that is intrinsic to the colonial foundations of the Americas we know today: the Doctrine of Discovery. From this false representation proceed two presuppositions that are equally erroneous. The first is that the territory was uninhabited when the Europeans arrived—in other words, that Indigenous peoples as non-Christians did not count as people in the imperial mind; the second, that the Indigenous peoples were inevitably doomed to disappear or, as the case may be, become assimilated—which comes down to the same thing. This representational subterfuge is based on the dehumanization of the Indigenous peoples—their existence does not count, or, if it does, it is doomed to extinction. In addition, it serves to conceal a reality that nonetheless persists: the continued appropriation of Indigenous land by colonial powers and settler societies. In his book *The Inconvenient Indian: A Curious Account of Native People in North America*, writer Thomas King identified land as the first priority of a colonizing enterprise that is still in operation: "The issue that came ashore with the French and the English and the Spanish, the issue that was the *raison d'être* for each of the colonies, the issue that has made its way from coast to coast to coast and is with us today, the issue that has never changed, never varied, never faltered in its resolve is the issue of land. The issue has always been land. It will always be land, until there isn't a square foot of land left in North America that is controlled by Native people."[14]

In the summer of 1990, the Oka Crisis or the resistance at Kanehsatà:ke reaffirmed the reality of this territorial issue and at the same time exposed the falsity of the presuppositions that both deny and normalize its existence. This exercises an undeniable rending power. When Quebec's human rights commission and Québécois poet Yves Boisvert, respectively, report a "collective shock" and a "shock of the real," it is precisely the event's antagonistic intensity to which they are referring. The force of the impact reveals the breadth of the rift between settler societies and Indigenous peoples and, more specifically, the Québec and Canadian societies' wilful ignorance of the fate of the First Nations. In this regard, scholars Dean Neu and Richard Therrien observed that "if we, as citizens, had had a better understanding of both the contested histories of settler society and our continuing complicity in genocidal practices directed at Indigenous peoples, the Oka stand-off would not have been seen as extraordinary at all."[15] We wish it would also be possible to suppose that, under these conditions, the political crisis would simply not have happened. Incidentally, because they possessed such an understanding, Indigenous people situated the event in a repetitive colonial history and a long history of First Peoples' resistance against colonial encroachment in its various guises.

Since events and conflicts become integral parts of community life, it remains critical to come back to Oka and the context of its emergence. This book was intended to imagine a space in which it would be possible to develop a shared narrative of the event, so as to launch a specific transformational action that would proceed in the direction of decolonization. After the event, the Tsi Niionkwarihò:ten Cultural Center in Kanehsatà:ke produced the magazine *Karihwatàtie,* whose name means "the continuing stories or events."[16] In the spirit of this publication, the process of reflection put forward in this book is not intended to be the last word, but rather a conversation to be furthered. The event goes on. In fact, the event will keep changing as long as it is reanimated, and how the narratives continue to develop will play a fundamental role in its future. This is the knowledge and consciousness that are behind the commemorations of the Kanien'kehà:ka resistance organized and held in Kanehsatà:ke in 2010, twenty years after the event, with a walk, an art exhibit, and the launch of two important books,[17] as well in 2015, with the 11 July webinar, "The Impact of the 1990 Occupation of Kanehsatà:ke and Kahnawà:ke," featuring Indigenous artists Rebecca Belmore, Ellen Gabriel, Martin Loft, Nadia Myre, and Skawennati, among other speakers. In 2015, the Idle No More bilingual campaign #MOHAWKUPRISING / #GÉNÉRATIONOKA invited people to share accounts, memories, and thoughts of the Mohawk resistance as a gesture of commemoration.[18] The pronounced involvement of Indigenous writers, filmmakers, and visual artists in the commemorations and representations of the event reminds us of Lee Maracle's reflection on Indigenous peoples' relationship to past events and the role of imagination in moving towards a future of their own design. According to Maracle, "it is our imagined direction that calls us to re-conjure old events, redraft them, pull the parts together from their disconnected places in our mind and our bodies and decide which ones are connected to the thread of direction we are determined to travel in. In so doing, the imagination reshapes reality and it becomes purposeful fiction."[19] Here, politics and literature appear as continously entangled.

Now that we have entered an era of reconciliation, with all the questions raised by this challenging concept, it is imperative, as argued Paulette Regan, that non-Indigenous people make an effort to "think more deeply about what it would mean to *fully* recognize and respect the *presence* and *humanity* of the people whose land we now share."[20] Such a reflection would inevitably lead to an in-depth interrogation of colonial concepts of territory and relations between the peoples. It would also, inevitably, foreground the deeply political questions of repatriation, reparation, and sovereignty.[21] In that respect, I also maintain that it is precisely because of its discordant, antagonistic, and violent character that the event of summer 1990 must continue to be seriously brought to mind, discussed, and reflected on. Indeed, the armed standoff is unlike positive intercultural experiences that, as incisively expounded by Stó:lō scholar Dylan Robinson in his sharp criticism of the Canadian Opera Company's remounting of the opera *Louis Riel*, can be "felt as a form of reconciliation."[22] The Oka Crisis was harsh, and the Kanien'kehà:ka armed resistance requires that we examine and transform settler-Indigenous relationships precisely in light of the "intractable settler colonial situation"[23] that still shapes our lives. Since words constitute concrete actions, a first gesture in acknowledging Indigenous presence and humanity with regard to the Oka Crisis would certainly be to answer the appeal made by Ellen Gabriel, Kanien'kehà:ka of the Turtle Clan in Kanehsatà:ke, when she asked that "an apology for the human rights abuses and all propaganda criminalizing the Mohawk people be given by the Government of Canada, the Government of Québec and the Municipality of Oka as quickly as possible in order to begin the process of reconciliation."[24] In the end, if knowledge and representation have been playing a fundamental role in the colonial project since its beginning, they can also be made to serve in a necessary, demanding process of decolonization. The Indigenous artistic expressions that have made a forceful entry into the public space since the time of the fateful conflict provide promising grounds for fostering that process, especially given their peculiar ability to reach out and maintain connections through thick layers of unease, conflict, and complexity.

ACKNOWLEDGEMENTS

I would like to acknowledge and thank the numerous people and groups who provided precious support through the research, writing, translating, updating, and editing process for this book. I am grateful for the places, resources, knowledges, and stories that were shared, as well as for the relationships and understandings that were created and have developed in the process.

First, this book would not have become what it is without the opportunities I had to visit and consult the archives at Kanehsatà:ke and Kahnawà:ke, and to engage in discussions that played a decisive part in my process of reflection. Heartfelt thanks go to Hilda Nicholas, director of the Kanehsatà:ke Language and Cultural Center, for granting me her trust and her invaluable support throughout the work of research. Whether by sharing knowledge and ideas, guiding the documentary research, organizing meetings and setting up connections, or welcoming me to a Mohawk language course, Hilda provided major and significant support. Our encounters and discussions, always very inspiring and motivating, gave me the means to refine my understanding of the 1990 resistance and its historical context, on the human level as well as the political. I am grateful for her vision, her patience, and her belief that something could come out of this initially vague research project. My sincere thanks to Ellen Gabriel for having considered and supported this project in various ways, including providing the benefit of her expertise, experience, diplomacy, and critical thinking to shed light on the fundamental issues of the Indigenous resistance and the colonial project from the perspective of Kanehsatà:ke in 1990 and beyond. Her unwavering commitment for justice and peace coupled with her insistence on the intractable nature of settler colonialism kept me focused on some of the most demanding aspects of this research. I also wish to wholeheartedly thank Linda Cree for her discreet but manifest presence over the years, and especially for her foreword. I am humbled and honoured by the words she summoned up to introduce this book. In Kahnawà:ke, I would like to thank the Kanien'kehá:ka Onkwawén:na Raotitióhkwa Language Center (KORLCC) for welcoming scholars and other visitors like me to the library, public presentations, and various exhibitions and activities. I am grateful to Thomas Deer, responsible for the library, for his advice and knowledge, and to Martin Loft, formerly supervisor of public programming, for the interest he took in this research project, for setting up key connections and introductions, and for sharing his reflections, knowledge, and anecdotes about Indigenous arts and politics. My gratitude more specifically for the generative opportunities he brought about through a rich and stimulating collabortion with the First People's Festival and the conference Regards autochtones sur les Amériques / Revisioning the Americas Through Indigenous Cinema / Visiones indígenas sobre las Américas, and my heartfelt thanks for the splendid artwork he contributed for the cover of this book.

It was important in this research to meet and discuss with other key actors of the Oka Crisis or Mohawk resistance, as well as with people engaged in storying the event in its aftermath. I would like to acknowledge and thank all the people who shared their thoughts and experiences over the years, informally and through more formal interviews. These people include Mary MacDonald and Harvey Gabriel in Kanehsatà:ke; Brian Deer, Phillip Deering, Roy Wright, Joe Delaronde, and Kahn-Tineta Horn in Kahnawà:ke; General John de Chastelain and Lieutenant-Colonel Robin Gagnon from the Canadian Armed Forces; the Honourable Marc David, Superior Court Judge; Pierre Lepage from the Commission des droits de la personne du Québec; Francine Lemay, French translator for *At the Woods' Edge*; and Darrell Dennis, Drew Hayden Taylor, Véronique Hébert, Catherine Joncas, Natasha Kanapé Fontaine, and Yves Sioui Durand from the Indigenous artistic scene. The thoughts you shared with me were extremely valuable in enhancing my knowledge, awareness, and understanding. Together with the people at the cultural centres mentioned above, they allowed me to realize the complexity and seriousness of this event, and the need to tackle it with respect and consideration. I hope this book is accurate and does justice to all the accounts I had the chance to listen to over the years.

The research process that led to writing and updating this book also consisted of meetings, discussions, and projects carried out in collaboration and partnership with various individuals and organizations who brought the academic world and the Indigenous arts community closer together, on occasions that generated a wealth of new ideas, reflections, and possibilities. Thanks to Maurizio Gatti and Louis-Karl Picard-Sioui for their innovative and impactful work in the field of Indigenous literature in Quebec, notably with the Carrefour international des littératures autochtones de la francophonie in 2008 and, subsequently, through

Kwahiatonhk!, the annual First Nation's Book Fair in Wendake. Regarding the conference-event Paroles et pratiques artistiques autochtones au Québec aujourd'hui [Indigenous voices and artistic practices in Quebec today] that I co-organized in 2008 with Chloé Charce, Anaïs Janin, Jonathan Lamy-Beaupré, and Gustavo Zamora Jiménez, I would like to thank the Cercle des Premières Nations de l'Université du Québec à Montréal (UQAM) and the Centre interuniversitaire sur les arts, les lettres et les traditions (CELAT). In connection with the international conference titled Regards autochtones sur les Amériques / Revisioning the Americas Through Indigenous Cinema / Visiones indígenas sobre las Américas that I co-founded with Claudine Cyr in 2009, my thanks go to the Groupe interdisciplinaire de recherche sur les Amériques (GIRA), as well as to Terres en vues / Land InSights. I wish to thank Réseau DIALOG, le Réseau de recherche et de connaissances relatives aux peuples autochtones, and more specifically Carole Lévesque, for their key support from 2009 to 2012. For the 2014 conference more specifically, thanks to the Laboratoire sur les récits du soi mobile and its director Simon Harel, the Wapikoni mobile and its director Manon Barbeau, as well as the Social Sciences and Humanities Research Council of Canada (SSHRC) for its Connection grant. I salute André Dudemaine's vision, diplomacy, and am absolutely grateful for the unique intellectual and creative possibilities he has opened up year after year within the Montreal First Peoples Festival, of which he is the co-founder and director. In relation to that conference, thanks to Audra Simpson for generously presenting her incisive and impactful academic work year after year, as well as to Reaghan Tarbell, Marion Delaronde, and the other people at KORLCC who contributed to make this event possible. Although I did not study these academic and cultural events per se, they have immensely nourished and shaped my understanding of the cultural context of the Mohawk resistance, and these insights consequently influenced my reading and interpreting of the written sources.

This book began its life as doctoral research I undertook at UQAM. I would like to thank my supervisor, Simon Harel, for his strong and steady academic support throughout the initial research process, as well as for the projects that grew out of it, in particular the graduate summer institute on Indigenous literatures of the Centre d'études et de recherches internationales at the University of Montreal (CÉRIUM) that I co-founded in 2013 with my colleague Sarah Henzi, and which also generously supported Lianne Moyes. My thanks are extended to my co-director, Denise Brassard, my other thesis committee member, Isabelle Miron, and my external examiners, Roxanne Rimstead from Sherbooke

University and Daniel Salée from Concordia University, who read through the first version of my research report and provided invaluable critical comments. The resources for exchange and investigation supplied by research centres and groups helped me enormously on the levels of ideas, networking, and courses of action. In this connection, I acknowledge the CELAT and the Groupe d'études et de recherches en sémiotique des espaces (GERSE) at UQAM, as well as the GIRA and the DIALOG Network at the Institut national de la recherche scientifique (INRS). In relation to these research groups, special thanks respectively to Charles Perraton and Maude Bonenfant; to Jean-François Côté, Claudine Cyr, and Frédéric Lesemann; and to Carole Lévesque and Daniel Salée.

Finally, all my gratitude and friendship to the UQAM's Cercle des Premières Nations and its coordinator, Gustavo Zamora Jiménez, as well as to all the members I worked with over the years, including Steve Boily, Philippe Charland, Widia Larivière, Mélanie Lumsdsen, Éric Pouliot, Marc Saindon, and Maxime Wawanoloath. I thank them for their commitment and creativity, their great hosting of students, their dynamic vision of Indigenous-settler collaborations, and the resulting learning and sharing opportunities. In 2013, I had the honour of presenting my research results in public alongside Ellen Gabriel, Widia Larivière, Pierre Lepage, Thibault Martin, and Alanis Obomsawin in a roundtable they had organized at UQAM. It is also thanks to them that I had the honour to present the French version of this book alongside a panel discussion with artists Charles Bender, Catherine Joncas, Mélanie Lumsden, Yves Sioui Durand, and Leticia Vera at the same university in 2015. Those were for me significant moments, and I am grateful to the Cercle des Premières Nations for making them happen.

This book was supported by the Social Sciences and Humanities Research Council of Canada (SSHRC) through a doctoral scholarship. It also benefited from support by the Réseau DIALOG and the GIRA on the research portion, and the Québec Parental Insurance Plan for the unrelated but nonetheless crucial maternity leave portion. My affiliation as a SSHRC postdoctoral fellow with the Department of Native Studies at the University of Manitoba later provided me with an academic context conducive to the pursuit of this book project. In that respect I would like to thank most sincerely my colleagues and mentors Warren Cariou, Niigaanwewidam James Sinclair, and the late Renate Eigenbrod. I salute their true generosity, their inspiring research, art, and activism, and am indebted to them for the great scholarly support and opportunities they have offered me over the last years. I also thank them, as I thank Taiaiake Alfred, for strongly and steadily supporting the CÉRIUM's summer institute on Indigenous literature, another venue that generated conversations on the Mohawk context more specifically. ·

I am grateful and excited to see this book appear in English. I wish to acknowledge the Presses de l'Université Laval for publishing the original research and welcoming the English version. My sincere thanks to the University of Manitoba Press, more specifically to David Carr, Glenn Bergen, Jill McConkey, and David Larsen, for welcoming my initial proposal and providing strategic assistance through the translating, editing, publishing, and dissemination process. I wish to thank the Canada Council for the Arts for the translation grant awarded to the Press, as well as Sue Stewart, the translator of this book, for her elegant, thoughtful, and precise work, and the anonymous reviewers for their reading and insightful comments. I am grateful for the doors this book might now open into a conversation with the Mohawk communities and the larger English-speaking world.

In addition to the people mentioned above, I would like to acknowledge other scholars and artists with whom I had the opportunity to exchange and collaborate at different points in the course of this work. Thanks to Nathalie Gagnon, Mathieu Li-Goyette, Michael Minor, Kathryn V. Muller, Sam McKegney, Rick Monture, Daniel Rück, Dagmara Zawadzka, and many others. Heartfelt thanks to my family, relatives, and friends for their optimism, humour, lively company, and unwavering support through the years. Many thanks to my sister, Catherine St-Amand, for her big heart and daunting efficiency, and to her partner, Gustave N'fonguem, with their children and extended family. I would also like to thank Michel, Sylvie, and Bertin, along with their partners and relatives, as well as Alexandre, Erin, Sean, Guylaine, Léonie, Brigitte, Naoko, Virginie, Alain. Love and thanks to Serge and Léon; my child, this book is for you. Lastly, I hope that this book will contribute to make a constructive change in how Quebec and Canadian societies relate to the Oka Crisis and how it came about, and, as a result, to their past and current histories as settlers and to their relationships with the Indigenous peoples with whom we share territory. I also wish that it will be relevant and useful to Kanien'kehà:ka and other Indigenous scholars, artists, cultural actors, and community members in their endeavors for the protection and flourishing of their lands and peoples. With respect and admiration, merci, niawenh:kówa.

NOTES

INTRODUCTION

1   99media, Les Altercitoyens, and GAPPA, *Je ne resterai pas une crise d'Oka.*

2   Months later I found in those same childhood souvenirs clippings of another tragic event, the École Polytechnique massacre of 6 Decembre 1989, in which an armed male student walked in and murdered fourteen women, mostly engineering students, in what he considered to be a personal fight against feminism. Québec, Ministère de la Sécurité publique, *Rapport d'investigation du coroner,* 7 and 14. I mention these clippings because the killings at Polytechnique were explicitly linked to the Mohawk women's resistance at Oka in a play by Véronique Hébert that I examine in Chapter 7 of this book.

3   Harel and St-Amand, *Les figures du siège.*

4   For an example, see First Nations Centre, *OCAP,* a document published by the National Aboriginal Health Organization (NAHO). The First Nations Centre was one of three centres within NAHO.

5   Eigenbrod, *Travelling Knowledges,* 43.

6   Ruffo, "Inside Looking Out," 174.

7   Pratt's work is discussed in Leclerc and Simon. "Zones de contact," 15–29; Mumford's work in Foster, "Of One Blood." See also Mumford, *Interzones;* and Pratt, *Imperial Eyes.*

8   Bainbridge and Nerenberg, *Okanada.*

9   Maracle, *Memory Serves,* 165.

10 Rickard or Richards, "Sovereignty" and "Visualizing Sovereignty."

11 McLeod, "Coming Home Through Stories," 18–19, 22–23. Subsequent references to this source will be identified by (McLeod 2001) following the reference in the body text.

12 See, for instance, Yves Sioui Durand, "Kaion'ni," 57–61.

13 Cariou, "Indigenous Literature," 580.

14 Cyr, "Cartographie événementielle," 371 f.

15 Episkenew, *Taking Back Our Spirits,* 15.

16 Ibid., 15–17.

17 Flahault, *La méchanceté,* 50–51.

CHAPTER 1: THE EVENT AND THE IMPOSSIBILITY OF NEUTRALITY

1   Idle No More, "The Story"; see also the collection *The Winter We Danced: Voices From the Past, the Future, and the Idle No More Movement,* edited by the Kino-nda-niimi Collective.

2   Newhouse, "Oka," 463.

3   Grégoire, "Notion d'événement," 167–86.

4   Québec, Ministère de la Sécurité publique, *Rapport d'enquête du coroner Guy Gilbert*, 9. Subsequent references to this source will be identified by (Quebec 1995) following the reference in the body text.

5   Another trial at the courthouse in Saint-Jérôme ended in the acquittal of one of the accused, Roger Lazore, and prison sentences for two other accused, Ronald Cross and Gordon Lazore. Regroupement de solidarité avec les Autochtones, *Le procès des Mohawks*, 8.

6   Ibid., 92.

7   Press release, quoted in Regroupement de solidarité avec les Autochtones, *Le procès des Mohawks*, 97.

8   Ciaccia, *Oka Crisis*, 355.

9   Canada, House of Commons, *Summer of 1990*, 1.

10   The Royal Commission on Aboriginal Peoples was estalished on 26 August 1991 by Order in Council P.C. 1991-1597 with the following mandate: "The Commission of Inquiry should investigate the evolution of the relationship among Aboriginal peoples (Indian, Inuit and Métis), the Canadian government, and Canadian society as a whole. It should propose specific solutions, rooted in domestic and international experience, to the problems which have plagued those relationships and which confront aboriginal peoples today. The Commission should examine all issues which it deems to be relevant to any or all of the aboriginal peoples of Canada. . ." (P.C. 1991-1597), https://qspace.library.queensu.ca/handle/1974/6874.

11   Canada, Royal Commission on Aboriginal Peoples, *People to People*.

12   Winegard, *Oka*. The book makes reference to the author's master's thesis, on which it is based, titled "The Court of Last Resort: The Canadian Forces and the 1990 Crisis."

13   Valaskakis, "Rights and Warriors," 1.

14   Chamberlin, *If This Is Your Land*, 1.

15   "Conceived in 1455, with the *Romanus Pontifex* papal bull, the international legal construct called 'the discovery doctrine' that spawned the concept of '*terra nullius or terra nullus*' consecrated the principle by which any Christian monarch who discovered non-Christian lands had the right to proclaim them his, since they belonged to nobody. Over the centuries, this doctrine became enshrined in national and international laws and politics and was promulgated through the dispossession and impoverishment of the Indigenous peoples." United Nations Permanent Forum on Indigenous Issues, 9th Session, 11th Meeting (AM); translation.

16   Wolfe, "Settler Colonialism," 387.

17   Chamberlin, *If This Is Your Land*, 28.

18   The name "Oka-Kanehsatake" itself refers to the fact that the Kanehsatake territory, which is not a reserve under the Indian Act, is fragmented within the Oka municipality, causing frequent jurisdictional disputes.

19   Redekop, "Hermeneutic of Deep-Rooted Conflict," 16–17.

20   Winegard, "The Court of Last Resort," f. 4.

21   Ibid., f. 10.

22   Roth et al., "Three Women," 51. See also Kalant, *National Identity*, 199–237.

23   Johnston, "One Generation from Extinction," 108.

24   Féral, *Théorie et pratique du théâtre*, 34.

25 Jonathan Culler, quoted in Feral, *Théorie et pratique du théâtre*, 34.

26 Ibid.

27 Fogelson, "Ethnology of Events," 134.

28 Romano, *L'événement et le temps*, 162–63. For the English translation of this book, see Claude Romano, *Event and Time*.

29 See, for instance, Salée, "L'évolution des rapports politiques," 326; Roth et al., "Three Women," 77–78; Stuart, "Mohawk Crisis," iv and 7–35; Conradi, "Uprising at Oka," 552–53; Kalant, *National Identity*, 200 and 240; Alfred, "De mal en pis," 33.

30 Alfred, *Heeding the Voices*, 1.

31 Romano, *L'événement et le temps*, 178.

32 Ibid., 176 and 162.

33 Fogelson, "Ethnology of Events," 135.

34 Neal B. Keating explains that the internal conflict was caused by dissension over the new gaming economy, smuggling, and the duty-free markets developed in the 1980s following neo-liberal reforms. In 1990, this dissension culminated in barricades and confrontations, and eventually fatal exchanges of fire, in addition to police and military intervention. Keating, *Iroquois Art, Power, and History*, 266. See also, among others, Johansen, *Life and Death;* and George-Kanentiio, *Iroquois on Fire*.

35 LaRocque, *When the Other Is Me,* 61.

36 Smith, *Decolonizing Methodologies*, 2.

37 Alfred (1991a; 1995; 1999; 2009; 2014) and Audra Simpson (2003; 2008; 2010; 2014; 2016). See also Goodleaf (1995); Gabriel-Doxtater and Van den Hende (1995); and Monture (2015).

38 Alfred, "Foreword," x.

39 Sefa Dei, "Rethinking the Role"; Kuokkanen, *Reshaping the University*; Mihesuah and Wilson, *Indigenizing the Academy*.

40 Eigenbrod, "A Necessary Inclusion," 10.

41 Coulthard, *Red Skin, White Masks*, 106.

CHAPTER 2: THE SIEGE IN ACTION

1 Kalant, *National Identity*.

2 Russell, "Oka to Ipperwash," 29.

3 See also Soussana, "Introduction," 9–24.

4 Winegard, "The Court of Last Resort," f. 3 and 208, and Simpson, *Mohawk Interruptus*, 152.

5 Delâge, "Autochtones, Canadiens, Québécois," 299–301.

6 Ciaccia, "Lettre du ministre John Ciaccia," 98.

7 Nora, "Le retour de l'événement," 300–1.

8 Kelman, "À l'âge du témoignage," 61.

9 Kalant, *National Identity,* 200.

10 Simard, "White Ghosts, Red Shadows," 333–69.

11 Kalant, *National Identity*, 222.

12 Ibid.

13 Jacques Parizeau, quoted in Kalant, *National Identity*, 183.

14 George Sioui, quoted in Kalant, *National Identity*, 239.

15 Ibid.

16 Quebec, Commission des droits de la personne du Québec, *Le choc collectif*, 9.

17 Gabriel-Doxtater and Van den Hende, *At The Woods' Edge*, 246. Subsequent references to this source will be identified by (Gabriel-Doxtater and Van den Hende 1995) following the reference in the body text.

18 See *Karihwatàtie*, Kanehsatà:ke, Tsi Niionkwarihò:ten Cultural Center, 39.

19 See also Simpson, *Mohawk Interruptus*, 154.

20 Muller, "Holding Hands With Wampum," f. 88.

21 Lainey, "Les colliers de wampum," 96–97.

22 The source material read "Enita, Ane8ariis, 8isekowa, Kekarontasha, Ottarakehte, Satiotenola, Kamon, 8arak8anentahon, Ni8aniaha, Tirdesha, and Cha8in." Thanks to Hilda Nicholas for the linguist guidance with regards to the spelling of names.

23 Fontaine, "Documents relatifs aux Droits du Séminaire," 93–94. The underlining is in the original text.

24 Muller, "Holding Hands With Wampum," f. 85–86.

25 York et al., *People of the Pines*, 84.

26 See Gabriel-Doxtater and Van den Hende, *At the Woods' Edge*, 100–24 and 133–34; and Parent, *Kanehsatake*.

27 York and Pindera, *People of the Pines*, 97. The Mohawk families who remained at Gibson had not yet seen the end of their troubles, since Ontario finally invoked the Land Settlement Act and its requirement of a time period to clear the assigned lots, in order to expropriate the families from the lands that had been set aside for them. Gabriel-Doxtater and Van den Hende, *At the Woods' Edge*, 164.

28 Rück, "'Où tout le monde est propriétaire,'" 32.

29 Rueck, "When Bridges Become Barriers," 243.

30 Ibid.

31 Rück, "'Où tout le monde est propriétaire,'" 32.

32 In his chapter "Seeing Red: Reconciliation and Resentment," Glen Sean Coulthard specified, in the context of the siege at Kanehsatake: "As Georges Erasmus, then national chief of the Assembly of First Nations, warned in 1988: 'Canada, if you do not deal with this generation of leaders, then we cannot promise that you are going to like the kind of violent political action that we can just about guarantee the next generation is going to bring to you.' Consider this 'a warning,' Erasmus continued: 'We want to let you know that you're playing with fire. We may be the last generation of leaders that are prepared to sit down and peacefully negotiate our concerns with you.'" Quoted in Coulthard, *Red Skin, White Masks*, 118.

33 Coulthard, *Red Skin, White Masks*, 116 and 117.

34   Québec, Commission des droits de la personne, *Audiences publiques sur les relations,* 3.

35   Winegard, "The Court of Last Resort," f. 154–55.

36   *Karihwatàtie,* Kanehsatà:ke, Tsi Niionkwarihò:ten Cultural Center, 37.

37   *Le Devoir,* 11 July 1990, 14.

38   *Le Devoir,* 12 July 1990, 12.

39   Quoted in Winegard, "The Court of Last Resort," f. 189.

40   Simmel, *Le conflit,* 48.

41   Ibid., 48–49.

42   *Le Devoir,* 14 July 1990, A8.

43   Agamben, *State of Exception.*

44   Harel and St-Amand, "Identités multiples," 3–4.

45   Simpson, *Mohawk Interruptus,* 153.

46   Fédération internationale des droits de l'Homme, *Crise d'Oka.*

47   Goodleaf, *Entering the War Zone,* 119–20.

48   Obomsawin, *Rocks at Whiskey Trench.*

49   *Le Devoir,* 14 July 1990, A8.

50   Winegard, "The Court of Last Resort," f. 203–4.

51   Ibid., f. 204.

52   Ibid., f. xxv.

53   Quoted in Pertusati, *In Defense of Mohawk Land,* 55.

54   Lisa Ford, quoted in "Introduction," 13.

55   Nettelbeck et al., paraphrasing and quoting Lisa Ford in "Introduction,"13.

56   Quoted in York and Pindera, *Peoples of the Pines,* 245.

57   Winegard, "The Court of Last Resort," f. 235.

58   Lieutenant-Colonel Robin Gagnon, interview with the author, Stanstead, Quebec, 4 February 2012.

59   Winegard, "The Court of Last Resort," f. 263.

60   Gagnon quoted in Winegard, "The Court of Last Resort," f. 236; Lieutenant-Colonel Gagnon said, "Following this incident, I understood that some people hoped that the army would arrive and immediately use force and, if necessary, start firing. This was out of the question." He also emphasized the importance of dialogue in resolving the conflict. *Le Devoir,* 17 October 1990, B1; (translation).

61   Winegard, "The Court of Last Resort," f. 248. *Le Devoir*'s front page for 28 August 1990 carried a similar declaration by Robert Bourassa, then Quebec's premier, as a subhead: "Bourassa States that Mohawks Negotiators Were Acting in Bad Faith" (translation).

62   Winegard, "The Court of Last Resort," f. 248.

63   On these questions, see Kalant, *National Identity,* 164–65, 172–75, 197–98.

64   Simpson, *Mohawk Interruptus,* 148.

65 Mohawk scholar Rick Monture discussed Thomas's interventions around and experiences of Oka, observing "that while Oka was an empowering event for many First Nations, it was also an extremely difficult time for Haudenosaunee leaders like Thomas who were responsible for upholding tradition in the face of a militant body of their own people who felt differently about what culture and sovereignty meant in the late twentieth century." Monture, *We Share Our Matters*, 192 ; see also189–93.

66 This statement is reported by Sauvageau et al. in *Les tribunes de la radio,* 113 (translation).

67 Bonspille-Boileau and Obomsawin, "Le film documentaire."

68 Rukavina. "Tracey Deer, Creator of *Mohawk Girls*."

69 Simpson, "The State Is a Man."

70 Foucault, "Of Other Spaces."

71 See Willow, "Conceiving Kakipitatapitmok."

72 *Karihwatàtie*, Kanehsatà:ke, Tsi Niionkwarihò:ten Cultural Centre, 35 and 34.

73 *Le Devoir,* 10 July 1990, A12.

74 *Karihwatàtie*, Kanehsatà:ke, Tsi Niionkwarihò:ten Cultural Centre, 38.

75 Pertusati, "Hermeneutic of Deep-Rooted Conflict," f. 19.

76 Pertusati, *In Defense of Mohawk Land*, 86.

77 Parker, "Certain Iroquois Tree Myths," 608.

78 Alfred, *Peace, Power, Righteousness,* xv.

79 A copy of this agreement was consulted in the archives of the Kanehsatà:ke Language and Cultural Center.

80 Excerpt from *The Constitution of the Iroquois Nations: The Great Binding Law.* http://www.indigenouspeople.net/iroqcon.htm (accessed 20 August 2017).

81 Le Breton, *Passions du risque,* 56–60.

82 Quoted in Pertusati, *In Defense of Mohawk Land*, 94–95.

83 Willow, "Conceiving Kakipitatapitmok," 262.

84 Ibid., 264.

CHAPTER 3: THE DISPUTED LAND: PERFORMING SOVEREIGNTY

1 Lepage, "La genèse d'un conflit," 103.

2 Winegard, "The Court of Last Resort," f. 200–4.

3 *Le Devoir,* 13 July 1990, 14.

4 Quoted in Swain, *Oka,* 132.

5 Peter H. Russell, "Oka to Ipperwash," 29–46.

6 Mike Harris quoted in Episkenew, *Taking Back Our Spirits*, 187.

7 Jones, "Research Report," 2.

8 Ibid.

9 Ibid., 31.

10   Lepage, "La genèse d'un conflit," 101.

11   Ibid., 102.

12   Simpson, "Under the Sign of Sovereignty," 108.

13   Savard, "Le légalisme à la sulpicienne," 127.

14   Pertusati, *In Defense of Mohawk Land*, 32.

15   Savard, "Le légalisme à la sulpicienne," 128.

16   Lepage, "La genèse d'un conflit," 101.

17   Quoted in Winegard, "The Court of Last Resort," f. 180–81.

18   Kalant, *National Identity*, 201–3.

19   Simpson, "Under the Sign of Sovereignty," 107.

20   *Karihwatàtie*, Kanehsatà:ke, Tsi Niionkwarihò:ten Cultural Center, 36.

21   Ibid., 33.

22   Taylor, *The Archive and the Repertoire*, 21. As Jolene Rickard expounded, it is also during key confrontational moments such at "the second Wounded Knee" and "the resistance by Kanien'kehà:ka communities at Oka" that the "Haudenosaunee performed sovereignty and created a physical record to be witness to these encounters." Rickard further added: "These events were important moments in the transference of Haudenosaunee notions of sovereignty and activism that culminated in a renewed desire to address an international audience." Rickard, "Visualizing Sovereignty," 470.

23   Quoted in Pertusati, *In Defense of Mohawk Land*, 9.

24   Butler, *Excitable Speech*, 154 and 158.

25   Simpson, "Under the Sign of Sovereignty," 119.

26   Ibid., 108.

27   Winegard, "The Court of Last Resort," f. 200–4.

28   Simpson, "Under the Sign of Sovereignty," 120.

29   de Certeau, *Practice of Everyday Life*, xix.

30   Ibid., 36 and xix.

31   Ibid., 38.

32   Simmel, *Le conflit*, 50.

33   Kalant, *National Identity*, 164–77.

34   Ibid., 184–85.

35   de Certeau, *Practice of Everyday Life*, 38.

36   Quoted in Pertusati, *In Defense of Mohawk Land*, 104.

37   Simpson, "Under the Sign of Sovereignty," 107–8.

38   Regarding the state's relation to Indigenous protest, see Gerald Taiaiake Alfred, *Wasáse*, and in relation to Mohawk refusal more specifically, see Audra Simpson, *Mohawk Interruptus*.

39   Lieutenant-Colonel Robin Gagnon, interview with author, Stanstead, Quebec, 4 February 2012.

40   *National Defence and the Canadian Armed Forces,* http://www.forces.ca (accessed 10 January 2014).

41   General John de Chastelain, email interview with the author, 26 April 2012.

42   Ibid.

43   Swain, *Oka,* 132.

44   Lieutenant-Colonel Robin Gagnon, interview with the author, Stanstead, Quebec, 4 February 2012.

45   Fenton, *Great Law and the Longhouse,* 5.

46   Pertusati, *In Defense of Mohawk Land,* 42–43.

47   Simpson, *Mohawk Interruptus,* 147–50; see also Goodleaf, *Entering the War Zone;* and Obomsawin, *Kanehsatake.*

48   Simpson, *Mohawk Interruptus,* 148.

49   Ibid.

50   Horn-Miller, "Emergence of the Mohawk Warrior Flag," f. iii and f. 12.

51   Ibid., f. iii, f. 95–111.

52   Deer and Kanatakta, "Pour mieux comprendre," 122 (translation).

53   Alfred, *Wasáse,* 127.

54   Desbiens, "Du wampum aux barricades," 73.

55   Regarding this aspect of political performance, see Taylor, *The Archive and the Repertoire,* xvii–xix.

56   Alfred, *Heeding the Voices,* 11.

57   Simpson, posted biography.

58   Simpson, *Mohawk Interruptus,* 158.

59   Ibid.

60   See foreword by Julien Freud, Simmel, *Le conflit,* 10–15.

61   Winegard, "The Court of Last Resort," f. 310.

62   Goodleaf, *Entering the War Zone,* 101.

63   Ibid., 103.

64   Quoted in Blue Cloud, "Resistance at Oka," 435.

65   Winegard, "The Court of Last Resort," f. 224.

66   Muller, "Holding Hands With Wampum," f. 40.

67   Blue Cloud, "Resistance at Oka," 535.

68   Quoted in Pertusati, *In Defense of Mohawk Land,* 50.

69   See the website of the Honoré-Mercier Bridge, http://pontmercierbridge.ca/en/, (accessed 9 June 2012).

70   Rueck, "When Bridges Become Barriers," 244.

71   Muller, "Holding Hands With Wampum," f. 93.

72   Ibid.

73   Willow, "Conceiving Kakipitatapitmok," 265.

74   Jenish, *St. Lawrence Seaway*, 30.

75   Simpson, "To the Reserve," f. 88.

76   Kakwiranó:ron Cook et al., *Kahnawake Revisited*.

77   Simpson, "To the Reserve," f. 88.

78   Ibid., f. 87.

79   Phillips, "Kahnawake Mohawks," f. ii.

80   Ibid., f. 48.

81   Alfred, *Heeding the Voices*, 1.

82   Kanienkehaka, "Statement of position."

83   Muller, "Holding Hands With Wampum," f. 61.

84   Ibid., f. 19.

85   Ibid., f. 20.

86   Simmel, *Le conflit*, 35.

87   Salée, "Enjeux et défis," 139.

CHAPTER 4: FROM THE SPECTACULAR TO THE DOCUMENTARY

1   Roth et al., "Three Women," 50.

2   Ibid.

3   Ferro, *Cinéma et histoire*, 13.

4   Ibid., 17.

5   Gagnon, *Fait d'armes*, 105–6.

6   At the time, the settler residents of Oka had wanted to prevent the opening of a centre for Indigenous clients, despite the fact that a similar establishment with a non-Indigenous clientele had been set up close by.

7   MacLaine and Baxendale, *This Land Is Our Land*.

8   Soussana et al., *Dire l'événement*, 23.

9   Albert Nerenberg, *Trailervision* website, http://www.trailervision.com/trailer.php?id=4 (accessed 8 July 2008).

10   Winegard, "The Court of Last Resort," f. 259.

11   Ibid., 286.

12   For examples of media strategies, see Collier, "War with the Army"; Roth et al., "Three Women."

13   General John de Chastelain, email interview with the author, 26 April 2012.

14   Quoted in *Voices From Oka*, video cassette consulted at the Kahnawà:ke Kanien'kehaka Onkwawén:na Raotitiohkwa Archives.

15   Nora, "Le retour de l'événement," 285–308.

16   Valaskakis, "Rights and Warriors," 36.

17   Truth and Reconciliation Commission of Canada, *Honouring the Truth,* 130.

18   Legacy of Hope, website, http://staging.legacyofhope.ca/wp-content/uploads/2016/03/Hope-Healing-2014_web.pdf (accessed 20 August 2017); and Lepage, *Mythes et réalités,* 26.

19   Truth and Reconciliation Commission of Canada, *Honouring the Truth*: Milloy, *National Crime.* For a discussion on colonial genocide and Indigenous peoples, see Hinton et al. *Colonial Genocide in Indigenous North America.*

20   Truth and Reconciliation Commission of Canada, *Honouring the Truth*, 1–2.

21   Ibid, 1.

22   Horn-Miller, "Emergence of the Mohawk Warrior Flag," f. 112.

23   Wolfe, "Settler Colonialism."

24   Truth and Reconciliation Commission of Canada, *Honouring the Truth*, 1.

25   Trudel, "La crise d'Oka," 129–35.

26   Barthes, *L'obvie et l'obtus,* 225.

27   Conradi, "Uprising at Oka," 553.

28   Felman, "À l'âge du témoignage," 58.

29   Dulong, "Qu'est-ce qu'un témoin historique" and *Le témoin oculaire*, 117–62.

30   Dulong, *Le témoin oculaire,* 165–68.

31   Felman, "À l'âge du témoignage," 56.

32   Horn et al., "The 1990 Oka Crisis."

33   Krupat, *Red Matters*, vii; Taylor, "Alive and Well," 29–37.

34   Taylor, *The Archive and the Repertoire*, 58.

35   Horn-Miller, "Emergence of the Mohawk Warrior Flag," f. 63.

36   Conradi, "Uprising at Oka," 547; italics ours.

37   Horn et al., "The 1990 Oka Crisis."

38   Horn-Miller, "Emergence of the Mohawk Warrior Flag," f. 64–65.

39   Ibid., 229.

40   Taylor, "Alive and Well," 36; Fagan, "Laughing to Survive," 251 f.

41   Roth et al., "Three Women," 78.

42   Ibid., 59.

43   Kinew, "Cowboys and Indians," 47–51. Subsequent references to this source will be identified by (Kinew 2010) following the reference in the body text.

44   Roth et al., "Three Women," 58–59.

45   Kalant, *National Identity*, 243.

46   Trudel, "De la négation de l'autre," 58.

47   Kalant, *National Identity*, 242.

48   Michaud, "De l'exotisme au réel," 111.

49   Horn et al., "The 1990 Oka Crisis."

50   Felman, "À l'âge du témoignage," 58.

51   Houba, "La parole errante."

52   Felman, "À l'âge du témoignage," 66.

CHAPTER 5: "A RECORD WE MADE OURSELVES"

1   Regarding Alanis Obomsawin's career, see Lewis, *Alanis Obomsawin,* and the website of the National Film Board of Canada, https://www.nfb.ca (accessed 12 June 2017).

2   The feature documentary *Our People Will Be Healed* "provides a glimpse of what action-driven decolonization looks like in Norway House, one of Manitoba's largest First Nations communities." Jesse Wente. Film Description.

3   Lewis, *Alanis Obomsawin,* 24–25.

4   Ibid., 29.

5   Ibid., 92.

6   From an article by Jerry White quoted in National Film Board of Canada, "Alanis Obomsawin," *Production Personnnel,* https://www.nfb.ca (accessed 19 July 2012).

7   Quoted in Lewis, *Alanis Obomsawin,* 93.

8   Dudemaine et al., "Table ronde sur le cinéma autochtone" (translation).

9   Quoted in Tremblay, "Alanis Obomsawin."

10   Bonspille-Boileau, *The Oka Legacy*, film description on the film's web page.

11   Bonspille-Boileau, *The Oka Legacy.*

12   On Skawennati's work, see Treva, "Skawennati's Timetraveller™."

13   For more details on Horn-Miller's impressive life story in relation to Oka and the Olympics, see Methot, "Canada 22/150."

14   St-Amand, "From Kahnawà:ke to Montreal Back and Forth."

15   Monture, *We Share Our Matters*, 179.

16   Bonspille-Boileau and Obomsawin, "Documentary Film."

17   Horn et al., "The 1990 Oka Crisis."

18   Bonspille-Boileau and Obomsawin, "Documentary Film."

19   Lewis, *Alanis Obomsawin,* 182.

20   Ibid., 156–94.

21   The book *La "chose indienne"* was published by Nota Bene publishers in 2015, based on Cornellier's doctoral thesis. The quotes that appear in my current book are taken from Cornellier's doctoral thesis "La 'chose indienne.'"

22   Cornellier, "La 'chose indienne.'"

23   Ibid., f. 147

24   Ibid., f. 160-65.

25   Rickard or Richards, "Sovereignty" and "Visualizing Sovereignty."

26   I refer here to Raheja, "Reading Nanook's Smile." This reflection is further developed and contextualized in Raheja's book *Reservation Reelism*.

27   Rickard, "Visualizing Sovereignty," 471.

28   Raheja, "Reading Nanook's Smile," 1163.

29   Ibid., 1161.

30   Simpson, posted biography.

31   Cornellier, "La 'chose indienne.'"

32   Bonspille-Boileau and Obomsawin, "Documentary Film."

33   Quoted in Lewis, *Alanis Obomsawin*, 137.

34   Alfred, *Peace, Power, Righteousness*, xvi.

35   Lewis, *Alanis Obomsawin*, 182.

36   See Garneau, "Les deux mémoires."

37   Quoted in Lewis, *Alanis Obomsawin*, 65.

38   Ibid., 63.

39   Raheja, "Reading Nanook's Smile," 1161.

40   Bainbridge et al., *Reel Injun*.

41   Raheja, "Reading Nanook's Smile," 1159–60.

42   Quoted in Lewis, *Alanis Obomsawin*, 138.

43   Leuthold, *Indigenous Aesthetics*, 199.

44   Bonspille-Boileau and Obomsawin, "Documentary Film."

45   Taylor, *The Archive and the Repertoire*, 34.

46   Lewis, *Alanis Obomsawin*, 183.

47   Bonspille-Boileau and Obomsawin, "Documentary Film."

48   Ferro, *Cinéma et histoire*, 25.

49   Dudemaine et al., "Table ronde sur le cinéma autochtone" (translation).

50   Alfred, *Peace, Power, Righteousness*, xviii.

51   Lyons, "Rhetorical Sovereignty," 453.

52   Estimates of numbers vary, with some at 1,500.

53   See the chapter "Cinema of Sovereignty" in Lewis, *Alanis Obomsawin*, 156–94.

54   For more on this type of representation, see the examples of Brisson, *Oka par la caricature;* and Trudel, "De la négation de l'autre," 53–66.

55   Conradi, "Uprising at Oka," 547.

56   For the complete text of the document, see Swain, *Oka*, 121–22.

57   Ibid., 123.

58   Winegard, "The Court of Last Resort," f. 215.

59   Swain, *Oka*, 122.

60   Ibid., 123.

61   Lewis, *Alanis Obomsawin*, 182.

62   Savard, "De la nation à l'autonomie gouvernementale," 46–47.

63   Muller, "Holding Hands With Wampum."

64   Taylor, *The Archive and the Repertoire*, xviii.

65   Raheja, "Reading Nanook's Smile," 1165.

66   Quoted in Lewis, *Alanis Obomsawin*, 110.

67   Bonspille-Boileau and Obomsawin, "Documentary Film."

68   Episkenew, *Taking Back Our Spirits*, 15.

CHAPTER 6: SETTLER LITERARY NARRATIVES

1   King, *The Inconvenient Indian*, xi–xii.

2   de Certeau, *Arts de faire*, 272.

3   Dickner, *Nikolski*, 178. Subsequent references to this source will be identified by (Dickner 2005) following the reference in the body text.

4   Scott, *The Obituary*, 141.

5   Trudel, "De la négation de l'autre," 61.

6   Farrow, *Ice Lake*, 381. Subsequent references to this source will be identified by (Farrow 2001) following the reference in the body text.

7   Lalonde has been generally presented and discussed as a Québécois writer. Although his work is analyzed in this book as part of the non-Indigenous corpus, it could have been explored in the Indigenous one as well. In 2004, Lalonde notably wrote the preface to the first extensive anthology of francophone Indigenous literature *Littérature amérindienne du Québec: Écrits de langue française*, which was edited by Italian scholar Maurizio Gatti. He also publicly discussed his Mohawk ancestry.

8   Lalonde, *Sept lacs plus au nord*, 16. Subsequent references to this source will be identified by (Lalonde 1993) following the reference in the body text.

9   Ruggeri, "L'image de l'Indien," 120 (translation).

10   Tremblay, "Une identité frontalière," 111.

11   Robert Lalonde, quoted in Tremblay, "Une identité frontalière," 111.

12   Tremblay, "Une identité frontalière."

13   Lacombe, "Embodying the Glocal," 41. On her part, literary scholar Petra Fachinger pointed out that "by discussing similarities between Indigenous people's stolen lives and history and those deprived by history through slavery, *Out of My Skin* points at two of the pillars of white supremacy," namely the subjugation of Indigenous peoples for the purpose of appropriating their lands and the enslavement of black people for the purpose of exploiting their labour. Fachinger, "Intersections of Diaspora."

14   Bannerji, "Oka Nada," 20.

15   Ibid.

16   McWatt, *Out of My Skin*, 52–53. Subsequent references to this source will be identified by (McWatt 1998) following the reference in the body text.

17   Noël, *Nous avons tous découvert.*

18   Boisvert, *Voleurs de cause*, 46. Subsequent references to this source will be identified by (Boisvert 1992) following the reference in the body text. All italics in quotes from this title were in the original text.

19   Boisvert, "R. Yves Boisvert, 216 and 217 (translation).

20   Hamelin, *Fabrications*, 166.

21   Ibid., 68.

22   Cyr, "Les défilés du *Columbus Day*," 106.

23   For a graphic response to the scenario of discovery that was reactivated through the 1992 celebrations, see Gord Hill, *The 500 Years of Resistance Comic Book*. For examples of creative criticism of Canada and Montreal's anniversaries, see Erik Ritskes's alternate "Canada 150" logo, which instead read "Colonialism 150"; Métis visual artist Christi Belcourt's hashtag "#Resistance150"; and the meeting of Indigenous artists called by Le Printemps autochtone d'Art 3 [3rd Indigenous Art Spring] to evaluate their practices in Quebec at the same moment as the Jacques-Cartier Bridge was illuminated in celebration of Montreal's 375th anniversary. Tremonti, "What Does Canada Mean"; Montpetit, "Zoom sur le Printemps autochtone d'art 3."

24   Cyr, "Les défilés du *Columbus Day*," 107.

25   York, *People of the Pines,* 67.

26   The original French statement was "Ils ont jusqu'au 9, après cette date ça va descendre." Elkas's statement refered to the barricades coming down but invited to read with another connotation, "descendre" someone also meaning to shoot them down.

27   Taylor, *The Archive and the Repertoire,* 28.

28   For a strong argument against the racialization of Métis and more largely Indigenous identities, see Anderson, *Métis.*

29   Trudel, "De la négation de l'autre," 59.

30   Handfield, "Les territoires imaginaires," f. 3.

31   Ibid., f. 1.

32   Bakhtin, *Problems of Dostoevsky's Poetics,* 97.

33   In a paper on the dispute's history, Mary Jane Jones wrote: "It hardly needs to be noted that none of the devices employed so far has resolved a complex situation in which the threads of so many enduring factional, tribal, ethnic, religious, linguistic, legal and constitutional issues are interwoven. It is equally obvious that the hearts and minds of people who labor under grievance, perceived or real, are not persuaded of the finality attributed to the doctrines of *res judicata, stare decisis* and the supremacy of Parliament." Jones, "Research Report," 1.

34   Lamy-Beaupré, "Je est un autochtone," f. 4 (translation).

35   Paré, *Exiguity,* 126.

36   Ibid.

37   For example, see the text *Les Canadiens français sont-ils des colonisés?* written by eminent French and North African writer and essayist Albert Memmi in response to Québécois intellectuals,

and published in 1972 in the new and revised edition of his *Portrait du colonisé* at L'Étincelle publishers in Montreal. Memmi, *Portrait du colonisé*.

38 Lamy-Beaupré, "Je est un autochtone," f. 6 (translation).

39 Plamondon, *Taqawan*, cover flap (translation).

40 Thérien, *Figures de l'Indien;* Chanady, *Entre inclusion et exclusion.*

CHAPTER 7: MOHAWK AND OTHER INDIGENOUS LITERARY NARRATIVES

1 Cariou, "Indigenous Literature," 580.

2 See, for instance, Armstrong and her seminal text "The Disempowerment of First North American Native Peoples and Empowerment Through Their Writing," 256–59.

3 Ruffo, *(Ad)dressing Our Words*, 14.

4 Goodleaf, "I Know Who I Am," 26.

5 McKenzie, *Before the Country.*

6 Armstrong, "Land Speaking," 183.

7 Goodleaf, "I Know Who I Am," 26.

8 Heath Justice, "Seeing (and Reading) Red," 109. For other discussions on Indigenous literatures, literary studies, and communities, see also Womack et al., *Reasoning Together,* and the position outlined by the Indigenous Literary Studies Association (ILSA).

9 Morrison, "Mediating Identity," 129–31.

10 Florent Vollant, quoted in *Journal de Québec*, 14 July 1990, 2.

11 St-Amand, "*Présence autochtone*," 152.

12 See Wickham, "Théâtre de guérison," 108; Sioui Durand and Weber, "Théâtre autochtone," among others.

13 Kanapé Fontaine, *Assi Manifesto*, 70.

14 Cariou and St-Amand, "Introduction," 9.

15 Hébert, "Oka," 63 (translation).

16 See Allen, "Decolonizing Comparison," 377–394.

17 Picard-Sioui, "Hannibalo-God-Mozilla," 52–53 (translation).

18 Quoted in Episkenew, *Taking Back Our Spirits*, 9.

19 Joe David, "How to Become an Activist in One Easy Lesson," 161. Subsequent references to this source will be identified by (David 1994) following the reference in the body text.

20 Ladner and Simpson, "This Is an Honour Song," 3.

21 David, "Razorwire Dreams," 22. Subsequent references to this source will be identified by (David 1992) following the reference in the body text.

22 Nettelbeck et al., *Fragile Settlements*, 6.

23 Cree, "Miroir, miroir," 304. Subsequent references to this source will be identified by (Cree 1990) following the reference in the body text.

24 Cree, "Mon pays rêvé," 23. Subsequent references to this source will be identified by (Cree 1995) following the reference in the body text.

25 Goodleaf, "Remember This!" 98. Subsequent references to this source will be identified by (Goodleaf 1995) following the reference in the body text.

26 Blue Cloud, *Native American Testimony*, 432–35. Subsequent references to this source will be identified by (Blue Cloud 1991) following the reference in the body text.

27 In her memoirs, Charlie wrote, "I was sitting here at the table with a friend of mine, all of sudden we heard this helicopter go over my roof. It was so close that we could see the soldiers that were in the helicopter, so we went outside to see which way they were going." Karonhiaion Annie Cecilia Charlie quoted in Rowe, "Saying goodbye." Karonhiaion Annie Cecilia Charlie passed away in 2017.

28 *Akwesasne Notes, Basic Call to Consciousness*, 102.

29 Another writer to watch for in relation to upcoming literary representations of the event is Mohawk scholar and activist Taiaiake Alfred, who in 2013 published online the first preview of "*a fictionalized oral history of the Mohawk community in Kahnawake and Akwesasne.*" With a focus on the twentieth century, his work in progress recounts "*the story of a Mohawk man who struggles to stay Onkwehonwe (indigenous) even as his life and the culture of his community changes radically.*" Alfred specifies "*that everything in it actually happened and exists as my memories or other people's stories or as traditional stories or legends—all interwoven.*" As such, references to Oka are likely to appear and would be relevant studying in terms of how the event could be symbolized through this particular literary form and authorial perspective. Alfred, "Smoke Is Still Rising," italics in original, http://numerocinqmagazine.com/2013/01/06/smoke-is-still-rising-fiction-tai-aiake-alfred/ (accessed 5 September 2017).

30 I am referring here to the narratives of the First Nations, but there are certainly Métis and possibly also Inuit writers who have published narratives that mention Oka.

31 Goeman, *Mark My Words*, 37.

32 Maracle, *Daughters Are Forever*, 134. Subsequent references to this source will be identified by (Maracle 2002) following the reference in the body text.

33 Nepinak, "The Oka Crisis in Manitoba," 141. Subsequent references to this source will be identified by (Nepinak 2010) following the reference in the body text.

34 Darrell Dennis, interview with the author, Barrie, Ontario, 21 May 2009.

35 Grégoire, "Notion d'événement," 180.

36 Alfred, "From Bad to Worse," 26.

37 Ibid.

38 According to the definition by the *Dictionnaire Larousse*, website, www.larousse.fr/dictionnaires/francais (accessed 12 July 2012).

39 Other works by Drew Hayden Taylor that mention Oka include "Someday," *The Baby Blues*, and *alterNatives*.

40 Taylor, "A Blurry Image," 232. Subsequent references to this source will be identified by (Taylor 2004) following the reference in the body text.

41 Keeshig-Tobias, "After Oka," 257.

42 Keeshig-Tobias, "From Trickster Beyond 1992," 262. Subsequent references to this source will be identified by (Keeshig-Tobias 2005b) following the reference in the body text.

43　O'Meara, "Let's Not Negotiate!!" 115. Subsequent references to this source will be identified by (O'Meara 1995) following the reference in the body text.

44　Cuthand, "Post-Oka Kinda Woman," 273.

45　LaForme, "Indians Have a Right," 99.

46　The story of this man, Randy Horne, is recounted in the 1997 documentary film *Spudwrench: Kanawake Man* by Alanis Obomsawin.

47　Maracle, *Sundogs*, 126. Subsequent references to this source will be identified by (Maracle 1992) following the reference in the body text.

48　Episkenew, *Taking Back Our Spirits,* 8.

49　Wilson, *Research Is Ceremony*, 87–88.

50　Episkenew, *Taking Back Our Spirits,* 8.

51　McKegney, "'pain, pleasure, shame. Shame': Masculine Embodiment, Kinship, and Indigenous Reterritorialization," *Canadian Literature* 216 (Spring 2013): 12–33, http://gateway. proquest.com.proxy.queensu.ca/openurl?ctx_ver=Z39.88-2003&xri:pqil:res_ver=0.2&res_id=xri:lion&rft_id=xri:lion:ft:mla:R04914678:0&rft.accountid=6180 (accessed 15 November 2017).

52　On this question, see Hinton et al., *Colonial Genocide.*

53　Altounian, *La survivance,* 6.

54　Damm, "what is it like," 127.

55　Baskin, "In the Spirit of," 14.

56　Darrell Dennis, interview with author, Barrie, Ontario, 21 May 2009.

57　Dennis, *Tales of an Urban Indian*, 34. Subsequent references to this source will be identified by (Dennis 2005) following the reference in the body text. To be noted, a French-language translation of this play was commissioned by the Ondinnok theatre company and performed in French in Quebec and France.

58　Episkenew, *Taking Back Our Spirits*, 154.

59　Ladner and Simpson, "This Is an Honour Song," 6.

60　Methot, "*A Quality of Light*: Review."

61　Episkenew, *Taking Back Our Spirits*, 16.

62　LaForme, "Indians Have a Right," 99.

63　Nettelbeck et al., *Fragile Settlements*, 17.

CONCLUSION

1　Quoted in Fagan, "Tewatatha:wi," 14.

2　Idle No More, "The Vision"; see also the Kino-nda-niimi Collective, *Winter We Danced.*

3　Richard, Petition "Indigenous and Northern Affairs."

4　Ahmed, *Cultural Politics of Emotions*, 44.

5　Alfred, *Wasáse,* 104.

6　Dulong, "Qu'est-ce qu'un témoin historique?"

7 Regan, *Unsettling the Settler Within*, 190.

8 Ibid., 191.

9 Tuck and Yang, "Decolonization," 1.

10 Leuthold, quoted in Lewis, *Alanis Obomsawin*, 137.

11 Paré, *Les littératures de l'exiguïté*,183.

12 For analyses of the type, see, for example, Hobb, "L'Autochtone dans *Le dernier été*," 231–52; Lacombe, "Embodying the Glocal"; Fachinger, "Intersections of Diaspora,"; Cornellier, *La "chose indienne."*

13 Cox and Heath Justice, "Introduction," 4.

14 King, *Inconvenient Indian*, 217.

15 Quoted in Regan, *Unsettling the Settler Within*, 108.

16 *Karihwatàtie,* 2nd ed., 2003, 3.

17 Simpson and Ladner, *This Is an Honour Song;* Gabriel-Doxtater and Van den Hende, *At the Woods' Edge.* The French translation of *At the Woods' Edge* was graciously offered by translator Francine Lemay, the sister of Corporal Marcel Lemay, who died on 11 July 1990, in a gesture that was part of what she describes as her path to reconciliation. Lemay, "20 ans après la crise."

18 Lamy, "Oka/Kanehsatake," 61.

19 Maracle, *Memory Serves*, 30.

20 Regan, *Unsettling the Settler Within*, 227.

21 See Tuck and Yang, "Decolonization"; Coulthard, *Red Skin, White Masks*; Alfred, *Wasáse;* and Simpson, *Mohawk Interruptus.*

22 Robinson, "Feeling Reconciliation," 280.

23 Nettelbeck et al., *Fragile Settlements*, 17.

24 Gabriel, "Epilogue," 347.

GLOSSARY

Haudenosaunee	Iroquois
Kaianere'kó:wa	Great League of Peace or Great Law of Peace
Kaionkeháka	People of the Great Pipe (Cayugas)
Kahnawà:ke	On the rapids (Kahnawake)
Kahnawa'kehró:non	People of Kahnawake
Kanehsatà:ke	On the sand dunes (Kanehsatake)
Kanehsata'kehró:non	People of Kanehsatake
Kanien'keha	Language spoken by Kanien'kehà:ka (Mohawk)
Kanien'kehà:ka	People of the Flint (Mohawks)
Onen'tó:kon	Under the pines
O'nientehá:ka	People of the Standing Stone (Oneidas)
Ononta'keháka	People of the Hill (Onondagas)
Rotinonhseshá:ka	Longhouse People
Rotisken'raké:ta	Warriors, Men; they who carry the burden of peace
Shenekeháka	People of the Great Mountain (Senecas)
Tehatiskaró:ros	People of the Shirt (Tuscaroras)
Teiotiokwaonhaston	It circles the people
Tiononte'kó:wa	Big Mountain
Tiohtià:ke	Where the group splits; Montreal

Sources: Brenda Katlatont Gabriel-Doxtater and Arlette Kawanatatie Van den Hende, *At the Woods' Edge: An Anthology of the History of the People of Kanehsatà:ke*, principal research by Louise Johnson (Kanehsatà:ke: Kanehsatà:ke Education Center, 1995), 379–81; and Kathryn V. Muller, "Holding Hands With Wampum: Haudenosaunee Council Fires from the Great Law of Peace to Contemporary Relationships with the Canadian State" (PhD thesis, Queen's University, 2008), 40.

BIBLIOGRAPHY

WORKS CITED

99media, Les Altercitoyens, and GAPPA. *Je ne resterai pas une crise d'Oka*. Online video. http://www.lebatondeparole.com/videos/amerindiens/je-ne-resterai-pas-une-crise-d-oka.html (accessed 15 November 2017).

Agamben, Giorgio. *State of Exception*. Translated by Kevin Attel. Chicago: University of Chicago Press, 2005.

Ahmed, Sara. *The Cultural Politics of the Emotions*. 2nd. ed. New York: Routledge, 2015.

Akwesasne Notes, rev ed. *Basic Call to Consciousness*. Introduction by John Mohawk. Premble by Chief Oren Lyons. Afterword by José Barreiro. Summertown, TN: Native Voices, 2005.

Alfred, Gerald R. (Taiaiake). "De mal en pis: la politique interne à Kahnawake dans la crise de 1990." In "Art, Politique, Idéologie," special issue, *Recherches amérindiennes au Québec* 21, no. 3 (1991[a]): 29–38.

———. "From Bad to Worse. Internal Politics in the 1990 Crisis at Kahnawake." *Northeast Indian Quarterly* 8, no. 1 (1991[b]): 23–31.

———. *Heeding the Voices of Our Ancestors: Kahnawake Mohawk Politics and the Rise of Native Nationalism*. Toronto: Oxford University Press, 1995.

———. *Peace, Power, Righteousness: An Indigenous Manifesto*. Don Mills: Oxford University Press, 1999.

Alfred, Taiaiake. *Wasáse: Indigenous Pathways of Action and Freedom*, 2nd edition. Toronto: University of Toronto Press, 2009.

———. "Smoke Is Still Rising: Fiction." *Numéro Cinq Magazine* 4, no. 1 (January 2013). http://numerocinqmagazine.com/2013/01/06/smoke-is-still-rising-fiction-taiaiake-alfred (accessed 15 November 2017).

———. "Foreword." In *Red Skin, White Masks: Rejecting the Colonial Politics of Recognition*, edited by Glen Sean Coulthard, ix–xii. Minneapolis: University of Minnesota Press, 2014.

Allen, Chadwick. "Decolonizing Comparison: Toward a Trans-Indigenous Literary Studies." *The Oxford Handbook of Indigenous American Literature*, edited by James H. Cox and Daniel Heath Justice, 377–94. Don Mills: Oxford UP, 2014.

Altounian, Janine. *La survivance. Traduire le trauma collectif*. Inconscient et culture Series. Paris: Dunod, 2000.

Anderson, Chris. *Métis: Race, Recognition, and the Struggle for Indigenous Peoplehood*. Vancouver: University of British Columbia Press, 2014.

Armstrong, Jeannette C. "Land Speaking." In *Speaking for the Generations: Native Writers on Writing*, edited by Simon Ortiz, 175–94. Tucson: University of Arizona Press, 1998.

———. "The Disempowerment of First North American Native Peoples and Empowerment Through Their Writing." In *An Anthology of Canadian Native Literature in English*, edited by Daniel David Moses, Terry Goldie, and Armand Garnet Ruffo, 256–59. 4th ed. New York/ Oxford: Oxford University Press, 2013.

Bainbridge, Catherine, and Albert Nerenberg. *Okanada: Behind the Lines at Oka*. Film. Produced by Ina Fichman. Montreal: Les Productions Maximage/Snap TV, 1991. VHS, 33 mins.

Bainbridge, Catherine, Neil Diamond, and Jeremiah Hayes. *Reel Injun*. Film. Montreal: National Film Board of Canada, 2009. 88 mins 21s.

Bakhtin, Mikhail. *La poétique de Dostoïevski.* Points, Essais Series. Paris: Éditions du Seuil, 1998.

———. *Problems of Dostoevsky's Poetics.* Edited and translated by Caryl Emerson. Introduction by Wayne C. Booth. Vol. 8, *Theory and History of Literature.* Minneapolis / London: University of Minnesota Press, 1999.

Bannerji, Kaushalya. "Oka Nada." In *A New Remembrance,* 20. Toronto: TSAR Publications, 1993.

Barcelo, François. *Les aventures de Benjamin Tardif, II.* Anjou: Editions Fides, 2013.

Barthes, Roland. *L'obvie et l'obtus.* Vol. 3, *Essais critiques.* Tel quel Series. Paris: Éditions du Seuil, 1992.

Baskin, Todd. "In the Spirit of." In *Steal My Rage: New Native Voices,* edited by Joel T. Maki, 14. Vancouver / Toronto: Douglas and McIntyre, 1995.

Beauvais, Johnny. *Kahnawake. A Mohawk Look at Canada and Adventures of Big John Canadian, 1840–1919.* Kahnawà:ke: Self-published, 1985.

Blue Cloud, Peter. "Resistance at Oka." In *Native American Testimony: A Chronicle of Indian-White Relations from Prophecy to the Present, 1492–1992,* edited by Peter Nabokov, 432–35. New York: Viking Penguin, 1991.

Boisvert, Yves. *Voleurs de cause.* Trois-Rivières: Écrits des Forges, 1992.

Boisvert, Yves, and Guy Sioui Durand. "Rêves, rituels, rapides, réserve, révolte, réveil, réjouissance." In *Aimititau! Parlons-nous!,* edited by Laure Morali, 211–41. Chronique Series. Montreal: Mémoire d'encrier, 2008.

Bonaparte, Warren. *The Wampum Chronicles.* Online. Accessed 15 March 2017. wampumchronicles.com.

Bonspille-Boileau, Sonia. *Qui suis-je?* Film. Montreal: Les Productions Via Le Monde, 2006. 10 mins.

———. *The Oka Legacy.* Film. CBC Firsthand. Developed and produced by Rezolution Pictures' Catherine Bainbridge, Christina Fon, Linda Ludwick, and Lisa Roth. Thursday June 2 2016, 44 mins. http://www.cbc.ca/firsthand/episodes/the-oka-legacy (accessed 15 August 2017).

Bonspille-Boileau, Sonia, and Alanis Obomsawin. "Documentary Film from Archiving to Storytelling: The Camera as a Witness of History." Roundtable moderated by Kenneth Deer. International conference Revisioning the Americas through Indigenous Cinema. Montreal and Kahnawà:ke, 17–19 June 2010.

Bouthillette, Benoît. *La trace de l'escargot.* Couche-tard Series. Chicoutimi: Éditions JCL, 2005.

Brisson, Réal. *Oka par la caricature: deux visions distinctes d'une même crise.* Quebec: Septentrion, 2000.

Butler, Judith. *Excitable Speech: A Politics of the Performative.* New York / London: Routledge, 1997.

———. *Le pouvoir des mots. Politique du performatif.* Translated by Charlotte Nordmann. Paris: Éditions Amsterdam, 2004.

Canada, House of Commons. *The Summer of 1990: Fifth Report of the Standing Committee on Aboriginal Affairs.* Ottawa: House of Commons, 1991.

Canada, Royal Commission on Aboriginal Peoples. *People to People, Nation to Nation. Highlights from the Report of the Royal Commission on Aboriginal Peoples.* Minister of Supply and Services Canada: 1996. http://www.aadnc-aandc.gc.ca/eng/1100100014597/1100100014637 (accessed 25 September 2013).

Cardinal, Gil. *Indian Summer: The Oka Crisis.* 16mm film. Montreal: Ciné Télé Action, 2006. 2 x 90 mins.

Cariou, Warren. "Indigenous Literature and Other Verbal Arts, Canada (1960–2012)." In *The Oxford Handbook of Indigenous American Literature,* edited by James H. Cox and Daniel Heath Justice, 577–88.

New York / Oxford: Oxford University Press, 2014.

Cariou, Warren, and Isabelle St-Amand, eds. "Introduction. Environmental Ethics through Changing Landscapes: Indigenous Activism and Literary Arts." *Canadian Review of Comparative Literature* 44, no. 1 (2017): 7–24.

Chamberlin, J. Edward. *If This Is Your Land, Where Are Your Stories? Finding Common Ground*, 2nd edition. Toronto: Vintage Canada, 2004.

Chanady, Amaryll. *Entre inclusion et exclusion. La symbolisation de l'autre dans les Amériques*. Bibliothèque de littérature générale et comparée Series. Paris: Honoré Champion, 1999.

Ciaccia, John. "Lettre du ministre John Ciaccia au maire d'Oka, M. Jean Ouellette, et à son conseil municipal, lundi le 9 July 1990." In "Les Mohawks," special issue, *Recherches amérindiennes au Québec* 21, nos. 1–2 (1991): 98.

———. *The Oka Crisis: A Mirror of the Soul*. Dorval: Maren Publications, 2000[a].

———. *La crise d'Oka: miroir de notre âme*. French-language translation by Suzanne Roch. Présent Series. Montreal: Leméac, 2000[b].

Clifton, James A., ed. *The Invented Indian: Cultural Fictions and Government Policies*. New Brunswick, NJ: Transaction Publishers, 1990.

Collier, Simone. "War with the Army." *Ryerson Review of Journalism* (Summer 1991). http://www.rrj.ca/m3844/ (accessed 6 October 2013).

Conradi, Alexa. "Uprising at Oka: A Place of Non-identification." In "Race, Ethnicity, and Intercultural Communication," special issue, *Canadian Journal of Communication* 34, no. 4 (2009): 547–66.

Cook, Kakwiranó:ron, and Karonhienhawe Dolormier. *Kahnawake Revisited: The Saint Lawrence Seaway I & II*. Video, DVD. Los Angeles: Millennium Productions/Kakari:io Pictures, 2009. 2 x 30 mins.

Cornellier, Bruno. "La 'chose indienne': cinéma et politiques de la représentation autochtone dans la colonie de peuplement libérale." PhD thesis, Concordia University, 2011.

———. *La "chose indienne." Cinéma et politiques de la représentation autochtone au Québec et au Canada*. Montréal: Nota Bene, 2015.

Coulthard, Glen Sean. *Red Skin, White Masks: Rejecting the Colonial Politics of Recognition*. Minneapolis: University of Minnesota Press, 2014.

Cox, James H., and Daniel Heath Justice. "Introduction. Post-Renaissance Indigenous American Literary Studies." In *The Oxford Handbook of Indigenous American Literature*, edited by James H. Cox and Daniel Heath Justice, 1–11. New York / Oxford: Oxford University Press, 2014.

Cree, Myra. "Miroir, miroir, dis-moi." *Relations* 566 (1990): 304.

———. "Mon pays rêvé ou la PAX KANATA." *Terres en vues* III, no. 4 (1995): 23.

Cuthand, Beth. "Post-Oka Kinda Woman." In *An Anthology of Canadian Native Literature in English*, edited by Daniel David Moses, Terry Goldie, and Armand Garnet Ruffo, 272–73. 4th ed. Don Mills: Oxford University Press, 2013.

Cyr, Claudine. "Cartographie événementielle de l'Amérique lors de son 500e anniversaire." PhD thesis, Université de Montréal, 2008.

———. "Les défilés du *Columbus Day* ou la négociation des identités culturelles dans l'espace public américain." In *Les figures du siège au Québec. Concertation et conflits en contexte minoritaire*, edited by Simon Harel and Isabelle St-Amand, 105–30. InterCultures Series. Quebec: Presses de l'Université Laval, 2011.

Cyr, Claudine, and Isabelle St-Amand. "Regards autochtones sur les Amériques / Revisioning the Americas through Indigenous Cinema / Visiones indígenas sobre las Américas." International conference program. Montreal, INRS, and Kahnawà:ke, 2010.

Damm, Kateri. "what is it like to be inside kane-satake t.c." In *Entering the War Zone: A Mohawk Perspective on Resisting Invasions*, edited by Donna K. Goodleaf, 127. Penticton: Theytus Books, 1995.

David, Dan. "Razorwire Dreams." In *Voices: Being Native in Canada*, edited by Linda Jaine and Drew Hayden Taylor, 20–31. Saskatoon: University of Saskatchewan, Extension Division, 1992.

David, Joe. "How to Become an Activist in One Easy Lesson." In "Canadas," special issue, *Semiotext(e)* 17 (1994): 36–38.

de Certeau, Michel. *The Practice of Everyday Life*. Translated by Steven Rendall. Berkeley and Los Angeles: University of California Press, 1988.

———. *Arts de faire*. Vol. 1, *L'invention du quotidien*. New edition produced and presented by Luce Giard. Folio essais Series. Paris: Gallimard, 1990.

Deer, Brian, and Kanatakta. "Pour mieux comprendre la crise d'Oka. Éveil du nationalisme et relations entre Kahnawake et les communautés voisines." Interview conducted by Pierre Trudel and Micheline Chartrand. In "Les Mohawks," special issue, *Recherches amérindiennes au Québec* 21, nos. 1–2 (1991): 118–25.

Deer, Tracey. *Club Native*. Film. Montreal: Rezolution Pictures and National Film Board of Canada, 2008. 48, 52, and 75 mins.

Delâge, Denis. "Autochtones, Canadiens, Québécois." In *Les espaces de l'identité*, edited by Laurier Turgeon, Jocelyn Létourneau, and Khadiyatoulah, 299–301. Sainte-Foy: Presses de l'Université Laval, 1997.

Dennis, Darrell. *Tales of an Urban Indian*. In *Two Plays: Tales of an Urban Indian. The Trickster of Third Avenue East*, 1–56. Toronto: Playwrights Canada Press, 2005.

———. *Contes d'un Indien urbain*. Translated by Olivier Choinière. Montreal: Compagnie Ondinnok/Centre des auteurs dramatiques, 2006.

Desbiens, Caroline. "Du wampum aux barricades: géographies du siège et espaces de réconciliation au Québec." In *Les figures du siège au Québec: Concertation et conflits en contexte minoritaire*, edited by Simon Harel and Isabelle St-Amand, 65–87. InterCultures Series. Quebec: Presses de l'Université Laval, 2011.

Dickason, Olive Patricia. "Precursors to the Summer of 1990." Unpublished manuscript. University of Alberta, n.d.

Dickner, Nicolas. *Nikolski*. Quebec: Alto, 2005.

———. *Nikolski*. Translated from the French by Lazer Lederhendler. London: Portobello Books, 2010.

Dudemaine, André, Rachel-Alouki Labbé, and Alanis Obomsawin. "Table ronde sur le cinéma autochtone au Québec." Paroles et pratiques artistiques autochtones au Québec aujourd'hui [Indigenous speech and artistic practices in Quebec today]. Montreal, Université du Québec à Montréal, 20–22 November 2008.

Dulong, Renaud. *Le témoin oculaire: les conditions sociales de l'attestation personnelle*. Paris: Éditions de l'École des hautes études en sciences sociales, 1998.

———. "Qu'est-ce qu'un témoin historique?" *Vox Poetica*. 20 January 2009. http://www. vox-poetica.org/t/dulong.html (accessed 18 January 2010).

Dunn, Willie. *The Ballad of Crowfoot*. Film. Montreal: National Film Board of Canada, 1968. 10 mins 18 secs.

Duran, Eduardo, and Bonnie Duran. *Native American Postcolonial Psychology*. New York: State University of New York Press, 1995.

Eigenbrod, Renate. *Travelling Knowledges: Positioning the Im/Migrant Reader of Aboriginal Literatures in Canada*. Winnipeg: University of Manitoba Press, 2005.

———. "A Necessary Inclusion: Native Literature in Native Studies." *Studies in American Indian Literatures (SAIL)* 22, no. 1 (2010): 1–19.

"Émission de radio—animateur Simon Bédard—crise d'Oka [Radio show—host Simon Bédard —Oka Crisis]." Accessed at Services documentaires du Conseil de la Nation Atikamekw. Class: Audiovisual documents; series: Documentation audio-visuelle, Box AV-18 File 13, n.d.

Episkenew, Jo-Ann. *Taking Back Our Spirits: Indigenous Literature, Public Policy, and Healing.* Winnipeg: University of Manitoba Press, 2009.

Fachinger, Petra. "Intersections of Diaspora and Indigeneity: The Standoff at Kahnesatake in Lee Maracle's *Sundogs* and Tessa McWatt's *Out of My Skin.*" *Canadian Literature*, 220 (Spring 2014): 74–91. http://go.galegroup.com.proxy.queensu.ca/ps/retrieve.do?tabID=T001&resultListType=RESULT_LIST&searchResultsType=SingleTab&searchType=AdvancedSearchForm&currentPosition=3&docId=GALE%7CA392177761&docType=Critical+essay&sort=RELEVANCE&contentSegment=&prodId=LitRC&contentSet=GALE%7CA392177761&searchId=R1&userGroupName=queensulaw&inPS=true (accessed 5 November 2017).

Fagan, Kristina Rose. "Laughing to Survive: Humour in Contemporary Canadian Native Literature." PhD thesis, University of Toronto, 2001.

———. "Tewatatha:wi. Aboriginal Nationalism in Taiaiake Alfred's *Peace, Power, Righteousness: An Indigenous Manifesto.*" In "Empowerment Through Literature," special issue, *American Indian Quarterly* 28, nos. 1–2 (2004): 12–29.

Farrow, John. *Ice Lake.* Toronto: HarperCollins, 2001.

Fédératon international des droits de l'Homme. *Crise d'Oka: mission d'enquête et d'observation sur les événements survenus à Kanesatake, Oka et Kahnawake (Québec, Canada), été 1990.* Paris: La Fédération, 1990.

Felman, Shoshana. "À l'âge du témoignage: *Shoah* de Claude Lanzmann." In *Au sujet de Shoah, le film de Claude Lanzmann,*

Bernard Cuau et al., 55–133. Paris: Belin, 1990.

Fenton, William Nelson. *The Great Law and the Longhouse: A Political History of the Iroquois Confederacy.* The Civilization of the American Indian Series. Norman: University of Oklahoma Press, 1998.

Féral, Josette. *Théorie et pratique du théâtre: Au-delà des limites.* Champ théâtral Series. Montpellier: L'Entretemps, 2011.

Ferro, Marc. *Cinéma et histoire.* Rev. ed. Folio Histoire Series. Paris: Gallimard, 1993.

First Nations Centre. *OCAP: Ownership, Control, Access and Possession.* Sanctioned by the First Nations Information Governance Committee, Assembly of First Nations. Ottawa: National Aboriginal Health Organization, 2007.

Flahault, François. *La méchanceté.* Paris: Descartes et Cie, 1998.

Fogelson, Raymond D. "The Ethnology of Events and Nonevents." *Ethnohistory* 36, no. 2 (1989): 133–47.

Foster, Tol. "Of One Blood: An Argument for Relations and Regionality in Native American Literary Studies." In *Reasoning Together: The Native Critics Collective,* edited by Craig S. Womack, Daniel Heath Justice, and Christopher B. Teuton, 265–302. Norman: University of Oklahoma Press, 2008.

Fontaine, Urgel, copy and interpretation. "Documents relatifs aux Droits du Séminaire et aux Prétentions des Indiens sur la Seigneurie des Deux Montagnes (1781 et 1788)." In "Les Mohawks," special issue, *Recherches amérindiennes au Québec* 21, nos. 1–2 (1991): 93–94.

Foucault, Michel. "Des espaces autres." In *Dits et écrits 1954–1988.* Vol. 4, *1980–1988,* edited by Daniel Defert and François Ewald in collaboration with Jacques Lagrange, 754–56. Bibliothèque des sciences humaines Series. Paris: Gallimard, 1994.

———. "Of Other Spaces: Utopias and Heterotopias." In Vol. 1, *Rethinking Architecture: A Reader in Cultural Theory,* edited by Neil

Leach, 330–36. New York: Routledge, 1997.

——. *The Essential Foucault: Selections from Essential Works of Foucault, 1954–1984,* edited by Paul Rabinow and Nikolas Rose. New York: New Press, 2003.

Francis, Daniel. *The Imaginary Indian: The Image of the Indian in Canadian Culture.* Vancouver: Arsenal Pulp Press, 1992.

Gabriel, Ellen. "Epilogue. Fraudulent Theft of Mohawk Land by the Municipality of Oka." In *This Is an Honour Song: Twenty Years Since the Blockades,* edited by Leanne Simpson and Kiera L. Ladner, 345–47. Winnipeg: Arbeiter Ring Publishing, 2010.

Gabriel-Doxtater, Brenda Katlatont, and Arlette Kawanatatie Van den Hende. *At the Woods' Edge: An Anthology of the History of the People of Kanehsatà:ke.* Principal research by Louise Johnson. Kanehsatà:ke: Kanehsatà:ke Education Center, 1995.

——. *À l'orée des bois. Une anthologie de l'histoire du peuple de Kanehsatà:ke.* Principal research by Louise Johnson. French-language translation by Francine Lemay. Kanehsatà:ke: Centre culturel et de langue Tsi Ronterihwanónhnha ne Kanien'kéha, 2010.

Gagnon, Réginald. *Fait d'armes à Oka.* Ottawa: Arion, 1994.

Garneau, Michèle. "Les deux mémoires de Pierre Perrault." *Protée* 32, no. 1, Spring (2004): 23–30.

Gatti Maurizio, ed. anthology. *Littérature amérindienne du Québec: Écrits de langue française.* Preface by Robert Lalonde. Cahiers du Québec / Littérature Series. Montreal: Hurtubise HMH, 2004.

George-Kanentiio, Douglas M. *Iroquois on Fire: A Voice from the Mohawk Nation.* Lincoln: University of Nebraska Press, 2008.

Goeman, Mishuana. *Mark My Words: Native Women Mapping Our Nations.* Minneapolis: University of Minnesota Press, 2013.

Goodleaf, Donna K. "I Know Who I Am." In *Entering the War Zone: A Mohawk Perspective on Resisting Invasions,* 26. Penticton: Theytus Books, 1995[a].

——. "Istah." In *Entering the War Zone: A Mohawk Perspective on Resisting Invasions,* 94. Penticton: Theytus Books, 1995[b].

——. "My Ribbon Shirt." In *Entering the War Zone: A Mohawk Perspective on Resisting Invasions,* x–xi. Penticton: Theytus Books, 1995[c].

——. "Remember This!" *Entering the War Zone: A Mohawk Perspective on Resisting Invasions,* 98. Penticton: Theytus Books, 1995[d].

——. *Entering the War Zone: A Mohawk Perspective on Resisting Invasions.* Penticton: Theytus Books, 1995[e].

Grégoire, Pierre. "Notion d'événement et plans de références: l'individu, les systèmes d'information et l'histoire-mémoire." In *Événement, identité et histoire,* edited by Claire Dolan, 167–86. Quebec: Septentrion, 1991.

Gronau, Anna, and Shelley Niro. *It Starts with a Whisper.* Film. Canada. Bay of Quinte Production. 27 min 30. 1993.

Habermas, Jürgen. *The Structural Transformation of the Public Sphere: An Inquiry into a Category of Bourgeois Society,* First MIT Press Paperback Edition. Cambridge, Mass.: MIT Press, 1991.

Hamelin, Louis. *Les étranges et édifiantes aventures d'un oniromane.* Quebec: L'instant même, 1994.

——. *La Constellation du lynx.* Montreal: Boréal, 2010.

——. *October 1970.* Translated by Wayne Grady. Toronto: Arachnide, 2013.

——. *Fabrications: Essai sur la fiction et l'histoire.* Montreal: Les Presses de l'Université de Montréal, 2014.

Handfield, Janie. "Les territoires imaginaires dans le triptyque *Cultures périphériques* d'Yves Boisvert." MA thesis, Université du Québec à Montreal, 2009.

Harel, Simon, and Isabelle St-Amand. "Identités multiples, identités assiégées : un point de vue critique sur la contingence." In *Les figures du siège au Québec. Concertation et conflits en contexte minoritaire*, 1–10. InterCultures Series. Quebec: Presses de l'Université Laval, 2011.

Hébert, Véronique. "Oka." *Inter: art actuel*, 122 (2016): 62–63.

Heath Justice, Daniel. "Seeing (and Reading) Red: Indian Outlaws in the Ivory Tower." In *Indigenizing the Academy: Transforming Scholarship and Empowering Communities*, edited by Devon Abbott Mihesuah and Angela Cavender Wilson, 100–23. Lincoln: University of Nebraska Press, 2004.

———. *Our Fire Survives the Storm: A Cherokee Literary History*. Minneapolis: University of Minnesota Press, 2005.

Higgins, Olivier, and Mélanie Carrier. *Québékoisie*. Film. Quebec: Mö Films, 2013. 80 mins 56 secs.

Hill, Gord. *The 500 Years of Resistance Comic Book*. Introduction by Ward Churchill. Vancouver: Arsenal Pulp Press, 2010.

Hinton, Alexander Laban, Andrew Woolford, and Jeff Benvenuto, eds. *Colonial Genocide in Indigenous North America*. Durham: Duke University Press, 2014.

Hobb, Sandra. "L'Autochtone dans *Le dernier été des Indiens* de Robert Lalonde: ou comment passer de la grande à la petite noirceur." *International Journal of Canadian Studies / Revue internationale d'études canadiennes* 41 (2010): 231–52.

Horn, Kaniehtiio, Rachel-Alouki Labbé, and Albert Nerenberg. "The 1990 Oka Crisis, Its Films and Its Aftermath: The Role of the Camera in Political Conflicts." Roundtable moderated by Joe Deom. International conference Revisioning the Americas through Indigenous Cinema, Montreal / Kahnawà:ke, 17–19 June 2010.

Horn-Miller, Kahente. "The Emergence of the Mohawk Warrior Flag: A Symbol of Indigenous Unification and Impetus to Assertion of Identity and Rights Commencing in the Kanienkehaka Community

of Kahnawake." MA thesis, Concordia University, 2003.

Houba, Pascal. "La parole errante des corps: pratiques de cinéma mineur." *Multitudes*, January 2003. https://www.cairn.info/ revue-multitudes-2003-1-page-135.htm (accessed 15 November 2017).

Idle No More. "The Story." http://www.idlenomore.ca/story (accessed 10 April 2017).

———. "The Vision." http://www.idlenomore.ca/vision (accessed 20 April 2017).

Jenish, D'Arcy. *The St. Lawrence Seaway, Fifty Years and Counting*. Manotick, ON: Penumbra Press, 2009.

Iskra. "Oka." *Bring The War Home* split w/ *Against Empire*. Album. CD. Rodend Popsicle Records. 2007.

Johansen, Bruce E. *Life and Death in Mohawk Country*. Golden, CO: North American Press, 1993.

Johnston, Basil H. "One Generation from Extinction." In *An Anthology of Canadian Native Literature in English*, edited by Daniel David Moses, Terry Goldie, and Armand Garnet Ruffo, 106–11. 4th ed. Don Mills: Oxford University Press, 2013.

Jones, Mary Jane. "Research Report on the History of Disputes at Oka/Kanehsatake." Report submitted to Indian and Northern Affairs Canada, 17 September 1990.

Kalant, Amelia. *National Identity and the Conflict at Oka: Native Belonging and Myths of Postcolonial Nationhood in Canada*. New York: Routledge, 2004.

Kanapé Fontaine, Natasha. "L'âme." Musique nomade. Wapikoni mobile. https:// soundcloud.com/musiquenomade/ natasha-kanape-fontaine-lame (accessed 12 November 2017).

———. *Assi Manifesto*. Translated from French by Howard Scott. Toronto: Mawenzi House Publishers, 2016.

———. "Kanehsatake/Oka: vingt ans après." Special issue, *Recherches amérindiennes au Québec* 39, nos. 1–2 (2009).

Kanienkehaka. "Statement of position and proposed agreement in principle, presented by the Kanienkehaka, August 22 1990." Archives, Kanehsatà:ke Language and Cultural Centre.

Karihwatàtie. 2nd ed. Kanehsatà:ke: Tsi Niionkwarihò:ten Cultural Center, Spring-Summer, 2003.

Keating, Neal B. *Iroquois Art, Power, and History*. Norman: University of Oklahoma Press, 2012.

Keeshig-Tobias, Lenore. "After Oka—How Has Canada Changed?" In *An Anthology of Canadian Native Literature in English*, edited by Daniel David Moses and Terry Goldie, 257–58. 3rd ed. Toronto: Oxford University Press, 2005[a].

———. "From Trickster Beyond 1992: Our Relationship." In *An Anthology of Canadian Native Literature in English*, edited by Daniel David Moses and Terry Goldie, 259–71. 3rd ed. Toronto: Oxford University Press, 2005[b].

Kinew, Wab. "Cowboys and Indians." In *This Is an Honour Song: Twenty Years Since the Blockades,* edited by Leanne Simpson and Kiera L. Ladner, 47–51. Winnipeg: Arbeiter Ring Publishing, 2010.

King, Thomas. *The Inconvenient Indian: A Curious Account of Native People in North America*. Toronto: Anchor Canada, 2013.

Kino-nda-niimi Collective, eds. *The Winter We Danced: Voices from the Past, the Future, and the Idle No More Movement*. Winnipeg: Arbeiter Ring Publishing, 2014.

Krupat, Arnold. *Red Matters: Native American Studies*. Philadelphia: University of Pennsylvania Press, 2002.

Kuokkanen, Rauna. *Reshaping the University: Responsibility, Indigenous Epistemes, and the Logic of the Gift*. Vancouver / Toronto: University of British Columbia Press, 2007.

Lackenbauer, P. Whitney. "Carrying the Burden of Peace: The Mohawks, the Canadian Forces, and the Oka Crisis." *Journal of Military and Strategic Studies* 10, no. 2 (2008): 1–71.

Lacombe, Michèle. "Embodying the Glocal: Immigrant and Indigenous Ideas of Home in Tessa McWatt's Montreal." In *Literature and the Glocal City: Reshaping the English Canadian Imaginary, e*dited by Ana María Fraile-Marcos, 39–54. New York: Routledge; Taylor & Francis, 2014.

Ladner, Kiera L., and Leanne Simpson. "This Is an Honour Song." In *This Is an Honour Song: Twenty Years Since the Blockades*, edited by Leanne Simpson and Kiera L. Ladner, 345–47. Winnipeg: Arbeiter Ring Publishing, 2010.

LaForme, Harry S. "Indians Have a Right to Be Happy Too." In *Voices: Being Native in Canada*, edited by Linda Jaine and Drew Hayden Taylor, 90–99. Saskatoon: University of Saskatchewan, Extension Division, 1992.

Lainey, Jonathan C. *La "monnaie des sauvages": les colliers de wampum d'hier à aujourd'hui*. Quebec: Septentrion, 2004.

———. "Les colliers de wampum comme support mémoriel: le cas du Two-Dog Wampum." In *Les Autochtones et le Québec: Des premiers contacts au Plan Nord*, edited by Alain Beaulieu, Stéphan Gervais, and Martin Papillon, 93–111. Montreal: Les Presses de l'Université de Montreal, 2013.

Lalonde, Robert. *Le dernier été des Indiens*. Paris: Éditions du Seuil, 1982.

———. *Sept lacs plus au nord*. Paris: Éditions du Seuil, 1993.

Lamy, Jonathan. "Oka/Kanehstake: 25 ans plus tard." In "Affirmation autochtone," edited by Jonathan Lamy, special issue, *Inter: art actuel*, 122 (2016): 61.

Lamy-Beaupré, Jonathan. "Je est un autochtone: L'ensauvagement dans les poèmes de Paul-Marie Lapointe, Patrick Straram and Denis Vanier." MA thesis, Université du Québec à Montreal, 2006.

LaRocque, Emma. *When the Other Is Me: Native Resistance Discourse 1850–1990*. Winnipeg: University of Manitoba Press, 2010.

Le Breton, David. *Passions du risque*. Traversées Series. Paris: A.M. Métailié, 1991.

Leclerc, Catherine, and Sherry Simon. "Zones de contact. Nouveaux regards sur la littérature anglo-québécoise." *Voix et Images* 30, no. 3 (2005): 15–29.

Legacy of Hope. Website. http://staging.legacyofhope.ca/wp-content/uploads/2016/03/Hope-Healing-2014_web.pdf (accessed 20 August 2017).

Lemay, Francine. "20 ans après la crise d'Oka. Mon voyage vers la reconciliation." *En Contact*, July 2010: 8–11.

Lepage, Pierre. "La genèse d'un conflit à Oka-Kanesatake." In "Les Mohawks," special issue, *Recherches amérindiennes au Québec* 21, nos. 1–2 (1991): 99–110.

———. *Mythes et réalités sur les peuples autochtones*. Montreal: Commission des droits de la personne and des droits de la jeunesse, 2009.

"Les Mohawks." Special issue, *Recherches amérindiennes au Québec* 21, nos. 1–2 (1991).

Leuthold, Steven. *Indigenous Aesthetics: Native Art, Media, and Identity*. Austin: University of Texas Press, 1998.

Lewis, Randolph. *Alanis Obomsawin: The Vision of a Native Filmmaker*. Lincoln: University of Nebraska Press, 2006.

Lyons, Scott Richard. "Rhetorical Sovereignty: What Do American Indians Want from Writing?" *College Composition and Communication* LI, no. 3 (2000): 447–68.

MacLaine, Craig, and Michael S. Baxendale. *This Land Is Our Land: The Mohawk Revolt at Oka*. Montreal: Optimum Publishing International, 1991.

MacLeod, Alec G. *Acts of Defiance*. Produced by Mark Zannis. Film/DVD. Toronto: National Film Board of Canada, 1992, 104 mins 34 secs.

Maracle, Lee. *Sundogs*. Penticton: Theytus Books, 1992.

———. *Daughters Are Forever*. Vancouver: Raincoast Books, 2002.

———. *Memory Serves: Oratories*. Edmonton: NeWest Press, 2015.

McKegney, Sam. "'pain, pleasure, shame. Shame': Masculine Embodiment, Kinship, and Indigenous Reterritorialization." *Canadian Literature* 216 (Spring 2013): 12–33. http://gateway.proquest.com.proxy.queensu.ca/openurl?ctx_ver=Z39.88-2003&xri:pqil:res_ver=0.2&res_id=xri:lion&rft_id=xri:lion:ft:m-la:R04914678:0&rft.accountid=6180 (accessed 15 November 2017).

McKenzie, Stephanie. *Before the Country: Native Renaissance, Canadian Mythology*. Toronto: University of Toronto Press, 2007.

McLeod, Neal. "Coming Home Through Stories." In *(Ad)dressing Our Words: Aboriginal Perspectives on Aboriginal Literatures*, edited by Armand Garnet Ruffo, 17–32. Penticton: Theytus Books, 2001.

McWatt, Tessa. *Out of My Skin*. Toronto: Riverbank Press, 1998.

Memmi, Albert. *Portrait du colonisé*. Preceded by *Portrait du colonisateur*. Preface by Jean-Paul Sartre, followed by *Les Canadiens français sont-ils des colonisés?* New edition revised and corrected by the author. Montreal: L'Étincelle, 1972.

Methot, Suzanne. "A Quality of Light. Review." *Quill & Quire*. http://www.quillandquire.com/review/a-quality-of-light/ (accessed 20 April 2017).

———. "Canada 22/150: Waneek Horn-Miller." Canadian Race Relations Foundation / Fondation canadienne des relations raciales. http://www.crrf-fcrr.ca/en/our-canada/150-stories/search-150-stories/item/25628-canada-22-150-waneek-horn-miller (accessed 10 November 2017).

Michaud, Carmen. "De l'exotisme au reel." In "Les Mohawks," special issue, *Recherches amérindiennes au Québec* 21, nos. 1–2 (1992): 111–17.

Mihesuah, Devon Abbott, and Angela Cavender Wilson. *Indigenizing the Academy: Transforming Scholarship and Empowering Communities*. Lincoln: University of Nebraska Press, 2004.

Miller, James R. *Skyscrapers Hide the Heavens. A History of Indian-White Relations in Canada.* 3rd ed. Toronto / Buffalo: University of Toronto Press, 2000.

Milloy, John S. *A National Crime: The Canadian Government and the Residential School System.* Winnipeg: University of Manitoba Press, 1999.

Montpetit, Caroline. "Zoom sur le Printemps autochtone d'art 3." *Le Devoir,* 30 March 2017. http://www.ledevoir.com/culture/actualites-culturelles/495132/zoom-sur-le-printemps-autochtone (accessed 20 April 2017).

Monture, Rick. *We Share Our Matters: Two Centuries of Writing and Resistance at Six Nations of the Grand River.* Winnipeg: University of Manitoba Press, 2015.

Morin, Robert. *Windigo.* Produced by Nicole Robert, written by Robert Morin. Film. Folsom, CA: Lux Films, 1994, VHS, 97 mins.

Morrison, Val. "Mediating Identity: Kashtin, the Media, and the Oka Crisis." In *Re-Situating Identities: The Politics of Race, Ethnicity, and Culture,* edited by Vered Amit-Talai and Caroline Knowles, 115–36. New York: Broadview Press, 1996.

Mouawad, Wajdi. *Anima.* Montreal / Paris: Leméac / Actes Sud, 2012.

Muller, Kathryn V. "Holding Hands With Wampum: Haudenosaunee Council Fires from the Great Law of Peace to Contemporary Relationships with the Canadian State." PhD thesis, Queen's University, 2008.

Mumford, Kevin. *Interzones. Black/White Sex Districts in Chicago and New York in the Early Twentieth Century.* New York, NY: Columbia University Press, 1997.

Nabokov, Peter, ed. *Native American Testimony: A Chronicle of Indian-White Relations from Prophecy to the Present, 1492–1992.* New York: Viking, 1991.

Nepinak, Douglas Raymond. "The Crisis in Oka, Manitoba." In *This Is an Honour Song. Twenty Years Since the Blockades,* edited by Leanne Simpson and Kiera L. Ladner, 125–63. Winnipeg: Arbeiter Ring Publishing, 2010.

Nettelbeck, Amanda, Russell Smandych, Louis A. Knafla, and Robert Foster, eds. *Fragile Settlements: Aboriginal Peoples, Law, and Resistance in South-West Australia and Prairie Canada.* Vancouver: University of British Columbia Press, 2016.

Nettelbeck, Amanda, Russell Smandych, Louis A. Knafla, and Robert Foster. "Introduction: Settler Colonialism and its Legacies." In *Fragile Settlements: Aboriginal Peoples, Law, and Resistance in South-West Australia and Prairie Canada,* edited by Nettelbeck et al., 3–18. Vancouver: University of British Columbia Press, 2016.

Newhouse, David. "Oka: A Political Crisis and its Legacy By HARRY SWAIN." *Canadian Public Administration* 54, no. 3 (2011): 461–63.

Niney, François. *L'épreuve du réel à l'écran. Essai sur le principe de réalité documentaire.* 2nd ed. Arts et cinéma Series. Brussels: De Boeck, 2002.

Noël, Francine. *Nous avons tous découvert l'Amérique.* Montreal / Arles: Leméac / Actes Sud, 1992.

Nora, Pierre. "Le retour de l'événement." In *Faire de l'histoire,* edited by Jacques Le Goff and Pierre Nora, 285–308. Bibliothèque des histoires Series. Paris: Gallimard, 1974.

Obomsawin, Alanis. *Incident at Restigouche.* Film. Montreal: National Film Board of Canada, 1984. 45 mins 57 secs.

———. *Kanehsatake: 270 Years of Resistance / Kanehsatake: 270 ans de résistance.* Film DVD. Montreal: National Film Board of Canada, 1993. DVD, 119 mins 25 secs.

———. *My Name Is Kahentiiosta / Je m'appelle Kahentiiosta.* Film. Montreal: National Film Board of Canada, 1995. DVD, 29 mins 50 secs.

———. *Spudwrench: Kahnawake Man / Spudwrench: l'homme de Kahnawake.* Film. Montreal: National Film Board of Canada, 1997. DVD, 57 mins 40 secs.

——. *Rocks at Whiskey Trench / Pluie de pierres à Whiskey Trench*. Film. Montreal: National Film Board of Canada, 2000. DVD, 105 mins 6 secs.

——. *Waban-Aki: peuple du soleil levant*. Film. Montreal: National Film Board of Canada, 2006. 104 mins 2 secs.

——. *The People of the Kattawapiskat*. Film. Montreal: National Film Board of Canada, 2012. 50 min.

——. *Trick or Treaty?* Film. Montreal: National Film Board of Canada, 2014. 1h 24 min.

——. *Our People Will Be Healed*. Film. Montreal: National Film Board of Canada, 2017. 97 min.

Office national du film du Canada. "Alanis Obomsawin." *Library and Archives Canada,* n. d. http://www.collectionscanada.gc.ca/femmes/002026-709-f.html (accessed 2 November 2008).

——. "Alanis Obomsawin." *Artisans de l'ONF,* n.d. http://www.onf-nfb.gc.ca/fra/portraits/alanis_obomsawin/ (acessed 19 July 2012).

O'Meara, Edee. "Let's Not Negotiate!" In *Entering the War Zone: A Mohawk Perspective on Resisting Invasions,* edited by Donna K. Goodleaf, 115–16. Penticton: Theytus Books, 1995.

Paré, François. *Exiguity: Reflections on the Margins of Literature*. Translated by Lin Burman. Waterloo: Wilfrid Laurier University Press, 1997.

——. *Les littératures de l'exiguïté*. Preface by Robert Major. BCF Series. Ottawa: Le Nordir, 2001.

Parker, Arthur C. "Certain Iroquois Tree Myths and Symbols." *American Anthropologist* 14, no. 4 (1912): 608–20.

Pertusati, Linda. *In Defense of Mohawk Land: Ethnopolitical Conflict in Native North America*. Albany: State University of New York Press, 1997.

Picard-Sioui, Louis-Karl. "Hannibalo-God-Mozilla contre le grand vide cosmique." In *Amun,* edited by Michel Jean, 49–75. Montréal: Les Éditions internationales Stanké, 2016.

Phillips, Stephanie K. "The Kahnawake Mohawks and the St. Lawrence Seaway." MA thesis, McGill University, 2000.

Philpot, Robin. *Oka: Dernier alibi du Canada anglais*. With a preface written twenty years after the Oka Crisis. Montreal: Les Intouchables, 2010.

Plamondon, Éric. *Taqawan*. Montreal: Le Quartanier Éditeur, 2017.

Pratt, Mary Louise. *Imperial Eyes: Travel Writing and Transculturation*. 2nd edition. London / New York: Routledge, 2008.

Propagandhi. "Oka Everywhere." Music recording. Netherlands: Recess Records, 1994.

Québec, Commission des droits de la personne du Québec. *Audiences publiques sur les relations entre les corps policiers et les communautés autochtones vivant au Québec*. Commission resolution adopted at the 344th hearing, 24 May 1990, Resolution COM-344-5.1, 1990.

——. *Le choc collectif: rapport de la Commission des droits de la personne du Québec*. Prepared by Monique Rochon and Pierre Lepage under the supervision of Jacques Lachapelle. Quebec: La Commission, 1991.

Québec, Ministère du conseil exécutif, Secrétariat aux affaires autochtones du Québec. Online. http://www.versuntraite.gouv.qc.ca/documentation/jugements.htm (accessed 6 October 2013).

Québec, Ministère de la Sécurité publique, Bureau du coroner. *Rapport d'investigation du coroner concernant le massacre à l'École polytechnique de l'Université de Montréal*. Quebec: Bureau du coroner, 1990.

——. *Rapport d'enquête du coroner Guy Gilbert sur les causes et circonstances du décès de monsieur Lemay*. Quebec: Bureau du coroner, 1995.

Québec, Secrétariat aux affaires autochtones du Québec. http://www.versuntraite.gouv.qc.ca/documentation/jugements.htm (accessed 6 October 2013).

Raheja, Michelle. "Reading Nanook's Smile: Visual Sovereignty, Indigenous Revisions of Ethnography, and *Atanarjuat (The Fast*

Runner)." American Quarterly 59, no. 4 (2007): 1159–85.

———. *Reservation Reelism. Redfacing, Visual Sovereignty, and Representations of Native Americans in Film*. Lincoln: University of Nebraska Press, 2011.

Rancière, Jacques. *Le destin des images*. Paris: La Fabrique, 2003.

Redekop, Vernon W. Neufeld. "A Hermeneutic of Deep-Rooted Conflict: An Exploration of René Girard's Theory of Mimetic Desire of Scapegoating and Its Applicability to the Oka/Kanehsatà:ke Crisis of 1990." PhD thesis, Saint Paul University, 1998.

Regan, Paulette. *Unsettling the Settler Within: Indian Residential Schools, Truth Telling, and Reconciliation in Canada*. Vancouver: University of British Columbia Press, 2010.

Regroupement de solidarité avec les Autochtones. *Le procès des Mohawks: non coupable*. Edited by Marc Drouin and François Saillant. Montreal: Centre d'information et de documentation sur le Mozambique et l'Afrique australe, 1992.

Rhythm Activism (RA). *OKA*. Cassette. Montreal: Les Pages Noir, 1990.

———. *OKA II*. Cassette. Montreal: Les Pages Noir, 1992.

Richard, Caitlyn. Petition "Indigenous and Northern Affairs Canada: Halt to the Land Development on Disputed Kanien'kehá:ka Territory." Change.org. https://www.change.org/p/indigenous-and-northern-affairs-canada-halt-to-the-land-development-on-disputed-kanien-keh%C3%A1-ka-territory (accessed 17 November 2017).

Richards, Jolene. "Sovereignty: A Line in the Sand." *Aperture Magazine* 139 (Summer 1995): 50.

———. "Visualizing Sovereignty in the Time of Biometric Sensors." *The South Atlantic Quarterly* 110, no. 2 (Spring 2011): 465–86.

Robinson, Dylan. "Feeling Reconciliation, Remaining Settled." In *Theatres of Affect*, edited by Erin Hurley: 275–306. Toronto: Playwrights Canada Press, 2014.

Romano, Claude. *L'événement et le temps*. Épiméthée. Essais philosophiques Series. Paris: Presses universitaires de France, 1999.

———. *Event and Time*. New York: Fordham University Press, 2014.

Roth, Lorna, Beverly Nelson, and Kasennahawi Marie David. "Three Women, a Mouse, a Microphone, and a Telephone: Information (Mis)Management during the Mohawk/Canadian Governments' Conflict of 1990." In *Feminism, Multiculturalism, and the Media: Global Diversities*, edited by Angharad N. Valdivia, 48–81. Thousand Oaks, CA: Sage Publications, 1995.

Rowe, Daniel J. "Saying goodbye to a fluent speaker." *The Eastern Door (Kahnawake Mohawk Territory)*, 23 March 2017. http://www.easterndoor.com/2017/03/23/saying-goodbye-to-a-fluent-speaker/ (accessed 15 November 2017).

Rück, Daniel. "'Où tout le monde est propriétaire et où personne ne l'est': droits d'usage et gestion foncière à Kahnawake, 1815–1880" ['Where everyone and no one is an owner': Rights of use and land management in Kahnawake, 1815–1880]. Translated by Marie-Ève Lampron. *Revue d'histoire de l'Amérique française* 70, nos. 1–2 (Summer-Fall 2016): 31–52.

Rueck, Daniel. "When Bridges Become Barriers: Montreal and Kahnawake Mohawk Territory." In *Metropolitan Natures: Environmental Histories of Montreal*, edited by Stéphane Castonguay and Michèle Dagenais, 228–44. Pittsburgh: University of Pittsburgh Press, 2011.

Rukavina, Steve. "Tracey Deer, Creator of Mohawk Girls, Fears Eviction from Her Native Kahnawake Where Show Is Set." *CBC News Postcast Series Montreapolis*, 3 April 2017. http://www.cbc.ca/news/canada/montreal/tracey-deer-creator-of-mohawk-girls-fears-eviction-from-her-native-kahnawake-where-show-is-set-1.3991142 (accessed 21 April 2017).

Ruffo, Armand Garnet. "Inside Looking Out. Reading 'Tracks' from a Native Perspective." In *Looking at the Words of Our People: First Nations Analysis of Literature*, edited by Jeannette Armstrong, 161–76. Penticton: Theytus Books, 1993.

Ruggeri, Paola. "L'image de l'Indien chez Robert Lalonde: avant et après la crise d'Oka." *Francofonia* 39 (2000): 113–24.

Russell, Peter H. "From Oka to Ipperwash." In *This Is an Honour Song. Twenty Years Since the Blockades*, edited by Leanne Simpson and Kiera L. Ladner, 29–46. Winnipeg: Arbeiter Ring Publishing, 2010.

Salée, Daniel. "Enjeux et défis de l'affirmation identitaire et politique des peuples autochtones au Canada: autour de quelques ouvrages récents." *International Journal of Canadian Studies / Revue internationale d'études canadiennes* 26 (2002): 139–61.

———. "L'évolution des rapports politiques entre la société québécoise et les peuples autochtones depuis la crise d'Oka." In *Les Autochtones et le Québec. Des premiers contacts au Plan Nord*, edited by Alain Beaulieu, Stéphan Gervais, and Martin Papillon, 323–42. Montreal: Les Presses de l'Université de Montréal, 2013.

Samian. "Injustice." *Face à soi-même*. Music recording. Rouyn-Noranda: Disques 7ième Ciel, 2007.

Sauvageau, Florian, Pierre Trudel, and Marie-Hélène Lavoie, eds. *Les tribuns de la radio: échos de la crise d'Oka*. Quebec: Institut québécois de recherche sur la culture, 1995.

Savard, Rémi. "De la nation à l'autonomie gouvernementale." Interview with Robert R. Crépeau. *Recherches amérindiennes au Québec* 25, no. 4 (1995): 45–52.

———. "Le légalisme à la sulpicienne." In "Kanehsatake/Oka: vingt ans après," special issue, *Recherches amérindiennes au Québec* 39, nos. 1–2 (2009): 127–28.

Scott, Gail. *The Obituary*. Toronto: Coach House Books, 2010.

Scott, James C. *Domination and the Arts of Resistance: Hidden Transcripts*. New Haven: Yale University Press, 1990.

Sefa Dei, George J. "Rethinking the Role of Indigenous Knowledges in the Academy."

International Journal of Inclusive Education 4, no. 2 (2000): 111–32.

Simard, Jean-Jacques. "White Ghosts, Red Shadows: The Reduction of North American Natives." In *The Invented Indian: Cultural Fictions and Government Policies*, edited by James A. Clifton, 333–69. New Brunswick, NJ: Transaction Publishers, 1990.

———. *La Réduction: l'Autochtone inventé et les Amérindiens d'aujourd'hui*. Sillery: Septentrion, 2003.

Simmel, Georg. *Le conflit*. Preface by Julien Freund. Paris: Circé, 2003.

Simpson, Audra. "To the Reserve and Back Again: Kahnawake Mohawk Narratives of Self, Home and Nation." PhD thesis, McGill University, 2003.

———. Biography as Katrin H. Lamon Resident Scholar, 2008–2009. https://sarweb.org/?resident_scholar_audra_simpson (accessed 19 July 2012).

———. "Under the Sign of Sovereignty: Certainty, Ambivalence, and Law in Native North America and Indigenous Australia." *Wicazo Sa Review* 25, no. 2 (2010): 107–24.

———. "Mohawk Citizenship-Formation in the Face of Empire." Paper presented at the international conference Revisioning the Americas through Indigenous Cinema, held in Montreal and in Kahnawake, 17–19 June 2010.

———. *Mohawk Interruptus: Political Life Across the Borders of Settler States*. London: Duke University Press, 2014.

———. "The State Is a Man: Theresa Spence, Loretta Saunders and the Gender of Settler Sovereignty." *Theory & Event* 19, no. 4 (2016). https://muse.jhu.edu/article/633280 (accessed 15 January 2017).

Simpson, Leanne, and Kiera L. Ladner, eds. *This Is an Honour Song. Twenty Years Since the Blockades*. Winnipeg: Arbeiter Ring Publishing, 2010.

Singer, Beverly R. *Wiping the War Paint off the Lens: Native American Film and Video*.

Visible Evidence Series. Minneapolis: University of Minnesota Press, 2001.

Sioui Durand, Yves. "Kaion'ni, le wampum rompu. De la rupture de la chaîne d'alliance ou le grand inconscient résineux." *Recherches amérindiennes au Québec* 33, no 3 (2003): 56–64.

———. "Y a-t-il un nouveau monde pour les Amérindiens?" In *Autochtonies: Vues de France et du Québec*, edited by Natacha Gagné, Thibault Martin, and Marie Salaün, 505–14. Mondes autochtones Series. Quebec / Montreal: Presses de l'Université Laval / DIALOG, Réseau de recherche et de connaissances relatives aux peuples autochtones, 2009.

———. *Mesnak*. Screenplay by Yves Sioui Durand, Robert Morin, and Louis Hamelin. Film. Montréal: K-Films Amérique, 2012. DVD, 96 min.

Sioui Durand, Yves and Pascale Weber. "Théâtre autochtone et mémoire du corps" [Indigenous Theater and Body Memory] Talks organized by Simon Harel, Isabelle St-Amand, and Pascale Weber as part of the SSHRC project "Expressions créatrices autochtones au Québec" and the Chaire d'études de la France contemporaine. Université de Montréal, 17 October 2016.

Skawennati. *TimeTraveller.* Episode 3. http://www.timetravellertm.com/episodes/episode03.html (accessed 10 November 2017).

Smith, Linda Tuhiwai. *Decolonizing Methodologies: Research and Indigenous Peoples*. 7th ed. London: Zed Books, 2004.

Soussana, Gad. "Introduction." In *Actualités de l'événement*, edited by Gad Soussana and Joseph J. Lévy in collaboration with Marcel Rafie, 9–24. Montreal: Liber, 2000.

Soussana, Gad, Alexis Nouss, and Jacques Derrida. *Dire l'événement, est-ce possible? Séminaire de Montréal pour Jacques Derrida*. Esthétiques Series. Paris: L'Harmattan, 2001.

St-Amand, Isabelle. *La crise d'Oka en récits: territoire, cinéma et littérature*. Quebec City, Quebec: Presses de l'Université Laval, 2015.

———. "*Présence autochtone*, une saga à contre-courant. Rencontre avec André Dudemaine." *Nouveaux Cahiers du Socialime* 18 (2017): 152–159.

———. "From Kahnawà :ke to Montreal Back and Forth: a Cinematic Journey." Interview with Tracey Deer. Conference "JE SUIS ÎLE" / "I AM TURTLE". *What Spaces are There for the Representation of First Nations and Inuit Artistic and Cultural Expression in the City?* Université de Montréal, 6 October 2017.

Stuart, Charles. "The Mohawk Crisis: A Crisis of Hegemony. An Analysis of Media Discourse." MA thesis, University of Ottawa, 1993.

Swain, Harry. *Oka. A Political Crisis and Its Legacy*. Vancouver / Toronto: Douglas and McIntyre, 2010.

Taylor, Diana. *The Archive and the Repertoire: Performing Cultural Memory in the Americas*. Durham: Duke University Press, 2003.

Taylor, Drew Hayden. "Alive and Well: Native Theatre in Canada." *Journal of Canadian Studies / Revue d'études canadiennes* 31, no. 3 (1996): 29–37.

———. "Someday." In *Fearless Warriors*, 87–97. Burnaby: Talonbooks, 1998.

———. *The Baby Blues*. Burnaby: Talonbooks, 1999.

———. *alterNatives*. Burnaby: Talonbooks, 2000.

———. "A Blurry Image on the Six O'Clock News." In *Our Story: Aboriginal Voices on Canada's Past*, edited by Tantoo Cardinal et al., 221–43. Toronto: Doubleday Canada, 2004.

Thérien, Gilles, ed. *Figures de l'Indien*. Cahiers du Département d'études littéraires Series. Montreal: Service des publications de l'Université du Québec à Montreal, 1988.

Tonkin, Elizabeth. *Narrating Our Pasts: The Social Construction of Oral History*. Cambridge: Cambridge University Press, 1992.

Tremblay, Emmanuelle. "Une identité frontalière. Altérité et désir métis chez Robert Lalonde et Louis Hamelin." *Études françaises* 41, no. 1 (2005): 107–24.

Tremblay, Odile. "Alanis Obomsawin, de l'autre côté des barricades, à jamais [From the other side of the barricades, forever]." *Le Devoir*, 19 July 2012. http://www.ledevoir.com/culture/cinema/194473/alanis-obomsawin-de-l-autre-cote-des-barricades-a-jamais.

Tremonti, Anna Maria. "What Does Canada Mean for Indigenous Communities." *The Current*. Segment produced by Samira Mohyeddin and Stephanie Kampf. 16 March 2017. http://www.cbc.ca/radio/thecurrent/the-current-for-march-16-2017-1.4026463/what-does-canada-150-mean-for-indigenous-communities-1.4027484 (accessed 10 November 2017).

Treva, Michelle. "Skawennati's-Timetraveller™: Deconstructing the Colonial Matrix in Virtual Reality." *AlterNative: An International Journal of Indigenous Peoples* 12, no. 3 (September 2016): 236–49.

Trudel, Pierre. "De la négation de l'autre dans les discours nationalistes des Québécois et des autochtones." *Recherches amérindiennes au Québec* 25, no. 4 (1995): 53–66.

———. "La crise d'Oka de 1990: retour sur les événements du 11 juillet." In "Kanehsatake/Oka: vingt ans après," special issue, *Recherches amérindiennes au Québec* 39, nos. 1–2 (2009): 129–35.

Truth and Reconciliation Commission of Canada. *Honouring the Truth, Reconciling for the Future.* Summary of the Final Report of the Truth and Reconciliation Commission of Canada. 2015.

Tuck, Eve, and K. Wayne Yang. "Decolonization Is Not a Metaphor." *Decolonization. Indigeneity, Education & Society* 1, no. 1 (2012): 1–40. http://decolonization.org/index.php/des/article/view/18630/15554 (accessed 15 January 2017).

United Nations. "Instance permanente sur les questions autochtones des Nations Unies." 9th session, 11th hearing—morning, 2010. http://www.un.org/News/fr-press/docs/2010/DH5019.doc.htm (accessed 25 September 2013).

Valaskakis, Gail Guthrie. *Indian Country: Essays on Contemporary Native Culture.* Aboriginal Studies Series. Waterloo: Wilfrid Laurier University Press, 2005.

Vizenor, Gerald, ed. *Survivance: Narratives of Native Presence.* Lincoln: University of Nebraska Press, 2008.

Vizenor, Gerald Robert. *Wordarrows: Native States of Literary Sovereignty.* Lincoln: University of Nebraska Press, 1978.

Wagamese, Richard. *A Quality of Light.* Toronto: Doubleday Canada, 1997.

Wente, Jesse. Film Description for the World Premiere, TIFF, Toronto International Film Festival, 2017. http://www.tiff.net/tiff/our-people-will-be-healed/?v=our-people-will-be-healed (accessed 20 August 2017).

Whitebean, Roxann. *Legend of the Storm.* Film. Self-distributed. Canada. 2015.

Whittall, Zoe. *Bottle Rocket Hearts.* Toronto: Cormorant Books, 2007.

Wickham, Philip. "Théâtre de guérison: Entretien avec Yves Sioui Durand." [*Healing Theater: Interview with Yves Sioui Durand*] JEU, 113, 2004, 104–12. https://apropos.erudit.org/fr/usagers/politiquedutilisation/ (accessed October 2017).

Willow, Anna J. "Conceiving Kakipitatapitmok: The Political Landscape of Anishinaabe Anticlearcutting Activism." *American Anthropologist* 113, no. 2 (2011): 262–76.

Wilson, Shawn. *Research Is Ceremony: Indigenous Research Methods.* Halifax and Winnipeg: Fernwood Publishing, 2008.

Winegard, Timothy C. "The Court of Last Resort: The Canadian Forces and the 1990 Crisis." MA thesis, Royal Military College of Canada, 2006.

———. *Oka: A Convergence of Cultures and the Canadian Forces.* Kingston: Canadian Defence Academy Press, 2008.

Wolfe, Patrick. "Settler Colonialism and the Elimination of the Native." *Journal of Genocide Research* 8, no. 4 (2006):

387–409. http://www.tandfonline.com/ doi/abs/10.1080/14623520601056240 (accessed 15 January 2017).

Womack, Craig S. *Red on Red: Native American Literary Separatism*. Minneapolis: University of Minnesota Press, 1999.

Womack, Craig S., Daniel Heath Justice, and Christopher B. Teuton, eds. *Reasoning Together: The Native Critics Collective*. Norman: University of Oklahoma Press, 2008.

York, Geoffrey, and Loreen Pindera. *People of the Pines: The Warriors and the Legacy of Oka*. Boston / Toronto: Little, Brown and Co., 1991.

OTHER REFERENCES

Agamben, Giorgio. *Ce qui reste d'Auschwitz. L'archive et le témoin*. Vol. 3, *Homo Sacer*. French-language translation by Pierre Alféri. Rivages poche / Petite Bibliothèque Series, 4th ed. Paris: Payot & Rivages, 2003.

———. *Profanations*. French-language translation by Martin Rueff. Rivages poche / Petite Bibliothèque Series, 3rd ed. Paris: Payot & Rivages, 2006.

Alfred, Taiaiake. "Then and Now, for the Land." *Socialist Studies: The Journal of the Society for Socialist Studies* 6, no. 1 (Spring 2010): 93–95.

Amos, Burton F. "Desperate Moves." In *Let the Drums Be Your Heart: New Native Voices*, edited by Joel T. Maki, 117–18. Vancouver / Toronto: Douglas and McIntyre, 1996.

Angus, Graham Scott. "Change Is Upon Us, So Call Me a Dreamer." In *Let the Drums Be Your Heart: New Native Voices*, edited by Joel T. Maki, 101–4. Vancouver / Toronto: Douglas and McIntyre, 1996.

Arcand, Bernard, and Sylvie Vincent. *L'image de l'Amérindien dans les manuels scolaires du Québec: ou, Comment les Québécois ne sont pas des sauvages*. Quebec: Cahiers du Québec / Hurtubise HMH, 1979.

Armstrong, Jeannette. "Rocks." In *Breath Tracks*, 21–24. Stratford: Williams-Wallace Publishers, 1991.

Armstrong, Jeannette, ed. *Looking at the Words of Our People: First Nations Analysis of Literature*. Penticton: Theytus Books, 1993.

Ashcroft, Bill, Gareth Griffiths, and Helen Tiffin. *The Empire Writes Back: Theory and Practice in Post-Colonial Literatures*. London / New York: Routledge, 1989.

Atwood, Margaret. *Survival: A Thematic Guide to Canadian Literature*. Toronto: McClelland and Stewart, 1996.

Baker, Annharte. *Indigena Awry*. Vancouver: New Star Books. 2012.

———. "I Shoulda Said Something Political." In *An Anthology of Canadian Native Literature in English*, edited by Daniel David Moses, Terry Goldie, and Armand Garnet Ruffo, 196–99. 4th ed. Don Mills: Oxford University Press, 2013.

Benjamin, Walter. *L'homme, le langage et la culture*. French-language translation by Maurice de Gandillac, 23–55. Bibliothèque Médiations Series. Paris: Denoël-Gonthier, 1974.

Biron, Michel, François Dumont, and Élisabeth Nardout-Lafarge, eds. *Histoire de la littérature québécoise*. Montreal: Boréal, 2007.

Boisvert, Yves. *La pensée niaiseuse ou Les aventures du comte d'Hydro*. Graphic design and production by Dyane Gagnon. Carré magique Series. Trois-Rivières: Éditions d'art Le Sabord, 2001.

Bonaparte, Darren. *A Lily Among Thorns: The Mohawk Repatriation of Káteri Tekahkwí:tha*. Illustrations by R. Kakwirakeron Montour. Ahkwesáhsne: Wampum Chronicles, 2009.

Bouvier, Laure. *Une histoire de Métisses*. Montreal: Leméac, 1995.

Couchie, Mike. "Oka Sights: Tanks for Everything." In *Let the Drums Be Your Heart: New Native Voices*, edited by Joel T. Maki, 119. Vancouver / Toronto: Douglas and McIntyre, 1996.

Dahl, Roy King. "Of Another World." In *Voices: Being Native in Canada*, edited by Linda Jaine and Drew Hayden Taylor, 6–19. Saskatoon: University of Saskatchewan, Extension Division, 1992.

Dallaire, François. *Oka: La hache de guerre.* Sainte-Foy: Éditions de la Liberté, 1991.

Damm, Kateri Akiwenzie. "Says Who: Colonialism, Identity and Defining Indigenous Literature." In *Looking at the Words of Our People: First Nations Analysis of Literature*, edited by Jeannette Armstrong, 9–25. Penticton: Theytus Books, 1993.

Dantec, Maurice G. *Cosmos Incorporated.* Paris: Albin Michel, 2005.

———. *Grande jonction.* Paris: Albin Michel, 2006.

Devrie, Laura. *Conflict in Caledonia: Aboriginal Land Rights and the Rule of Law.* Vancouver: University of British Columbia Press, 2011.

Doxtater (Horn Miller), Kahente. "From Paintings to Power: The Meaning of the Warrior Flag Twenty Years after Oka." *Socialist Studies: The Journal of the Society for Socialist Studies* 6, no. 1 (Spring 2010): 96–124.

Doyle-Bedwell, George H. "Whose Face Anyway? Images of First Nations Protest and Resistance in Kahnawake and Kanesatake, Kanien'kehaka Territory 1990: A Study in the Social Construction of Voice and Image." MA thesis, Dalhousie University, 1998.

Dupuis, Renée. *Quel Canada pour les autochtones? La fin de l'exclusion.* Montreal: Boréal, 2001.

Erasmus, Georges. "Vingt ans d'espoirs déçus et les solutions que nous préconisons." In "Les Mohawks," special issue, *Recherches amérindiennes au Québec* 21, nos. 1–2 (1991): 7–28.

Fife, Connie. "A New World Poem" and "A Room in Charlottetown." In *Poems for a New World,* 40–45; 83. Vancouver: Ronsdale Press, 2001.

Foucault, Michel. *Discipline and Punish: The Birth of the Prison.* Translated from the French by Alan Sheridan. New York: Vintage, 2012.

Gabriel, Miranda. *War of Life.* Video. Montreal: Wapikoni mobile / Les Productions des Beaux Jours / National Film Board of Canada, 2007. 7 mins 8 secs.

Gatti, Maurizio. *Être écrivain amérindien au Québec. Indianité et création littéraire.* Preface by François Paré, Cahiers du Québec / Littérature Series. Montreal: Hurtubise HMH, 2006.

Ginsburg, Faye, and Audra Simpson. "The Oka Crisis. The Power of a Woman with a Movie Camera." In *Alanis Obomsawin. 270 Years of Resistance. Essays, Articles and Documentation*, 18–32. Montreal: National Film Board of Canada, 2008.

Greer, Allan. *Mohawk Saint: Katherine Tekakwitha and the Jesuits.* Oxford / New York: Oxford University Press, 2005.

Guilbeault-Cayer, Émilie. "*Une image vaut mille mots*: la crise d'Oka de 1990 et sa représentation par une photographie." *Conserveries mémorielles: Une collectivité en images. Mémoire et (ré)interprétations du passé québécois et canadien* 4 (2007): 65–79. http://cm.revues.org/194 (accessed on 15 November 2017).

———. *La crise d'Oka: au-delà des barricades.* Quebec: Septentrion, 2013.

Hamelin, Louis. *Le joueur de flute.* Montreal: Boréal, 2001.

Harel, Simon. *Espaces en perdition.* Vol. II, *Humanités jetables.* InterCultures Series. Quebec: Presses de l'Université Laval, 2009.

Hill, Susan M. "Travelling Down the River of Life Together in Peace and Friendship, Forever: Haudenosaunee Land Ethics and Treaty Agreements as the Basis for Restructuring the Relationship with the British Crown." In *Lighting the Eighth Fire: The Liberation, Resurgence, and Protection of Indigenous Nations*, edited by Leanne Simpson, 23–45. Winnipeg: Arbeiter Ring Publishing, 2008.

——. *The Clay We Are Made Of: Haudeno-saunee Land Tenure on the Grand River.* Winnipeg: University of Manitoba Press, 2017.

Horn, Kahn-Tineta. *Mohawk Warriors Three: The Trial of Lasagna, Noriega & 20-20.* Kahnawà:ke: Owera Books, 1994.

Hudon, Marc. "La crise d'Oka: rumeurs, médias et icône. Réflexion critique sur les dangers de l'image." *Cahiers de géographie du Québec* 38, no. 103 (1994): 21–38.

Iser, Wolfgang. *How to Do Theory.* How to Study Literature Series. Malden, MA: Blackwell Publishing, 2006.

Kanesatake Emergency Measures Committee. "Breaking All Barriers: A Healing Process for Kanesatakeró:non." Grant application to Health Canada and Department of Indian Affairs and Northern Development. 3 October 1990, n.p.

Keller, Elizabeth Andrea. "Anglos with Feathers: A Content Analysis of French and English Media Coverage in Québec on the Oka Crisis in 1990." MA thesis, University of British Columbia, 1996.

King, Thomas, Cheryl Calver, and Helen Hoy, eds. *The Native in Literature: Canadian and Comparative Perspectives.* Toronto: ECW Press, 1987.

Krupat, Arnold. *The Turn to the Native: Studies in Criticism and Culture.* Lincoln: University of Nebraska Press, 1996.

Lajoie, Andrée, Jean-Maurice Brisson, Sylvio Normand, and Alain Bissonnette, eds. *Le statut juridique des peuples autochtones au Québec et le pluralisme.* Le droit aussi Series. Cowansville: Éditions Yvon Blais, 1996.

Lamy-Beaupré, Jonathan. "Du stéréotype à la performance: Les détournements des représentations conventionnelles des Premières Nations dans les pratiques performatives." PhD thesis, Université du Québec à Montréal, 2012.

LaRocque, Emma. "Here Are Our Voices—Who Will Hear?" In *Writing the Circle: Native Women of Western Canada,* edited by Jeanne Perreault and Sylvia Vance, xv–xxx. Edmonton: NeWest Publishers, 1990.

Larose, Roger. "La crise d'Oka à la télévision : l'éloge du barbare." PhD thesis, Concordia University, 2000.

Lepage, Pierre. "Oka, 20 ans déjà! Les origines lointaines et contemporaines de la crise." In "Kanehsatake/Oka: vingt ans après," special issue, *Recherches amérindiennes au Québec* 39, nos. 1–2 (2009): 119–26.

Maracle, Lee. "Oratory on Oratory." In *Trans. Can.Lit: Resituating the Study of Canadian Literature,* edited by Smaro Kamboureli and Roy Miki, 55–70. Waterloo: Wilfrid Laurier University Press, 2007.

McIntosh, Peggy. "Les privilèges des Blancs: au-delà des apparences." http://psac-ncr. com/fr/privileges-blancs-dela-apparences (accessed on 10 November 2017).

McKegney, Sam. "Writer-Reader Reciprocity and the Pursuit of Alliance Through Indigenous Poetry." In *Indigenous Poetics,* edited by Neal McLeod, 43–60. Waterloo: Wilfrid Laurier University Press, 2014.

McNab, David T. *No Place for Fairness: Indigenous Land Rights and Policy in the Bear Island Case and Beyond.* Montreal and Kingston: McGill-Queen's University Press, 2009.

Mercredi, Duncan. "Blue Collar Indian." In *Voices: Being Native in Canada,* edited by Linda Jaine and Drew Hayden Taylor, 115–25. Saskatoon: University of Saskatchewan, Extension Division, 1992.

Michaud, Yves. *La violence.* Que sais-je? Series. Paris: Presses universitaires de France, 1986.

Monture-Angus, Patricia. *Thunder in My Soul: A Mohawk Woman Speaks.* Preface by Mary Ellen Turpel. Halifax: Fernwood Publishing, 1995.

Parent, Armand. *Kanesatake: Life in Kanesatake as Told by Rev. Armand Parent 1870–1878.* Excerpt of the biography *The Life of Rev. Armand Parent. Eight years among the Oka Indians.* Kanehsatà:ke: Kawennénhas Project Production, n.d.

Patrick, Rena. "Oka Man." In *Steal My Rage: New Native Voices*, edited by Joel T. Maki, 73. Vancouver / Toronto: Douglas and McIntyre, 1995.

Picard-Sioui, Louis-Karl. *Chroniques de Kitchike: la grande débarque*. Wendake: Hannenorak, 2017.

Ponting, J. Rick. "Internationalization: Perspectives on an Emerging Direction in Aboriginal Affairs." *Canadian Ethnic Studies / Études ethniques au Canada* 22, no. 3 (1990): 85–109.

Ransen, Mort. *You Are on Indian Land*. DVD. Montreal: National Film Board of Canada, 1969. 36 mins 48 secs.

Robinson, Eden. "Terminal Avenue." In *An Anthology of Canadian Native Literature in English*, edited by Daniel David Moses, Terry Goldie, and Armand Garnet Ruffo, 595–600. 4th ed. Don Mills: Oxford University Press, 2013.

Rogers, Janet. *Peace in Duress*. Vancouver: Talon Books, 2014.

Ruffo, Armand Garnet, ed. *(Ad)dressing Our Words: Aboriginal Perspectives on Aboriginal Literatures*. Penticton: Theytus Books, 2001.

Said, Edward W. *Orientalism*. New York: Vintage Books, 2003.

———. *L'orientalisme. L'Orient créé par l'Occident*. French-language translation by Catherine Malamoud, preface by Sylvestre Meininger and Tzvetan Todorov, afterword by Claude Wauthier. Paris: Seuil, 2005.

Sehdev, Robinder Kaur. "Lessons from the Bridge. On the Possibilities of Anti-Racist Feminist Alliances in Indigenous Spaces." In *This Is an Honour Song: Twenty Years Since the Blockades*, edited by Leanne Simpson and Kiera L. Ladner, 105–23. Winnipeg: Arbeiter Ring Publishing, 2010.

Sévigny, Hélène. *Lasagne: l'homme derrière le masque*. Saint-Lambert: Sedes, 1993.

Simpson, Audra, and Andrea Smith, eds. *Theorizing Native Studies*. Durham and London: Duke University Press, 2014.

Sioui Durand, Guy. "Jouer à l'Indien est une chose, être un Amérindien en est une autre." In "Quand les Autochtones expriment leur dépossession. Arts, lettres, théâtre," special issue, *Recherches amérindiennes au Québec* 33, no. 3 (2003): 23–35.

Sioui Durand, Guy, ed. "Indiens Indians Indios." *Inter, art actuel*: 104 (2009–2010): 4–7; 28–33; 38–39; 42–47.

St-Amand, Isabelle. "Discours critiques pour l'étude de la littérature autochtone dans l'espace francophone du Québec." In "L'autochtonie en dialogue: l'expression littéraire autochtone au-delà des barrières linguistiques," special issue, *Studies in Canadian Literature / Études en littérature canadienne* 35, no. 2 (2010[a]): 30–52.

———. "Retour sur la crise d'Oka. L'histoire derrière les barricades." In "Institution 1959–2009," special issue, *Liberté* LI, no. 4 (2010[b]): 81–93.

———. "L'influence des intellectuels mohawks dans la recherche sur la crise d'Oka." *Cahiers DIALOG*, "Actes de colloque. L'activisme autochtone: hier et aujourd'hui." No. 2011-01, edited by Carole Lévesque, Nathalie Kermoal, and Daniel Salée, 10–12. Montreal: DIALOG / Institut national de la recherche scientifique, 2011.

Teuton, Sean Kicummah. *Red Land, Red Power: Grounding Knowledge in the American Indian Novel*. Durham: Duke University Press, 2008.

Voices From Oka—A Native Recounting of the Mohawk Siege on 1990. VHS. Sydney, AU: Barricade Productions, 1990. 30 mins.

Wagamese, Richard. *The Terrible Summer*. Toronto / Los Angeles: Warwick Publishing, 1996.

Wheeler, Sue. "Pickling Beets, Anniversary of Oka." In *Solstice on the Anacortes Ferry*, 60. Vernon: Kalamalka Press, 1995.

Williamson, Peter. "So I Can Hold my Head High: History and Representations of the Oka Crisis." MA thesis, Carleton University, 1997.

INDEX